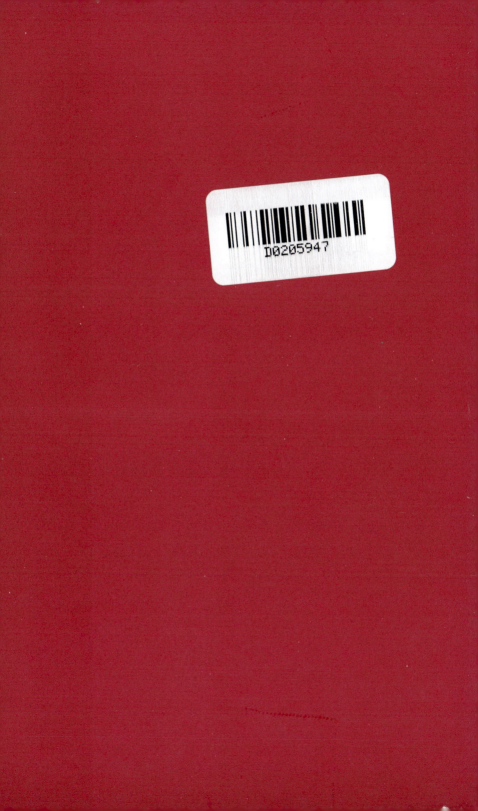

UGO FOSCOLO
POET OF EXILE

UGO FOSCOLO

Poet of Exile

GLAUCO CAMBON

Princeton University Press · Princeton, New Jersey

Copyright © 1980 by Princeton University Press
Published by Princeton University Press, Princeton, New Jersey
In the United Kingdom: Princeton University Press,
Guildford, Surrey

All Rights Reserved
Library of Congress Cataloging in Publication Data will be
found on the last printed page of this book

This book has been composed in VIP Bodoni

Clothbound editions of Princeton University Press books
are printed on acid-free paper, and binding materials are
chosen for strength and durability

Printed in the United States of America by Princeton
University Press, Princeton, New Jersey

In memory of Alice De Micheli,
my lycée teacher in Milan,
and for my students in both countries

CONTENTS

ACKNOWLEDGMENTS

In slightly different form, Chapter I of this book, along with the pages Chapter III devoted to a discussion of the sonnet "To Zacynthos," appeared as an independent essay in *Mosaic*: A Journal for the Comparative Study of Literature and Ideas, published by the University of Manitoba Press, Volume IX, No. 1 (Fall 1975), pp. 132-42, to whom acknowledgment is herewith made.

For invaluable encouragement to develop that first attempt into a more systematic exploration of Foscolo's literary experience and accomplishment, I am deeply indebted to my friends Austin Warren of Providence, R.I., Francis Fergusson of Kingston, N.J., Giovanni Cecchetti of U.C.L.A., Joy Potter of the University of Texas, Eugenio Montale, Cesare Segre, Sergio Antonielli, and Giancarlo Buzzi of Milan, and to my wife and fellow scholar, Marlis Zeller Cambon.

Special thanks are due to the following persons and institutions for gracious help in my research: Dr. Luca Badaloni, Director of Leghorn's Biblioteca Labronica "Guerrazzi" and Curator of its Foscolo MSS/ collection; Dr. Gennarelli and her fellow librarians at the Biblioteca Nazionale of Florence, MSS department; the staff of Milan's Archivio di Stato; the staff of Milan's Biblioteca Civica "Sormani," and the staff of Rome's Biblioteca Nazionale Centrale. Travel to Italy for direct consultation of those source treasuries was made possible by grants of the American Council of Learned Societies, of the Fulbright Commission, and of the Research Foundation of the University of Connecticut, in 1975 and 1976. For assistance in obtaining my relevant Fulbright travel grant in 1976 I am indebted to Dr. Cipriana Scelba, Director of Rome's Commissione per gli scambi culturali Italia-U.S.A.

Whatever its presumable gaps, this book would not have

reached its substantially improved present form without the careful suggestions of Professor Nicholas Perella of the University of California at Berkeley, who painstakingly read the original typescript, and of Professor Olga Ragusa of Columbia University, its second exceptionally knowledgeable reader. Finally, I should like to thank Professor Mario Praz of Rome for his memorable tea-talk and for his gift of a photograph of the fine portrait of Foscolo by F. Fabre, which is part of Praz's unique collection of Empire style art objects in his apartment at Via Zanardelli. That photograph is reproduced by kind permission of Professor Praz.

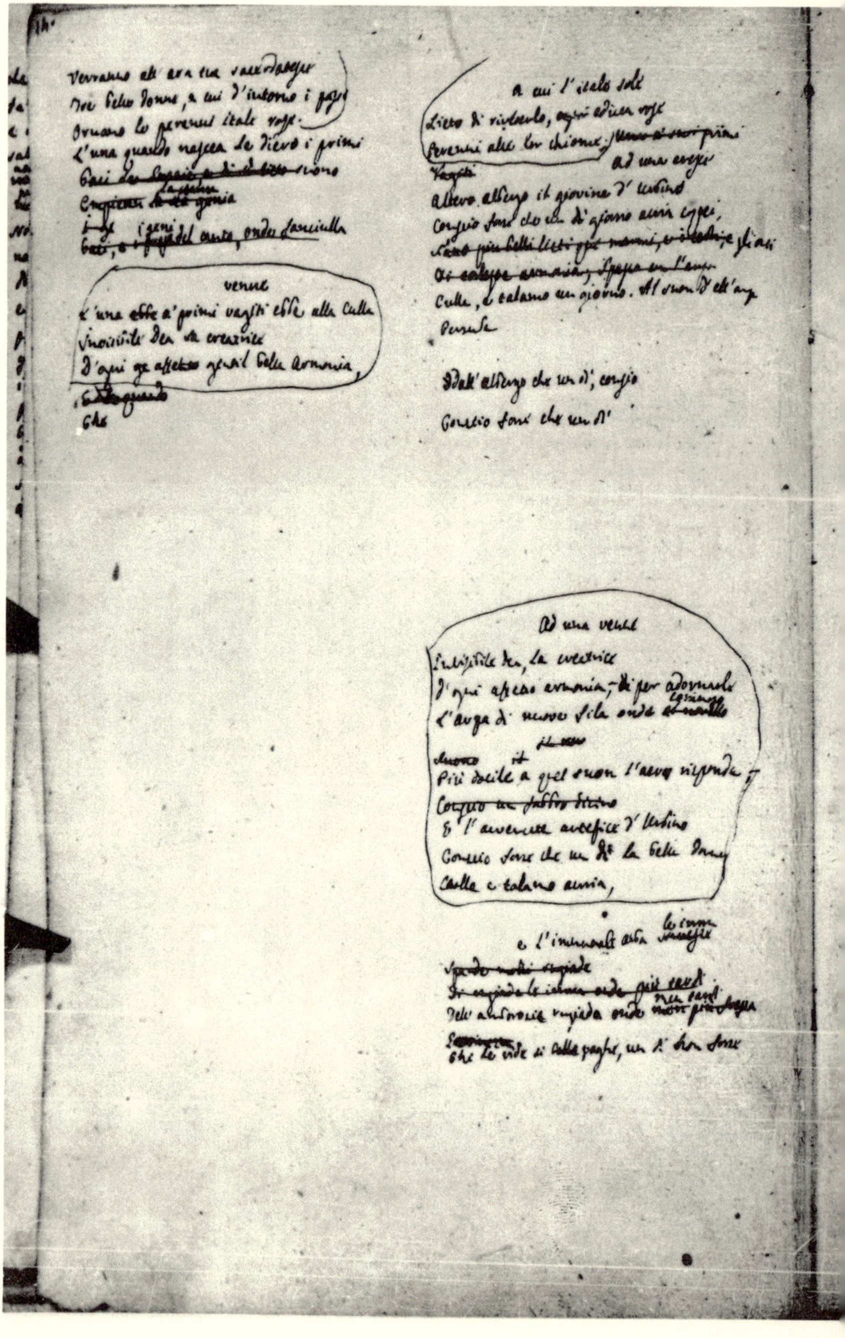

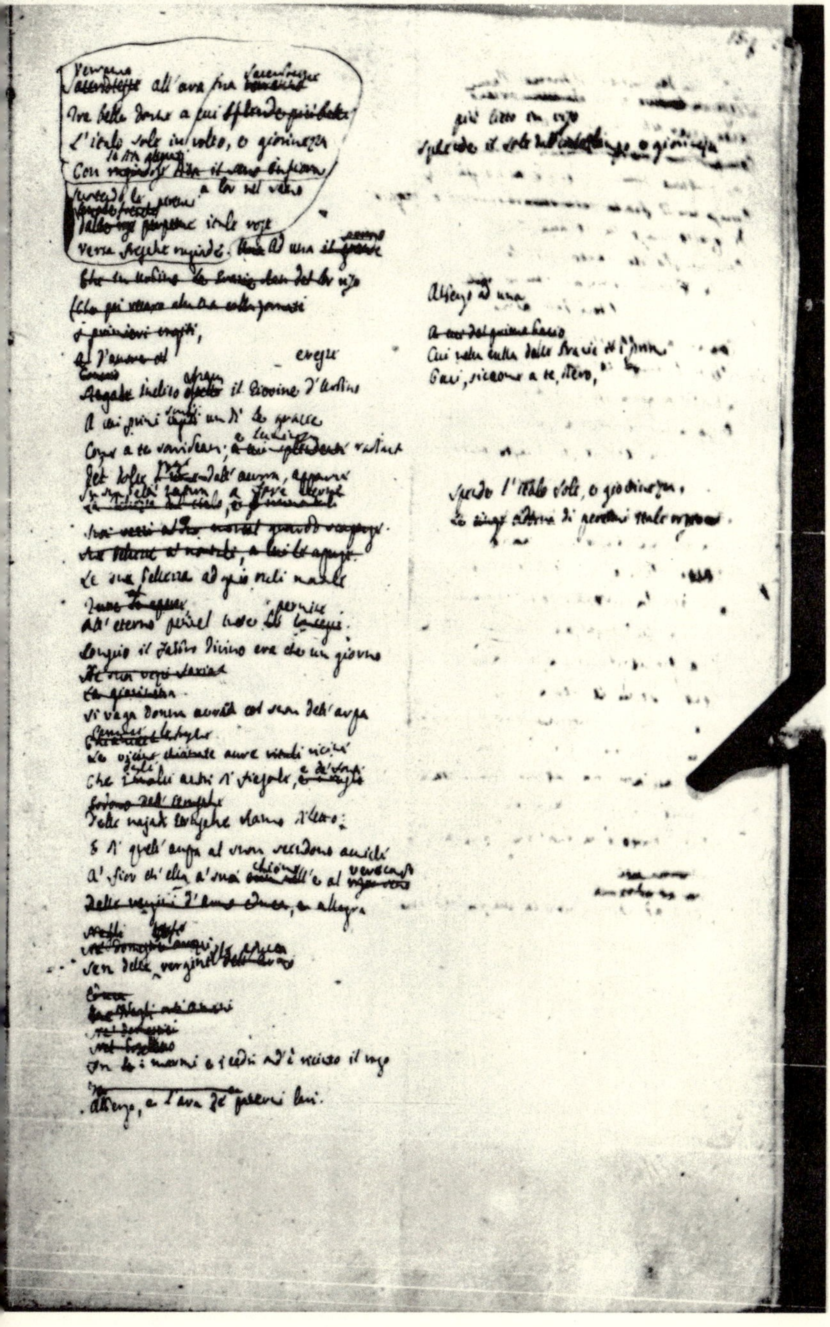

CHAPTER I

Introduction:
The Poetry of Exile

For our Western tradition, the literature of exile begins with two very different sources: the Old Testament on the one hand, and Ovid's *Tristia* and *Epistulae ex Ponto* on the other. Interdiction of his Roman *aqua et ignis* wrought a metamorphosis on the jolly author of *Ars Amatoria*; he now wrote letter upon letter in verse from the ice-caked harbor of Tomis on the black Sea, from the winter of his life, reiterating both his guilt and his innocence in turn, in desperate flattery of Augustus and desperate entreaty, from among the shaggy, breech-clad, dagger-happy barbarians of Sarmathian and Gothic extraction who made him feel like the actual barbarian because his Latin was incomprehensible to them. To this day his obsessive plea echoes in our mind as the voice of one who has faced a destructive cultural situation and, to survive, has mobilized his extreme resources—in the terror that they too (language, imagination, tradition) might fail him.[1] It is a very personal voice, at times endearingly petulant, in turn wily, peevish, hopeful and dejected, and instinct throughout with the diplomacy of despair—the true, and poetically redeeming, note that rings out from his repeated gestures of abject

---

[1] Two relevant passages, among others, are *Tristia* v, vii, lines 40-68, and *Tristia* v, x, 33-44. I am referring to the Loeb Classical Library volume: *Ovid–Tristia, Ex Ponto*, tr. by A. L. Wheeler. London: Heinemann, and Cambridge: Harvard University Press, 1924, 1965.

confession, from the self-abasement of his flatteries to Augustus, the unresponsive demigod.

If after reading Fustel de Coulanges one wants a final illustration of what the ancient city meant to its children, one should turn to exilic Ovid, who struggles so hard not to lose twice the city he has already lost once. It has become for him an invisible city, a city of the mind, a memory and an exchange of signs across an otherwise unbridgeable distance; and his *raison d'être* is to reaffirm his fidelity to it. In the last resort, it is of course literature, the written word, that saves Ovid and makes him, the unrecalled exile, a hero of language. His values, those that make him humane rather than just human, have been put to the supreme test by the predicament of exile, and he has to keep the City alive in himself if he wants to live. Hence the inextricable nexus between absent City and rejected citizen, between community and individual, from the individual's own side; language makes the nexus reciprocal because it is Ovid's one inalienable possession, the gift of the City he has lost:

> ne tamen Ausoniae perdam commercia linguae,
>   et fiat patrio vox mea muta sono,
> ipse loquor mecum desuetaque verba retracto,
>   et studii repeto signa sinistra mei.
> Sic animum tempusque traho, sic meque reduco
>   a contemplatu summoveoque mali.
> Carminibus quaero miserarum oblivia rerum:
>   praemia si studio consequar ista, sat est.[2]

As the preceding part of this poem makes clear, fear of losing his very language after losing his city springs from the daily

---

[2] *Tristia* v, vii, 61-68: "Yet for fear of losing the use of the Latin language, and so that my voice will not grow dumb in its native sound, I talk to myself and revive obsolete words, and revert to the ill-starred practice of my art. In this way do I drag out my life and time, in this way do I manage to withdraw from contemplation of my troubles. Through song I endeavor to forget my wretchedness: and if I do obtain such a reward, it is enough." (Tr. mine.)

spectacle of those descendants of Greek colonists who have given up both speech and fashions of Hellas.

How paramount the city values are to civilized man we also know from so many pages of the Bible, where the lamentations by the waters of Babylon convey the predicament of a whole community uprooted from its Jerusalem. Once the nomadic people has been chosen for sedentary civilization, collective exile becomes to the enslaved Jews what removal from Rome means to one gifted individual, Ovid. Both are radical situations, both impose a grim existential challenge: will you preserve your identity? The poetry elicited by this predicament amounts to a kind of victory in defeat, and it countervails, if it does not justify, the doom visited upon the respective protagonists. Something of each paradigmatic situation, and of the correlative literary response, reappears in Dante's medieval career, which would be unthinkable apart from the wound of unjust banishment and without the Biblical and classical models that went into the imaginative reshaping of his singular experience. Once the Tuscan poet saw himself struck by the same fate that had hounded the Hebrews and afflicted the once carefree Ovid, he recognized in the sudden blow an affinity of election. The persona he projected in the *Divine Comedy*, a sinning wanderer in the wilderness, took on the traits of the peculiar people, Jacob's people, chosen *because* peculiar, and the penitential stance went hand in hand with the vatic. But from Ovid, temperamentally alien though he was, Dante inherited the individual emphasis, the vindication of self as a center of experience, which he was the first and possibly the only poet to weave with striking results into the large pattern of a cosmic opus. St. Augustine mediated between classical and Scriptural sources, to be sure; and, as a result, the prophet and the penitent, the communal spokesman invested with a sacred mission and the citizen of human contingency, the type and the individual make themselves heard in the semantic chords of Dante's music, consonant as it proved with David's harp as well as with Ovid's or Virgil's lyre. And—again like Ovid—

our Florentine exile turns to language as his sacred trust.
Whether we read his major poem, or his treatises, or his letters, we can hardly miss this note. The fury, of course, was
neither Ovidian nor Virgilian; for that, he had the Biblical
prophets at hand; but most of all his own eagle-gnawed liver
and his heart, love-devoured. Dante's Florence, a creation of
love and hate, is neither Ovid's Rome nor the Bible's
Jerusalem, though it has something of both, and much more.
It is both everyday city and Holy City, both Egypt and Promised Land.

Even in the sketchiest bird's-eye view, the landscape of
Western literary history unfolds as one defined by certain rare
landmarks which prove ultimately essential to the total ap-
prehensible shape of the terrain. To translate into less
metaphoric terms: the literature of exile reflects an exceptional experience, but without it our literary heritage would
be vastly different and immeasurably poorer. Whether this
flies in the face of any comfortable theory of gradual continuity or homogeneous quality in literary tradition is not my
present concern. I am quite prepared to entertain the paradox
that, in literature as well as in other cultural domains, exceptions in the last resort determine the norm—any "norm" of
course having to be periodically redefined by either upheav-
als or cumulative erosions. Anthropologically speaking, the
collective experience of the Jewish people is the exception:
nomadism, Covenant, Promised Land, exile, diaspora—and
through the literary vehicle of the Bible it has become
exemplary to a huge part of mankind. Artistically and biographically, we do not expect every writer to go through the
ordeal of exile; in fact we insist on the necessity of cultural
roots, of close contact between writer and community; but the
phenomena which contradict or at least qualify this symbiotic
ecology of art—like those I have been surveying so far—do
give us pause. In the long run it may be pretty hard to say
whether the exile imposed on Solzhenitsyn by the Soviet
bureaucrats will blight or enhance his creative vein. Several
decades ago, political banishment failed to dry up Thomas

Mann's vein; and the American expatriates (first Henry James, then Ezra Pound and T. S. Eliot, along with Irishman Joyce)[3] successfully passed the test of self-uprooting. Here let us marginally note how, not unaccountably, Pound and Eliot pioneered in the conversational style which has in Ovid's epistolary poetry its remote fountainhead;[4] how, again, they and Joyce looked up to Dante's example; and how questions of language, of the meeting or attrition of cultures, are intrinsic to their preoccupation and accomplishment. Vatic utterance, stimulated by their Biblical and Dantesque affinities, sooner or later came to characterize the work of Eliot and Pound.

Perhaps it is unfair to equate the condition of freely chosen expatriation with exile under duress—which was the lot of the three classical prototypes I touched upon to begin with. Neither the Old-Testament Jews, nor Ovid or Dante, had a choice. Jerusalem, Rome, and Florence respectively were .taken away from them by unappealable fiat. Nor would it do justice to Ovid's *Grenzsituation* (to say it in Karl Jaspers' words)[5] to compare his actual way of life as an outcast among barbarians to Pound's and Joyce's wanderings and residences among civilized peoples who shared with them the basic European tradition, and to James's or Eliot's privilege of taking up residence in what was the original homeland of their

---

[3] One remembers Stephen Dedalus' motto: "silence, cunning, and exile."

[4] Not only Ovid's, but also Horace's epistolary verse and satires come to mind in this connection. In his comments on his own free translation of Propertius ("Homage to Sextus Propertius"), Pound said that the Roman poets of the imperial age were culturally our contemporaries, this being one reason why he gave Propertius, as a mask of himself, an English voice attuned to prosy cadences and style and free of any archaism. Disenchantment can be a defense—whether against exile or against the corruption of the times.

[5] Literally, a "threshold situation," a predicament which strains our moral or intellectual resources to the utmost. It is interesting to remember that Karl Jaspers, the modern German philosopher, began as a psychiatrist.

own native language. Yet an uprooting is still an uprooting, no matter how circumstantially muffled the trauma may be; James and Eliot never forgot their native land, and Joyce and Pound looked upon it with fierce ambivalence to the end. Besides, Pound's spontaneous expatriation became a forced exile in 1941 when he was denied return to America, and this aggravation was compounded in 1945 when American military authorities put him in the notorious cage at the Detention Training Camp near Pisa—the *Pisan Cantos* being the unpremeditated literary upshot. Here it seems fair to observe that forced exile has reappeared elsewhere in twentieth-century society as a consequence of ideological fanaticism, to judge from Nazi and Stalinist or neo-Stalinist actions. We thought that we had left the Dark Ages far behind in our dim historical past, but history has a way of being unpredictable, however providential some of its unplanned byproducts, including exilic poetry, may come to seem in retrospect. History can be also ironic: Pope Boniface VIII thought of himself as the chosen instrument of Providence, without possibly anticipating the reason why posterity would eventually agree with him—that reason being the *Divine Comedy*, which his high-handed actions helped to instigate.

If Pound leads us back to Dante and the Bible and the Latin or Greek classics, he also reminds us of the post-Enlightenment conditions that have confronted the countless many and the gifted and articulate few in our disconcerting time to make a new "medieval" literature possible. Up to now it would have been sensible to say that while the ancient and medieval writers were sometimes *chosen* by exile, against their wish, modern writers from Romanticism on tended quite often to *choose* exile as a vital act and a theme; but cases like Mann or Mandelstam or Singer or Solzhenitsyn have reversed the trend. At any rate there can be little doubt that the "lost generation" had its direct ancestry in the Romantic generation of Byron, Keats, and Shelley, to whose obvious names I now claim the privilege of adding the less widely known one of their contemporary, Ugo Foscolo.[6] He was somehow, as E. R. Vincent has said,[7] a Byron in reverse, starting his existential itinerary from the Greek island of Zante (the Homeric Zacynthos, still under Venetian rule in 1778, when Foscolo was born to an Italian father and a Greek mother), to pursue it through a progression of exiles which was to end with his death at Turnham Green near London in 1827.

The Hellas Byron went to die for became Foscolo's lifelong myth—in an Italian version, to be sure, because apart from the fact that his father was an Italian, Italy provided the longest and decisive station of his earthly pilgrimage. He was still a child of ten when his father died and the family moved from the Dalmatian town of Spalato (now Split) to Venice. Here Ugo grew up to be a learned, fiery young man with radical ideas nurtured by such disparate sources as Alfieri and Rousseau. He greeted Napoleon as a liberator in 1796, but suffered a bitter disappointment a year later when the Corsican general, after putting a forcible end to the thousand-year old Venetian Republic, handed over its territories to the Austrian Empire at the bargaining table of Campoformio. Now the former citizen of the "Most Serene Republic" had to leave his adoptive city and ancestral homeland, to avoid political persecution at the hands of the counterrevolutionary pro-Austrian police. This second exile differed from the first, which took place in 1784 when his father left Zante for

[6] Croce considered him a true European, for reasons that go beyond the biographical vicissitudes I am now summarizing. See Croce, *Poesia e non poesia–note sulla letteratura europea del secolo XIX*. Bari: Laterza, 1922, 1955. Pp. 72-86 (chapter on F.; English tr. Douglas Ainslie, *European literature in the nineteenth century*. London: Chapman and Hall, Ltd., 1925), and Karl Kroeber, *The Artifice of Reality–Poetic Style in Wordsworth, Foscolo, Keats, and Leopardi*. Madison: U. of Wisconsin Press, 1964. Foscolo was by temperament and achievement a member of the "visionary company," and he showed an affinity for English literature even before moving to England, where he acted as a cultural liaison officer of sorts.

[7] E. R. Vincent, *Ugo Foscolo—an Italian in Regency England*. Cambridge: at the University Press (Great Britain), 1953.

Spalato; it was consummated in full adult consciousness, it entailed leaving mother and siblings behind, namely his whole remaining family, and it left him to his own devices in Napoleon-dominated Lombardy, not a culturally foreign country, of course, but still a new land in every other way. The Cisalpine Republic that came into being there under French sponsorship drew Foscolo to itself, like many other Italian liberal patriots, as the only hope for nationwide political emancipation, and he brilliantly served as an officer of the Cisalpine army in many a hard campaign. Meanwhile, as the French Republic turned into the Napoleonic Empire and the Cisalpine Republic accordingly changed into the Italian kingdom under a French Viceroy, its capital, Milan, became another Venice for Foscolo, who now enjoyed a rising reputation as the author of the Wertherian epistolary novel *The last Letters of Jacopo Ortis* (1798) (written in the aftermath of departure from enslaved Venice) and of the terse *Odes* and *Sonnets* (1802, 1803), then of *The Sepulchers* (1806). This singular protest poem was sparked by the author's reaction against French sanitary regulations on burial practices (Edict of St. Cloud, 1804), but his poetic temper submerged the polemical occasion in wave after wave of prophetic vision, culminating in the scene of blind Homer groping his way into the Trojan necropolis to awaken the voice of the dead heroes there for his deathless song.

The first fifteen years of the new century, which correspond to the span of Napoleon's empire, are the time of full fruition for Ugo Foscolo the poet and the man. He goes from love to intense love; he fights in Napoleon's armies because Napoleon is the lesser of two evils, but openly criticizes the Emperor's political impositions on democratic ideals; he takes an active interest in public life, and briefly teaches at Pavia University (1809), only to become a casualty of his own refusal to compromise with political expediency; he follows up the success of his fiction and verse with the unfinished rhapsody, *The Graces*, and an equally unfinished translation of the *Iliad*; he pioneers in literary criticism. All of this helps us to appreciate what it must have meant for our Greco-Venetian refugee to face a third exile when the Empire fell in 1815 and once again he had to leave a whole world behind—since he, an officer in Viceroy Beauharnais' Italian army, turned down the option of swearing allegiance to the reinstated Austrian occupying power shortly before Waterloo.

After a short stay in Switzerland, Foscolo found a new home in hospitable England, thanks to the good offices of an English Italophile litterateur, W. S. Rose, whom he had known in Florence. The story of Foscolo's eleven years in England has been beautifully told by E. R. Vincent, and one can do no better than refer to that biography. Those were in effect the years of Foscolo's decline, despite the heartening welcome he had from literate and affluent English society. No new poetry to speak of came from his pen, though he kept tinkering with *The Graces* and the *Iliad*'s translation.[8] (At the same time, his vein flowed forth in a different direction—he freelanced as literary critic and historian in journals like *The Edinburgh Review, The Westminster Review, the Quarterly Review, The European Review*, to illustrate the Italian heritage for an eager English readership. So this, the third main period of his life, was not altogether sterile; on the contrary, we owe to it the fine essays on Petrarch and Dante, among

---

[8] Foscolo's *Esperimento di traduzione dell'Iliade di Omero* had been published by Bettoni in Brescia in 1807, but the project kept him busy far beyond that date and well into his last years. The complete part of the project, with the variants, has been published in the *Edizione nazionale delle opere di U. F.*, a long, committee-directed scholarly enterprise in many volumes, the publisher being Le Monnier of Florence. *Le Grazie*, despite the author's tireless self-editing, remained unfinished though not incomplete at his death, and its entire publication, posthumous of course, has engaged the guessing and the polemical skills of generations of scholars. May I refer to Vincent, U. F., and Fubini (see fn. 12) in this regard. The essential structure of the rhapsody consists of three hymns (respectively to Venus, Vesta and Pallas Athena) celebrating the graces of civilization and dedicated each to a lovely young lady who cultivates an art (in the order, dancing, apiculture, music). The three Hellenic goddesses of beauty and harmony are thus personified and at the same time depicted as forms of the creative process.

others, and they would be enough to insure a niche in the nation's memory for the man of whom later Risorgimento patriots (many of whom were to follow him to England during the ups and downs of Italy's struggle for liberty and unification) said that he had "given his country a new institution: exile."

The political implications of that expression do have a clear counterpart in tone and themes of Foscolo's work, yet, as I hope to show further on, there are deeper resonances to be overheard in his writing. His youthful persona, Jacopo Ortis, opens his fictional self-portrait by saying that he is now a man without a country (*"senza patria"*), and he ends a suicide for political as well as sentimental reasons à la Werther. Shortly after, the death by suicide of Foscolo's brother, Giovanni, inspires one of his greatest sonnets, *In morte del fratello Giovanni* (1803), where the desperate option is implicitly exorcised by the Stoic persona. A later tragedy on Ajax likewise turns on suicide as the inevitable conclusion for a certain type of man in a certain situation. Another sonnet, *"Che stai?"* (Why do you tarry?), the twelfth and last of the series, styles its self-addressing author a *"senza patria,"* and the same epithet applies to the fictional mask of Didimo Chierico, Didymus the Clergyman, whom Foscolo projected as the translator of Sterne's *Sentimental Journey* (1805), a work clearly meant, in our writer's inner economy, to offset the Sturm-und-Drang extremism of *Jacopo Ortis*:

> As a boy, circumstances led to my being trained in a seminary; then nature stopped me from becoming a priest: it would have caused me remorse to go on, and shame to go back: and since I practically despise whoever changes his way of life, I peacefully wear this tonsure and this black suit: this way I can either take a wife, or seek a bishopric. I asked him which solution he would choose. He answered: I haven't thought of it; a man without a country cannot decently be either a priest, or a father.[9]

[9] I am translating my text from *Opere di Foscolo*, a cura di Mario Puppo.

Self-irony and humor, worn as a mask by the death-haunted poet, counterbalanced his self-destructive tendencies and helped to enrich his literary gamut. The predicament of being "without a country," which destroys the fictional Jacopo Ortis, is accepted by Didymus and enables Ugo to dissociate exile from inevitable death; he now lives in a delicate balance which allows him to face his own uprootings without flinching—as witness the Stoic *Sonnets*—or even (it's the case of *The Sepulchers*) to place his individual destiny within the objective framework of mankind's historical instability, for history viewed without a transcendent guarantee is a cumulation of exiles, a parade of cemeteries. Plus the reiterated struggle to wrest precarious life from perennial death, the heroic continuity of civilization, a human thing, a feat of memory, memory (Mnemosyne) banking on tombs as testimonials:

Siedon custodi de' sepolcri, e quando
Il tempo con sue fredde ali vi spazza
Fin le rovine, le Pimplée fan lieti
Di lor canto i deserti, e l'armonia
Vince di mille secoli il silenzio.

They sit to watch the sepulchers, and when
Time with its cold wings there sweeps away
Even the last ruins, the Pierian sisters gladden
The desert wastes with their singing, and harmony
Overwhelms the silence of a thousand ages.

(*The Sepulchers*, 230-34)[10]

These are neither the conventional Muses of rococo or neoclassical *décor*, nor the Disquieting Muses of De Chirico, but

---

Milan: Mursia, 1973. Page 535 ("Notizia intorno a Didimo Chierico"). It has been pointed out that at about the same time Foscolo also took an interest in the urbane work of Horace.

[10] A recent translation of *I Sepolcri*, by Thomas G. Bergin, has been published in 1971 by The Bethany Press at Bethany, Conn. The translation of excerpts here given is mine.

they are closer to the latter—they radiate a halo of weird, numinous hilarity over the frightening void to which the landscape of human history (as Ozymandias knows) periodically returns. Old Rocky Face, instructed in Vico's theory of cycles, looks forth and listens—and Hyperion's *Schicksalslied* fills the space. Contemplation of man's collective fate reconciles man to individual calamity—especially if, like Hölderlin or Foscolo, he feels invested with the mission of song, that sole possible victory over ravaging time:

> E me che i tempi ed il desìo d'onore
> Fan per diversa gente ir fuggitivo,
> Me ad evocar gli eroi chiamin le Muse
> Del mortale pensiero animatrici.

> And me, whom the complexion of the times
> And steadfastness in honor drive to flee
> Through alien peoples, me may the Muses summon
> To evoke all heroes, for the Muses only
> Forever breathe life into human thought.
> *(The Sepulchers*, 226-29)

Personal reality, the self as such, is far from denied in *The Sepulchers*; the self is not submerged without a trace in the vistas of history; on the contrary, he is very much there when surfacing in the waves of the epic hymn to reaffirm his commitment to his own hopeless-hopeful destiny—which is more a matter of moral choice than of external imposition, as the above lines show with their variation in a new key on Dante's topical *"l'essilio che m'è dato, onor mi tegno"* (the exile imposed on me I hold as an honor). The passage quoted here initially recalls the opening lines of the Sonnet on the death of Foscolo's brother:

> Un dì, s'io non andrò sempre fuggendo
> di gente in gente, mi vedrai seduto

su la tua tomba, o fratel mio, gemendo
il fior de' tuoi gentili anni caduto.

One day, should I stop wandering forever
from one nation to another, you will see me seated
at your tomb, O my brother, there to mourn
over your gentle youth cut down in its prime.

The chord set up by this juxtaposition contains a dissonance: in the sonnet, written a few years earlier, the self appears as "I," whereas in the *Sepulchers* he is an objectified "Me," first as the victim of fate and of his own resolution and independence, then as the hopefully chosen vehicle of the goddesses of poetry. The "I" of the sonnet holds private conversation with the victim of self-inflicted, untimely death; the self of *The Sepulchers* summarizes all his private woes to purge them in the catharsis of poetry, which is conceived as a communal mission, as the commemoration and redemption of mankind's woes. In the sonnet, conversation with the beloved shade takes place as a parenthesis in the restlessness of exile; in the *Sepulchers*, the condition of poetry is directly connected with the condition of exile, which seems to be necessary to the poetical investiture, and which, anyhow, is felt to be something that brings the individual man, as singer, closer to the rest of mankind. The vicissitudes of mankind are themselves a sort of perennial exile, a perpetual loss of the *ubi consistam*, of the sacred grounds and roots to be restored by collective effort, by communal memory—through the proper single vessel, the rhapsode.

Homer's figure, the archetypal poet in his civilizing mission, is evoked at the end by prophetess Cassandra and thereby placed in a perennial future, out of a mythical past, to resolve in himself all the poets, Foscolo included, who have made themselves heard in this concentrated epos of civilization. Exiled Dante, wandering Petrarch, and roving Alfieri were among them; and even in this regard does Homer recapitulate (or forecast) an essential trait of theirs, for he appears in Foscolo's grand evocation as a wandering beggar:

> . . . Un dì vedrete
> Mendico un cieco errar intra le vostre
> Antichìssime ombre, e brancolando
> Penetrar negli avelli, e abbracciar l'urne
> E interrogarle. Gemeranno gli antri
> Secreti, e tutta narrerà la tomba
> Ilio raso due volte e due risorto . . .

> . . . One day you will see
> A blind beggar roam among your ancient shades,
> And grope his way into the burial chambers,
> And embrace the urns, and interrogate them.
> At this, a moan will issue from the secret
> Vaults, and the whole tomb will tell the story
> Of Ilion twice razed and twice rebuilt . . .
>
> (*The Sepulchers,* 279-285)

The poet, as an exile, is a marked man, and therefore *sacred:*

> . . . Il sacro vate,
> Placando quelle afflitte alme col canto,
> I prenci Argivi eternerà per quante
> Abbraccia terre il gran padre Oceàno.
> E tu onore di pianti, Ettore, avrai
> Ove fia santo e lacrimato il sangue
> Per la patria versato, e finché il Sole
> Risplenderà su le sciagure umane.

> . . . The sacred bard,
> Soothing the hurt of those souls with his song,
> Will make Greek princes immortal through all
> The lands that father Ocean embraces.
> And you, Hector, will be honored by tears
> Wherever blood shed for one's homeland is

> Holy and revered, and as long as the sun
> Keeps shining on the disasters of mankind.
>
> (*The Sepulchers*, 288-295, the end)

The adjective *"sacro,"* so climactically used by the dramatis persona (Cassandra) in this finale which reconciles patriotism, the religion of motherland, with the religion of mankind at large, has the same ring its German equivalent *heilig* acquires in Hölderlin's likewise Hellenizing (and Pindaric) odes.

The poet, as a marked man, begins in the role of a scapegoat, and if he has the strength to resist the temptation of Werther, of Jacopo Ortis, of Giovanni Foscolo, he becomes Ugo Foscolo, who survives to tell the story because he has accepted the branding mark of his destiny as an initiation. In ancient Latin the word *sacer* could refer either to the criminal set apart by his crime (Law of the Twelve Tables) or to the privileged person or object marked for cult and reverence. In Foscolo's myth, the haunted Romantic persona undergoes a *consecration* precisely by choosing his fate as an outcast to convert it into an election: vatic poetry. Hence the vatic stance, which goes with the solemn diction, in a style quite germane to Keats as well as to Milton (the latter writer being acknowledged by Foscolo as his own stylistic counterpart).[11] Fate in the form of repeated exile has stripped him bare as he, going forth from country to country, shed a world each time; now he reaps his reward, by donning the robe of the poet-prophet. Like Didymus' ironic garb, this mantle emblazons a liberating distance—but also a passionate intensity vis-à-vis the turmoil of experience.

---

[11] In a review article on Ippolito Pindemonte's translation of the Odyssey, dating from 1810 and now available in Vol. VII of the *Edizione Nazionale*, pp. 197-230. In this context, talking of the general problem of translation, Foscolo digresses to criticize his own experiment as a translator of the Iliad, and says (p. 210) he has been better at writing essays on the question than at conveying Homer's own spirit in his version, because Nature seems to have made him "an apter follower of Pindar and Milton than of Virgil and Homer."

According to Mario Fubini, who has written the best study
of Foscolo's poetry to date,[12] this vatic persona appears only
in *The Sepulchers*, while in the great sonnets, deeply inspired
by exile though they may be, it would be only the private lyrical persona that speaks. They, according to Fubini, are the
harvest of Foscolo's youth, while *The Sepulchers* expresses his
full ripening. The statement needs qualification if we keep in
mind the sonnet to Zante (written three years earlier, in
1803), where already the persona dons the cursed-sacred
garments of the *vates:*

> Tu non altro che il canto avrai del figlio,
> o materna mia terra; a noi prescrisse
> il fato illacrimata sepoltura.

> Of your son, you will get nothing but the song,
> O my motherland; fate decreed for us
> only an unmourned burial in the end.

That is the last tercet, which antiphonally seals, epitaph-like,
the surging movement of personal memory that had delved
into the communal past to attain mythic status. The native island, a paradise forever lost, can never be "touched" again
(to say it in the intense words of Line 1) but only re-collected;
it is an intangible image, beyond reach except in song, and in
the awareness of its wandering child it is inseparable from the
doom of exile. The doom is also a consecration to poetry, the
last return. Ulysses-like and Homer-like, the Zacynthian
persona recalls his mythic beginning in the act of anticipating
his unmourned end. As we shall see in Chapter III, style sustains this mental movement to perfection; and prolepsis acti-
vates the whole structure, converting utterance from the mode
of reminiscence to the mode of anticipation.

[12] Mario Fubini, *Ugo Foscolo*. Florence: La Nuova Italia, 1962. (Fubini's first study of F. appeared in 1928.) At p. 188 he has this to say of
Foscolo: ". . . only his being an exile, an Italian, a poet, could enable him
to feel the universal human sorrow as his own intimate sorrow."

The conspicuous recurrence of this rhetorical module in Foscolo's best poetry warrants close consideration. In the sonnet to Zante, it operates with salient pervasiveness. To begin with, the climactic vocative *"Zacinto mia"* (O my Zacynthos) rings out long after the essential completion of its relevant clause (Line 1) and after a whole dependent clause (Line 2) has had a chance to intervene. The vocative itself comes as a surprise, in a way, because the governing and the relative clauses preceding it could very well stand on their own feet grammatically and semantically; they would make sense by themselves. Yet when the *in-voked* name appears, it changes everything, it refocuses on itself the whole syntactic structure completed so far: everything now points to Zacynthos, everything gravitates on "my" Zacynthos, and only Zacynthos, as a supervening grace, can make sense of the seemingly self-contained world where she has appeared. The delayed-action effect amounts to an epiphany in the given context, and epiphany will elicit a theophany in turn when, shortly after, the goddess Venus surfaces from the remembered waters of Zacynthos. The proleptic pattern may be defined as inversion compounded with retardation of some kind and the attribution of climactic importance to the member accordingly shifted to last position in a clause or syntagm. It is intrinsic to the hypotactical chain of our sonnet's first part as well as to the isolated last tercet. The names of Venus and Ulysses, no less than the hieratically un-named Homer, all come at the end of their respective clauses, and so does the vocative *"o materna mia terra"* (O my motherland), so symmetrical to the first one, in the last tercet. What in less strong hands might have remained a conventional figure of speech, Foscolo refashions into a propulsive device of utterance. Combined with the many enjambments, it energizes discourse by keeping it in forward motion from idea to idea, each climax becoming a hinge, each provisional goal a new departure. In this way a purely personal memory—childhood spent lounging on the shores of a Mediterranean island—can release a flood of historical and mythical memories, of which it becomes a part.

Combined with apostrophe, prolepsis characterizes other fine sonnets of Foscolo's, notably the already quoted *"In morte del fratello Giovanni"* and the sonnet to Evening (*"Alla Sera"*):

> Forse perché de la fatal quïete
> tu sei l'immago, a me sì cara vieni,
> o Sera, . . .

> Perhaps because you are the very image
> of the ultimate quiet, you are so welcome
> to me, O Evening, . . .[13]

where the maternal function is taken over by Death, the promise of peace after so much tumult, the ultimate exile which now appears as a homecoming. Less pervasively, but still significantly, the proleptic pattern (with or without apostrophe) propels the feverish transitions of *The Sepulchers*, from scene to scene of European history down to the crowning evocation of Homer in the act of wresting life from a penetrated tomb—as if the whole poem were one gigantic prolepsis, gravitating on that absolute image. Utterance surges forward toward its apogee by moving backward in time—

[13] Because the imagery of this sonnet is so antiphonal to that of the Zacynthos sonnet, I am appending here my free translation (see also the Appendix to the present book:

"Perhaps because you are the very image of the ultimate quiet, you are so welcome to me, O Evening, and whether the summer clouds blithely court you along with the mild breezes or through the snow-ridden air you bring disquieting, long darkness to the world, you always alight as a presence invoked, and softly win secret access to my heart. You make me roam with my thoughts along the way that leads to eternal nothingness; meanwhile this wretched age flees, and with it go the herds of worries that devour me in its wake; and while I contemplate your peace, there slumbers within me the warlike spirit, its roars hushed."

mythic-historical time, the memory of the West. And memory is prophetic—it disinters mankind's future from mankind's past, not just the foregone fictional future of Troy, or of any other city. The figures of Homer and of Cassandra, who prophesies Homer's coming to the still dancing youths of intact Troy, are complementary, and they converge in the vatic persona of Foscolo.

This happens most ostensibly in *The Sepulchers*, but it was foreshadowed in the sonnet to Zante, where the figure of Fate partly functioned in a Cassandra-like way, and where again personal memory delved into its ethnic source. "A Zante" is indeed a culmination of poetic maturity and a portent of things to come for its author, both existentially and artistically. We have glimpsed some of its seminal relevance to the later *Sepolcri*, and we shall see (in Chapter IV) how it relates to the still later opus, the unfinished *Le Grazie*, which Foscolo wrote mainly in the shadow of Napoleon's impending collapse, and on the eve of his own last exile.

But I can at least point out the recurrence of the island theme in Part III of *The Graces*. As a novel celebration of Zacynthos it already crops up in Part I, but in Part III it becomes a myth of Atlantis, the vanished continent which now can dawn only on the sailor as a mirage. It is a world suspended beyond reality, the last refuge of Pallas Athena and of the Graces, the powers of civilization perpetually exiled by human recklessness or brutality and eternally committed to the immunity of art. Once again, the island forever lost is the sanctuary of imagination, and there Pallas and the Fates weave a magic veil for the Graces, a synaesthetic *Gesamtkunstwerk* that depicts reality and generates cosmic harmony, conquering Time and its ravages. This is Foscolo's version of Paradise, sustained by longing and not by faith, unlike Dante's, in the face of stark science. It is a man-made paradise; it is poetry trying to capture its own essence: poetry, that is, on the making of poetry. Perhaps Foscolo's failure to write more poetry (apart from his work on the translation of the *Iliad*) in his not altogether fruitless English exile

should not be blamed on that exile itself. The poet of history
had achieved the myth of meta-history and thereby completed
his cycle; now he could commit his creative powers only to
critical prose, moving among several languages since exile
had sharpened his ear.

Exile prompted him to correlate different cultures to his
own Mediterranean heritage; it also spurred him to "keep his
erasers in order," this being the only way to keep faith with
the initial vision. Europe had come a long way from the time
when exiled Ovid could feel it as a half-comical degradation
to have to learn the language of the host country. In the same
context, Foscolo's activity as a translator (whether of Sterne
or of Catullus, Sappho, and Homer) bears scrutiny. Along
with his essays on translation, it mediates between his poetical and his noteworthy critical contributions, extending
from the golden Milanese period to the silver Londoner one.
There are invaluable technical observations to be gleaned
from this part of Foscolo's work, and they place him in the
forefront or even well in advance of his age, since his vatic
stance goes hand in hand with a keen consciousness of his
craft; this in turn makes him intolerant of classicist Aristotelian rules which he resents for having hamstrung the Italian
genius from the high Renaissance on. His Greekness, though
preeminently Apollonian, has a Dionysian touch, like an
intimation of things to come in European culture. The
philologist in him, as the essay on Homer's Zeus shows,[14]
was as perceptive as the critic; and as a critic, whether of his
own work or of the work of others, again he proved how the
recognition of affinities between oneself and one's brethren
need not blur objective vision.

We have something to learn from his statement that
Dante's chief quality was a swiftness of language and im-

[14] More easily than in the exhaustive *Edizione Nazionale*, this piece of
sensitive erudition which holds a clue to Foscolo's poetics as well can be
found in *Opere di F.*, pp. 420-27 ("Su la traduzione del cenno di Giove,"
On the translation of Zeus' nod).

agery, or that to Petrarch[15] the Italian language, so exactingly
shaped into polished verse, was (as a consequence of the
man's wandering life) "both native and foreign." These judg-
ments are fairly self-descriptive on Foscolo's part, yet perfectly relevant to their historical subjects. Again in *Epochs of
the Italian Language* (1818) he insists on dynamism and
rapidity as the native virtue of that tongue, though he places
ancient Greek above even Italian in the matter of "harmony."
Then in an unsigned piece on modern Italian writers,[16] which
he did for Hobhouse as a commentary on *Childe Harold's Pilgrimage*, Book IV, he defines his own achievement in terms of
rhythmical mimesis (against Doctor Johnson's dictates), for
his hendecasyllables are supposed to bear a unique stamp; he
wants a different melody, whether vocalic or consonantal,
from each line, and a different harmony from each sentence.
And he goes on to say that the intellectual tension his writing
demands from the reader is of one piece with the vehemence—also physical—of his conversation; poetry to him
was evidently gesture and dance, a kinetic instinct. One
could also profitably read his foreword to the *Experiment of
translation from the Iliad* (1807) for the pointed remarks on
style,[17] which seem to anticipate those of an Ezra Pound.

[15] The original English text as published in 1821 (*Essays on Petrarch*)
can be found, along with the Italian translation by Ugoni, in *Edizione
Nazionale*, vol. X. The Italian text alone is reprinted in *Opere di F.*, which
also includes the Italian text of *Epochs of the Italian Language*. The revealing statement on the ambivalent nature of the Italian language to Petrarch
is at p. 64 of *Edizione Nazionale*, vol. X: "At the same time that he im-
proves the materials in which the Italian language already abounded, he
seems to create it afresh, for it was in reality both native and foreign to
him."

[16] The *Essay on the Present Literature of Italy* is to be found, both in its
English and in its Italian versions, in *Edizione Nazionale*, vol. XI, Part II.

[17] See Note 8. In the foreword Foscolo names imagery, style, and passion as essential to both poet and translator, translation being for him contiguous to poetry as such. While he declines to define the element of passion, he analyzes style to break it down into the three components of
harmony, *movement*, and *color*; harmony results both from the "absolute

Whether engaged in repossessing his complex heritage through poetry, criticism, or literary historiography, he never ceased revitalizing the great tradition which was to him a matter of life and death. The lesson of exile, coming to him from Dante and Petrarch and the Bible, fostered constant exercise of critical judgment as the accompaniment—or antiphon—to the ascetically cultivated poetical gift which enabled him to dream of his Zacynthian "pre-existence"[18] while squarely facing the wounds and blights of existence.

---

sound" of words and from their rhythmical combinations, movement dwells in verbs because they express action, and color attaches to nouns. Furthermore, he makes much of the connotative function of language ("accessory and concomitant ideas"), which gets lost in dictionaries and in most translations. Finally, he postulates an elective affinity between author and translator, calling it a "harmony of souls" bestowed by Nature alone and to be discovered only by experiment. If we dissolve the element of "passion" into the tangibles of imagery and style as defined by Foscolo, we shall move in a very Poundian sphere indeed, the more so as the exercise of translation as self-discovery or self-masking was intrinsic to Pound's work no less than to Foscolo's. The relevant passage is to be found in vol. cit. of *Ediz. Naz.* cit. p. 210.

[18] The expression coined by Hugo von Hofmannsthal (*"Präexistenz"*) to define what Blake would have called innocence, a basic myth to Romantics and moderns alike, seems strikingly apt for the condition evoked and cherished in Foscolo's Zacynthos sonnet; a condition forever lost yet mentally reattainable in poetry, with the help of the "Graces."

CHAPTER II

The Demon of Suicide and
the Demon of Fiction

If we are to believe Foscolo's love letters to her, Countess Antonietta Fagnani Arese, that naughty Milanese beauty who irritated him into some of his finest writing, said teasingly that he was a little novel in the flesh.[1] And a novel in the making, if we want to translate her humorous expression in a way that does justice to its larger implications. Ugo Foscolo, restless exile, patriot, soldier, scholar, poet, Byronic lover, was himself the stuff of which Romantic novels are made, and he knew it so well that he kept trying to pour his whole incandescent life-experience into some adequate narrative, from *The Last Letters of Jacopo Ortis* on. However, in the intimacy of drawing room or boudoir, Antonietta did not call him "un personaggio da romanzo," a character fit for a novel, as she well might have if she had tried to fit him into the mold of an available idiom. She called him a novel as such. The metaphor was more than a society quip or *bon mot*, and more than

---

[1] The actual expression he quotes (or refers to) from their conversation in three of the letters he wrote her between 1801 and 1803 is *"un romanzetto ambulante,"* a little novel going around on two feet. The letters in question are respectively numbered 158, 210 (where he begins: "You are right, perhaps I am like this because my life is a continuous novel [*un continuo romanzo*] . . ."), and 273 in Vol. I of Foscolo's *Epistolario*, ed. by Plinio Carli (in *Edizione Nazionale*, Vol. XIV, Florence: Le Monnier, 1949). In that volume the letters to Antonietta, including two she wrote Foscolo to accompany her translation of *Werther* and to request restitution of her correspondence, are printed together to emphasize their dramatic sequence.

a simple idiosyncrasy of the kind that the private language of lovers can foster. It was attuned to his rapid style. It both revealed the large scope of his personality and good-humoredly punctured his (however sincere) addiction to heroic roles and melodrama. Above all, it wittily stated that convergence of life and literature which operated at the center of Foscolo's concerns.

Countess Arese can be credited with her share of wit and insight, despite (or because of) the fact that she cynically played her men one against the other in the game of love. Besides, it is hard to see how Ugo Foscolo of all lovers could have become so passionately involved in her if she had been just a mindless, ravishing brunette beauty with wealthy leisure at her command, instead of an intelligent and pretty cultivated woman who, in the patriarchal society of her conservative class, place, and age, had to use marriage as a shield and duplicity as a weapon for her urge to live a fuller life than convention allowed. The role of Aspasia was dangerous; and if we grant exceptional men like Foscolo, Byron, or Goethe the right to fulfill themselves at the expense of several women's feelings, we might as well concede that a true Aspasia is as rare as a good poet. The poet at any rate seems to need her in some form. Giacomo Leopardi—Foscolo's direct literary descendant—certainly did, no less than his physically more fortunate master.

Readers of good poetry, then, should acknowledge their debt to women like Antonietta Fagnani Arese, or Fanny Targioni Tozzetti (the inspirer of Leopardi's "Aspasia" lyrics). That is the very debt which the purveyors of that poetry could not bring themselves to admit—except by writing their verse and prose in fierce or desolate protest. Foscolo's occasionally patronizing words to his Antonietta (whom, at the height of their liaison, he credits with much heart and little imagination) surely do little justice to her mind—which he seems to respect far more, despite himself, when he lashes out at her infidelity in the parting letter—last but one of the series, undated but probably written in February 1803, and numbered

284 by Plinio Carli.[2] Here Foscolo, in cold rage, calls her "a feminine Lovelace"—referring to a notorious character in Richardson's *Clarissa Harlowe*, the book which, along with *Pamela*, had started in eighteenth-century Europe the clamorous tradition of the epistolary novel. That tradition of course included, in a straight line of succession, Rousseau's *La nouvelle Héloïse*, Goethe's *Werther*, and Foscolo's own *Jacopo Ortis*.

Pinpointing the above-mentioned convergence of literature and life, Ortis is named in this letter (he had actually appeared in many as the author's alias); as for *Werther*, which Foscolo variously recognized as a kindred book and a model source at least for the reshaping of his own novel, Antonietta was apparently translating it for him at the time of their passion.[3] The Arese translation, which Foscolo rated above the ones then in print, was never published (and he was probably reworking it for a while); but he mentions it honorably in his January 16, 1802 letter to Goethe.[4] This letter announces the

[2] *Epistolario* I, p. 410.

[3] See Letter 283, p. 410 of *Epistolario* I, dated January 14, 1803. It is by Antonietta and it accompanies her completed translation of *Werther*. A much decried scurrilous phrase seals this not altogether unfriendly farewell.

[4] *Epistolario* I, p. 129, No. 86. The relevant part of this letter reads as follows: "You will receive from Mr. Grassi the first small volume of a modest work of mine which your *Werther* perhaps originated . . . Countess Antonietta Aresi [sic], my eternal and only lady friend, translated *Werther* from its last edition into the style of *Ortis*: and this will be the only Italian version to be spared mutilation by the ignorance of translators or by the preposterousness of governments. . . ." Plinio Carli, the editor of Foscolo's letters for the *Edizione Nazionale*, appends very informative footnotes on scholarly discussions of this letter's authenticity and on historical and bibliographical references, including one to a book by F. Zschek, dated 1894, which discusses this letter in the framework of a comparison between *Werther* and *Ortis*. Since Foscolo elsewhere (Letter of Sept. 1808 to Bartholdy, and Bibliographical note prepared for the Zurich 1816 edition of *Ortis*) makes *Werther* much less influential on *Ortis*, and emphasizes the differences between the two books, most scholars came to agree that the 1802 letter to Goethe reflects an unguarded youthful enthusiasm. In 1973,

arrival, by private delivery, of a complimentary copy of *Le ultime lettere di Jacopo Ortis* (1801 edition, Mainardi publisher)—and that copy was duly preserved in Weimar's Goethe Archive. Goethe's opinion of the handsome tribute is not known, or at least did not prompt a reply to Foscolo (whose name fails to appear, for instance, in Eckermann's *Gespräche mit Goethe*); a strange omission in view of Goethe's keen interest in contemporary Italian literature, for whose sake he eventually took up the cudgels when it came to defending Manzoni's artistry. Perhaps the by now classically oriented genius of Weimar did not want to be admired for the radical work of his *Sturm-und-Drang* youth, as the epistolary exchange with Schiller in those very years[5] may confirm. He was, let us remember, cool to Hölderlin and hostile to Kleist.

On our part, in any case, we can hardly fail to notice the decisive intersections, at the beginning of the new century, in Foscolo's life and work. Given his strong autobiographical bent, his sense of history, and his political commitment, we can hardly discount the juncture of certain shocks at the moment of his literary flowering between the last years of the eighteenth century and the first years of the nineteenth: Napoleon's ambiguous role, with the destruction of any hope for

---

however, Giorgio Manacorda has made a cogent case for F.'s acquaintance with Michiel Salom's Italian translation of *Werther* (publ. in 1788 and 1796); an earlier translation, by Gaetano Grassi, had appeared in 1782). Manacorda's book, *Materialismo e masochismo–Il "Werther," Foscolo e Leopardi* (Florence: La Nuova Italia, 1973), also spotlights the psychoanalytical implications of certain linguistic and thematic elements in *Ortis*, and the agreement with some of my own independent findings is remarkable.

[5] The only reference to *Werther* in the rich exchange is to be found in Schiller's letter to Goethe of February 19, 1795 (p. 86 of Emil Staiger's edition: *Der Briefwechsel zwischen Schiller und Goethe*, Frankfurt am Main: Insel Verlag, 1966). And this is what is said: "[Körner] finds in *W. Meister* all the strength that was in *Werther's Sorrows*, but controlled by a virile spirit and purified into the quiet grace of an accomplished work of art." The letters, we should keep in mind, reach well into the spring of 1805, and they touch upon every work of the two correspondents as well as on most exponents of the European culture of the time.

Venetian liberal patriots; the suicide, in real life, of Foscolo's own brother, Giovanni, and of the Paduan student Girolamo Ortis; Antonietta Arese's comet-like visitation from 1801 to early 1803, which coincided with the reworking and completion of *Ortis*. The novel had been originally written (Part I) in 1798, in the wake of the Campoformio treaty (1797); interrupted by the political vicissitudes of 1799 which saw Italy invaded by Austrian and Russian forces during Napoleon's expedition to Egypt; "completed" by an Angelo Sassoli at the behest of the original publisher, Marsigli of Bologna; then resumed by Foscolo after Napoleon's return, and finally printed in 1802.[6] Foscolo had trouble with pirated editions and fakes—an odd compliment to him, to be sure, if rather unwelcome.

If ever the making of a novel could itself be a novel in the making, such was the case with *Le ultime lettere di Jacopo Ortis*; and since the fictional suicide, Jacopo, is Foscolo's self-portrait, we are sent back once more to Countess Arese's teasing quip about her fiery poet lover. It would not be until 1817 that the final authoritative edition could appear, in London, with further changes (including the division of the story in two parts), but in this regard the turning point had occurred with the Milan edition of 1802. If Goethe presided over the development of the book with his long-standing

[6] A detailed discussion of these adventurous circumstances surrounding the rise of Foscolo's romantic novel is to be found in Giovanni Gambarin's eighty-four-page Introduction to his critical edition of *Ortis*, Vol. IV of *Edizione Nazionale*, published in Florence in 1955 and including the 1798 edition, Sassoli's arbitrary Epilogue, and the definitive London edition of 1817 (with the variants and afterword of the 1816 Zurich edition). Apropos of the Sassoli "Epilogue" an epoch-making reassessment has come in 1970, and it cannot be ignored. Mario Martelli's article, "La parte del Sassoli," in *Studi di filologia italiana* XXVIII, pp. 177-251, uses painstaking linguistic and stylistic analysis to prove that Sassoli must have worked on F.'s own directions, for "the basic elements of F's compositional technique—juxtaposition of quotes, dismemberment of quotations, reuse of the greatest possible number of elements from the text quoted—are to be found . . . both in S.'s conclusion of *Ortis* and in F's other works."

example, Antonietta Arese gave it the central impulse with her intervention in Foscolo's life; the crucial intertwining of these concomitant stimuli is documented also by the fact that some of the fictional letters Jacopo Ortis addresses to his friend Lorenzo Alderani (the Wilhelm of *Jacopo Ortis'* Werther) closely mirror some of the letters Ugo Foscolo was actually writing at the time to his bewitching mistress and translator of *Werther*. This is true in particular of Ortis' July 19 letter to Teresa, his beloved, which in the 1802 edition markedly changes from its first version in the incomplete 1798 edition (where it was numbered XLV and happened to be the very last part penned by Foscolo himself).[7] The changes overwhelmingly reflect phrases and ideas from Foscolo's own letters to Isabella Roncioni (a real life model of chaste Teresa he had had to give up in Florence) and to Antonietta herself, as Giovanni Gambarin has pointed out in a detailed footnote to his critical edition.[8] For instance, the 1802 version introduces the motif of Jacopo's request of his beloved's portrait as a souvenir—a request Foscolo made to Isabella Roncioni in his parting letter of 1801 from Florence, and also to Antonietta in several letters.

In one of these,[9] probably written in December 1801 or January 1802, he talks of an exchange of portraits and dwells on the way he would like to have them done, fashions, posture and all. Here is what he envisages for her:

[7] My references here will be to Gambarin's critical edition; but it should be kept in mind that the novel is also available in *Opere di F.* and as a separate book with foreword by Carlo Muscetta (Turin: Einaudi, 1973). Both follow the 1817 London edition. Franco Gavazzeni instead, in *U. F., Opere, Tomo I* (Naples: Ricciardi, 1974), includes the Milan edition of 1802. Two recent English translations of *Ortis* are by Douglas Radcliffe-Umstead (in the series North Carolina Studies in the Romance Languages and Literatures) and, respectively, by Dale McAdoo and Anthony Winner (included in the volume *Great European Short Novels* Vol. I, Ed. with Preface and Introduction by A. Winner. New York: Harper and Row, 1968. Pp. 253-390).

[8] *Edizione Nazionale*, Vol. IV, p. 219.

[9] *Epistolario* I, p. 363: Letter 249 (numbered XCVII in the Arese sequence). Translation mine.

. . . I still don't know what to suggest about your portrait. I would long to have it in a melancholy attitude,
picturesque but not romanesque, and in the background
[sic] some tree of a dark green, like cypress or oak. For
the rest, leave it to the painter: if he is a real artist and
has ever been in love, he'll be able to do much better
than what I could tell him. And which painter, seeing
you so beautiful, could not bank on your divine physiognomy? Don't put on your head any coiffure, or French
rags, or flowers. Let your hair go as it stands, and nature
will make it much lovelier than your hairdresser could
ever do with all his art. The arm naked, and the dress
white; if you want a shawl, the fittest color would seem to
be the black; or if it were to stand out too sharply on the
white, choose one that is less violent but tending to the
pathetic. I'd like for you to have a book on your knees or
in your hand: *Werther*, or *Ortis*, and have the painter put
small capital letters in the pages, so one may see that
you have either one of these two books . . .

Antonietta's portrait is already painted here, and the disappointment expressed in the following letter[10] at the preliminary sketch the painter (a lady) had done, only enhances the
vividness of Foscolo's own verbal brushwork:

No, no, the more I think of it the more I dislike that
drawing: you hold the book too awkwardly; I would want
you seated with the book loosely opened on your knees;
the arm then would be stretched and the hand would
have something soft and nonchalant. Do consult more
carefully yesterday's letter; in fact, why don't you copy
that pictorial article and have the painter read it . . .

Taken together in their sequence, or even each by itself, the
two letters are also quite a lively portrait of Ugo Foscolo,

[10] *Epistolario* I, p. 365: Letter 250 (XCVIII Arese sequence). Translation
mine.

showing his intimate side, playful and vehement in turn, and
if the second one is signed "Il tuo Ortis" (Your Ortis), the
obsessively passionate and self-destructive aspect—the one
that chiefly went into the novel, very cathartically—is not allowed to hold unchallenged sway; Didymus tempers him into
self-irony or supersedes him in joyful release:

> . . . Now I'll tell you my life after your last kiss. I took
> the way of the old city ramparts, and I made love to
> yesterday's utterly beautiful sun. Back home, a bit tired,
> I took three or four cups of tea, and then lay down, but
> had no chance to sleep. I have chatted with [my broth-
> er's] teacher until evening, and he was fondly advising
> me not to get up so early any more, because the air of
> this season and sky is most fatal, so much so as he be-
> lieves I have spent my hours in walking and philosophiz-
> ing. Thus from story to story night came, and that Chal-
> dean face did so many crazy things, and said such
> strange ones, that I laughed to split my sides. . . . It was
> months since I had had such a laugh, unless you except
> the *story of the Church* with which my *Scimiotta* (Monkey
> pet) made me laugh while I ate *panettone* (Milanese
> Xmas cake). Then supper time came . . . or rather, I
> made it come around seven; my little family had already
> supped. Therefore I got up to take a stroll; but who
> knows how, at nine or shortly before I found myself in
> bed, at ten I was asleep; I woke up this morning after
> six; I had my servant (mine and not mine) light the fire,
> where I am now writing you and sipping a piping hot tea;
> and may the Lord God bless you. . . .

That is the breezy finale of the first letter, a true hymn to joy,
while the second letter, after the "pictorial" beginning, harps
on possible rivals or disturbers of the amatory peace in comi-
cally violent, self-parodying terms, only to subjoin that
"Werther and Jacopo Ortis are the two only real honest men
on earth," for the others are despicable "courtly polished

rabble" who "play satellite to your planet [meaning obviously Antonietta]" and "talk very badly of anybody, who do no good because they have no virtue, and do no evil because they do not have the courage." "Yet," Foscolo goes on, "Werther and Ortis, despite their heart, talent and honesty, are not preferred to certain wretches who act as pimps to women in order to satisfy their lust, and sell their honor to men in order to foster their vices. Hooray! As for me, I'd say goodby to all society and all belles if I had to be soiled by such wretches.—I am obviously on a preaching stunt. Never mind: when on earth shall I come to stay with you? You are wrong if you think letters are enough for me. . . . "

Whichever way we approach it, the pulsing knot of life and literature, image and passion, reading, living and writing, appears harder and harder to disentangle: their interplay is so complex. On the one hand, these letters give us as nearly unreflected an experience as was possible for such a cultivated writer as Foscolo to have. They actually show the urgency of all but instant communication rather than the niceties of elaborate composition, and we may regard them in part as "sources" for the novel that was still in progress during the first year of Foscolo's love affair with Countess Arese. On the other hand, the letters cannot help being literary prose of a frequently high order; their addressee was a most provocative Muse, the same who, in that very period, elicited from her exuberant worshiper the *Ode all'amica risanata* (Ode to His Lady on Her Recovery)—one of Foscolo's enduring lyrics, a memorable celebration of feminine beauty and capriciousness. And nothing of what he wrote her, be it ever so intimate and circumstantial, could fail to respond in style to that thoroughly enjoyed yet repeatedly elusive Aphrodite.

Moreover, the letters as such, and what they reveal of the liaison that prompted them, bask in the reflected light of the novel in progress—*Jacopo Ortis' Last Letters*—as well as of *Werther. Werther,* we saw, had hovered on the creative horizon of *Ortis* in its 1798 inception (Letter XLV of the 1799 edition has a direct reference to Goethe's book along with others,

Clarissa included), but it re-entered Foscolo's creative orbit even more forcefully when, having resumed work on his own interrupted book, he could have Antonietta Arese as officiating mediator between the German text and his literary consciousness. Life mirrored literature and the nexus between Foscolo's own work and that of an inspiring literary model, just as much as literature fed on his turbulent life.

The resulting constellation of interacting forces is emblematized by him in that letter which contains directives for the prospective painter of Antonietta's portrait. That letter is life directly experienced—and at the same time, literature. It utters an intimate message and grasps a living image; the image in turn, statically conceived as a tableau à la Gainsborough, and abounding in color as Foscolo's poems rarely are (but then note how the *Ode to his Lady on her Recovery* antithetically seizes her image as pure motion), fixes the important elements of Foscolo's creative life in that feverish phase: with Antonietta as presiding Muse, holding the key to his communion with Nature in the background and congenial literature (Goethe) in the foreground. She is actually projected as part of Nature herself, a privileged, culminating part, to be sure, the crown of creation. In the mentioned farewell letter to Isabella Roncioni, as well as in the corresponding first redaction of Ortis' letter to Teresa at the end of the novel's 1798 draft, the request of a souvenir portrait entails no such painterly and emblematic elements as this paramount real life missive to Antonietta does.

Needless to say, the portrait motif, which at its best embodies the endeavor to rescue a significant image, figure or situation from the erosion of time, was to be found also in *Werther*, and will be found in Mme. De Staël's *Corinne* (known to Foscolo) as well as, decades later, in a novel related to *Corinne*: Melville's *Pierre*. What Foscolo does with it in his epistolary exchange with Countess Arese finds little counterpart in *Jacopo Ortis* (where Teresa herself, the chaste, sad, unpossessible sweetheart, is the painter), and places these letters as a whole much above the level of mere source material or side illustration for the novel's composition. I will return to this question eventually; at the moment what matters is the work of narrative art which Aphrodite Antonietta helped to elicit. Its "intertextual" or analogical relationship to Goethe's exemplary novel never ceased busying Foscolo's critical awareness, as we can see from the detailed comparison he draws between *Ortis* and *Werther* in the 1817 *Notizia Bibliografica*,[11] a disguised self-descriptive account he published on the occasion of his novel's definitive London edition.

Thematic analogy is no consequence of servile imitation on Foscolo's part, but rather a deliberate choice springing from a recognition of affinity. The affinity extended to the existential predicament and real life cues; the epistolary form and the theme of suicide as catastrophe seemed viable enough,[12] instead of preemptive, to the eager Italian writer who needed models to emulate, whether classical or modern, in his urge to shape the inner turmoil of a restless, adventurous life into the kind of incisive formulation that would make a difference in Italian literature, indeed shake it from Arcadian complacency. Foscolo's own Arcadian phase, which accounted for the repudiated youthful lyrics (their Ossianic dark shudders notwithstanding), was already overcome by his forceful if rhetorically Alfierian tragedy, *Thyestes*, of 1796 (a great success on the Venetian stage). In a sense, Thyestes' liberty-minded suicide foreshadows Jacopo Ortis', who significantly quotes Dante's purgatorial episode of Cato:[13] "libertà va cercando, ch'è sì cara/ come sa chi per lei vita rifiuta (He is

[11] See Gambarin's critical edition of *Ortis*, pp. 477-541.

[12] For the relevance of the suicide theme (and act) to the European Romantics in general (including Foscolo), see H. G. Schenk, *The Mind of the European Romantics—an essay in cultural history* (New York: Ungar, 1966), p. 64, and Chapter VII, "The Lure of Nothingness," pp. 58-65.

[13] Dante, *The Divine Comedy*, Purg. I, 71-72. For an exemplary treatment of the *Sturm und Drang* movement as a whole, and of *Werther*'s revolutionary implications, see Roy Pascal, *Der Sturm und Drang* (Stuttgart: Alfred Kröner Verlag, 1963). Originally published in English as *The German Sturm und Drang* (Manchester: Manchester University Press, 1953).

seeking liberty, which is so precious, / as those well know
who for its sake repudiate life). Both gestures symbolically
purge an existential despair at the stagnation Foscolo sensed
all around him, but by the same token enact a preliminary to
rebirth.

Here it pays to observe the preponderance of the political
element as description, discussion and motivation, in *Ortis'*
Part I—an element which sharply differentiates Foscolo's
novel from its great German model even though it does not
lead to a successfully unified poetical treatment of the largely
autobiographical character. Libertarian political passion entered neither *Werther's* compass nor that of its immediate artistic predecessor, *La Nouvelle Héloïse*, as a motivating element; it came into *Ortis* from revered Alfieri's example and
it was no matter of mere literary infatuation. Indeed one of
the reasons why *Werther* is the greater work of art is the
avoidance of political passion as such, regardless of the
noteworthy admixture of social critique into what is after all a
subversive *Sturm-und-Drang* novel rather than just a pathetic
bourgeois idyll.[14] Instead of impoverishing Goethe's book,
that basic lack of a political protest—due no doubt to the
chronology of *Werther* (1774) which, unlike *Ortis* (1798,
1802), antedates both the American and the French
Revolution—makes for better focus, more sustained narrative

---

[14] I refer to, and quote from, the following edition of *Werther: Goethes
Werke*, Hamburger Ausgabe, Band 6 (Romane und Novellen, ed. Erich
Trunz. Hamburg: Christian Wegner Verlag, 1963). In this volume *Werther*
comes first, and the editor's exegetical, historical and bibliographical notes
in the Appendix are excellent. They also refer to studies of *Werther* and
Ortis. A distinguished and handy English language edition is: Goethe, *The
Sorrows of Young Werther, and Novella*, tr. by Elizabeth Mayer and Louise
Bogan, Foreword by W. H. Auden (New York: Random House Vintage
Books, 1973). Another fine translation is: Goethe, *The Sorrows of Young
Werther. The New Melusina Novelle*, Introduction by Victor Lange, tr. (New
York: Holt, Rinehart and Winston, Inc., 1949). In both editions, of
course, Macpherson's "Ossian" text which Werther reads to Lotte in the
climactic scene (In Goethe's own translation) is given in the original ver-
sion, from which I shall also quote later on.

development, and richer treatment of the dominant love motif within the chosen narrower compass.

One follows with growing interest the peripeteia of Werther from the joyous effusions of his first contacts with the idyllic world of Waldheim—which afford him a refreshing communion with living Nature no less than with her well attuned human denizens—to the blossoming of his love for Lotte, which, instead of fulfilling the initial auspices of natural and human harmony, gradually turns into a growth of destructive alienation, a ripening to death.[15] The expansion of consciousness at first makes Werther say *Yes* to the world—it happens to be an Edenic world—and gives that world a chance to live in his consciousness, from its cosmic perspective of forest, field, valley, river, mountain, and sky down to the minimal creatures and events which alert his perception to the verge of ecstasy. In keeping with the intrinsic freedom of the letter form, style in such moments effortlessly heightens into rhythmical prose, sustained by waves of musical anaphora:

. . . *Wenn* das liebe Tal um mich dampft, und die hohe Sonne an der Oberfläche der undurchdringlichen Finsternis meines Waldes ruht, und nur einzelne Strahlen sich in das innere Heiligtum stehlen, ich dann im hohem Grase am fallendem Bache liege, und näher an der Erde tausend mannigfaltige Gräschen mir merkwürdig werden; *wenn* ich das Wimmeln der kleinen Welt zwischen Halmen, die unzähligen, unergründlichen Gestalten der Würmchen, der Mückchen, näher an meinem Herzen fühle, und fühle die Gegenwart des Allmächtigen, der uns nach seinem Bilde schuf, das Wehen des Alliebenden, der uns in ewiger Wonne schwebend trägt und erhält; mein Freund!

[15] An intimation of the destructiveness to come can already be seen in the nearly morbid excitement with which Werther responds to the joyful messages of nature toward the end of the May 10 letter: "But I founder on that, I succumb to the sovereign power of these phenomena."

wenn's dann um meine Augen dämmert, und die Welt
um mich her und der Himmel ganz in meiner Seele ruhn
wie die Gestalt einer Geliebten—*dann* sehne ich mich
oft und denke: Ach könntest du das wieder ausdrücken,
könntest du dem Papiere das einhauschen, was so voll,
so warm in dir lebt, dass es würde der Spiegel deiner
Seele, wie deine Seele ist der Spiegel des unendlichen
Gottes!—Mein Freund—Aber ich gehe darüber zug-
runde, ich erliege unter der Gewalt der Herrlichkeit
dieser Erscheinungen.[16]

. . . *When* the lovely valley steams around me, and the
high sun rests on the surface of my wood's impenetrable
darkness, and only single rays sneak into the inner
sanctum, and I then lie down in the high grass near the
brook's falls, and closer to earth a thousand small herbs
become perceptible to me; *when* I feel the teeming of the
little world between grass stalks, the numberless, unfathomable shapes of the mites, of the midges closer to
my heart, and feel the presence of the Almighty, who
made us in his image, the blowing wind of the All-
loving, who carries and sustains us in perennial delight;
o my friend! *when* then twilight gathers around my eyes,
and the world about me and the sky wholly rest in my
soul like the figure of a beloved woman—then do I often
sigh and think: O could you only express all this again,
could you infuse onto the paper what in you lives so
fully, so warmly, so that it would become the mirror of
your soul as your soul is the mirror of infinite God!—o
my friend—But I founder on that, I succumb to the
sovereign power of these phenomena.

Whispering or rich spirant alliterations conspire with the cadence created by the insistent end-verbs sealing clause after

---

[16] *Goethes Werke*, Vol. 6, *Werther*, Part I, May 10 letter, p. 9. Translation mine.

clause to create a syntactical crescendo effect. The specific resources of the German language generate a chiasmic design to make live microcosm and God-pervaded microcosm hinge on the sentient "I" of the writer persona through the pivotal verb *fühle* (I feel), while the persona's soul (*"deine Seele"*) becomes a central mediator between the inspired writing which should mirror it on paper and the inspiring Godhead of whom it in turn is the mirror. The pulsing prose achieves a unique intensity, and critics[17] have accordingly noted the affinity between such lyrical effusions in *Werther* and the coeval *Sturm und Drang* hymns (especially *Ganymed*) freely uttering the ecstatic transport of a lay religiousness disentangled from any church.

But our main concern now is to realize how motifs spontaneously coming up so early in the story become clues to later developments of structural and thematic import, for Goethe is nothing if not a profoundly organic writer. For instance, when world and sky, an all-encompassing reality (one could almost say a cosmic womb), are internalized by the speaker persona as "the figure of a beloved woman," the simile prophesies Werther's falling in hopeless love with Lotte, in whom all the God-suffused beauty of living nature will come to a focus for him. She will be the emotional and aesthetic epitome of the All, and her hold on him (as inner image) will be unshakable. He cannot have her in the circumstances of a relative human world to which she is committed, but since she is by then his absolute, and he wants nothing less than an absolute, he will then have to kill himself—thereby attaining a negative absolute, death, a love death consecrated to her. Erich Trunz, who has appended an insightful commentary to his critical edition of the novel, aptly says that this love death for Werther is an *"Entgrenzung,"* a liberation from the constraining finite—an inverted fulfillment of sorts, I would add, foreshadowing many a *Liebestod* in

---

[17] See *German Sturm und Drang* and *Goethes Werke* 6.

German literature and music, but differing to some extent from the more extremely nihilist implications of Jacopo Ortis' suicide.

The death-wish looming in Werther's lovesick mind when he realizes that Lotte cannot be his other than in friendship—because she marries and loyally loves her sensible, thoughtful Albert—prompts a recurrence of scene and rhythm in the August 18 letter to friend Wilhelm, in which it is inevitable to overhear the direct echo of the May 10 letter in mournful key. At the outset we have once again the surging syntax scanned by the heightening repetition of temporal clauses introduced by *Wenn*, and the energizing view of the living world in panoramic as well as in microscopic scale. The awareness of creative natural forces underneath, a joyful dynamism, is retrospectively colored by sadness at the loss of such communion—for now "a curtain has been pulled open before my soul, and the spectacle of endless life changes under my eyes into the abyss of the eternally yawning grave . . ."; Nature the tireless creative force becomes Nature the voracious destroyer:

> Himmel und Erde und ihre webenden Kräfte um mich her: ich sehe nichts als ein ewig verschlingendes, ewig wiederkäuendes Ungeheuer.[18]

> Sky and Earth and their busy forces all around me: I see nothing but an eternally devouring, eternally ruminating monster.

The vision of a sustaining Nature invested by divine afflatus and benevolence, which ecstatically climaxed the May 10 letter on a note of defeat before the inexpressible, has made way for the infernal revelation of the irrational dark powers that underlie the deceptive grace and majesty of visible phenomena—a transmogrification already hinting at Schopen-

---

[18] *Goethes Werke*, Vol. 6, pp. 51-53. Translation mine.

hauer's and Melville's Weltanschauung, and, before them, at Foscolo's own, in *Jacopo Ortis*.

Goethe will overcome the impasse in the integrative vision of *Faust*, whose *Erdgeist* (Spirit of the Earth) demonically unites in himself the destructive and the creative powers that here in polarized separation haunt Werther's doomed mind. Within the scope of this novel, let us go on to observe how the rhythmical scansion and darkening tone of this August 18 letter forecast the funereal Ossian passages which Werther will read to Lotte (in Goethe's own translation) toward the end, to express his own lugubrious passion and finally snatch a kiss before the final catastrophe. In Werther's own confession, the conversion to a sinister view of reality, and to a deathbound approach, is marked by the fact that Ossian supersedes Homer in his literary taste. Homer had presided, along with the Bible, over the earlier scenes of an idyllic world amounting to an objective, warm reality, while sunny Homer's disappearance from the horizon heralds the advent of a night of the soul under the sign of Ossian: the night of the self-involved, tendentially worldless and therefore self-destructive subjectivity.

Thus the literary references conspire with the development of imagery and style to articulate the theme, and there is a perfect convergence in this case when hymn is eventually metamorphosed into dirge. Rhythm and tone of Goethe's Ossian well suit the fateful occasion—Werther's kiss and his decision to die—while clearly recalling, in the changed key, Werther's early effusions of May 10 and his transition from ecstatic contemplation of the living universe to the horror of its demoniac destructiveness in the August 18 letter. A musical permutation occurs from the very start:[19]

Stern der dämmernden Nacht, schön funkelst du im Westen, hebst dein strahlend Haupt aus deiner Wolke, wandelst stattlich deinen Hügel hin. Wornach blickst

[19] *Ibid.*, pp. 108 ff.

du auf die Heide? Die stürmenden Winde haben sich
gelegt; von ferne kommt des Giessbachs Murmeln; rau-
schende Wellen spielen am Felsen ferne; das Gesumme
der Abendfliegen schwärmet übers Feld. Wornach
siehst du, schönes Licht? Aber du lächelst und gehst,
freudig umgeben dich die Wellen und baden dein lieb-
liches Haar. Lebe wohl, ruhiger Strahl. Erscheine, du
herrliches Licht von Ossians Seele!

   Und es erscheint in seiner Kraft. Ich sehe meine ge-
schiedenen Freunde, sie sammeln sich auf Lora, . . .

Star of descending night! fair is thy light in the west!
thou liftest thy unshorn head from thy cloud; thy steps
are stately on thy hill. What dost thou behold in the
plain? The stormy winds are laid. The murmur of the
torrent comes from afar. Roaring waves climb the distant
rock. The flies of evening are on their feeble wings; the
hum of their course is on the field. What dost thou behold, fair light? But thou dost smile and depart. Thy
waves come with joy around thee: they bathe thy lovely
hair. Farewell, thou silent beam. Let the light of
Ossian's soul arise!

   And it does arise in its strength! I behold my departed
friends. Their gathering is on Lora, . . .

Now that the infectious vogue of Ossian is a matter of literary
archaeology, we might well feel that this episode, with the
emphasis it receives from the extended quotation (over six
pages), from the climactic placement and function, and Lotte's tearful response, dates *Werther* beyond salvage—were it
not that the structural reasons I just mentioned concur with
deft handling and seminal value of theme to make us recon-
sider.

   It is Werther, not Goethe, who succumbs to literature, just
as in *Inf.* v it is Paolo and Francesca, not Dante, who succumb to (meretricious) literature; just as, later on in Euro-

pean writing, it will be "Tristan," not Thomas Mann, who succumbs to literary and musical seduction, and again Aschenbach, not Thomas Mann, who lets literature strengthen the call of homoerotic love to death. Werther, the overly sensitive mind, the potential creator, is dominated by Ossian; Goethe dominates Ossian by incorporating the dirge in his own language and fictional context. Incidentally, I tend to agree with Roy Pascal, who sees in Werther certain problems of the creative spirit who is made vulnerable by his very creativity, rather than with Erich Trunz, who sees him merely as the artist manqué because he fails to commit himself to the initially cultivated art of painting.

Werther is not just the man of feeling, this side of reason and of objective creativity; he is a spontaneous artist in his letters and an intentional one in what is fictionally purported to be his translation from Ossian (Goethe being, of course, the actual translator). That solemn, tearful scene, then, though it may grate on a modern reader's taste, must be seen also as Werther's swansong as an artist—the limited artist he can be. One touch of parody, and we would have Thomas Mann's Tristan instead of Goethe's terribly serious Werther. Make friend Wilhelm, the dutiful reporting voice, a bit more detached; make him sarcastic, and he would play Mephistopheles to the budding Faust that Werther is. But Faust is involved in open experience, not in absolutist love-death. Analogously, the need to pursue his radical theme to the bitter end prevented Foscolo from augmenting his dosage of Sternian ingredients in *Ortis* to the point where humor, the Didymean antidote, would have stopped poor Jacopo from taking that last destructive step. It was in the nature of the theme that these *Sturm-und-Drang* heroes should be taken seriously by their authors and, above all, by themselves. If these novels date in some regards, then after all greater works of literature tend to date: Othello's jealousy, Achilles' wrath, Hamlet's perplexity, Lear's and Goriot's paternal folly, Emma Bovary's dreamy yearning, need our cooperation to be taken

as seriously as they are supposed to be; we need only remember that a reader of Robert Graves' sophistication has seen
the *Iliad* as intentional satire.

The obvious lack of parody in Goethe's presentation of his
hero in *Werther* (the novel as such is not devoid of humorous
touches, at least in Part I) does not imply lack of criticism;
the writer lets him follow his path to self-destruction, and that
is an implicit criticism, not an invitation to imitate Werther's
example, as some readers actually did. The latter grotesquely
brought the work of art back to one occasional source in real
life—the suicide of Mr. Jerusalem, whose yellow waistcoat
and blue jacket were also donned by Werther and became as
famous for decades as Gautier's red waistcoat was to be
somewhat later, for different reasons. The inner logic that
brings Werther to suicide is sustained by many an artful
touch in the handling of narrative incident, dialogue, imagery, and word-play, as we already saw in part when touch-
ing on the organic growth of the overall theme. We saw that
Werther's initial opening to a new life gradually becomes a
ripening for death, and he himself characterizes the process
when he says toward the end, in the December 10 letter: "It is
necessary that nothing should be harvested before it is
ripe,"[20] though he says it in a seemingly casual way. The
curve of his "ripening" develops against the background of
the seasonal cycle: the joyful first letters are penned in
spring, and the suicide is consummated in December of the
following year; the handsome old walnuts he so much
cherished in the parsonage (letter of July 1st, Part I) are eventually chopped down (letter of Sept. 15, Part II), and it is an
intimation of waste and death. When Werther says to
Wilhelm "Mir wäre besser, ich ginge" (It is better for me to
go),[21] he is punning in a macabre way. When Werther says to
Lotte, at the end of Part I, "We shall see each other again,"[22]
that auspicious expression carries a funereal overtone to be

[20] *Ibid.*, p. 101.   [21] *Ibid.*, pp. 100 and 101.
[22] *Ibid.*, p. 57; letter of September 10.

borne out later by his last passionate message to her: "We shall be! We shall see each other again!"[23]—for here he specifies that he dies for her and he feels sure that he will be reunited to her in death, or in another world. When it is autumn around him in Nature, it is autumn in his soul,[24] and winter cannot be far behind. Shortly later (November 30) he meets the deranged youth who seeks flowers in winter and finds none.[25] Intimations of world repudiation and suicide have cropped up almost from the start, and they have counterpointed even the early happy messages, for Werther feels like a prisoner in a world that has no use for his higher forces, which he thinks must remain unused and disguised, to rot away; only with his deceased lady friend (letter of May 17, first year) could he be wholly himself and rise above the level of mere social pleasantry and heartiness. His (largely unachieved) potential is what sets him apart and condemns him to suicide since he cannot fully express it; here we have the theme of the artist's alienation from bourgeois society, long before Flaubert, Mann, and Joyce.

In such a carefully orchestrated development, the cues and inner echoes never sound contrived. Such is the case with the motif of the pistols, which Werther asks of Albert once in the early phase (occasioning a heated discussion of the ethical merits of suicide) and then again later, to use them for killing himself. The same goes for the episodes which could be mistaken for accessory, and work instead as figures (or counter-figures) of Werther's own destiny, since it is strictly through his perception that we are exposed to them: the young handyman who kills his lady out of jealousy, and the young madman at large in the fields. In both cases Werther recognizes alternative destinies to his own, choices he must discard: killing Albert, who stands legally and emotionally between Lotte and himself, and yielding to the seduction of gentle madness. The episodic characters thus introduced are

---

[23] *Ibid.*, p. 117; letter of December 22.
[24] *Ibid.*, p. 76; letter of September 4.   [25] *Ibid.*, p. 88.

artistically realized in their own right, thanks to the dramatic
and epic gift Goethe shares with his beloved Shakespeare;
otherwise they could not convincingly perform their structural
function of thematic reinforcement through mirroring and enrichment. In retrospect, even the masterly and ostensibly
joyous scene of the dance in Part I, when Werther first gets to
know Lotte (in a quite casual way), takes on ominous implications, not just because of the storm that breaks out (it's very
un-Virgilian meteorology after all), but on account of its
breathless crescendo; Werther and Lotte whirl around as if
caught in a storm of their own, from which Lotte can escape,
and Werther cannot. And all the time, needless to say, the
symbolic dimension makes itself felt as a natural projection of
the straight narrative. The dance scene is first and foremost a
lovely verbal picture of social behavior, which advances the
plot while adding to the character portrayal of both Werther
and Lotte.

No one, in short, can read *Werther* today as mere sentimental effusion, of mainly historical interest. It is too subtly
organized—and formally organic—for that. The vegetal imagery conspires with the year-cycle framework to give it a firm
warp and woof. And, in this context, Werther's self-portrayal
achieves a dramatic climax in the Christological references of
November 15, 21, and 30,[26] which find a most striking echo
in his farewell letter to Lotte[27] penned just before his suicide,
between eleven and twelve p.m.:

> Hier, Lotte! Ich schaudre nicht, den kalten, schreck-
> lichen Kelch zu fassen, aus dem ich den Taumel des
> Todes trinken soll! Du reichtest mir ihn, und ich zage
> nicht. All! All! So sind alle die Wünsche und
> Hoffnungen meines Lebens erfüllt!

> Here, Lotte! I am not shuddering at grasping the cold,
> fearsome cup from which I must drink the tumult of

---

[26] *Ibid.*, pp. 85-91.   [27] *Ibid.*, p. 123.

death! You are offering it to me, and I do not tremble.
All! All! Thus are fulfilled all the desires and hopes of
my life!

The chalice motif had come up, as a forceful existential protest, in the November 15 letter:[28]

Was ist es anders als Menschenschicksal, sein Mass
auszuleiden, seinen Becher auszutrinken?—Und ward
der Kelch dem Gott vom Himmel auf seinem Menschen-
lippe zu bitter, warum soll ich grosstun und mich stel-
len, als schmeckte er mir süss?

Is it anything but human destiny to fill one's measure of
suffering, to empty one's cup?—And if the cup (chalice)
tasted too bitter to the Heaven-sent God on his human
lips, why should I act grandly and pretend it tastes sweet
to me?

His religious feeling, wholly heretical, can only express itself
in "a whole litany of antitheses";[29] and in fact, in the Nov. 21
letter, it is Lotte who gives him the cup "full of poison" from
which he drinks his destruction.[30] Place this alongside the
Nov. 15 reference in the immediately preceding letter, and
the final Dec. 13 letter to Lotte quoted above, and you will
have a rendingly dissonant chord: one Gospel image through
its dizzy variations gives the graph of Werther's abysmal
swaying "zwischen Sein und Nichtsein,"[31] so that the Hamle-
tic despair can find its fearful release in the Golgotha cry:

Mein Gott! mein Gott! warum hast du mich verlassen?

My God! my God! why hast thou forsaken me?

[28] *Ibid.*, p. 86.
[29] *Ibid.*, p. 87; letter of November 22.
[30] *Ibid.*, p. 86.
[31] *Ibid.*, p. 86. The expression means "between being and non being."

Werther can identify with Christ in his non-Christian way because he has his own Olive Garden and his Calvary; the language of prayer becomes one and the same thing with the language of protest and despair; it is as if the individual could come to know himself only in utter repudiation and abandon, in the curse of individuality. Werther can identify with Christ because he—like Christ—wants to go back to the Father; but he does not know this Father, this arch, inscrutable Protestant God:

> Vater, den ich nicht kenne! Vater, der sonst meine ganze Seele Füllte und nun sein Angesicht von mir gewendet hat, rufe mich zu dir! Schweige nicht lange! Dein Schweigen wird diese dürstende Seele nicht aufhalten—Und würde ein Mensch, ein Vater, zürnen können, dem sein unvermutet rückkehrender Sohn um den Hals fiele und riefe: "Ich bin wieder da, mein Vater! Zürne nicht, dass ich die Wanderschaft abbreche, die ich nach deinem Willen länger aushalten sollte. Die Welt ist überall einerlei, auf Mühe und Arbeit Lohn und Freude; aber was soll mir das? mir ist nur wohl, wo du bist, und vor deinem Angesichte will ich leiden und geniessen."—Und du, lieber himmlishcher Vater, solltest ihn von dir weisen?[32]

> Father, whom I do not know! Father, who once filled my whole soul and now has turned his face away from me, call me to you! Be silent no more! Your silence will not stop this thirsty soul—And could a man, a father, indeed be angry when his unexpectedly returning son threw his arms around his neck and called out: "Here I am again, father! Do not be angry if I cut short the wandering that according to your will I should have borne longer. The world is the same all over, for toil and work,

---

[32] *Ibid.*, p. 90; letter of November 30.

wages and joy; but what matters that to me? I am well only where you are, and in your presence only will I suffer and rejoice."—And you, dear heavenly Father, you should cast him away?

The suicide is a prodigal son presumptive, and in competition with Christ rather than in imitation of him, so that Werther can appropriate His last cry of anguish without falling back on the established religion—and yet the whole book vibrates with religious feeling, of such a personal nature that we have no trouble recognizing here a forerunner of the existentialist attitude instigated by modern man's loss of the reassuring old creeds.

It is this religious feeling that powers the recurrent wavelike rhythms of *Werther* as they move from the hymnic to the elegiac tone and back again to a hymn in the teeth of despair: Werther's final letter to Lotte, who turns out to be his true godhead and will presumably answer the desolate question that God the Father, unknown and absent, has left unanswered. The crowning of this strong drive toward a feminine godhead will be seen in *Faust*, whose Part II ends with the glorification of redeeming-redeemed Gretchen in the sight of Mary, both translated into "das Ewig Weibliche." Here in *Werther*'s final sequences, it is significant that twice, when an impassioned appeal to the absent God takes shape, that father figure is superseded by Lotte in a comparably exalted capacity. Her deification springs from the absolutist claim of an unfulfilled Eros, for whom the all becomes nothing without her, and she—visually epitomized in her black eyes— invades the all:

Wie mich die Gestalt verfolgt! Wachend und träumend füllt sie meine ganze Seele! Hier, wenn ich die Augen schliesse, hier in meiner Stirne, wo die innere Sehkraft sich vereinigt, stehen ihre schwarzen Augen. Hier! ich kann dir es nicht ausdrücken. Mache ich meine Augen

zu, so sind sie da; wie ein Meer, wie ein Abgrund ruhen
sie vor mir, in mir, füllen die Sinne meiner Stirn. . . .[33]

How her form pursues me! In waking or in dreaming she
fills my whole soul! Here, when I close my eyes, here in
my forehead, where the inner power of vision unites,
stand her black eyes. Here! I cannot express it for you.
If I close my eyes, there hers are; as a sea, as an abyss
they rest before me, in me, and fill the senses of my
forehead. . . .

Just as Laura obsesses Petrarch, Lotte obsesses Werther,
and there is a touch of the demonic as well as of the divine in
the surreal visionary climax reported here; in Werther's subjective world she supersedes God the Father, that God who
used to "fill" him while she is the only fullness he now knows.
The ambiguities of erotic-religious experience are conveyed
with rare force by the web of recurrent-developing imagery
allied to the surging rhythms of a prose which repeatedly as-
pires to the condition of music. Although Werther declares
himself unable to render this deep experience in adequate
words, he manages to do it so well that his expression projects
for us a tangible, dynamic infinity, the divine-demonic essence of Lotte, goddess of love and death, nocturnal, unseizable and inescapable, funereal and splendid. This "Entgrenzung"[34] of Lotte—a prefiguring of Werther's own submersion
in death—has little to do with the plain, reasonable, if sensitive, and practical Lotte of real life, and the discrepancy is
underlined by Goethe himself by way of juxtaposition, as we
see by comparing this letter with the previous one featuring
Lotte's own innocently solicitous words to her friend. It all
bears out the intrisic critique Goethe implants in the self-

[33] *Ibid.*, p. 92; letter of December 6.

[34] This word, which might be awkwardly rendered in English as "un-
limiting" or release from limits, infinite expansion, is used by Erich Trunz
in the interpretive essay appended to his critical edition of *Werther* to convey the quality of the suicidal hero's feeling about his own death.

description of his tragic hero. It is as if he resumed, to bring it to a head, the troubadour tradition of doomed love, from Cavalcanti to Petrarch, while looking forward to a different solution, as his later fiction was to attest. Werther's extreme subjectivism is its own doom; the later Goethe will have left this crucial phase behind, just as the mature Dante was to leave behind his Cavalcantian phase of death-ridden, subjectivized love. Love in the Western world, certainly in the literary one, had had a long heterodox tradition, as Denis de Rougemont pointed out;[35] and through whatever modifications it has led, chiefly with Goethe but also Rousseau before and Foscolo after him, to the confessional strain of modern writing.

The very passionate intensity Goethe injected into the confessions of his own *enfant du siècle* testifies to the closeness of creature to creator in this model case, where bringing forth the fictional child was also an act of necessary repudiation, and the repudiation, a saving exorcism. Werther secretly haunted Goethe, and only in his old age, when writing the *Trilogy of Passion*, could the poet bring himself to welcome back the prodigal son of his own stormy youth. Likewise Ugo Foscolo, for whom the writing of *Le ultime lettere di Jacopo Ortis* amounted to a cathartic endeavor, spent the rest of his literary life neutralizing that confessional character, Jacopo Ortis, whose self-destructive bent paradoxically supplied him with the quick of creativeness, and called forth the ironic Didymus, an anti-self terribly needed in the saving dialectic of imagination. There was so much to kill in the domain of his turbulent self, and so much to revive, that only by this symbolic sacrifice could Ugo Foscolo liberate himself for the exceptional task awaiting him. Out of this total negation the difficult limited affirmations historical flesh is heir to could arise. The initial claim to an unqualified fulfillment, to an emotional infinite, would thus make the limited fulfillments possible, for both writers. *Ortis* is not born as a mere literary

[35] Denis de Rougemont, *Love in the Western World*. New York: Doubleday, 1940, 1955.

imitation of *Werther*; at any rate it takes courage to snatch the club from the hands of Hercules, and Foscolo was the first to acknowledge his debt to the formidable German model, which helped him to channel and release his creative powers instead of stifling them—as might have happened to a less vigorous talent.

Foscolo was also the first to analyze in detail the similarity along with the telling differences between *Ortis* and *Werther*, in his bibliographical notice appended to the 1817 London edition of the novel that had suddenly made him famous almost a score of years before. The comparison is as penetrating and straightforward as we could expect from a man of his temper, who had not hesitated to enter a direct confrontation with Goethe's early masterpiece when the circumstances of his own life had impelled him to voice his "heroic furies" through the mask of Jacopo Ortis and thereby control them. The analogy of conception and vehicle acted as a stimulant on Foscolo's inventive talent, which found repeated incentive in extant literature (whether as translator-critic or conscious imitator) for the expressive release of his tumultuous experience. He is as literary as a writer can afford to be precisely because he is as personal as one could ever be; he needed molds to contain and shape that lava. In this again he resembles Ezra Pound, and certainly his impact on the Italian literary scene was revolutionary, and far from short-lived. But if he looms larger on the Italian horizon, he demands to be placed in a European perspective too, if only because of the enduring enrichment he had brought to poetry and of the tireless experimentation that marked his intense career—an experimentation we are in a better position to evaluate after Ezra Pound.

Ortis, as its author indicates, differs from *Werther* not just because the political element plays such a large part in it that it precedes and almost forestalls unhappy love as the motivation of suicide, but also because it is a story contained within a narrower compass of development, and jerkier in narrative treatment. In *Werther* we follow the organic development of the hero's attitude from joyful expansiveness to brooding despair through a tragic *peripeteia* of sorts, though the seeds of alienation were there to begin with; in *Ortis* instead, the chips are down from the start, for the axe has fallen on the protagonist's hopes for a better or simply viable world:

Il sacrificio della patria è consumato.

The sacrifice of our fatherland is consummated.

That opening clause of the novel (which refers to Napoleon's ruthless bartering of Venice's freedom in 1797 for the political advantages a settlement with Austria would afford) already hints at the final sacrifice which Jacopo will consummate in his own person when even the love of Teresa will be denied him, and he will see no reason to cling to an uprooted life. Thus, properly speaking, in *Ortis* we have no dramatic development because we have no reversal of situation and attitude, no *peripeteia* to say it in Aristotelian terms; it is a more static novel than its German counterpart, and Jacopo Ortis' "tragic monologue," as Angelo Jacomuzzi has aptly called it,[36] is already an epilogue, a predetermined catastrophe which the episode of Teresa can only temporarily delay; one could graphically abstract it as a descending curve with a rebounding tract in the midst, or, in more concrete terms, one could describe it as a positive reversal *manqué*.

The painful realization of defeat for his liberal ideals, supported by objective description and philosophizing interludes, passes into the reawakening of hope when Teresa appears, but the ecstatic moment makes way for another disappointment and then nothing is left but suicide—a gesture compounded of Plutarchian as well as Wertherian aspects, but still significant as a radical challenge to a world which has no providential God to illuminate it and no human justice to sustain it either. In this sense, *Ortis* in the literary sphere

[36] Angelo Jacomuzzi, *Il monologo tragico di Jacopo Ortis*. Torino: Fògola editore, 1974.

amounts to an extremer act of contestation than its poetically
richer and more coherent model. Cheated in his revolutionary
hopes (a terrible thing for an aspiring young man who has
seen the initial promise of the French Revolution, that revolution to which Goethe's *Werther* and the whole Sturm und
Drang movement were only tentatively pointing), robbed of a
country he loved, and forced to renounce the one thing which
might have reconciled him to this existence—a great love, itself frustrated by the political circumstances—Jacopo Ortis
flings his body in bloody protest at the world, and at God himself if such an entity be conceivable anymore.

Werther's ultimate sacrifice is preceded by prayer, heretical of course, but sublime; Ortis argues with God or "God"
only to blaspheme, blasphemy being his only way to acknowledge a possible godhead. This reflects the overall
physiognomy of each novel, *Werther's* being clearly more focused and narratively modulated, with the consequence that
its Pietist inspiration ultimately reabsorbs the concurrent
Sturm-und-Drang ideology, with which it seemed bound to
clash. Pietism transforms protest into prayer and violence itself into a strange gentleness, while *Ortis* seesaws between
gentleness and violence for the same reason that its Christian
and biblical component conflicts with its Jacobin, materialist,
ultimately Hobbesian[37] ideology without ever bringing such
tense polarity to a resolution. As happens with so many disaf-
fected Catholics, blasphemy, that verbal violence, becomes a
negative verification of God's presence, or a stratagem to
summon him back from an unendurable absence. Werther
never accuses his "unknown Father," he actually makes his
suicide a sacrificial offering in which the person of the priest
and the person of the victim are one, and God the Father and
God the Mother—in Lotte—are also one. His self-removal
from the world of flesh and blood is a way of seeking God be-

[37] For a recent assessment of Thomas Hobbes's impact on Italian
thought (through Vico), with cursory but emphatic acknowledgment of Foscolo's part in the contact, see Ferruccio Focher, *Vico e Hobbes*. Naples:
Giannini, 1977.

yond the established creeds. Ortis instead quarrels with God because he cannot find Him, and the contradiction between the letters in which he invokes or praises God, and those which describe his desolate, infernal view of nature and history as a product of blind forces, is nearly schizoid; it actually pulls his mind apart at the seams and goes a long way toward justifying his suicide.

The later work of Foscolo will show no such destructive tension between the ancestral creed and the stark image of reality that modern science has begun to formulate; Foscolo will accept the latter and stoically build on it what can be called a newfangled humanism deprived of any metaphysical guarantees. Thus *I Sepolcri*, thus *Le Grazic*, works where characteristically we find no reference to a Christian God, and therefore no blasphemy; the Greek gods that populate these poems are cherished fictions, cultural data, ciphers of man-made values. Thus the storm of *Ortis* was cathartic to Foscolo in a different way than *Werther* proved cathartic to Goethe, for the German poet evolved a kind of humanism steeped in an immanent spiritualism (and the end of *Faust* II actually comes pretty close to a neo-Catholic mythology), while Foscolo made a pretty radical choice between his received transcendent faith and the bare world-view conveyed by Enlightenment philosophy. When Jacopo Ortis, toward the very end, in his letter to Teresa asks God to annihilate him, he is in effect annihilating God:

T'amai dunque t'amai, e t'amo ancor di un amore che non si può concepire che da me solo. E' poco prezzo, o mio angelo, la morte per chi ha potuto udir che tu l'ami, e sentirsi scorrere in tutta l'anima la voluttà del tuo bacio e piangere teco—io sto col piè nella fossa; eppure tu anche in questo frangente ritorni, come solevi, davanti a questi occhi che morendo si fissano in te, in te che sacra risplendi di tutta la tua bellezza. E fra poco! Tutto è apparecchiato: la notte è già troppo avanzata— addio—fra poco saremo disgiunti dal nulla, o dalla in-

comprensibile eternità. Nel nulla? Sì, sì; poiché sarò
senza di te, io prego il sommo Iddio, se non ci riserba
alcun luogo ov'io possa riunirmi teco per sempre, lo
prego dalle viscere dell'anima mia, e in questa tremenda
ora della morte, perché egli m'abbandoni soltanto nel
nulla. Ma io moro incontaminato, e padrone di me
stesso, e pieno di te, e certo del tuo pianto! Perdonami,
Teresa, se mai—ah consolati, e vivi per la felicità de'
nostri miseri genitori; la tua morte farebbe maledire le
mie ceneri. . . .[38]

I loved you then I loved you, and I still love you with a
love that can only be conceived by myself. It is a small
price, o my angel, to die when one has heard you say
that you love him and felt his whole soul flooded by the
delight of your kiss, and wept with you—I have one foot
in the grave; yet you even now return, as you used to,
before these eyes which dying come to rest on you, on
you who sacred shine with all your beauty. And before
long! All is prepared: the night wears on—goodbye—
before long we shall be divided by nothingness, or by
the incomprehensible eternity. In nothingness? Yes—
Yes, yes; since I shall be without you, I pray almighty
God, if He reserves no place where I can be reunited to
you forever, I pray Him from my deepest soul, and in
this dreadful hour of death, that He may only abandon
me in nothingness. But I die untainted, and self-
possessed, and full of you, and sure of your tears! Forgive me, Teresa, if ever—ah console yourself, and live
for the happiness of our poor parents; your death would
cause my ashes to be cursed. . . .

Consider the equivalence of "nothingness" and "incomprehensible eternity," and the resolution of religion in
nihilism; consider the idea that Jacopo and his beloved

---

[38] *Edizione Nazionale*, vol. IV, p. 472. Translation mine.

Teresa will be separated, instead of united, by death, and compare this tolling insistence on the word "nulla," nothingness, with the quite different tone and tenor of Werther's final letter to Lotte, which rings with the certainty of reunion in the beyond, echoing triumphantly, in the funereal context, the earlier words "We shall be! We shall see each other again!" Jacopo's final words are an utter denial of the Beyond, and a protesting assertion of this world's values—the "incomprehensible eternity" is really nothing when compared to the fleeting plenitude of Jacopo's timebound consciousness in his last moments.

To ask God for annihilation is itself blasphemy, since God is traditionally, for a Christian mind, the creator and preserver of being; and blasphemy indeed had occurred earlier in the novel:[39]

Midnight

I used to send my thanks to the Godhead, and my prayers, but I never feared it. Yet now that I feel the whole flagellation of misfortune I fear and beseech it.

My intellect is blinded, my soul is prostrate, my body is buffeted by death's languor.

It is true! the wretched need another world, different from this one where they eat a bitter bread, and drink water mingled with tears. The imagination creates that world, and the heart is consoled. Virtue, always unhappy down here, holds out by the hope of a reward— but woe to those who in order not to be rascals need religion!

I have knelt in a little church at Arquà, because I felt that God's hand weighed on my heart.

Am I perhaps weak, Lorenzo? May Heaven never let you feel the need for solitude, for tears, and for a church!

[39] *Ibid.*, pp. 377-78 (letter of June 2, 1798); pp. 382-83 (letter of July 7, 1798). Translation mine.

Two a.m.

The sky is stormy: the stars few and pale; and the moon half buried in the clouds beats at my windows with livid rays.

Dawn

Lorenzo, don't you hear? your friend is invoking you: what a sleep! a ray of daylight is glimmering and perhaps only to revive my pain in blood—God does not hear me. He actually condemns me at every minute to the agony of death; and He compels me to curse my days which are not stained by crime.

What? if you are *a strong, intolerant, jealous God, who avenges the iniquities of the fathers on the sons, and who visits in his fury the third and the fourth generation,* shall I hope to appease you? Send into me—but not into anyone else—your anger which *kindles in hell the flames* that shall burn millions and millions of peoples to whom you did not make yourself known.—But Teresa is innocent: and instead of deeming you cruel, she worships you with most sweet serenity. I do not worship you, because in fact I fear you—and I feel that I need you. Do, do strip yourself of the attributes in which men have clothed you to make you like themselves. Aren't you the Consoler of the Afflicted? And was not your Divine Son called *the Son of Man?* Hear me then. This heart feels you, but do not be offended at the moan Nature wrings from man's lacerated inside. And I murmur against you, and cry, and invoke you, hoping to free my soul—free it? but how, if it is not full of you? if it has not implored you in prosperity, and only runs to you for help, and asks for your arm's support now that it is downcast in misery? if it fears you, and has no hope in you? Neither does it hope or desire anything but Teresa: and I see you in her alone.

Here, o Lorenzo, here comes from my lips the crime for which God has withdrawn His look from me. I have

never worshiped Him as I worship Teresa.—Blasphemy!
The equal of God, she who at a mere gust will be bones
and nothing? You see man humiliated. Shall I then put
Teresa before God?—Ah! from her a beauty celestial
and immense radiates, omnipotent beauty. I measure
the universe with one glance; I contemplate eternity with
astonished eyes; everything is chaos, everything fades,
and sinks into nothingness; God becomes incomprehensible to me; and Teresa is always before me.

The emotional charge is unmistakable, and it affects everything Foscolo is appropriating from *Werther*—notably the
motif of the unknown God, who no longer fills the soul of
Jacopo because Teresa takes over and becomes his godhead;
but, unlike Werther, Jacopo Ortis experiences an eclipse of
God into chaos and nothingness, and no wonder, considering
the shaken faith that the midnight entry voices with its ruthless critique of popular religion and its intellectual destruction of the idea of a Beyond in anthropological terms. Jacopo
has a bitterer cup to empty than Werther (and the chalice
motif likewise echoes in several passages of *Ortis*), his
Gethsemane is more excruciating, because it will lead to
nihilism or at least a totally irreligious stance, sharply contrasting with the very personal faith Werther is left with in his
supreme moments.

As against the hymnal rhythm that surges from Werther's
fictional pen in ample waves of liberated prose, Ortis' lines
achieve a hammering and often staccato effect with their repeated questions and exclamations—just as the total narrative structure of *Ortis* tends to the staccato versus the legato
shape of *Werther*. Even the lovely 2 a.m. entry, with its utter
brevity and powerful synaesthetic image of the moon beating
at the windows, contributed to syncopate the rhythmic form of
a prose which is the portrait of a "lacerated inside," of an intense, torn mind, caught between irreconcilable values and
struggling to free itself from those it no longer finds viable
even if it has a residual attachment to them, because they are

part of its background. And this is where the persona Jacopo Ortis coincides with his creator Ugo Foscolo—never mind how carefully he tried to dissociate himself from the identity of his tormented creature in his public pronouncements on the novel, for instance this:

> But would Ortis seem any longer the twenty-year old youth who feels his passions so strongly and quickly, to the point where he can never find a way to develop them? If instead of concentrating the excessive warmth of his style according to his way of feeling and conceiving, he had endeavored to expand it conformably to art's dictates, the readers would have seen the *author* in him instead of *the man*; . . .[40]

The fact is, that in *Ortis'* case the persona is much closer to the author than in the case of *Werther*, both novels clearly having a strong confessional touch to begin with, the mark of ebullient adolescence weathered in imaginative minds that must come to terms with a crucial alternative to which their projected heroes succumb: All or Nothing. The sacrifice of Werther and Jacopo Ortis, consummated as it was on the white page, enabled their creators to survive.

The issue will arise anew in twentieth-century existentialist literature, whether of a Christian or of an atheist bent, Chestov or Camus, Berdiaev, Sartre, Sylvia Plath, or Pavese. Pavese's liking for Foscolo as well as for German romantic literature is far from accidental, and far from accidental is the resemblance of many pages from his diary, *The Job of Living* (posthumously published, and kept until the eve of his bitter end—suicide) to much in *Werther* and in *Ortis*. The *Ortis* sequence excerpted above comes to mind when one reads Pavese's diary entries from the last years, in Rome: short impressionist touches of *paysage moralisé* alternating with self-searching meditations and barely sketched essays. To be

---

[40] *Ibid.*, p. 527 ("Notizia bibliografica"). Translation mine.

sure, in Pavese's case the coincidence of writer and persona became total, for self-sacrifice was consummated in the flesh after its vicarious enactment in the personae of novels like *Among Women Only*; Foscolo and Goethe instead, having faced the incommensurables of a culture in the process of secularization and of a burgeoning youth that could accept only absolutes, committed suicide by proxy at the outset of their career, not at the sunset. And that, too, may be a comment of sorts on the distance modern Western culture has travelled since their stirring time, if Alfred Alvarez[41] can be adduced as a side witness. In Ortis' end was Foscolo's beginning, while in Pavese's end was Pavese's end; the reversal is symptomatic.

To continue with Foscolo's attempt to dissociate himself from his Ortis persona (in response to H. Meister's remark that, vis-à-vis *Werther*, *Ortis* evinced a franker, more individual, Southern-style warm touch, but still left something to desire, namely a more continuous development of motifs, the succession of feelings proving perhaps "too sudden and rapid"), he comes closer to the truth when he says:

> . . . the vigor and freshness of expression springs from spiritual vehemence and practical use of language, rather than from a premeditated method of writing. Therefore whoever happened to say that the style of this booklet pleases precisely because it has no style (in the scholastic sense of the word), would perhaps hit the mark. One never reads; one always hears; nor does one hear the orator or the narrator, but the young man who speaks impetuously and in so doing betrays the various colors of his voice and the changes of his physiognomy.[42]

I shall return to this statement further on, but for the time

[41] Alfred Alvarez, *The Savage God, a Study of Suicide*. New York: Random House, 1972.

[42] *Edizione Nazionale*, IV, p. 483. Translation mine.

being let me observe that when Foscolo characterizes Jacopo Ortis' style as close to the informal oral delivery one would not expect in canonic literary language, and moreover as rapid and impetuous, he is characterizing himself, "rapidity" being, in Foscolo's own definition, not just the prerogative of effusive youth, but the high mark of Dante's style, and of the Italian language at its best. Rapidity, impetuousness, narrative staccato, are the distinctive traits of Foscolo's Pindaric style in the lyrical poetry for which he is best known, even if one must allow for the difference between the Latinate color of the poems' lexicon and the somewhat plainer tone of *Ortis'* vocabulary. Jacopo Ortis was the uncompromising youth at the center of Ugo Foscolo's personality, just as Didymus was the smiling wise man he hoped to become, both projections of one intense, rich center of experience.

When Ortis "writes," he writes Foscolo, pure Foscolo, Foscolo in his untamed turmoil, the chaos in which God sinks so that the new man may rise; and he writes the beginning of a literature to come, a literature that will wait long after Ugo's death to follow suit. Through Jacopo Ortis, Foscolo felt free to be free, criminally free, more extremely free than any of his officially Romantic successors in Italian literature ever dared to be; so free that he himself felt afraid of that freedom later on, when he penned his *Lettere dall'Inghilterra* for prospective publication,[43] and there, having donned the mask of wise Didymus, condemned the novel of his volcanic youth as dangerous to the new youth; and yet so free that in 1817 his *Ortis* style exemplified for him the perilous liberties which threaten formal disruption just because they insure, for the strong writer, a live, new form, on the brink of the *informal*:

> His style suddenly takes various colors from the multiplicity of objects; his thoughts are disorderly: and yet the style always keeps one tenor, thanks to the individual's character; and disorder forms a whole which might

[43] *Edizione Nazionale*, v. *Prose varie d'arte*, a cura di Mario Fubini. Florence: 1951. Pp. 237-454.

be defined as harmonically composed of dissonances.[44]

Or, in Wallace Stevens' words a century and a half later, "a violent disorder is an order." I daresay that in this critical aside Foscolo shows the extent of his poetical boldness just as much as he had eighteen years earlier when lending his blood to the phantom of Jacopo Ortis. Again, he refers to critics who objected to the hyperbolic tension of expressions like this:

Tu mi hai inchiodata la disperazione nel cuore . . .

You have nailed despair into my heart . . .[45]

One should not forget that the dominant taste in Italian letters was still Arcadian when Foscolo wrote *Ortis*, and that the necessary violence in style and ideas must have upset readers accustomed to blander fare. That his violence could be liberating only few could recognize—and we have seen that Foscolo himself, years later, felt uncomfortable about his criminally confessional novel.

The manner was no less disruptive than the matter was subversive—a difficult heritage to live with even for somebody as temperamentally honest as the exile from Zante was. In view of his waverings vis-à-vis his own brainchild, which it took him almost a score years to accept for the "dangerously" innovative work it was (and even so, under the protective mask of authorial lie, for he refused to accept responsibility for the *Notizia bibliografica*), I incline to look on Jacopo Ortis as Foscolo's "man of the underground," the demonically destructive alter ego whom he kept confronting,[46] his William Wilson, on whom, of course, creativity also depended. This explains both his recurrent identification with him in the let-

----

[44] *Edizione Nazionale*, IV, p. 496. Translation mine.

[45] *Ibid.*, p. 404. Letter of September 17, Part II.

[46] For this thematic area in the European novel from Goethe on, see Maurice Beebe, *Ivory Towers and Sacred Founts–the Artist as Hero in Fiction from Goethe to Joyce*. New York: New York University Press, 1964.

ters to Antonietta and in the coeval poems until 1803, and his subsequent attempts at dissociation from Ortis in favor of the gentler Didymus mask. It is one thing to have "overcome" the inner demon by way of objectified fiction, and another to have to confront that permanently conjured reality, that voice crying out for absolutes. If writing is cathartic, it is also spellbinding. And shocking: the formal and thematic liberties Jacopo Ortis afforded Ugo Foscolo could be as shocking in his time as automatic writing has been in ours. Jacopo Ortis, man of the underground, iconoclastic accuser, can have a dark, Satanic voice, like Byron's Manfred and Cain before the fact, and is thus a prototype of the Satanic strain in European literature:

> . . . But I have lost you [Teresa], and you steal away from me, you yourself. Ah if you only loved me as I love you!
>
> Yet, Lorenzo, in such fierce doubts, and in so many torments whenever I ask the advice of my reason it confronts me by saying: *You are not immortal*. So then, let us suffer; and to the utmost—I will, I will get out of life's hell; and I alone am enough for that: at this idea I laugh at chance, and at men, and almost at God's omnipotence.[47]

The Satanic, nihilist implications of that laughter stand out even more sharply if we keep in mind the angelic beginning of the letter, all suffused by the remembrance of Teresa's one kiss. And the satanic destructiveness rings out in a dissonant chord with the thought of Teresa in the follow-up to this letter, the May 28 one:

Often I imagine the whole world deranged, and the Sky,

Even though Beebe does not mention Foscolo, his name jumps from the page, as it were, in Part One where the talk is of "the divided self" and of "the 'I' as Hero—the Confessional Novel, 1785-1869." (Pp. 21-64).

[47] *Edizione Nazionale*, IV, p. 375. Letter of May 27. Translation mine.

and the Sun, and the Ocean, and all the globes in flames
and nothingness; but even if among the universal ruin I
could once more clasp Teresa—just once more in these
arms, I would invoke the destruction of the universe. [48]

Frequent alternation of short to long letters, and of descriptive to ratiocinative ones (like the one reporting Jacopo's conversation with old poet Parini in Part II, first section, covering the pilgrimage through Italy's patriotic shrines), combines with the contrast of rare lyrical interludes to the prevalently stormy or dejected tenor of the prose to make the story pulsate feverishly between light and shadow, effusion and knotted up contraction. The June 2 letter in Part I (mentioned above) depicts a desperate Jacopo who is criminally insane (in his wishful thinking) in the midst of a sinister Nature from which he has torn the veil. But the far longer February 19 and 20 letter in Part II,[49] echoing the earlier one, orchestrates the theme more massively and profusely in a searing argument of Jacopo with himself, about everything—his unhappiness, the unreliability of man, nature and history, his right to kill himself in protest, and compassion as the only genuine virtue, since all other virtues are "usuraie," usurer virtues. The monologue—a clear anticipation of Schopenhauer (and of course Leopardi) in its logical tenor—unfolds breathlessly from a hectic sequence of questions and answers which aim at refuting any philosophical justification of existence, to a nadir of nightmare, to a funereal peace of meditative release, and it well samples the endless debate Foscolo was conducting with himself about these existential issues.

Comparison with the later essay *On the limits of Justice*,[50] which arose as an academic address to the young law graduates of Pavia University during Napoleon's rule, spotlights the double answer Foscolo could give to the same

[48] *Ibid.*, p. 375. Translation mine.

[49] *Ibid.*, pp. 430-39. Translation mine.

[50] *Edizione Nazionale*, VII. *Lezioni, articoli di critica e di polemica, 1809-1811*, a cura di Emilio Santini. Florence: 1933, 1967. Pp. 165-186.

question—whether or not life and society made sense—
depending on the private or public context. His private, underground, Ortis self is free to say *No, in thunder*; his public
self, mindful of his mental power on other lives, departs from
the same Hobbesian view of life as a jungle to arrive at a qualified justification of organized society, at least under the new
dispensation. The public-minded essay is admirably woven
and compact; the private confession delegated to Jacopo Ortis
is convulse and subordinates logic to passion, but it brings us
closer to the desperate truth Foscolo was facing through his
demonic persona:

> . . . But the debts you have to Society?—Debts? perhaps
> because it drew me out of Nature's free womb, when I
> had neither reason nor free will to consent, nor strength
> to oppose it, and it brought me up among its needs and
> prejudices? Lorenzo, . . . you would be as convinced as
> I am, if you felt my wounds; may heaven spare you
> those!—Did I contract those debts of my own accord?
> and shall my life pay, as if I were a slave, for the evils
> Society procures for me, only because it calls them
> benefits? and let them be benefits: I enjoy them and pay
> for them as long as I live; and if in the tomb I am no good
> to society, what good do I get from it in the tomb? O my
> friend! every individual is a born enemy of Society, be-
> cause Society is the necessary enemy of individuals.
> Suppose all mortals were interested in abandoning life,
> do you think they would bear it just for my sake? and if I
> commit a deed which damages the many, I am punished;
> while I'll never have a chance to revenge myself of their
> actions, even though they may amount to utter damage
> for me. They can well claim me as a child of the great
> family: but I in turn, renouncing the common goods and
> duties, can say: I am a world in myself: and I intend to
> emancipate myself because I miss the happiness you
> promised me . . .
> . . . Why do I live? what good am I to you, I a fugitive

among these cave-ridden mountains? what honor to myself, to my country, to my loved ones? Is there a difference between these solitudes and the tomb? My death would be the terminal point of my troubles to me, and the end of your anxieties about me. . . . Ah yes! I still live; and the only spirit of my days is an obstinate hope that always reanimates them, and which I still try not to listen to: I cannot—and if I want to disabuse it, it changes into infernal despair.—Your marriage vows, Teresa, will also be my death sentence—but as long as you are free; and our love is so far at the mercy of circumstances—of the uncertain future—and of death, you will always be mine. I talk to you, and look at you, and embrace you: and it seems to me that from far away you feel my kisses and my tears. But once your father has offered you as a propitiatory victim on God's altar—when your weeping will have returned peace to your family—then—not I—but despair alone, and by itself, will annihilate man and his passions. And how can my love be extinguished, while I live? and how can its sweet lure fail to seduce you secretly? but then they will no longer be sacred and innocent. I will not love, once she is of somebody else, the woman who was mine—I love Teresa immensely; but not Odoardo's wife—alas, while I write perhaps you are in his bed!—Lorenzo!—alas Lorenzo! here is that demon persecuting me; he returns to harass me, to press me, to assail me, and he blinds my intellect, and even stops my heart throbs, and makes me all ferocity, and would want the world to be finished with me.—Cry, all of you—and why does he push a dagger into my hands, and goes before me, and turns back to see if I am following him, and shows me where I must stab? Are you coming from Heaven's lofty revenge?—And thus in my fury and superstition I prostrate myself on the dust horribly to beseech a God whom I do not know, whom at other times I candidly worshiped, whom I did not offend, of whom I always doubt—and then I tremble, and worship him. Where am I seeking help? not in me, not in men: the Earth I have bloodied, and the Sun is black.

At last here I am at peace!—What peace? weariness, burial drowsiness. I have wandered among these mountains. There is no tree, no shack, no grass. It is all briars; jagged and livid boulders; and here and there many crosses marking the spots where wayfarers were murdered. Down there is the Roja, a torrent which when the ice thaws rushes headlong from the Alps' entrails, and for a long stretch has split this immense mountain in two. There is a bridge near the seashore that connects the path. I have stopped on that bridge, and I have gone as far as I could with my eyes; and ranging over two walls of very high cliffs and cavernous ravines, one just glimpses, superimposed on the heads of the Alps, other Alps of snow steeped in the sky, and everything whitens and fades—from those wide open Alps there descends the north wind in wavy gait, and through those jaws it invades the Mediterranean. Nature sits here solitary and menacing, and drives all the living from this its kingdom.

These are your boundaries, Italy! but they are daily transgressed on every side by the persistent greed of nations. Where are then your sons? . . . .

. . . The universe is a system of balances. Nations devour one another because one could not subsist without the corpses of the other. I looking out on Italy from these Alps cry and shake, and invoke revenge against the invaders; but my voice is lost in the still live shudder of so many deceased peoples, when the Romans raped the world, sought beyond the seas and deserts new empires to lay waste, violated the gods of the conquered, chained utterly free princes and peoples, until, not finding anything more to bloody their swords, they turned them against their own entrails. Thus the Israelites slaughtered the peaceful inhabitants of Canaan . . . Thus Alexander. . . . Thus the Spartans. . . . Thus the ancient Italians tore one another to pieces until they were swallowed by Rome's fortune. . . . Oh how much smoke of human pyres encumbered the sky of America, oh how much blood of numberless peoples who bore no fear or envy to the Europeans, was brought by the Ocean to sully our beaches with infamy! but that blood will be avenged one day and will fall on the children of the Europeans! . . . The earth is a forest of wild beasts. . . .

Meanwhile we pompously call virtues all those actions that help the security of men in power and the fear of men who serve. . . . Lorenzo, do you know where true virtue still lives? in us few weak or illstarred men; in us who, after experiencing all errors, and feeling all the woes of life, can pity and succor. You, Compassion, are the only virtue! the others are all usurer virtues. . . .

But while I look from on high upon the follies and fatal misfortunes of mankind, don't I feel all the passions, and weakness and tears, the only elements of man? Don't I sigh daily for my motherland? . . . O Nature! do you perhaps need us wretches, and consider us like the worms and bugs which multiply and teem under our eyes without knowing why they live? . . . Why then am I fleeing? . . .—Ah no! I will return to you, sacred lands which first heard my infant cries. . . . Since all is clothed in sadness for me, if nothing else I can hope but the eternal sleep of death—you alone, o my woods, will hear my last lament, and you alone will cover my cold corpse with your peaceful shade . . . and if passion survives the sepulcher, my sorrowing spirit will be comforted by the sign of that heavenly girl who I thought was born for me. . . .

Of course the meandering chain of emotional associations ends in consolation of a kind—like *The Sepulchers*—but it is the consolation of death, a return to the womb, motherland as womb, death as womb, Nature inaccessible and cruel on the one hand, sheltering and motherly on the other—and see the March 14 letter, after midnight:[51]

> Shine, yes, shine, Nature, and soothe the worries of mortals. You will no longer shine for me. I have already felt all your beauty, and I have worshiped you, and I have fed on your joy; and as long as I saw you beautiful and beneficent you told me with a divine voice: Live.—But in my despair I then saw your hands dripping with blood; the fragrance of your flowers was full of poison to me, and bitter your fruits; and you appeared a devourer of your children whom you lured with your beauty and gifts toward grief alone.

Many considerations offer themselves upon reading the long excerpt and its internal reverberations in the book. Thematically, it bears out once more the decline of the Father-god figure and the rise of a new deity, Nature—an impersonal, indifferent principle, truly omnipotent in its power vis-à-vis all living creatures, tangible yet inaccessible, beautiful yet cruel, and personifiable in feminine form (as will happen with Leopardi) because it bears and sustains the creatures it then destroys, and it reabsorbs them in its womb-like sepulture. Thus a chain of images connects this newfangled (and archaic) Nature goddess, so Lucretian and scientifically modern yet so archetypal, with Teresa the beloved, unpossessible girl, and with Ortis' mother (both come up in the long meditation I excerpted above, and not so marginally either). The resolution of all these images into the negative one, death, occurs a bit later:[52]

> Let us tear the mask from this phantom that wants to terrify us.—I have seen frightened children go into hiding

---

[51] *Edizione Nazionale*, IV, p. 448. Translation mine.
[52] *Ibid.*, p. 451. Letter of March 19. Translation mine.

at the altered countenance of their nurse. O Death! I look at you and question you—not things themselves but their appearances trouble us: who do not dare call you, still face you fearlessly! You still are a necessary element of Nature—to me now all your horror vanishes, and you seem like the evening sleep, the quiet after day's work.

A genuine mythopoeic process is at work here; and without wanting to lead it back to the biographical vicissitudes of Foscolo the man, who was orphaned of his father during childhood, and passionately clung to his mother even when torn from her by political necessity, I will note how it is at this level that we can touch the inner motivation and genesis of *Ortis*, beyond its surface incoherence.

Even the patriotic motif, which to a modern reader might sound so dated and rhetorical, takes on a new significance when viewed within the iconic chain of mother-female-nature-beloved-death motifs. Motherland is mother, it is cradle and tomb, dwelling and sustenance, joy and frustration; Teresa becomes its most viable synecdoche. In such a perspective, the long letter dated Feb. 19 and 20 acquires central value for an understanding of the whole novel, whose basic themes and development it recapitulates with dramatic power.

The debt to *Werther*'s Aug. 18 letter envisaging Nature as devourer is fully repaid; anticipations of Melville's and of Leopardi's tragic vision of existence ring out, in Foscolo's own voice. A voice not to be silenced or outdone, it keeps on a high register, at times skirting shrillness, yet it modulates from inner dramatic dialogue to hallucinated vision, to prophecy and elegy. Two tragedies, *Aiace* and *Ricciarda*, will follow *Ortis* in due time. Meanwhile, in the novel's prose we are reading, the infernal pitch reached with the Macbethian image of the obsessive dagger and with the eclipse of reality in blood and black sun makes way for a Dantesque scene tangentially reminiscent of *Inferno* XIII, the wood of the suicides.[53] Between the two excruciating moments, a strong pause, orthographically marked, signals a panting silence into which the convulsed voice of nightmare had to sink before it could rise again in "funereal peace" to utter the awesome majesty of a mountain wasteland after having conveyed the horror of a subjective chaos haunted by a Doppelgaenger demon.

The former was the hell of alienated self, world-destroying; the latter is the "hell" of objective, resistant, rocky reality, thus actually much less of an inferno than the Dantesque analogy would suggest. Into the former state one sinks, and to the zero point, the nadir of consciousness; into the latter state *and* place one rises, and a world is recomposed, in weird beauty. The transition is thus from chaos to cosmos, from hell to an initial purgatory, which, true to Dante's conception, Foscolo too envisages as a mountain, though he has Jacopo stop midway on the steep slopes. From blindness (the black sun) to a dizzy, terrifying, yet sobering sight: the vistas of Nature at its most sublime, and of history—a part of Nature itself, space modulating into time. Howl becomes dirge, and dirge, elegy; the rhythms of the voice mark the transition, if we actuate them in our listening-uttering (on the author's own cue), for the dynamic shape of utterance just before the climactic pause is defined by driving exclamations and questions, by short, overlapping clauses, in a jerky resilience, like a reiterated gasp, to be resolved at full volume in the crescendo of the phrase "the Earth, I have stained it with blood, and the Sun is black." After the pause, instead the

---

[53] Comp. Foscolo's descriptive lines here: "Non v'è albero, non tugurio, non erba. Tutto è bronchi; aspri e lividi macigni . . ." (No tree is here, no shack, no grass. All is briars and dry sticks; harsh and bleak boulders . . .) and the following three lines from Dante (*Inf.* XIII, 4-6): "Non fronda verde, ma di color fosco;/ Non rami schietti, ma nodosi e 'nvolti;/ Non pomi v'eran, ma stecchi con tosco." (No green foliage, but of darksome color; no straight branches, but knotty and twisted; no fruits were there, but poisonous sticks.)

key-word "peace" determines the phrasal rhythm; the initial exclamation has a relaxing effect on the whole ensuing paragraph, and no hectical rhetoric shapes the utterance, couched as it is in quiet, affirmative clauses which succeed one another without clashing or interrupting, till they reach their grand cumulative effect through the "peace" of an object-absorbed vision. The expressionist "black sun" of inner derangement and turmoil has made way for the whiteness of the snow-capped Alps, a terrifying challenge, but also a reassuring certainty that the world is there, after all, for the self-torn, self-involved subject who had earlier seen himself as an uprooted, self-contained, destructive individual self.

Compared with the far less public and far less historically minded pronouncements of *Werther*, this eloquence might sound a bit too rhetorical in modern ears—I mean the eloquence of the long passage on Italy's misfortunes, on the cannibalistic fierceness of history's jungle ("Earth is a forest of wild beasts"), and on the falseness of socially approved "virtues" versus the only one that deserves the name, compassion born of such destructive knowledge. Granting Foscolo's irrepressible bent for eloquence as a mode of expression, we should pay attention to the inner structuring of Jacopo's voice in this basic "letter"—as we saw, it ranges the whole gamut of tones, and its articulation hinges on the crucial transition marked by the pause discussed above. Until then, the voice had been whirling around in a maelstrom of contestations and self-absorbed nightmare; after that, it emerges from silence to utter a different vision, funereal yet susceptible of rational control, existentially moored in the crucified self but gravitating on the objective, communal theme. Self-transcendence thus marks a kind of catharsis within the doomed horizon of the persona's consciousness. Undeniably, the confessional stance has touched bottom here as Jacopo inwardly drinks his bitter cup to the dregs, and then it begins to change into a (passionately, bitterly) gnomic, almost vatic stance. The full-fledged metamorphosis will come about only in *The Sepulchers*, where the vatic and epic stance includes the per-

general.[54] These expressions are put on Parini's lips, but it is Jacopo who avowedly feels "clinging to the steep cliff of life" to follow "a light glimpsed from afar" and never to be reached; and further on Jacopo writes that he often dreamed of being rescued by his old mother from the imminent plunge into the abyss—the plunge being a fancied consequence of the confirmed impossibility to change the world by successful action. The view from a perilous mountain offers the fascination of death and the dizziness of terrifying, if liberating, realizations. In a way, the dizzy spell of December 4 is overcome by the direct confrontation with the abyss in the letter of February 19-20; moreover, the earlier situation is a haunting fantasy, while the later one is anchored to a concrete natural scenery.

Materializing the ancestral vertigo, so to speak, makes it possible to overcome it, even if here the overcoming does not lead to joy, or to the renewed acceptance of life, but to the acceptance of death. The news of Teresa's marriage[55] just seals this decision; it is the last straw; and tranquillity succeeds turmoil until the envisaged deed is consummated:

> . . . I see the goal: I have already decided everything in my heart—the way, the place—nor is the day far away.
>
> What is life for me? time devoured my happy moments; I only know it in the feeling of grief; and now even illusion abandons me—I meditate on the past; I dwell on the days to come; and I see only nothingness . . . If in life is grief, what is left to hope for? nothingness; or another life still different from this one.— Therefore I have decided; I do not desperately hate myself; I do not hate the living. I have been seeking

---

[54] *Edizione Nazionale*, IV, pp. 410-19. Letter of December 4, from Milan. Translation mine.

[55] *Ibid.*, p. 439. Letter of March 5 from Rimini, the part supposedly penned at 11 p.m. Translation mine.

peace for a long time; and reason always points to the grave . . .

I am calm, imperturbably calm. Illusions have vanished; desires are dead: hopes and fears have left my mind free. No alternately joyful and sad phantoms confuse my imagination; all is calm. . . .

Even if there is some unlikely seesawing between the utterly nihilist (if Pascalian) utterance of March 20:

I do not know either why I came into the world; or how, or what the world is; or what I am myself. . . . On every side I only see infinities which absorb me like an atom[56]

and the resurgent invocations to God in the Wednesday, March 21 letter, preceded by an interval of convulsive yearnings,[57] the last letter, addressed to Teresa,[58] is dictated by that very unearthly calm, in its splendid beginning, as of a dead man returning to see reality:

I have visited my mountains, I have visited the lake of the five springs, I have said farewell forever to the woods, the fields, the sky. O my solitudes! o brook which first taught me the house of that celestial girl! how many times have I scattered flowers on your waters which passed by her windows! how many times I have strolled with Teresa along your banks, while intoxicated by the delight of adoring her, I emptied the cup of death in big draughts. . . .

O sacred mulberry tree! I adored you too. . . .

This last written communication from the imminent suicide rehearses in memory the ecstasy of May in the previous year, when Jacopo enjoyed Teresa's company, contemplating her in

[56] *Ibid.*, p. 455. Translation mine.
[57] *Ibid.*, p. 457. Translation mine.
[58] *Ibid.*, pp. 457-60. Translation mine.

her sleep,[59] rediscovering Nature's beauty from the hilltop in the afterglow of that joy,[60] escorting her to a mulberry tree, hand in hand,[61] then stealing a kiss from her,[62] and living for a short while in that fleeting happiness,[63] before realizing that Teresa could never be his. The echoed vision is a high point of the novel's art; the poignancy of its resurgence matches the intensity of its genesis; it is a phantom sunrise in the night of the soul. The vision is attached to, and released by, sensuous details like the mulberry tree; Foscolo's handling of the original scene bears scrutiny.

Paradise glimpsed, touched and lost finds its expressive counterpart in a prose passage which, taken by itself, would rank as a prose poem, and placed in narrative context enhances our awareness of the narrator's predicament:

Oh how many times I have taken the pen in hand again, and I haven't been able to go on: I feel a bit calmer and I resume writing to you.—Teresa lay under the mulberry tree—but then what can I tell you that is not entirely contained in these words? *I love you*. At these words everything I saw seemed to me a laughter of the universe: I gazed at the sky with thankful eyes and it seemed to open wide to welcome us! ah me! why did not death come? and I have invoked it. Yes; I have kissed Teresa; the flowers and the trees in that moment exhaled a sweet smell; the breezes were all harmony; the brooks plashed from afar; and everything radiated beauty in the splendor of the moon which was full of the infinite light of Divinity. Elements and beings rejoiced in the joy of two love-inebriated hearts—I have kissed that hand and kissed it over and over again—and Teresa embraced me

[59] *Ibid.*, p. 360, letter of May 12.

[60] *Ibid.*, pp. 361-63, letter of May 13.

[61] *Ibid.*, p. 364, letter of May 14, morning.

[62] *Ibid.*, p. 365, letter of May 14, 11:00 a.m.; pp. 366-67, letter of May 14, evening.

[63] *Ibid.*, p. 367, letter of May 15.

trembling all over, and poured forth her sighs into my
mouth, and her heart throbbed on this breast: gazing at
me with her big languid eyes, she kissed me, and her
wet lips, unsealed, murmured on mine—alas! for all of a
sudden she wrested herself away from my bosom as if
terrified: she called her sister and got up running to meet
her. I have prostrated myself to her, and reached out as
if to clutch her gown—but I dared not retain her, or call
her back. Her virtue—and not so much her virtue, as
her passion—awed me: I felt and feel the remorse of
having first excited her innocent heart. And it is remorse—remorse at treason! Ah my cowardly heart!—I
have approached her in a tremor.—I cannot be yours,
ever!—and she uttered these words from the depth of
her heart and with a glance that seemed to blame herself
and pity me. As I accompanied her along her way, she
no longer looked at me; nor did I have the courage to
speak a word to her. At the garden's iron gate she took
Isabellina from my hand and leaving me: Goodbye, she
said; and turning back after few steps,—goodbye.

I remained in ecstasy: I would have kissed her foot-
prints: one arm of hers hung, and her hair shining in the
moon's rays fluttered softly: but then, scarcely did the
long driveway and the thick shadow of the trees allow me
to glimpse her waving long skirts which still gleamed
white from afar; and after I lost her, I sharpened my ear
hoping to hear her voice.—And departing, I turned
around with open arms, as if to console myself, toward
the star of Venus; it too had vanished.[64]

Unlike the letter dated May 12, which after a lively and sensuous beginning gets bogged down in dime-novel rhetoric by
waving capitalized abstractions like Virtue, Youth, Beauty,
and Misfortune in the eyes of the reader, this one, apparently
resuming the same theme (erotic bliss skirted, or attained

---

[64] *Ibid.*, pp. 366-67, letter of May 14, evening. Translation mine.

only fleetingly, in the sphere of contemplation) succeeds in bringing its subject to life, and almost rescues the earlier passage, from which it takes its cue, from those dated banalities. On May 12 Jacopo told his rapture upon gazing at Teresa asleep in all her beauty, and his understandable refraining from the embrace that would have been physically so easy ("I have not dared! I have not dared!"), while now, on May 14, he describes the joy of that preliminary consummation which is a kiss, given and returned in full responsiveness by the no longer sleeping beauty. The variation on the theme has a heightening effect. Jacopo's getting within close reach of his yearned-for happiness marks the high point of the story's countermovement and justifies by contrast his relapse into final misery.

In both scenes Teresa is pictorially visualized, first as an immobile goddess enveloped in awe, and then as a throbbing, conscious, nimble being who is subjectively and not just objectively alive, in an acceleration of movement which ends in disappearance. Teresa's few words—fully motivated by the concrete situation in which she finds herself long before anything like a women's liberation movement can begin to be conceivable—effectively convey her predicament in one with Jacopo's; what should join them separates them forever, any deft compromise being out of the question for people of their kind. They are the All-or-Nothing young lovers, a rare but credible breed. Teresa's abrupt "I cannot be yours, ever!" establishes her as a character in her own right, with a tactic that is the reverse of Goethe's in depicting for us his charming Lotte through Werther's protracted account.

Goethe gives Lotte ample room and time to manifest herself, and he endows her with many an endearing trait, making her motherly, sociable, and coquettish in turn; however, when she turns down Werther's advances by calling herself "the property of another man,"[65] we as readers are at

[65] *Goethes Werke*, Vol. 6, *Werther*, Part II, p. 102, letter of December 20: "Warum denn mich, Werther? just mich, das Eigentum eines anderen? just das? Ich fürchte, ich fürchte, es ist nur die Unmöglichkeit, mich zu

a loss to decide whether this expression is merely symptomatic or implicitly critical of the wretched status quo. We are not sure that Goethe himself, for all his *Sturm und Drang* aggressiveness (as shown in his Rousseauvian and Pestalozzian treatment of the children's problem, or in his turning of the tables against preconception and information that parade as knowledge), is aware of the feudal and early bourgeois patriarchalism that reduces women to chattel status. Foscolo is not either, to judge from the comments he makes many years after on the role assigned to Teresa;[66] but there can be no doubt that, when summoning her to life in the novel, he sees and portrays her as a victim of the social order, as well as of the particular historical circumstances which dissuade her father from giving her hand in marriage to a poor prospect like the political refugee Jacopo Ortis.

In a sense, Jacopo Ortis, as Foscolo's persona, truly awakens his sleeping beauty with the kiss that is to seal his fate; for it is that kiss which animates Teresa into full consciousness and makes her exist as a subject, rather than as a mere object, of experience. Unlike Lotte, Teresa in this capacity remains tangential to the story, because Foscolo had a far narrower compass to grant her, and she could be realized only by narrative foreshortening. The latter is a structural device that amounts to Foscolo's signature, if we but think of his avowed cult of "rapidity" and quick transitions; so much so that it marks him as the essentially lyrical or meditative, but not epic, writer. The epic breath, the gift for sustained narration, was paramount instead among Goethe's gifts. Foscolo himself said that he lacked the power to translate Homer

---

besitzen, die Ihnen diesen Wunsch so reizend macht." (Why me, Werther? just me, the property of another man? just that? I am afraid, I am afraid it is only the impossibility to possess me that makes this desire of yours so very keen.)

[66] See *Edizione Nazionale*, IV, "Notizia bibliografica," where Foscolo criticizes his own novel both by itself and by comparison with *Werther* and with Rousseau's *La nouvelle Héloïse*. His reservations on the characterization of Teresa, and on other aspects of *Ortis*, are of great interest anyway.

adequately, because his own affinities were rather Pindaric and Miltonic.[67] In this case, the lyrical or Pindaric bent has served Foscolo well; it has enabled him to differentiate himself from his great model and thereby compete with him more freely.

One striking detail which shows Foscolo's mettle both in devising his own narrative or scenic incidents and in emulating a cherished source is the concluding paragraph of the May 14 letter, where Teresa's beauty appears in one last flash, immediately to fade from her worshiper's visual field as a tacit fluttering whiteness. It climaxes the whole letter's movement, with faultless rhythm and unerring vision; nor does it suffer by comparison with an analogous finale in Goethe's novel, the end of Part I and of the Sept. 10 letter, which rings with reiterated intimations of loss on Werther's part ("I shall not see her again! . . . We shall see each other again!"):[68]

". . . Farewell, Lotte! Farewell, Albert! We'll see one another again."

"Tomorrow, I think," she specified jokingly.—I felt that "tomorrow"! Alas, she did not know, as she withdrew her hand from mine.—They walked away along the alley, I stood where I was, looked at them in the moonlight and threw myself on the ground and cried myself dry and jumped to my feet and ran to the terrace and still saw there below in the shade of the high linden trees her white dress shimmer toward the garden gate, I stretched my arms, and it vanished.

[67] *Edizione Nazionale*, VII, pp. 209-10, in the article "Sulla traduzione dell'*Odissea*" (On the translation of the *Odyssey*). Here, in discussing Ippolito Pindemonte's newly published Homeric version, Foscolo refers to his own translation of *Iliad*, Canto I, which had appeared in print in 1807.

[68] *Goethes Werke*, Vol. 6, p. 59. Translation mine. Comp. *Ortis*, letter of May 14, evening, as quoted in my translation above. The correspondence between the two episodes was noticed by Mario Martelli in 1970. See fn. 6, above.

The driving rhythm of Goethe's clauses combines with the
emotional tenor to mark a sentimental drift; Foscolo's rhythm
and tenor here stand out as more sober, and contemplative.
Not only so; but the Italian writer can turn to account this
motif a few pages later, to extract from whiteness its funereal
implications:

> . . . Then I turn my eyes on the clusters of pinetrees
> planted by my father on that hill near the parsonage
> door, and I see a white gleam through the wind-stirred
> branches: my headstone. . . . Perhaps Teresa will come
> alone at dawn to remember sadly. . . .[69]

The semantic permutation goes one step further when, in the
long late letter of Part II from the Alps, Jacopo sees the
snow-capped Alps gleam whitely above him, in that half-
hellish, half-purgatorial scene which marks his longest epistolary effusion. And the semantic radiations do not stop here;
just as Teresa registers most durably on her admirer's consciousness as she fades from his sight, because then she is
pure image, beyond the possibility of possession, just so, on a
kindred key, he will write her:[70]

> . . . my heart believed you to be all its own; you have
> loved me, and you love me—and now that I lose you,
> now I call death for help. . . .

The lofty motif reverberates laterally in the letter of March
14, midnight,[71] when the same words are addressed to Nature, the almost personified object of so many outlets:

> Shall I then be ungrateful to you? shall I prolong my life

[69] *Edizione Nazionale*, IV, p. 373, letter of May 25, toward the end.
Translation mine.

[70] *Ibid.*, p. 458, letter of Wednesday, March 21, 5 a.m. Translation
mine.

[71] *Ibid.*, p. 449, letter of March 14, midnight. Translation mine.

to see you so formidable, and blaspheme? No, no.—By transforming yourself, and blinding me to your light, aren't you abandoning me yourself, and ordering me at the same time to abandon you?—Ah! now I look at you and sigh; but I still cherish you for the memory of past sweetness, for the certainty that I shall no longer have to fear you, and because I am about to lose you.—

That provides an unmistakable iconic link between Teresa and Nature, the Nature of which she is, as I said before, a living synecdoche; hence a further proof that Ortis' true godhead is feminine.

Within the ambit of the novel itself, one climactic image has thus proven susceptible of ramifying developments which tend to cover most of the fictional space available, and thereby to impart a secret poetical coherence to the uneven and at times disjointed narrative. Nor does this iconic fruitfulness stop at the compositional and chronological boundary of *Jacopo Ortis*. About a decade later Ugo Foscolo was working at his last poetical project, *Le Grazie*, whose endless variants have kept scholars quite busy. Though the poem must rate as technically "unfinished," its basic structure is clear. Of the three hymns that compose it, the second, addressed to Vesta, celebrates the art of dance—and the poet had a lovely lady of his acquaintance in mind. Here is how he envisages her at the very end of the section:[72]

Often for future ages, should the Italian

[72] At this writing, the critical edition of *Le Grazie* by Francesco Pagliai, completed by Mario Scotti, is due to appear before very long as a volume of *Edizione Nazionale*, the announcement having been made at Florence in May 1979. However, since the passage I quote here has reached its presumably final form, I can refer the reader to the Chiarini text as used by Mario Puppo at p. 68 of *Opere di F*. Moreover, Saverio Orlando publishes the same passage in his critical edition of 1974 (U. F., *Le Grazie–Carme ad Antonio Canova*, Ed.cr. a cura di S.O. Brescia: Paideia editrice, 1974), at pp. 123-24, directly checked on the MS of the Biblioteca Nazionale in Florence (Fascicolo VI, p. 11). Translation mine.

language be ever bequeathed to our descendants
intact (it's yours, O Graces, to preserve!),
in my verse I try to portray the sacred
dancer, less beautiful when she sits to rest,
less beautiful than you, gentle musician,
less lovely than you are when you converse,
o keeper of the bees. But if she dances,
look! the whole harmony of the sound flows forth
from her sovereign body, and from her smiling
lips; and a motion, an act, the smallest gesture
imparts a sudden beauty to her glances.
And who can then depict her? While I endeavor
to capture her with intent eyes, she flees,
and those roundels she had been slowly tracing
she now speeds to the utmost: skimming in flight
the flowers, there, she is gone; I scarcely see
the fleeting veil flash white among the myrtles.

Not only the key verb *biancheggiare*, which I have variously
rendered as "gleam white" or "gleam whitely" or "whiten" or
"flash white" as in the present instance (where swiftness of
accelerating motion is of the essence), but the whole scene
echoes the impeccable finale of the May 14 letter which
shows Teresa's white dress fluttering away in the distance
among the trees. The emotional tone naturally differs: where
the novel dramatized a heart-rending loss, the later poem
contemplates the unseizable nature of beauty in motion; but,
in both cases, the unpossessible, and transitory, body becomes an undying image, and it can therefore be said that
when Jacopo loses Teresa he is like Foscolo failing to capture
the dancing Cornelia, and the loss and failure are the birth of
the poetic image.

Since the ultimate implications of the love scene from *Ortis*
come to light in the passage from *The Graces*, it is permissible
to use that splendid passage as a retroactive illumination of
the earlier prose which was its seedbed. *The Graces* is every-

thing *Ortis* is not, and Mario Fubini has rightly termed the unfinished poem a paradisal stage of Foscolo's art versus the "infernal" accent of the novel and some of the coeval verse. Yet unhappy Teresa, painter and musician, intact beauty doomed to a marriage of convenience, is already a Grace tangentially present in the hopeless universe of Jacopo Ortis, and the inversion of tone in the poetical development of her image beyond the compass of the novel but stresses the inner affinity of the Gestalt. In the novel, possession denied is loss, and loss is despair; in the later poem, possession is never the point, and not to possess is not to lose; contemplation rescues the fleeting moment from transitoriness, making it "a joy forever", as Keats would say. The enduring rapture of poetry supersedes the doomed rapture of carnal love, and we approach that modern threshold of artistic consciousness where "poetry is the subject of the poem" for the writer so absorbed in his developing vision that his thought becomes analogous to that of the self-contained Aristotelian God, *noësis noëseos*. The process would not have been possible if the suffering of earth and flesh had not impelled the struggling artist to seek this liberation: "art for art's sake" is out of the question here. The dynamic nature of poetic vision—poetry as process—is well borne out in the climactic passage from *The Graces*, where the body of the dancer is aesthetically nothing (in a way) as long as it remains still, but quickens into matchless splendor when it moves, at a swifter and swifter pace, till she is pure motion, intangible yet totally present like the Athikte of Valéry's *L'âme et la danse*,[73] and then no one "can tell the dancer from the dance." Retrospectively, a similar pattern will be seen to operate in the sequence of *Ortis* letters from May 12 through May 14: first we see, through Jacopo's eyes, an immobile Teresa, unstirred in her sleep, pure object and

---

[73] Paul Valéry, *Eupalinos ou l'Architecte, L'Âme et la Danse*. Paris: Gallimard, *nrf*, 1923. Athikte, the dancer contemplated by Socrates in this Platonically conceived dialogue, is, according to her Greek name, "the Unattainable."

static pictorial image, and then we see and hear her in motion, unattainably beautiful, a white vision receding to vanishing point.

The power of imagery both within the synchronic range and along the diachronic line of development concurs with the animating rhythms to raise *Ortis*'s prose to a high level—the level, of course, at which it can sustain comparison with *Werther*'s germane, if partly divergent, achievement. But another concomitant factor is to be seen in the handling of literary references. By this I do not mean the outspoken tribute of *Ortis* to "Homer, Dante and Shakespeare, three masters of all superhuman talents" (*Ortis*, May 13 letter) and of *Werther* to Homer in its first part and to Ossian in its latter part. Nor do I have in mind the irrevocably dated device of sanctioning the fictional hero's destiny by obviously linking it to a cherished, fateful book, whether Lessing's *Emilia Galotti* (which is mentioned at the outset of *Werther* and found among Werther's possessions at the end) or Plutarch's *Parallel Lives*, often mentioned by Jacopo Ortis and then conspicuously present in his bloodstained room. Such a subsumption of life (fictional, yet to be experienced as "real" in the reading transaction) to normative literature was a battle cry two centuries ago, for the books thus canonized in that writing emblazoned the revolt of passion against abstract reason, or at least (in the case of Plutarch) the desperate dignity of a Stoic stance against whatever cowardly accommodations the pressure of the times dictated. On modern ears, clearly, the device is wasted, and it has outlived its rhetorical function. But such is not the case when Foscolo weaves unacknowledged quotations or deft allusions into his impassioned prose.

We have already seen an example of this in the analogically Infernal and Purgatorial landscape he sets up in the long letter of Feb. 19-20, which also contains an effective Shakespearian allusion from *Macbeth*. Other Shakespeare references can be overheard in Jacopo's treatment of the Lauretta episode,[74] a story within the story, and Sterne has

[74] *Edizione Nazionale*, IV, p. 369, letter of May 25, communication of

prompted its insertion. Appropriate lines from Dante's *Inferno* or *Purgatorio* punctuate the epistolary narrative from time to time, to reinforce its dominant tenor. Biblical references from the *Psalms* and topical parts of the Old and New Testament vie with excerpts from Alfieri's tragedies to connote the predicament of Jacopo *moriturus*, especially toward the end.

The high point of this art, however, comes where the source used remains hidden and is thus allowed to operate by direct appropriateness and expressiveness on the immediate level, and by added resonance supervening with literary recognition afterwards—a practice honored in our time by Eliot, Montale, and Pound, among others, and already familiar to the Latin classics, and to Dante. In the May 12 letter, for instance, Jacopo emphasizes his erotic restraint-cum-rapture vis-à-vis sleeping Teresa by inlaying his prose with quotes or close paraphrase from Petrarch's verse on haunting, unattainable Laura:

> *Io la ho più volte veduta* a passeggiare e a danzare; mi sono sentito sin dentro l'anima e la sua arpa e la sua voce; la ho adorata *pien di spavento* come se l'avessi veduta *discendere dal paradiso*. . . .[75]

> *I have often seen her* stroll and dance; I have heard deep in my soul her harp and her voice; I have adored her *full of awe* as if I had seen her *descend from paradise*. . . .

The pinpointing force of the expressions I italicize in this excerpt can only be felt by collating the Italian text with its Italian source:

> *I' l'ho più volte* (or chi fia che m'il creda?)

---

the news of Lauretta's death as a liberation from long misery. The conversation Jacopo reports from his meetings with the poor mentally deranged girl makes one think of Ophelia.

[75] *Ibid.*, p. 360, letter of May 12. Translation mine.

ne l'acqua chiara, e sopra l'erba verde
veduto viva. . . .

Many a time (and who will believe me?)
in the clear water, and on the green grass
have I seen her alive . . .[76]

Quante volte diss'io
allor *pien di spavento*:
Costei per fermo *nacque in Paradiso*!

How many times
did I say then, *full of awe*:
She *was* certainly *born in Paradise*![77]

This is no precious literary game; the references are functional, they do not disturb the fluency of narrative, while deepening its resonance to encompass an analogy between Jacopo's privileged-hopeless situation with regard to Teresa and Petrarch's predicament vis-à-vis Laura. The *Canzoniere* poems thus laid under contribution are among the finest and best known of Petrarch's works and they would be topical to any moderately cultivated Italian. From Foscolo's vantage point in time, the modern story of Jacopo and Teresa reproduced to a large extent the old tale of Petrarch and Laura, and of all troubadour love in the Western world, as he, Foscolo, clarifies also contextually by making Arquà, Petrarch's last home, a landmark in his narrative, and by explicitly referring to Petrarch shortly before and after the present page. But it is here, where Foscolo lets the voice of the fourteenth-century poet echo in his own prose without explicit pointers, that the impact becomes pervasively stronger, discretion being the best part of mastery. Petrarch bestows ritual sanction on Ortis' narrative; Jacopo's account of his own experience ac-

[76] Francesco Petrarca, *Canzoniere*, Canzone 129 (Di pensiero in pensier, di monte in monte), Stanza IV.
[77] *Ibid.*, Canzone 126 ("Chiare, fresche e dolci acque"), Stanza V.

tualizes Petrarch. When subtlety yields to naive rhetoric, as happens in the last part of this May 12 letter, we have an object lesson in the difference between the good and the bad use of literature for literary purposes.

If Petrarch brings to poetical focus the moment of rapt admiration when Jacopo experiences Teresa's beauty as unresponsive (because immersed in sleep) and unattainable, Dante takes over as a hidden presence in Jacopo's lines when that limited contact and consummation, a kiss, finally takes place.[78] Very astutely, Foscolo here has counterpointed Paradisal consummation with its Infernal antitype, thus setting up a dissonant chord that already insinuates the tragic end of Ortis (and, in a way, of Teresa herself who will be denied her true love):

> *Vi amo.* A queste parole *tutto ciò ch'io vedeva mi sembrava un riso dell'universo*: io mirava con occhi di riconoscenza il ciélo etc. . . .

> *I love you* [Teresa's words to Jacopo]. At these words *everything I saw seemed a laughter of the universe*: I gazed at the sky with grateful eyes etc. . . .

The second phrase I italicized comes verbatim from *Par.* XXVII, 3-4:

> *Ciò ch'io vedeva, mi sembrava un riso*
> *dell'universo*; per che mia ebbrezza
> entrava per l'udire e per lo viso.

> *What I saw seemed to me a laughter*
> *of the universe*; so that my inebriation
> came through my hearing and through my sight.

Jacopo Ortis' ecstasy at eliciting from Teresa a confession of

---

[78] *Edizione Nazionale*, IV, p. 366, letter of May 14, evening. Translation mine.

love, and a responsive kiss, is thus effectively compared to the ecstasy Dante experiences when Beatrice's intercession earns him the accolade of the great Apostles in Heaven and heightens his perceptual powers to superhuman liveliness. But soon after comes the dark antiphon, cannily disguised:

> . . . *ho baciata* e ribaciata quella mano—e Teresa mi abbracciava *tutta tremante*, e trasfondea i suoi sospiri *nella mia bocca*, e il suo cuore palpitava su questo petto: mirandomi co' suoi grandi occhi languenti, *mi baciava* . . .

> . . . *I have kissed* that hand again and again—and Teresa was embracing me, *trembling all over*, and effused her sighs *into my mouth*, and her heart throbbed on this breast: gazing at me with her big languishing eyes, she kissed me. . . .

The cue I italicize comes from *Inf.* v, where Francesca da Rimini, beautiful and damned, speaks for herself and her lover Paolo:

> Quando leggemmo il disiato riso
> esser *baciato* da cotanto amante,
> questi, che mai da me non fia diviso,
> *la bocca mi baciò tutto tremante*[79]

> When we read of the much desired smile
> being *kissed* by such a lofty lover,
> this man, who will never be parted from me,
> *kissed my mouth, trembling all over*

Even though Jacopo will never possess Teresa, either in marriage or in adultery, and even though (unlike Paolo and Francesca) they will be parted forever, infernal misery will follow that kiss. The suggestive reverberations have already

[79] Dante Alighieri, *Divine Comedy*, *Inf.* v, 133-36. Translation mine.

been heard in the previous letter,[80] where Jacopo contemplated from a hill the wistful sunset:

Cantano flebilmente gli uccelli *come se piangessero il giorno che muore* . . .

The birds are singing plaintively *as if to mourn the dying of the day* . . .

Purge. VIII starts with a memorable sunset, reminding the poet of the faraway bell

che *paia il giorno pianger che si muore.*[81]

which *seems to mourn the dying of the day.*

The skillful writer has immersed this Dantean reminiscence into the flow of a descriptive prose which seems to embody in its largo rhythm the very ebbing of sunlight and the gathering of starlit night. The overall imagery effortlessly absorbs the intentional echo of a formidable source which, if too extrinsically used, would dwarf its user. In other words, the expressive power of Foscolo's own prose here is independent of the great literature he turns to account. Foscolo's writing intersects, instead of paralleling or mirroring, Dante's, and the effect is to emphasize the divergence of dramatic situation within the consonance of tone, for Jacopo Ortis, after taking in so much of the visible world from mountain to valley to plain, from animal life to human activity, turns to the sky and to himself against a graveyard scene, and the symphony of peace ends in the presentiment of his own death. Dante the purgatorial pilgrim, on the other hand, caught between the homesickness of earth and the call of heavenly peace, hears and sees in the sunset scene an intimation of purified life, while Ortis' only release is final death, the annihilation of a

---

[80] *Edizione Nazionale*, IV, p. 362, letter of May 13. Translation mine.
[81] Dante Alighieri, *Divine Comedy*, Purg. VIII, 6. Translation mine.

"useless life," which makes a mockery of the initial invocation to God.[82]

The remarkable passage works as an interlude between the two climactic encounters with Teresa (May 12 and May 14), and it appropriately ends with her name:

. . . In my sobbing I invoked Teresa.

The passage thereby works as a functional narrative link, and not as a set piece of descriptive and lyrical prowess, strong as its claim to representative excellence could be on this level by itself. It also rehearses in advance the movement of Jacopo's mind away from an initially invoked God the Father to the Lucretian certainties of uncreated, indestructible, perennially self-transforming matter; one can also overhear Lavoisier's formula in the funereal words:

Have peace, o naked remains: matter has returned to matter; nothing diminishes, nothing grows, nothing is lost down here: everything is transformed and reproduced—o human lot! less unhappy than others is he who does not fear it.[83]

Clearly the peace Jacopo envisages in his Thomas Gray-like address to the denizens of the country churchyard is the peace coming from the sheer cessation of existence, and not from the glory of Heaven, even though shortly after the outset[84] he had asked God if He took delight in His work when He gazed at a spring evening. In the sunset scene we are thus witnessing a sunset of God, who is reduced to a mere aesthetic idea, intermittently glimmering from afar on a world He cannot save or sustain. The stark contrast between the address to a divine Creator at the beginning, and the acceptance of materialism at the end, verges on incoherence, were it not

[82] *Edizione Nazionale*, IV, p. 363, letter of May 13. Translation mine.
[83] *Ibid*. Translation mine.   [84] *Ibid*., p. 362.

that Jacopo's mind in its wandering does voice, in between, a yearning for "something celestial" as he looks up from sun-reddened earth to darkening sky.

A mediation is thus introduced, even if the narrator pro-tagonist is not made to realize the full import of his own men-tal shift—perhaps because Ugo Foscolo does, and tries to keep his book on the plane of experience, this side of ar-gumentative logic. The experienced dilemma was no doubt very much with Foscolo when he composed *Ortis*, and his confessional persona registers it without always managing to bring it to dramatic focus; this is one of the novel's discon-tinuities, and, oddly enough, one of its points of interest. The negative solution Jacopo Ortis eventually tries when he asks God to annihilate him appears as the deep-set yearning of Ugo Foscolo for a sheltering nothingness in the coeval sonnet *Alla sera*,[85] which transfigures Evening into a motherly death goddess bestowing the gift of nirvana. The sonnet is contigu-ous to the passage from the novel I have been discussing; Mario Fubini has aptly remarked that it was Jacopo Ortis who wrote that and the other sonnets, while Foscolo wrote *The Sepulchers*, and Didymus, *The Graces*.

The sometimes jarring discontinuities, the unresolved ideological tensions in *Ortis*, were acknowledged by the author himself, who, as we saw,[86] described his novel as a "harmony of dissonances." He also said that the style is style-less (in the sense of rejecting any scholastic standard of classicist decorum) and approaching the spoken word; moreover, knotty with ellipses which leave much to the reader, and astir with the turmoil of the fictional character's youthful mind. The correspondence between character and style is verifiable, and if a modern reader may occasionally take exception to some too obviously literary or vociferous peaks of this highstrung style, its alternations between con-

[85] *Opere di F.*, p. 12.

[86] *Edizione Nazionale*, IV, "Notizia bibliografica," *passim* for this and the following references.

vulsiveness and elegiacal cadence (the latter to be especially noticed in the "letter" under examination) must count among its successful traits. *Jacopo Ortis* is no mere period piece.

One reason why it escaped that common fate of so many hopeful works was, to be sure, the choice of the epistolary convention. By Foscolo's time, after Richardson and the others whom he acknowledges as predecessors in the sub-genre, this was already a convention, yet a very recent one, less than a century old, and still rife with its original charge of anti-conventionalism. Foscolo's own remarks on Rousseau's stylistic treatment of Saint-Preux and Julie, which according to the Italian writer failed to match the intended object through excessive salon-like sophistication, are instructive.[87] He also said that ·while his admired Goethe in *Werther* could rely on a developing tongue for his medium, he, Foscolo, had to jolt an old established language from its academic ruts. In this, as in other respects, Foscolo is the pioneer of that Italian Romanticism which failed to give him full credit for what he had done.

Rejuvenation is no easy feat, nor easily recognized. Nor were the implications of Foscolo's seminal work in fiction quickly realized. The cue he gave was ignored for generations; the plotty "historical novel" and the "impersonal," clinical Naturalist novel had to dominate the nineteenth century (in Italy as well as in Europe at large) before writers like Svevo and Pirandello, the *La Voce* innovators like Slataper, Papini, Jahier, and then Pavese,[88] could emerge. Their

[87] *Ibid.*

[88] For the significance of Svevo and Pirandello as novelists, see Renato Barilli, *La linea Svevo-Pirandello*, Milan: Mursia, 1972. For the revaluation of Foscolo's prose by the *La Voce* writers, see Pino Fasano, *Stratigrafie foscoliane*, Rome: Bulzoni, 1974, pp. 182-83; also *Ardengo Soffici, l'artista e lo scrittore nella cultura del 900*, Atti del convegno di studi, Poggio a Caiano, Villa Medicea, 7/8 giugno 1975, a cura di Geno Pampaloni. Firenze: Centro Di, 1976, p. 107, paper by Aldo Rossi. These critics, however, refer to the Didymus aspect of Foscolo's work and not to the Ortis aspect as I do; an aspect which is obviously paramount to the confessionally and existentially oriented writers I have in mind. For Pavese's affinity

work—however unintentionally to a large extent—reactivated the operative principles of *Jacopo Ortis*. First-person narrative, vindication of subjective experience, open form, approximation of an oral style, testimonial stance—these are the principles, and they define the new art of fiction in Italy above and beyond the individual differences. Similarly, as Walter Jens has observed,[89] the epistolary style of *Werther* presaged the new fiction of our century in the German tongue, from Grass to Böll and Frisch. This parallel development in German and Italian writing is to be traced back to two congenial sources that were originally linked, across sharp language barriers, by one of the most liberating acts of self-affiliation in modern European literature.

Seeking liberation in self-inflicted death, Jacopo Ortis is the dawn of his century, strangely foreshadowing the "ripeness" that at the next century's noontide hour would bring Cesare Pavese, author become character, to rehearse the same gesture in his own person. But the invocation of death at the peak of rapture, on Jacopo's part, is an antiphon to suicide, a metaphor of ecstasy, the counterpart of Eros absolutized. The same tone, the same imagery, the same theme come to life in one of the finest letters Foscolo wrote to Antonietta Arese in the heyday of their love:[90]

> Devo io dirti il mio unico voto? . . . quando i tuoi sospiri si trasfondono nella mia bocca, e mi sento stretto dalle tue braccia . . . e le tue lagrime si confondono alle mie . . . e . . . sì; io invoco la morte! il timore di perderti mi fa desiderare che la vita in quel sacro momento si

to Foscolo, see the sparse references in Gian-Paolo Biasin, *The Smile of the Gods, a thematic study of Cesare Pavese's works*. Ithaca, N.Y.: Cornell University Press, 1968.

[89] Walter Jens, *Deutsche Literatur der Gegenwart*. Munich: Piper Verlag, 1962. *Passim*, esp. chapter III. Also: Wolfgang Kayser, "Wer erzählt den Roman?" in *Die Vortragsreise*, Bern: Francke Verlag, 1958, pp. 82-101.

[90] *Epistolario* I, p. 227, letter No. 162. Translation mine.

spenga in noi insensibilmente, e che un sepolcro ci
serbi congiunti per sempre . . .

Must I tell you my one deep wish? . . . when your sighs
are transfused into my mouth, and I feel clasped by your
arms . . . and your tears mingle with mine . . . and . . .
yes; I invoke death! the fear of losing you makes me wish
that life in that sacred moment may imperceptibly ebb
away from us, and one sepulcher keep us united forever
. . .

The similarity involves specific verbal elements like the use
of the expression "e[Teresa] trasfondea i suoi sospiri nella
mia bocca" in the novel, so close to "i tuoi sospiri si trasfon-
dono nella mia bocca" in the letter; a *transfusion of sighs*, followed by a con-fusion of tears in the letter, and by the wish
for an extinguishing of life and a union in death, while the
novel stops short of such erotic ecstasy which is the mark of
consummation—since Jacopo and Teresa stay this side of the
carnal barrier which Tristan and Isolde, or rather, Ugo and
Antonietta, have crossed.

Both the letter to Antonietta and the "letter" of Jacopo
Ortis in the version finally sanctioned by the editions of 1802
and 1817 were written in 1801; the letter to Antonietta certainly was, since it dates from the beginning of that liaison,
and as for the novel, comparison with the first and incomplete
draft (which as we saw dates from 1798 and was surrepti-
tiously published in 1799 with a "completion" by Angelo
Sassoli) shows that the detail of Jacopo's kiss to Teresa was
introduced only in the second draft, the one we know from the
1802 edition. The 1798 draft had Jacopo and Teresa part
company after the meeting at the mulberry tree with no more
than coy verbal contact (Sappho and Petrarch acting as literary chaperons). The whole crucial sequence of "letters" from
May 12 through May 14 was initially shrunk into one far less
rich, far less dramatically modulated, "letter." It was obviously Antonietta's love that inspired our writer to flesh out his

novel and bring it to completion. This biographical fact would be of little interest if it did not throw light on the problem of the complex relation between literature and life which has emerged in connection with Pavese and above all Foscolo; the relation in turn becomes relevant to a finer understanding of literature as such once we agree that it cannot be mechanistically conceived.

It is not a matter of ascertaining what private event in the writer's life determined which literary endeavor and result, but rather of recognizing that in a life like Ugo Foscolo's, which was so intensely oriented on the written word as to be inconceivable apart from the power of verbal signs, every significant experience became a literary stimulus or was intended from the start as a potential literary event. Conversely, it was the word, especially the written word, that shaped his turmoil and justified his existence. No one can suspect Ugo Foscolo of art-for-art's-sake indulgence, nor does his work ever smack of decadent aestheticism; to say it with Arnaud Tripet, it was his "inquiétude" that made him yearn for an appeasing "forme."[91]

To be more specific, probing into the relationship of art and life can hardly lead us to posit an awkward ratio between incommensurables (such as what Foscolo felt, did, and said with Antonietta, and what he wrote thereafter in the domain of fiction); we are interested in what and how he wrote more than in what the occasion for the writing was, especially since that occasion is always manifold to begin with. We are actually investigating the connection between two verbal experiences: one—the novel in progress at the time—intentionally literary and fictional; the other—Foscolo's letters to

[91] Arnaud Tripet, *L'Inquiétude et la Forme–Essai sur Ugo Foscolo.* Lausanne: L'Aire, Coopérative Rencontre, 1973. After Fubini's classical study, this has been so far the most striking modern reading of Foscolo's *oeuvre*. Its existentialist orientation finds support in a fine ear for poetry, earning the approval of a critic as hard to please as Mario Praz is. See Praz's review article on recent Foscolo scholarship, "Il Foscolo come Omero," in the Rome daily *Il Giornale* (Literary page, July 26, 1975).

Antonietta—intentionally personal and confessional. The two
verbal experiences are extant in documentary evidence; in
other words, they are available *texts*. The confessional text
has fed into the literary text; once again, "life" has served
"literature," because "fiction" feeds on "truth." We have
seen the eloquent reverberations of Foscolo's letter to Antonietta onto Jacopo's "letter" to Lorenzo about Teresa. But
there is more. If it is tenable to say that literature feeds on
life, fiction on fact, in Foscolo's case the reverse is also true:
life imitates art (to modify Wilde's dictum) at least as much as
art imitates life. Life or, rather, "life," which in our case can
be equated with the confessional text seen in its intentional-
ity, namely, as an act of verbal communication from a given
"I" to a given "Thou," the communication involving far more
than practical matters, for it expresses a total experience—
the "I" 's *élan* toward the "Thou" and the "Thou" 's presence
in the "I." Obviously, "life" in the case on hand is the letter,
and literature is the "letter"; the "letter" mirrors the letter,
yet the letter in turn reflects the "letter."

If the adoption of the epistolary convention in the novel
brought fiction as close as possible to the *letter* of life (and
thereby enhanced the novel's illusionary power, its very essence as fiction), the love letters penned by the novelist in his
real life context could not help echoing the fictional situations
and the expressive richness of the imaginary missives that his
persona was "writing" in the intermittences of his bona fide
private writing. The missives to Antonietta did not only re-
orient and enrich the novel in progress; they also used it as a
basic reference for their own purposes. The feedback from
Jacopo Ortis to these passionate messages which in turn had
been feeding lifeblood to the restless phantom Jacopo can be
pinpointed in more than one way. Several letters to Antonietta are signed "Il tuo Ortis," Your Ortis; Jacopo Ortis is
mentioned along with Werther as the only honest person in a
fatuous society which keeps that type at arm's length because
it has little use for his sincerity and uprightness; *Ortis* or
Werther is interchangeably suggested as an emblematic detail

to be included by the painter in the portrait Ugo solicits from Antonietta. To complicate matters further, Ugo encourages her to finish her translation of Goethe's novel, and we have seen that his dedicatory letter to Goethe praises that translation, by then obviously completed, far and above those which were available in Italian so far.

A network of literary intersections innervates Ugo's and Antonietta's exchange of messages; it could be plausibly said that they live their love under the sign of literature, and in this too they, the real life characters, mirror the behavior of those fictional characters who people the pages of their favorite novels. Werther and Lotte, Jacopo and Teresa can hardly refrain from reading or quoting their exemplary authors in the climactic moments of their unconsummated love. Jacopo and Werther die with Plutarch and Lessing (*Emilia Galotti*) respectively in sight. In the first redaction of *Ortis'* Part I, Jacopo's Letter No. XLV to Teresa,[92] a sorrowing adieu, recommends *Werther, Amalia, Virginia*, and *Clarissa* to her attention; they are his gifts to her and are supposed to express the essence of Jacopo's and Teresa's frustrated passion. When Jacopo accompanies her to the mulberry tree, she expatiates on Petrarch as *genius loci*, and he answers in kind by reading Sappho's *Odes* to her. We have seen to what length Goethe goes in actualizing Werther's reading of Ossian to Lotte, prior to that fateful stolen kiss which Foscolo's novel mirrors in the mulberry scene without, however, actually quoting for his readers' benefit the texts that inspire the two lovers. And at the end of the liaison, Ugo lashes out at Antonietta by calling her a Lovelace in skirts, from Richardson's then fashionable novel, *Clarissa*.

What we have agreed to define the confessional text, the letter, is obviously permeated by the literary text, by the "letter," to the point where the two definitions become almost interchangeable. The letter has a strong literary (or fictional) component and the "letter" a confessional one, which is emphasized at the expense of the fictional aspect when Ugo, by

[92] *Edizione Nazionale*, IV, pp. 72-73.

signing his letters to Antonietta as "Ortis," indicates that this is the true essence of his real character. In the novel as such the confessional component is undeniable, but intentionally connotative in Ugo's letters to his belle which are signed "Ortis" or otherwise stress the Ortis side: the connotative function of literature becomes denotative, tilting their tenor from the confessional toward the literary, the fictional sphere. At the same time, when the fictional character Ortis takes over the epistolary communication, the act reverberates on the novel from which the character is extrapolated, and makes the confessional function of that novel denotative instead of just connotative—in other words, it suggests a reading in the confessional key, it tells us that Jacopo Ortis is the real self of his author, whatever the factual discrepancies.

The interplay becomes well nigh hopelessly intricate when we realize that to introduce Jacopo Ortis in the letters to Antonietta means to relativize the absolutist, since he can be only one of Ugo's self-projections in a context which admits of a Didymus aspect, i.e., of the humor and irony, also at his own expense, which Ugo Foscolo liberally injects in these letters. The Didymean spice is conspicuously lacking in the pages of *Jacopo Ortis*, even though that book takes many a cue from Laurence Sterne's writing.[93] Jacopo's ideological and erotic passion could not brook the tempering action of humor or the corrosive one of irony. It is noteworthy that Sterne came to the forefront in Foscolo's literary experience

[93] Sterne was an early favorite of Foscolo's, who refers to him (directly or covertly) at several points in his writings. In 1813 he published in Pisa his translation of Sterne's *Sentimental Journey*, with the title *Viaggio Sentimentale di Yorick lungo la Francia e l'Italia*, and he credited this work to the fictional persona "Didimo Chierico" (Didymus, clergyman). The relevant postscript to the translation formulates the Didymean poetics of humor which comes to the fore in so much of Foscolo's post-*Sepulchers* work. On Foscolo's use of Lawrence Sterne's literary cues, see Mario Fubini; Introduction to the critical edition of U. F., *Prose varie d'arte*, Edizione Nazionale, v (Florence: 1951), a volume containing the translation from Sterne and the later *Lettere scritte dall'Inghilterra*. See also Fasano, *Stratigrafie foscoliane*.

when he left Italy for France, as an officer of the Cisalpine
army stationed there for a prospective invasion of Britain; it
was then that he began translating *Sentimental Journey* and in
so doing projected his anti-self, or anti-Ortis self, of Didymus
as translator.

Sterne helped him to forget Antonietta—but her function
in Ugo's creative career was accomplished by now, both because this love had revitalized *Ortis* as a book, and because it
had sprouted into another, though unintentional, novel: the
Letters to Antonietta, which grew in the shadow of the intentional novel, *Jacopo Ortis*, much as a gorgeous flower plant
will grow, untended, where the wind blew from a well-cared-
for garden. The letters to Antonietta are comparable to
Pavese's diary in two important respects: one, that they give
us much of the private Foscolo (as *The Job of Living* records
much of the private Pavese), and, two, that they end up as a
novel with the author as main character and narrator (as
Pavese's diary does). In other words, they started taking
shape as intentional confession-communication (as letter[s])
and they became fiction ("letter"). When Mr. Giuseppe
Argentieri assembled them in what makes up the dominant
part of a handsome volume,[94] he did realize that they were a

---

[94] U. F., *Lettere d'amore*, a cura di Giuseppe Argentieri. Verona: Edizioni speciali del Club degli Editori, 1970. Edition not for sale, reserved
for members of the club. With an introduction by G. A. The autograph
manuscripts of these Letters are lost; they were first published by the re-
nowned philologist, Giovanni Mestica, from extant copies, in 1884. *Lettere
amorose di U. F. ad Antonietta Fagnani*, a cura di G.M., con un discorso.
Firenze: Barbera, 1884, pp. XCII-356. Moralistic scruples stemming from
the convention of the age led editor and publisher to offer what was a textu-
ally incomplete edition. The Letters' relevance to F.'s epistolary novel was
pinpointed, through a table of concordances, in the Introduction to the important 1887 critical edition of *Jacopo Ortis* by G. A. Martinetti and C. A.
Traversi (printed in Saluzzo by Fratelli Lobetti-Bodoni for Enrico Molino,
Rome, pp. CCXCIV-457). In 1949 Lanfranco Caretti noticed the "fictional
nature" (*carattere romanzesco*) and artistic merit of the letters to Antonietta
(in *Belfagor* IV, 6, "Sulle lettere del Foscolo all'Arese," pp. 679-93, then
reprinted in: *Studi e ricerche di letteratura italiana*, Firenze: La Nuova
Italia. 1951, pp. 277-311). Caretti also questions Plinio Carli's chronolog-

seedbed of Foscolo's literary masterpieces, but he failed to see that this byproduct of Ugo's pen amounted to a masterpiece in its own right.

Simple chronological arrangement[95] suffices to bring out the letters' narrative quality. They add up to a self-contained cycle (in a time span of roughly two years, more or less equal to *Ortis'*), they tell the story of a great, fitful love from its expansive beginnings to its bitter aftermath, and they portray the narrator protagonist with modulated effusiveness while obliquely but effectively portraying also his correspondent, against the background of Milan high society in early Napoleonic times. Since the focus is consistently on Ugo's love and its vicissitudes, inner and outer, this novel, which wrote itself as if a literary elf had played a trick on its unsuspecting author, manages better overall unity than the planned novel with whose second compositional phase its writing overlapped.

The very nature of that confidential communication which a love letter is forced Ugo to keep out of these vivid pages the long political and philosophical arguments which went into the making of *Ortis*, though incidental historical notations do crop up to counterpoint the prevalent private tenor with their poignancy. Ugo knows that this love, or any love for that matter, cannot last forever, and he knows that the political instability of the times may contribute to its demise, with the result that a *carpe diem* memento tolls to enhance both the joy and the anguish of the unfolding experience. The time of narration and the time of experiencing coincide even more closely than in *Ortis*, without any need for editorial manipulation; no Lorenzo Alderani has to intervene, all that was required for the narrative to cohere was the posthumous, un-

---

ical ordering of the Letters. Other scholars to note the independent importance of these Letters were Giuseppe De Robertis (in "Linea della poesia foscoliana," *Saggi*, Firenze: Le Monnier, 1953) and Sergio Romagnoli (in "Le lettere all'Arese e il 'Giornale' bergamasco di U. F.," *Ottocento tra letteratura e storia*. Padova: Liviana editrice, 1961, pp. 41-63).

[95] The arrangement, however, appears also in *Epistolario* I.

foreseen editing by Argentieri. I have elsewhere called Pavese's diary a *roman-vérité*[96] but the definition applies to this epistolary cycle of Foscolo's as well.[97]

Because they are essentially private, both diary and letter can be the matrix of modern fiction; and the occasional nature of his letters to Antonietta allowed our poet freely to tell his own story, in a kind of lay confession to a woman who was priestess, goddess, and demon in turn. Nothing less would have done, to elicit so much from him. These intermittences of the heart, unknown to him, ended up by composing a whole narrative, which was unpremeditated as a novel yet not as confession. While he was writing *Ortis* with his right hand, he wrote *Letters to Antonietta* with his left, and it is not as if the one hand ignored what the other did. On the contrary, the two narrative images thus taking shape mirrored each other, sometimes faithfully, more often with a canny distorting effect. We have seen above some of the mutual mirrorings in a faithful vein; now let us look at the distortions.

[96] "Truth as Fiction: Pavese's Diary," in *Michigan Quarterly Review*, winter 1977. Vol. XVI, 1. pp. 1-10.

[97] Sibilla Aleramo's *Amo dunque sono* (I love, therefore I am) arose in the same way, and was accordingly published by her in 1927. More recently, Reverend Lorenzo Milani's letters to his mother, published by Mondadori (Milan: 1973) under the editorship of Alice Milani Comparetti, elicited the following comments from Pier Paolo Pasolini: "Instinctively I have read Reverend Lorenzo Milani's *Lettere alla mamma* [Letters to Mother] as one reads an epistolary novel: namely, ignoring whatever documentary value the book may have (and it would be a minor document at that). And just as I have not used the *Letters* to complement [Rev. Milani's] *The Pastoral Experience*, I have not resorted to *The Pastoral Experience*, and to the other writings, to complement the *Letters*. I have filled in the gaps and the long suspenseful pauses between letter and letter novelistically. I have made reconstructions and established connections; I have made suppositions and attempted interpretations, exactly as one does with a work of fiction in its relations to autobiographical reality and culture . . ." P. P. Pasolini, *Scritti corsari*. Milan: Garzanti, 1975, p. 185. Translation mine. Pasolini, it will be remembered, was an outstanding Italian poet, novelist and movie director, while Reverend Milani was an apostle of evangelical Christianity within the Catholic Church. See also: Helene Hanff, *84, Charing Cross Road*. New York: Viking Press, 1975.

Actually the latter have been touched upon to some extent when the present discussion concerned the letters' use of the Ortis persona or their restriction of subject matter to private rather than to political themes, and their different approach to love. If erotic repression and sublimation is the keynote of *Ortis*, the letters to Antonietta glow with erotic consummation, thereby attaining a fullness and a richness which the novel can emulate only negatively, by exasperating the pain of renunciation. Teresa as woman is confined in the novel to a role which keeps her at an idealized distance, and, but for the fleeting sensuous effusiveness Foscolo grants her under the shade of the mulberry tree, she would remain a phantom. We have seen that she owes her artistic resurrection in the second edition of the novel to the Antonietta letters and to the experience they convey; the difference between first and second draft of this *Ortis* scene is the difference between failure and success, and one can only admire Foscolo's solution in making quick flight and disappearance follow the instant of blissful abandon. But Antonietta on her part inhabits the verbal scene that Ugo's messages to her have created; if he keeps the center of the stage, it is also true that she is never out of sight.

And she exists in her own right, not just as a projection of Ugo's outpourings. One remembers his tender words and his words of rage, one is captivated by his descriptions of the secret rendezvous place, one feels with him the undercurrent of future loss, the impossible resignation. Ortis is in him, as he tells her in the first letter, but suicide is out; it is harder to live than to die, therefore Ugo will live. There is one separation and reconciliation before the final parting; the glory of the flesh is also a fervor of the mind, plenitude is grasped, rather than skirted. The unworldly Ugo must come to terms with the mundane sphere, like Alceste confronted by his Célimène in Molière's *Misanthrope*. But when he hymns her (and he knows that those hymns, whether in prose or verse, are not wasted on the translator of Goethe) it is clear that no price was too high to pay for such a fulfillment. Perhaps there were the makings of a Stendhal in this Foscolo, who later became so prudish as to condemn (in his *Lettere dall'Inghil-terra*) Laclos and throw the shadow of ethical disapproval on his own *Ortis*. Certainly the *Lettere ad Antonietta* read like a fine psychological novel or *nouvelle*, and it is here, not in *Ortis*, that Foscolo equals Goethe's psychological finesse in *Werther*.

The writer that Ugo could not help being asserts himself in that seminal tenth letter[98] which I have excerpted before, and which should now be read in its entirety against the foil of the corresponding *Ortis* "letter" to which it gave a powerful vitalizing cue:

> *Friday, 5 pm. . .*
>
> Prepare *a thousand* kisses, for tonight I'll come and suck them from your heavenly mouth. O moments of paradise! I await you with such anxiety; you last so little! and then you leave me again to this terrible emptiness, to this deep sadness, to this forgetfulness of the whole world. . . .—Do you know, that Wednesday the mail went out without any letters for my mother?
>
> O my philosopher lady! you moved me so the day before yesterday with your letter penned among sorrows: and truly you are right: the prime of life fades so soon! And we two, Antonietta, have only few years left; we feel too much; and the soul devours our body, while with most people it is the body that devours the soul. On the other hand your poor health, which does endear you to me even more, does not promise you many happy hours . . . , and as for me, mishaps, and sad experience, and men's wickedness, and melancholy which dominates all my faculties, warn me that the time of pleasure is almost over for me. Never mind: we love each other, and loyally, ardently; isn't that enough? Must I tell you my only deep wish? . . . when your sighs are transfused into my

[98] Numbered x in the Antonietta Arese sequence, this letter is to be found at pp. 227-28 of *Epistolario* I, and its numbering in the overall progression of Foscolo's letters as published here is 162. Translation mine.

mouth, and I feel clasped by your arms . . . and your
tears mingle with mine . . . and . . . yes; I invoke death!
the fear of losing you makes me wish that life in that sacred moment may imperceptibly ebb away from us, and
one sepulcher keep us united forever . . . —Let O let me
get you away from these thoughts . . . why should I em-
bitter the joy of your youth? . . . why should I pour my
melancholy on the delight allotted to your angelic soul
and your celestial beauty?

What was your opinion of my way of loving? has it improved, or have you been disappointed? did you believe
me to be more ardent? more discreet?, have you involved yourself with me more through fatality than out of
vocation? And now what do you think?—What a throng
of questions! But they are so quickly answered that I
hope they won't annoy you; and you are so naive that you
will not be embarrassed in telling me the truth. As to
me, I find in you more than I expected: I suspected in
you a lot of whim and little feeling, and I was deceived
in this. . . . I also find a certain delicacy I haven't discovered in any other woman, and a goodness unaccountably combined with your rare intelligence (talent). So
long. So long. Turn over, and read more attentively
these other lines.

Before eight o'clock I will pass by . . . If the first window is open I shall come into Teresina's room . . . and if
not . . . —the window will be open, my heart tells me.
. . . Were it shut, I . . . will come anyway.

The Catullus of *Vivamus, mea Lesbia, atque amemus . . .
da mihi basia mille . . . nobis, semel cum occiderit brevis lux/
nox est perpetua una dormienda*[99] hovers behind the first part

[99] In the Loeb Library edition, volume containing the poems of Catullus,
Tibullus and the Pervigilium Veneris (London: Heinemann, and Cambridge, Mass.: Harvard University Press, 1966), this poem, with en face
translation by F. W. Cornish, is numbered V and appears at pp. 6-9. The
meaning of lines excerpted in my quotation is: "Let us live, o my Lesbia,

of the letter, but not as a programmatic allusion, rather as a natural convergence. The intimate chitchat that follows the poetical effusion, and the final tryst announcement, bring the message down to a quotidian, piquant, practical level, yet it is this that makes it viable for narrative purposes. Brilliant set pieces of lyrical tone without such modulations would not add up to a novelistic cycle of the kind I have been trying to evidence. The self narrator pulls many stops, and they do not all have to be of the deep sort we hear when the memorable saying of souls that devour their bodies rings out. The voice ranges all the way from a Tristan-like register invoking a Liebestod to a piquancy straight from rococo boudoirs; it is almost as if Richard Strauss, with Hofmannsthal's help, rehearsed his Wagner to offset him with Italianate or French comedy tunes and scenes.

Shortly after, Letter No. XII[100] again parallels the intense tone of *Ortis*, with comparable force:

> I saw you coming toward me, as simply dressed as I saw you yesterday morning . . . and like a pilgrim I have visited those places where we have walked, and where you have sat down, and the spot of that kiss. . . . (O my soul; I still feel my lips wet and sweetly smelling). . . . There is no remedy. This devouring fire, immense, can no longer keep within my bosom. I feel it burst from all my senses, from my eyes, from my hands . . . it is necessary for me to see you . . . I have already abandoned any prudence . . . let me see you! . . . —My imagination has risen to such a pitch that it fashions paradisal delights, and infernal torments. . . .

Some of this force is of course missing from the related pages

---

and let us love . . . give me a thousand kisses . . . suns can set and rise again, but for us, once our short day is over, there will be one long perpetual night to sleep through. . . ."

[100] *Epistolario* I, p. 230. Translation mine.

of *Ortis* (May 14 letter, beginning of May 15 letter) which have to take the road of renunciation, while here the fire of liberated libido keeps feeding on itself, ravenously, in a dramatic crescendo seldom equalled. Letter XIV[101] plays on yet another register, the meditative one, and makes Antonietta maieutic to Ugo:

> Peace to poor Ortis—and couldn't you, my woman, bring another one to birth . . . and perhaps a better one? I thank you, heavenly creature, for the sensations you afford me, I gather them in my heart as precious things; one day they will keep me company in my solitude. . . . I shall write with my imagination full of these blissful days I am living with you; and all my ideas and words will have that truth and warmth which one vainly seeks by studying and which one finds only having felt the passions.
>
> Yet I must begin to study again. I promise that to myself every day, and then I always resort to tomorrow . . . since we cannot become great through deeds, let us try with writings.

The prophecy will be fulfilled, and meanwhile it casts its long shadow on the fleeting present, a fullness of the senses and of the mind is enjoyed in the awareness of its impermanence. It is also a way of projecting the present experience into future literature, and acknowledging Antonietta as a Muse in the flesh, like those Boccaccio collectively acknowledged in the introduction to the *Decameron*'s Fourth Day.

If we listen carefully, here Ugo is talking to himself just as much as to Antonietta, and he is already taking leave of her, because he knows that he will have to lose her sooner or later, and living in the awareness of this transitory condition, he is saying to her what Ortis says to Teresa and to Nature; essentially, "I lose you and in losing you I have you forever;

---

101 *Ibid.*, p. 235. Translation mine.

plenitude cannot last, except as image." This is what imparts such a poignancy to these letters, even to their seemingly trifling parts—the trysts, the jealousy, the inner serenades to drawn shutters. Fictional time and "real" or compositional time coincide, to make the lived-imagined moment that much more intense; and its correlative dimension, its breathing space, is a projection into a dialectical future, which sharpens the uniqueness of the present experience and inverts the traditional perspective of narrative. Epic fiction unfolds against a vista of the past and it brackets the uttering or writing "I"; confessional fiction of the kind Foscolo writes here makes that "I" central and situates its narrative in a lived present against an intermittently anticipated future which negates that present and thereby intensifies its experiential value.

Besides, this is not fiction but "fiction," a reality imaginatively experienced, the utmost of truthfulness from a man who lives in and for the imagination; just as Ortis' letters are "letters"; and fiction becomes truth so that truth may reinvent itself. Letter and "letter," time and "time," author and character, coincide in the unintentional novel. In this total identification which enables him to write in perfect good faith, because his public is as intimate and as important as his own self can be, Ugo tests his Ortis persona, which is so much of him and yet not all, and will become Didymus to survive. The *Letters to Antonietta* are really the anti-*Ortis*, Foscolo's way to cope with his own underground self, the youthful, the criminal, the unappeasable Jacopo. It is criminal, in a way, to want the infinite and to want it to last. In *Ortis*, Jacopo confesses to a secret crime he is tormented by; he once accidentally killed a man who had failed to dodge his galloping horse on a country road. That "crime" stands for the total crime of Jacopo Ortis, his repressed yet huge libido that wants all of reality (Italy, Mother Earth, Teresa) for itself.

There is a subterranean reading of the novel that says No to reality as given and Yes to the self, then No to everything. The crime is the No, and the Yes of the transgression; suicide is only the last transgression, but writing as such is a transgression for Jacopo Ortis, since it will commemorate his revolt. It actually *is* his revolt. As for Ugo, when he writes to his Antonietta he transgresses too, not by revolting but by conspiring privately, and we, the readers, become posthumous accomplices by violating his secret. Writing is transgression, secrecy and fulfillment, and so is life at this point.

And what a fulfillment it was! "The whole world has vanished under my eyes, and all my passions only conspire to make you even more beautiful and worthy of love in my eyes. . . ." That is Letter No. XVIII.[102] Antonietta is his All, and if a touch of psychological ratiocination (as in Letter XXX)[103] makes him momentarily relativize the emotional absolute that she is, it is only because he plays proud Pygmalion to her—yet, as we have seen before, that rapport can be inverted, and in Letter No. L[104] he calls her "mother"; Letter XVI,[105] however, will be signed "Your Daddy"—he is her teacher of love.

The absolute of love is counterpointed, not offset, by the absolute of glimpsed death; Letter XXXII,[106] teetering between the pronoun of cold estrangement ("Voi") and the pronoun of intimacy ("Tu") as a reaction to the complications that have intervened, returns to the keynote:

I shall die . . . but I will leave you. I shall tell myself even with one foot in the grave: I have abandoned her because I have loved her with the whole violence and truth of love.

[102] *Ibid.*, pp. 241-42, letter numbered 170 in the general order of the collection. Translation mine.

[103] *Ibid.*, pp. 254-55, letter numbered 182 in the general order of the collection.

[104] *Ibid.*, pp. 280-81, letter numbered 202 in the general order of the collection.

[105] *Ibid.*, pp. 291-92, letter numbered 208 in the general order of the collection.

[106] *Ibid.*, pp. 257-58, letter numbered 184 in the general order of the collection. Translation mine.

For, as Letter XLI says[107]

> From passion to passion, from impetuousness to impetuousness. . . . I think I have as it were abused the feeling of life.

No wonder that he thinks of suicide, impersonating his persona:

> What a cold, angry day . . . it really looks like a season for suicide. This reflection is not mine, it is of poor Ortis.[108]

Life mirrors literature; unlike Ortis, however, Ugo recovers from his suicidal obsession and passes into a self-humorous mood in the following letter,[109] only to return to his self-tormenting attitude shortly later:

> Alas how many hardships still await me! Exiled from my homeland, a stranger to the whole world, removed, and forever, from you . . . what other shelter will be left?—I am perhaps my own executioner. I should close my eyes when the curtain of the future opens, and not devour my present with the fear of the future. . . .[110]

This is the letter signed "Il tuo papà," Your Daddy, as if to underline the desolate momentary wisdom which has brought self-knowledge. Ugo is an early victim of the *mal du siècle*, from which, unlike the heroes of De Musset, Stendhal, and

[107] *Ibid.*, p. 270, letter numbered 193 in the general order of the collection. Translation mine.

[108] *Ibid.*, pp. 285-86, letter numbered 205 in the general order of the collection. Translation mine.

[109] *Ibid.*, pp. 286-90, letter numbered 206 in the general order of the collection.

[110] *Ibid.*, p. 291, letter numbered 208 in the general order of the collection. Translation mine.

others, he suffers long before Napoleon's disappearance from the scene. He takes opium to sleep (Letter LXIV and passim);[111] he sways between inner turmoil and languor:

> My soul is in a storm . . . it is true. . . . I still feel alive, and for you alone, for you . . . but everything else moans in languor and apathy. My imagination is dead: my head is utterly empty.[112]

But if she is his unrenounceable All soon to be renounced, when she asks him to leave her he concludes on a note of all-givingness, for he in turn will possibly be her All:

> Send me your *Werther* as you go on translating it; it will be the company of my solitude. . . . Should you ever be with child because of me, or in whatever trouble, come into my arms. We shall share bread and tears. I shall be to you a father, spouse, brother, friend, servant. . . . I shall be all, all, to you. . . .[113]

The temporary reconciliation after this crisis will change that, as we saw, and the need for a complete rapport will be eventually projected onto other women, one of whom in particular, Quirina Mocenni Magiotti of Florence, will keep up a faithful correspondence with Ugo through the years of exile. She is bride, sister, friend, and Muse to him—from beyond the impassable gap that her marital predicament and his political vicissitudes have thrown between them. At times his letters to her sound like the continuation of those to Antonietta, to an Antonietta, of course, in whom he could occasionally see the giver and receiver of an Eros capable of sub-

---

[111] *Ibid.*, pp. 302-03, letter numbered 216 in the general order of the collection.

[112] *Ibid.*, p. 305, letter numbered 218 in the general order of the collection. Translation mine.

[113] *Ibid.*, p. 311, letter LXX, numbered 222 in the general order of the collection. Translation mine.

DEMONS OF SUICIDE AND FICTION   115

limating itself into Agape. Quirina, the *Donna gentile*, would
eventually bequeath to the Leghorn library many of his *Le
Grazie* manuscripts (and letters), with her own editorial observations. She was the keeper of his soul, if such a thing was
possible. Antonietta, on the other hand, could never be
Quirina except in Ugo's moments of self-deception; she could
be faithful only to herself, could only be the "Eternal
Feminine" as incarnated in the "beautiful moment" that cannot be fixated. She, like her later avatar Lucietta, is there
only to be lost; Quirina instead cannot ever be lost because
she eludes possession. She is the paradoxical "wife" of
paradoxical Didymus—whom Antonietta helped to be born
on the ashes of Ortis.

A letter to Lucietta of December 1813 deserves quotation
for its insistence on the word "to lose," the art our exiled poet
and warrior was forever relearning:

> I have also lost my prized independence, and soon hav-
> ing to lose my homeland, if I lose you too, I shall have
> nothing left to lose on earth. But I cannot help losing
> you.[114]

The letters to Antonietta make up an epistolary novel *ex-
post-facto*, but they can also be considered as a chapter in the
longer epistolary novel Ugo spent all his life writing. He was
himself a *romanzo*, a novel, as she had told him one day, and
it took him a long time to tell his story. Though he occasionally claimed the privilege of educating Antonietta to the art of
subtler love, it was she who educated him, and in this she
had only one rival, the Greco-Venetian woman of letters,
Isabella Teotochi Albrizzi, who became the catalyst and incidental subject of an unfinished novel. The *Sesto Tomo dell'io*

[114] Translation mine. I get my quotation from the Argentieri edition, p.
228. The text is also available in *Edizione Nazionale*, XVII (*Epistolario*, IV).
A similar expression ("I must lose you," Bisogna pur ch'io ti perda") recurs
in the Jan. 1814 letter to Lucietta, numbered 1438 by Plinio Carli in *Epistolario* V.

(Sixth Volume of the Self)[115] remained at the inchoate stage; a pity, considering its brilliant inception, notably the pages where Temira, priestess of love, after initiating the hero to carnal pleasure tells him not to expect undying love on earth. The humor, the sensuous frankness and strength of these pages, augured well for the unwritten sequel. One reason for the lack of a sequel was that at the time of writing (1801) "Temira" (as she appears in the narrative) was a past episode, and Antonietta ("Psyche") was taking over. In any case the Temira pages rate as another chapter of the *roman vècu* and *inachevè* we have been scanning, with the *Lettere scritte dall'Inghilterra* (Letters written from England)[116] as a further chapter, featuring a Didymus poised between the two modern cultures he had come to compare with Jamesian tact, while the countless letters to Quirina make up the last chapter. All in all, an "open work" of sorts.

It is thus possible to read most of Foscolo's prose as one long unfinished novel, or as the brilliant project for one. It could not ever find its completion. The mind that received its decisive shock from Napoleonic Antonietta, the mind committed to the fullness of the present experience, and yet unable to ignore the presentiments of an uncertain future, went on exfoliating itself, tirelessly, from love to love, from exile to exile, from page to searing page. There was so much to tell, and so little time to tell it in. And the letter was the suitable form for this never ending self-revelation which managed to keep at bay the destructive demons conjured in earlier days.

---

[115] In *Edizione Nazionale*, v, pp. 1-26. For Isabella Teotochi Albrizzi's role in Foscolo's life, see Antonio Piromalli, *Saggi critici di storia letteraria*. Florence: Olschki, 1967, pp. 1-42.

[116] *Edizione Nazionale*, v, pp. 237-454.

CHAPTER III

Vatic Exorcism: the Lyrics
and *The Sepulchers*

The disabused modern ear might occasionally withhold response from Foscolo's vatic utterances and misjudge his muscular verse as decorative or bombastic. Such were the unanticipated risks he took when inditing his *I Sepolcri* hymn (1806)[1] with outright fondness for mythological or historic names coupled with classicist lexical choices. *Ortis* had pointed another way with its espousal of the epistolary open form, so germane to the language of passion and unobstructed observation. It would be possible to play off the courtly style of his 1803 *Poems*[2] (the two odes and the twelve sonnets) against the romantic freedom of the *Ortis* prose, and thereby

[1] This poem, consisting of 295 unrhymed hendecasyllables, was written in 1806 and published in 1807 by Bettoni in Brescia, Lombardy. It will be found at pp. 25-32 of *Opere di F.*, with the author's notes following at pp. 33-38. For a better understanding of the poem itself, and of Foscolo's own literary disposition, it should be kept in mind that he was aroused into writing *The Sepulchers* by the (to him) infuriating Edict of St. Cloud (1804), which forbade burials within city walls and prescribed standardized cemeteries in the countryside, to cope with sanitary problems. The St. Cloud Edict had been recently extended to Italy.

[2] To be found at pp. 5-18 of *Opere di F.*, which also lists the several original editions. A "Poesie Varie" (Various Poems) appendix to the Odes and Sonnets follows at pp. 19-21, comprising two poems from the subsequent years in which Foscolo served as an officer of the Italian division stationed on the Channel with the Napoleonic army poised there for a prospective invasion of Britain.

dismiss the poems as a regression from the newly cleared path toward an authentic confessional art, as if the lesson of Rousseau and Goethe (*Werther*'s Goethe) had been repudiated for a renewed obeisance to the decrepit dictates of a finicky classicism. But such writers as Foscolo, once they venture out on their own to discover that they are goats rather than sheep, can hardly return to the fold.

As in the case of Hölderlin and Keats, his Hellenic myth and bardic style are existential mythopoeia. Foscolo's own approach to the classical matrix recalls Goethe's pilgrimage to Rome, "antiker Form sich nähernd";[3] and to give up the *Ode all'amica risanata* (Ode to his Lady Friend On Her Recovery)[4] would be almost as crucial a loss as giving up the exquisite *Roman Elegies* of the German master.

We are safely past Verlaine's injunction against eloquence,[5] and any suspicion of the vatic stance in poetry will be dispelled by the example of Yeats and Pound, who emerged from a *Symboliste* initiation to achieve the unsuspected revival of what *Symbolisme* seemed to have buried forever. Foscolo's public concerns, one soon realizes upon reading his 1803 and 1806 poems, are rooted in his personal experience, and if he chooses to convey them in the literary vehicle by now germane to Revolutionary and Imperial taste, as well as to an Italian tradition of long standing, he has ex-

[3] Literally, "approaching ancient Form." This is the title appearing in the 1876 Leipzig edition of Goethe's collected works for a small part of his lyrical poetry which, in the most authoritative recent edition (*Goethes Werke*, Hamburger Ausgabe. Hamburg: Christian Wegner Verlag, 1948, 1960; Vol. I, ed. Erich Trunz, *Gedichte und Epen*) is differently and more chronologically distributed. Some of these unrhymed couplets imitating the classical elegy are to be found in the Hamburg edition, under the subtitle "Vermischte Epigramme," in the section devoted to poems of the "classical phase" (*Die Zeit der Klassik*, pp. 157-294), which also contains the great "Roman Elegies" (*Römische Elegien*). There is a marked affinity between the latter and Foscolo's Odes.

[4] *Opere di F.*, pp. 9-11.

[5] Paul Verlaine, "Art Poétique," from *Jadis et Naguère*, in p. V, *Oeuvres Poétiques Complètes*. Paris: Gallimard, Bibliothèque de la Pléiade, 1951, p. 206.

cellent reasons—*pace* Mme. de Staël. One should turn to
Foscolo's rejoinder in the unfinished *Lettere dall'Inghilterra*
to settle the question.[6] And one should also take into account
the favorable response of some Italian Romantics to Foscolo's
example; a response of decisive weight, especially considering that rejection of the time-hallowed classical mythology in
favor of historical truth and Christian revelation stood at the

[6] See *Lettere Scritte dall'Inghilterra*, in *Edizione Nazionale*, v, and in
particular pp. 358-379: "Appendice al Gazzettino No. 1," i (Il gazzettino
contro la metafisica e la lettera della poesia moderna, p. 358), ii (Frammento sui romanzi, p. 368). The same authoritative edition is reproduced
in *Opere di F.*, where the part that interests us here goes from p. 593 to p.
603, and is supplemented by Edoardo Sanguineti's notes and commentary
in the Appendix, pp. 1186-1226. In this part of the *Letters from England*
Foscolo polemizes against the romantic vogue of poetry attuned to
metaphysical speculations in the German style and to Northern mythology.
This vogue was helped in Italy, as is well known, by Madame De Staël's
intervention on the Italian literary scene with her two articles published in
the *Biblioteca Italiana* of Milan (January 1816, June 1816). In these writings, which stirred great controversy and contributed to the rise of Italian
romanticism, the French writer applied to the seemingly stagnant Italian
cultural situation the ideas already set forth in her book on Germany (*De
l'Allemagne*), where she held up rising German culture as a mirror to the
smug sophistication of French rationalism and *salon* culture. Her lament
over the failure of modern Italy to live up to past glory had already been
voiced in the 1807 novel, *Corinne ou l'Italie*, where she mythifies herself as
a poetess crowned in the Capitol—and in that role Foscolo takes her to task
in *Letters from England*, objecting to her inadequate knowledge of Italian
literature. It is interesting to notice that while Foscolo took up the cudgels
for Classicism against Mme. De Staël, he failed to see that her plea for
broader literary horizons and deeper commitment in fiction and poetry alike
was quite consonant with his attitude. She of course was insufficiently in-
formed and missed the fact that men like Foscolo himself, and Alfieri,
Cesarotti, and Bertola before him, had been championing a similar cause
and fostering better knowledge of modern European developments in literature. The details of this momentous episode in Italian literature are lucidly
given by Prof. Grazia Avitabile in Chapter ii of her book *The Controversy on
Romanticism in Italy* (New York: Vanni, 1959), while an earlier, and fun-
damental study is G. A. Borgese's *Storia della critica romantica in Italia*
(Milan: Il Saggiatore, 1965, rep. from 1905 ed.), and further essays and
bibliography appear in L. Caretti's and G. Luti's anthology, *La letteratura
italiana*, L'Ottocento (Milan: Mursia, 1973), p. 105 ff., "Il romanticismo."

center of their emphases along with the plea for a more democratic language and a more open form in poetry and drama
alike. Behind these differences there was a perceptible affinity: the heartfelt commitment of Ugo Foscolo, and of his
Romantic brethren who rose on the literary horizon after his
exile, to the ethical implications of literature, hence to the
liberal, patriotic Italian cause, against the so-called Holy Alliance's reactionary absolutism.[7]

That truth engaged both passion and intellect, and because
Foscolo—with his flair for new talent—sensed it in Carlo
Porta, in Silvio Pellico, in Ludovico di Breme, in Giovanni
Berchet, and in Alessandro Manzoni at the inception of their
career, when they were still unknown and their Romantic
cause still this side of official·formulation, he corresponded
with some of them in a friendly way. With Porta in particular
he entertained a warm friendship, and as for Manzoni, who
was destined to be the leader of that group and an interna-
tionally acclaimed poet, playwright, and novelist, Foscolo in-
serted a reference to that budding author's first significant
poem ("In morte di Carlo Imbonati," On the Death of C.I.) in
his own coeval *I Sepolcri* (The Sepulchers, 1806, publ.
1807).[8]

[7] The "Holy Alliance" of the Continental monarchies, established at the
Vienna Congress of 1815 with the purpose of upholding official Christianity
and political repression against any resurgence of the revolutionary principles that seemed to have gone underground with Napoleon's downfall, had
nothing to do with the evangelical, democratic interpretation of Catholicism
that the Italian romantics favored, notably Manzoni, Berchet, and Silvio
Pellico, the playwright who later became famous throughout the world for
the stoicism with which he bore long-term imprisonment at the notorious
Spielberg jail and for the unresentful candor with which he told the experience in a book called *Le mie prigioni* (My Imprisonment). Pellico, it will be
remembered, was to be acclaimed by Melville as an exemplary figure in
Clarel (1876).

[8] *Opere di F.*, pp. 37-38, where, in the notes to *The Sepulchers*, Foscolo
quotes a passage on Homer from Manzoni's earlier poem *In morte di Carlo
Imbonati* (1806) to praise the budding author who was to become the tower-
ing figure of Italian Romanticism. Curiously enough, toward the end of his
life Foscolo (1827) criticized the by now famous Manzoni for having at-

Foscolo's eloquence surges forward from a hot center of vision, yet his stately style does not inevitably make for public utterance or declamatory tone. It is versatile, it can take a turn for the intimate, and then the verse makes a strange music, seemingly ancient, disquietingly new:

Qual dagli antri marini
l'astro più caro a Venere
co' rugiadosi crini
fra le fuggenti tenebre
appare, e il suo viaggio
orna col lume dell'eterno raggio;

sorgon così tue dive
membra dall'egro talamo,
e in te beltà rivive. . . .

As from the secret seacaves
the star most dear to Venus
with dewy hair appears

---

tempted and failed to reconcile dramatic poetry and historical truth in the widely discussed tragedy *Carmagnola* ("Della nuova scuola drammatica italiana," in *Edizione Nazionale*, XI, *Saggi di letteratura italiana*, Part II, ed. Foligno, pp. 559-618. The essay remained long unpublished in the rough-draft form in which the author left it). Of the other Romantic writers I mention in connection with Foscolo, Carlo Porta, also a friend of Manzoni, was to become the greatest poet in the Milanese dialect and is now recognized as one of the important satirical poets in nineteenth-century Italian literature; Giovanni Berchet has a place in the anthologies, including the *Penguin Book of Italian Verse*, for his elegiac poetry on medieval or politically topical subjects, but he is more important for his impassioned formulation of Romantic literary doctrine in the essay *Lettera semiseria di Grisostomo*, largely inspired by the Schlegels, Goethe, and Vico; Ludovico di Breme was an erudite clergyman whose critical acumen stirred further investigation on the new ideas then ripening, and caused G. Leopardi to redefine his advocacy of classical myth in *Discorso di un italiano sulla poesia romantica* (1818). These and other litterateurs wrote in journals like *Biblioteca Italiana* and *Il Conciliatore*. See Foscolo's letters in *Epistolario*, passim.

> among the fleeting darkness, to effuse light's
> perennial ornament along its way;
>
> just so do your divine
> limbs rise from the sick bed,
> and beauty in you revives. . . .

That is the "Ode all'Amica Risanata," the poem written for Antonietta Arese's recovery from an illness which had temporarily confined that eager beauty to a lonely bed. It differs both from the coeval letters' plain, if superbly articulate, style of amorous conspiracy, and from the prose of *Ortis*, which has no such mythological trappings and lexical privileges to remove it and its object into an inaccessible sphere of veneration. But this is the point, of course: to address the loved woman as a fitful goddess, with the intimacy a "Tu" form implies (and in Stanza 13 the intimacy will be strengthened: ". . . your secret abode/ where to me alone you appear, a priestess . . ."), yet to distance her from the rapt contemplators through the devices of the formal if light-footed ode rhythm, of the Latinate or Hellenizing diction, and of the mythic personifications European poetry had cherished from the days of the Petrarchan dispensation to those of Alexander Pope and beyond. Thus we find the ministering Hours of stanzas 4 and 5, who used to serve medicines to the bedridden beauty and now instead bring her the paraphernalia of her restored dominion: an Indian silk dress, the cameos and embossed jewelry, and the white buskins and amulets which will again make her "a Goddess" (st. 5), the cynosure of young admirers. One only has to look at the paintings of David or Appiani and Ingres, or visit Mario Praz's personal collection of Empire style art and interior decoration (with maybe a glance at his matchless *History of Furniture*),[9] to realize that this is no stale literary convention but an accurate description

[9] Mario Praz, *La Filosofia dell'Arredamento*. Milan: Longanesi, 1964. English translation by William Weaver, *An Illustrated History of Interior Decoration from Pompei to Art Nouveau*. New York: Braziller, 1964, and London: Thames & Hudson, 1964. Mario Praz has also written on Foscolo

of the high fashions of the day; and if precious, not inane. Ear and eye of the poet celebrant at the altar of his latter-day Aphrodite cannot help caressing their object, whom he is arraying in sacred vestments for the love rite—but they are the vestments and ornaments of the time, for she is a particular embodiment of Aphrodite, a passing splendor in timebound flesh (st. 1, st. 9) whom he will rescue from mortality in song (st. 16).

No decorative detail fails the central evocative function. The rhythm dances forward with flexible vigor, banking on a resilient syntax which both accentuates and overflows the stanzaic pattern—itself a uniquely viable model for such a dynamism, for it seals five short seven-syllable lines (alternately rhyming and rhymeless, paroxytone and proparoxytone) with a longer one, the standard Italian hendecasyllable, which fulfills the repeatedly arrested (and pause-enhanced) impulses of the five shorter lines with a free if measured sweep, aided by rhyme. The metric mold itself was inherited from the Arcadian rococo school of eighteenth-century memory, but the result is far livelier. It is thematically appropriate that the godlike woman's return to her Venus role should mark a high point of the poem (sts. 5-6-8) with the sensuous, kinetic conjuring of her dance and "perilous song."

Thus the musical development vindicates the prelude, and what might have otherwise remained an ornamental simile of the idle kind (st. 1) becomes a propulsive device. Rhythm and vision keep moving forward, and the woman-goddess is caught in unceasing motion, from the moment she rises from her sick bed like the star of Venus from the sea (st. 1) to the moment when the celebrant persona remembers her mortality

---

and Byron (*Rivista di Letterature Moderne e Comparate*, June 1962, pp. 177-84), and on Foscolo (in *Sulle orme di U. Foscolo. Florilegio di Critica*, ed. G. La Rocca Nunzio. Bergamo: Gli Amici dei Sacri Lari, 1962, pp. 111-120). For our purposes, one should also consult Praz's contribution to *Arte Neoclassica*, Atti del Convegno, 12-14 ottobre 1957. Venezia-Roma: Istituto per la Collaborazione Culturale, 1964 (Praz's paper is "La fortuna del gusto neoclassico e di Antonio Canova).

("beltà fugace," fleeting beauty: st. 9) in the very act of suspending it. She is first evoked as an analogue of Venus Anadyomene, though the poet tactfully avoids making that point explicitly; he lets the mythic status accrue to her from the cues of direct perception itself: star rising from the sea = woman rising from her temporary eclipse. An exchange of attributes takes place, for the star has anthropomorphic traits (the "dewy locks" of Ossianesque cast) while the woman has "divine limbs," both being lights in an otherwise dark world, and both under Venus' patronage. Patronage or, actually, occult identity: star and woman do not just represent Venus, they are Venus' emanations one on the cosmic, the other on the human scale. Significantly, both are identified by reference to Venus-Aphrodite, but neither is named directly in the poem. And if the woman is first worshipped as goddess ("Dea," st. 5) only to be subsequently demoted to the role of priestess (st. 13), stanzas 10-14 unfold a contrapuntal argument. The presently adored woman is only mortal, but so were the famed goddesses of Greece after all, whom the Foscolian persona considers to have been mere posthumous apotheoses of women in the flesh: Artemis a real, "mortal" huntress; Bellona the war goddess a formidable Amazon; Aphrodite herself a historical queen of Cythera and Cyprus.

And when the demystified goddess recurs in the poem (sts. 13-14), in inverse symmetry to the initial imaginative *élan* which raised her priestess to divine status, the event is marked by the pivotal verb *apparire* (to appear), a clear echo of the first stanza where the star of Venus was said to *appear*:

> fra le fuggenti tenebre
> appare . . . (st. 1)

> amid the fleeting darkness
> appears . . .

> agli arcani tuoi lari
> ove a me sol sacerdotessa appari (st. 13)

over your household shrine
where to me alone you appear, a priestess.

Perhaps only in Dante[10] and in Tasso[11] had that verb found
such radiant emphasis. The act of appearing, in all these instances, amounts to an apparition, but an apparition of reality, not of phantoms. To *appear*, in other words, means here
to show oneself, to show forth, to manifest one's essence in
the very act of entering our range of vision. Such semantic
heightening, which is a recovery of the verb's root meaning,
occurs most clearly in Stanza 1 of Foscolo's Ode, where the
verb *appare* (appears) is syntactically focused by its placement at the beginning of the line, immediately after the "fleeting darkness" it offsets, and without any nominal predicate to
qualify it. It sheds any qualification, it shines in its absoluteness; and it retains something of that semantic strength when
it recurs later on (st. 13) in conjunction with the predicate
"sacerdotessa" (priestess). Actually in the latter context the
relevant noun wavers between a predicative and an apposi-
tional function, while the verb tends to reconcentrate semantic energy upon itself by taking the climactic position, at the
end of line and phrase. An epiphany is involved, a luminous
event, exactly as in Dante's sonnet and in Tasso's ottava

[10] First lines of the well-known *Vita Nuova* sonnet, "Tanto gentile e
tanto onesta pare/ La donna mia quand'ella altrui saluta . . ." (So gentle
and so chaste my lady shows herself/ When greeting somebody . . .).

[11] Torquato Tasso, *Gerusalemme liberate*, Canto III, Stanza 21, final
couplet:

"e, le chiome dorate al vento sparse,
giovane donna in mezzo al campo apparse."

"and, loosening her gold hair to the wind,
she showed herself a young woman in the battlefield."

As I pointed out in my "Fairfax Versus Wiffen: Tasso's Clorinda in
Elizabethan and in Romantic Garb" (*The Rarer Action, Essays in Honor of
Francis Fergusson*, ed. Cheuse and Koffler. New Brunswick, N.J.: Rutgers
University Press, 1970, pp. 191-201), both translators of Tasso's poem fail
to reproduce that climactic verb. Foscolo, incidentally, knew Wiffen's
work but had strong reservations on its accuracy and style.

rima. The etymological kinship between English *shine* and German *Erscheinung* comes to mind, like that other kinship, which could hardly be lost on Foscolo's Greek ear, between *phàino* (I show) and *phos* (light).

Unquestionably the poem stakes a great deal on verbs in general—those carriers of energy, as Foscolo acknowledged in a statement I have already referred to. In each case, concentration of energy in a salient verb happens to be enhanced by the overall sequential design. Thus in the first two stanzas, quoted above, the Anadyomene cluster of images (Venus-star-woman) banks on the semantic progression of *appare* (appears, line 5)—*sorgon* (rise, line 7)—*rivive* (revives, line 9). A good dancer needs a good backbone, and there is nothing overly soft or unduly stiff about the verbal backbone of this poem, which is as lithe as its protagonist. It would not be a minuet she dances in stanzas 6 to 9, but a free solo dance on the verge of wildness:

fra il basso sospirar vola il tuo canto

più periglioso; o quando
balli disegni, e l'agile
corpo all'aure fidando,
ignoti vezzi sfuggono
dai manti, e dal negletto
velo scomposto sul sommosso petto.

All'agitarti, lente
cascan le trecce, nitide
per ambrosia recente,
mal fide all'aureo pettine
e alla rosea ghirlanda
che or con l'alma salute April ti manda.

through the low-keyed sighing flies your song
most perilous; or when
you try a dance, and as you entrust

your nimble body to the air
unknown charms issue from
your mantles and the unchecked
veil ruffled on the palpitating bosom.

At your commotion, slow
your locks fall, shining
with ambrosial fluid, ever
reluctant to the golden comb
and the roseate wreath
which April sends you with the boon of health.

As the poem bodies her forth, this dancer is all vocal and kinetic energy, and conventional decorum crumbles in the presence of her savage grace. When she returns to the salon after her illness, she takes over, she becomes the center of attention and polarizes the elegant society around her, frightening the women and charming the men. She has the fitfulness and occasional cruelty of the true goddess—a vessel of Eros not Agape. No wonder that wild Artemis the huntress, and Bellona the war goddess, should follow up in close sequence before Aphrodite finally reappears to clinch the point about the queenly woman (st. 10-14). No wonder either that the force of language should press against the dykes of set meter and at times overflow them by sweeping over two or three stanzas with one syntactical wave. And as if to remind us that his pagan godheads are no conventional décor, Foscolo in St. 13 has Venus take the form of a statue for her matchless devotee to put wreaths on, only to say next that the goddess once was a queen in flesh and blood (st. 14):

regina fu, Citera
e Cipro ove perpetua
odora primavera
regnò beata, e l'isole
che col selvoso dorso
rompono agli Euri e al grande Ionio il corso.

a queen she was, on Cythera
and Cyprus where perennial
Spring perfumes the air
she reigned in bliss, and on the islands
which with their wooded backs
break the streams of the windswept Ionian sea.

A multiple accomplishment, even apart from the sober splendor of those lines that delineate a legendary landscape in
terms of sheer physical dynamism; for the emphatic inversion
"regina fu" (a queen she was) at the same time removes
Aphrodite from the mythical sphere and revaluates her on the
level of human experience. She, whose statue you are now
worshipping, was really just a queen, a mortal human being
like you, and her later apotheosis was pure fiction. Yet a
queen she was, and what a queen! Mortality, no matter how
painful, has its unique rewards; we have no use for the sham
immortality men often seem to take so literally; that "immortality" can be seen in the lifeless statue, compared to which
you, lady, are the true goddess because only life is divine,
and life can only exist in time, in mortality, like the star, like
your radiant flesh, deathbound. Yet you can get a longer
lease of life through the memory of posterity, and that is
something I, the poet, can confer.

Accordingly, you will be "divine" as an image in the mind
of the living long after your demise. To be divine is not to be
literally deathless; it is to embody a perfection of living form
for the time allotted by nature, and then perhaps to survive
the rotting flesh as an incorruptible image traversing the consciousness of generations. By the time the celebrant persona
in the last stanza promises this to his beloved, the epithet
"divina" has acquired its strongest focus after several semantically wavering occurrences: "divine limbs" (*divine membra*)
in St. 2, "you, a Goddess" (*te, Dea,*) in St. 5, "the world calls
her [Artemis] a goddess (*Diva il mondo la chiama*), St. 11.
There can be no doubt now about the limits and intensity of
this attribute, for it simply defines the highest peak of aes-

thetic fulfillment a mortal creature can achieve, and that
which makes her worthy of posthumous remembrance, a
coveted survival. The poet of *The Sepulchers* already looms
here with his sharp anthropological reduction of myth to
human experience excluding any transcendent metaphysics;
the earnest reader of Hobbes, Machiavelli, and Vico knows
that values come from below, not from above. The poetry
thrives on these denials instead of withering away as so many
conventional classicists would have feared. By showing us
the existential roots of myth, Foscolo is destroying plaster
gods and topical stereotypes, the arsenal of classicist tradition, only to dramatize the historical and mental process from
which they sprang; and by the same token he is reacclimatiz-
ing those gods to the disenchanted mind of the new age.
Knowledge replaces superstition, and in so doing it claims
the whole vistas of civilization for its proper domain, the
study of man.

From the very moment Venus has been ideally shattered as
a statue to be returned to her human origins, a new breath
widens the scope of the poem. We are no longer in the early
nineteenth-century salon of Antonietta Arese, during the first
years of Napoleon's precarious empire, but in the open
spaces of the Greek sea where Venus rose, Anadyomene
idea, and in the open perspective of an unqualified future
which will receive the memory of today's perishable goddess
to immortalize her as we have immortalized the vague memory of Cythera's long vanished queen. And the poet officiates;
he has the bardic investiture from native Greece, the cradle
of poetry itself:

Ebbi in quel mar la culla,
ivi erra ignudo spirito
di Faon la fanciulla,
e se il notturno zefiro
blando sui flutti spira,
suonano i liti un lamentar di lira (st. 15).

> I had my birth in that sea,
> and there, a naked spirit,
> Phaon's sweetheart roams on,
> and if the nightly breeze
> mild blows on the waves,
> the shores resound with a lamenting lyre.

The uncanny melody of these lines, where the Italian language shows its vocalic and alliterative mettle, again transports us into a region where the imaginary is accepted as such, *and therefore* as a legitimate kind of reality: Sappho's heartbreak still haunts Foscolo's native sea, but only after suffering a sea-change into song, the love song he inherits and translates into the cognate Italian language, next in the succession line. To celebrate beauty even among the intermittent threats of war (st. 12) and in spite or because of its mortality is a worthwhile function for the keeper of civilization's values. We are cast into a particular time and place, and only a recognition of this limitation enables us to transcend the limits of time and space—in song, memory, Mnemosyne. Beyond the poet of the Ode there dawns the poet of *The Sepulchers*, as we saw, and beyond that, the indefatigable and gloriously defeated rhapsodist of *The Graces*.

It would seem that the poem answers in advance the notorious objections of strict Romantics by showing that "the death of one god is the death of all" and that "Phoebus [or Aphrodite] was/ a name for something that never could be named."[12] That something mobilizes the timeless array of Olympian deities and demons in the fight for historical truth; they enter the poem as stylizations of as many social and mental events, like the miracle of birth, the passing of inexorable time, the outbreak of war, the ecstasy and cult of consoling beauty in the midst of disorder and bloodshed. If the Hellenic gods are dead, so is the Christian one; but that impartial *Goet-*

---

[12] Wallace Stevens, *Notes Toward a Supreme Fiction*, Part I ("It Must Be Abstract"), poem No. 1. *The Collected Poems of W.S.* New York: Knopf, 1957, pp. 380-81.

terdaemmerung admits of a resurrection of sorts, to be
enacted in communal memory; and that memory is delegated
to the individual singer who has gone back to the roots of personal and collective history and thereby accepted his investiture. When Ugo Foscolo of Zante places his autobiographical
persona at the conclusive turn of the poem, he is giving us an
acknowledgment of cultural responsibility. Poetry is a cultural act, a cognitive function, not a superstructural embellishment of life for soporific purposes. The truth that the
human mind descries cannot be taken for granted in Neoclassical fashion as if it were an unquestionable set of axioms
supported by a timeless "Reason" or by a venerable "Authority." Both forms of humanism are defunct, and Foscolo—
along with his brethren Keats, Byron, Goethe, and
Hölderlin—propounds in their place an existential humanism
which is called upon to test the received as well as the newly
formulated verities.

That verification can only originate in the dedicated self,
"full of the native/ sacred air," (st. 16), who reattains the
original shudder of discovery in the presence of the sacred
because he has disposed of all factitious "sacredness." Unlike Keats, then, Foscolo can posit on a stronger basis the
dilemma "truth versus beauty," that stinging dissociation of
sensibility the Enlightenment rationalism had inflicted upon
the European mind torn between the legacy of religious-
aesthetic humanism and the inflexible urgings of the new science. The old beauty is stale and the way to authentic beauty
lies through the truth-singed landscape that has repelled so
many. To realize that the ancient fictions were just fictions is
to repossess them as part of mankind's ceaseless *paideia*. The
resulting clarity of mind will enable the imagination to do its
work—to rediscover reality as an invention. So much for the
conceivable misreading of this Ode as a mere exercise in deft
salon gallantry, rococo style.

Even so, along with its companion piece (the "Ode to
Luigia Pallavicini fallen from a horse" which dwells on the
physical precariousness of feminine beauty rather than on its

power—it was written at Genoa in 1800 during the Austrian siege, in the lull of battle), the Ode to beauty healed seems to offset the twelve sonnets that make up the second part of Foscolo's slim book of lyrics. For, as Fubini has said, these sonnets sound as if they had been written by Jacopo Ortis himself; they are haunted by the thought of death, and, with the exception of the Zante sonnet, they mostly shun mythological references. The odes move in a privileged sphere which can envisage mortality itself as the substance of divine status; the sonnets either dread or covet annihilation. Their style, though unmistakably Foscolian harks back to Alfieri,[13] Petrarch, and the *Dolce Stil Nuovo*, instead of to Pindar and Alcaeus. Thus Sonnet II, starting on a deliberate Latin cue,[14] goes on to echo Petrarchan passages,[15] and finally closes on a clear Alfierian-Ortisian note:

Che se pur sorge di morir consiglio,
a mia fiera ragion chiudon le porte
furor di gloria, e carità di figlio.
     Tal di me schiavo, e d'altri, e della sorte,
     conosco il meglio ed al peggior m'appiglio,
     e so invocare e non darmi la morte.

For if there rises in me the will to die,
such fierce reasoning finds its way blocked

---

[13] Vittorio Alfieri, the eighteenth-century playwright of European fame who spent his last years in Florence with the Countess of Albany, is remembered in *The Sepulchers* for his patriotic spirit. Foscolo knew him personally, and was familiar not only with his tragedies but also with his stark, angular sonnets ultimately traceable to a freely interpreted Petrarch.

[14] From a couplet by Maximianus: *Non sum qui fueram: periit pars maxima nostri:/ Hoc quoque quod superest languor et horror habet.* And Foscolo, translating: *Non son chi fui; perì di noi gran parte:/ Questo che avanza è sol languore e pianto* (lines 1 and 2, Sonnet II). Maximianus in turn took his cue from Propertius.

[15] See *Dall'Ortis alle Grazie*, note pp. 57-58, lines 3-4: *E secco è il mirto, e son le foglie sparte/ del lauro*; cfr. Petrarch, Poem No. 269 *(Canzoniere*, Part II): *Rott'è l'alta colonna, e 'l verde lauro, . . .*

by frenzy of glory and filial devotion.
Thus a slave to myself, and to others, and to chance,
I know the better choice yet cling to the worse,
and I can only invoke, not seize the boon of death.

The deft intarsia of quotations (to which also belongs the
Ovidian-Petrarchan last line but one)[16] manages to survive its
literary debt and achieve a personal tone. It is certainly better
on the whole than the other markedly Alfierian piece of the
collection, Sonnet VII ("Il proprio ritratto," Self-portrait),
whose final line must nevertheless rank as prophetic:

Morte, tu mi darai fama e riposo.

Death, you will give me both fame and repose.

If literary tension occasionally makes for rhetorical noise
not music (as is the case with No. III, a protest against the
proposed educational bill of the Cisalpine Republic that
would have abolished the teaching of Latin; and incidentally
elsewhere), the flaws remain sporadic. They cannot obscure
the accomplishment of this concise autobiography in verse,
which if sequentially read will yield a clue to the inner struggle Foscolo was waging against the Ortis side of his own self,
rather than simply confirm his avowed Ortis vocation. Sonnet
I, "Alla sera" (To Evening),[17] sighs for the peace of death as

[16] *Video meliora proboque, deteriora sequor* is a line from Ovid's
Metamorphoses, VII, 21, already rendered by Petrarch as "E veggio il meg-
lio ed al peggior m'appiglio" in his Canzone No. 264, last line of the envoi.
It is a particularly dramatic poem, ending on a somber note of unresolved
struggle, and therefore germane to the tone of Foscolo's sonnet despite the
different situation involved. As later with Eliot and Pound, or Montale, the
use of a concealed quote in a poem transforms the source in the very act of
anchoring the poem to it; the source is thereby rediscovered, and here actually Foscolo, while creatively appropriating Petrarch, is critically em-
phasizing Petrarch's dramatic aspect over and above Petrarch's well known
melodiousness.

[17] *Opere di F.*, p. 13. See also S. Orlando's commentary in *Dall'Ortis*

a blessing, and the somber note rings out again in the following piece as we saw; but the last sonnet, No. xii,[18] provides the Stoic antiphon toward which the whole sequence has been meandering: if literal action is hopeless, let the action of free literature bear witness to the dignity of man:

> Figlio infelice e disperato amante,
> e senza patria, a tutti aspro e a te stesso,
> giovine d'anni e rugoso in sembiante,
> che stai? Breve è la vita e lunga è l'arte;
> a chi altamente oprar non è concesso
> fama tentino almen libere carte.

> Unhappy son, desperate lover, with
> no country, harsh to all and to yourself,
> young in years and wrinkled in visage, why
> hesitate? Life is short and long is art;
> who cannot see his way to high deeds, shall
> at least try the rewards of a free pen.

The calling of literature in the service of truth (Foscolo is not envisaging himself as a poet laureate) is far from easy to obey, as the previous sonnet clarifies by lamenting the cherished Muse's desertion. It can only find food in searing experiences—loss of country, loss of family, loss of love, betrayed ideals—and sustenance in an unflagging commitment, the exact reverse of the literature as idyllic escape and courtly entertainment which had held sway in Italian circles throughout the eighteenth-century Arcadian phase. Foscolo's ears sought another music, of the less comfortable kind.

It would, if attained, free him from the temptation to follow

---

alle Grazie, pp. 56-57, and Mario Fubini's in *Metrica e poesia* (Milano: Feltrinelli, 1962), pp. 63-65. There are no known variants.

[18] *Opere di F.*, p. 18, and *Dall'Ortis alle Grazie*, pp. 71-72. See also Fubini, *U.F.*, for an evaluation of this and other sonnets, in Chapter iv, pp. 127-64.

the example of his fictional hero Jacopo and of his brother in the flesh, Giovanni, with whom Ugo's Byronic persona holds a posthumous conversation in the memorable Sonnet X ("In morte del fratello Giovanni"):[19]

Un dì, s'io non andrò sempre fuggendo
di gente in gente, mi vedrai seduto
su la tua pietra, o fratel mio, gemendo
il fior de' tuoi gentili anni caduto.
    La madre or sol, suo dì tardo traendo,
parla di me col tuo cenere muto:
ma io deluse a voi le palme tendo;
e se da lunge i miei tetti saluto,
sento gli avversi Numi, e le secrete
cure che al viver tuo furon tempesta,
e prego anch'io nel tuo porto quiete.
    Questo di tanta speme oggi mi resta!
Straniere genti, l'ossa mie rendete
allora al petto della madre mesta.

One day, should I stop wandering forever
from one nation to another, you will see me seated
at your tombstone, my brother, there to mourn
the flower of your youth cut down in its prime.
    Now mother only, dragging on her years,
comes to talk of me with your silent ashes,
while I reach out my disappointed hands
to you, and if I greet home from afar
I feel the hostile powers and the hidden
worries that to your life were such a storm,
and I long for the peace your haven gave.
    This is what now remains of so much hope!
But then, o foreign people, do return
my bones to the sad bosom of my mother.

[19] *Opere di F.*, p. 17, and *Dall'Ortis alle Grazie* pp. 68-69. Fubini's interpretation of this sonnet (in *U.F.*) is probably the most sensitive one we have, though he does not go into technical details.

The poem gains by the tact the persona shows in avoiding any direct reference to his brother's suicide and correspondingly avowing his own yearning for the peace death grants after a life of torment. The suicide is seen almost as an act of fate, an inevitable death, and the survivor realizes he has little to live for except the promise of that final exile which will put an end to all exiles. The tender dialogue with the dead brother also happens to be a lucid confrontation with personal destiny, and that destiny is seen as the outcome of the most painful choice: not to die. Death would be easy, survival is hard. The verb denoting the speaker's attitude toward death is "prego," I pray, like "invoco," invoke, in other sonnets; the verbal choice, as so often in Foscolo, captures several divergent meanings to conflate them into a semantic chord. On the one hand, to pray for death implies a rejection of life, since all is vanity; on the other hand, it also entails a renunciation of self-inflicted death, the hope for a death that will come only when the time is right, like a ripening. The hostile deities ("gli avversi numi") that personify uncontrollable circumstances can at least be generically named, as well as the inner enemies ("secrete cure") that undermine the self. Not so the nameless power that regulates life's cycle and has nothing more to do with the personal God of childhood devotions. The contemplation of unfathomable cosmic rhythms, while definitely superseding any residual biblical view, allows a religious aura to persist around the however unconventionally used word "prego" (I pray).

Despair is stoically ritualized into a religious act of sorts, a submission (albeit of the agnostic kind) to the power that looms beyond our existential horizon. Everything hinges on the word "pray" and its direct object "quiet" (quïete), which is suggestively prolonged by dieresis not so much to fit the given prosodic pattern as to activate its own deeper phonic and semantic resources. The same thing happens in "Alla sera" (To Evening), as we shall see. The emphasis such a word claims in the expressive cosmos of Foscolo's stormy persona is a matter of focal placing rather than quantitative recurrence, and we can see that also by correlating the haunting line in question with the thematically analogous one from Sonnet II, already quoted:

e so invocare e non darmi la morte.

and I can only invoke, not seize the boon of death.

Intertextual harmony arises between "invocare" (to invoke) and "prego" (I pray); likewise, "morte" (death) attains heightened significance in its counterpart "quïete" (quiet). Whatever was explicit gesture in the earlier line (and poem) becomes implicit in the later one, with an Adagio effect:

"e prego anch'io nel tuo porto quïete."

Any residual shrillness or loudness (the dangers besetting Foscolo's forceful diction) is purified into the grave, internalized, penetrating tone that marks the achieved transition from despair to serenity (of the negative kind).

In the opening sonnet of the series, "Alla sera" (To Evening), the decisive word (with attendant clusters) provides the departure rather than the resolution for the whole movement:

Forse perché della fatal quïete
tu sei l'immago a me sì cara vieni
o sera!

Perhaps because you are the very image
of the ultimate quiet, you are so welcome
to me, O evening!

For this introductory sonnet, so soothingly begun, ends on a dissonant chord:

e mentre io guardo la tua pace, dorme
quello spirto guerrier ch'entro mi rugge.

and while I contemplate your peace, there slumbers
the warlike spirit in me, its roars hushed.

The very last word is "rugge," roars, the epitome of that
lifelong turmoil our haunted persona has been trying to exorcise, and by its climactic placement it counteracts or at least
qualifies the overall tenor. The everlasting peace of annihilation is glimpsed through the momentary peace of day's end,
and that nirvana promise becomes temporary, and cyclical,
fruition for the moment of twilight, magically poised as it is
between pitiless light and disquieting darkness. The transition between the two cosmic extremes conveys the borderline
event of consciousness experiencing its own gradual extinc-
tion; the experience projects a mythic personification, the
goddess Evening, a dawn in reverse. Yet her motherly sua-
sion fails to silence for good the "roar" of rebellious existence. While the semantic and syntactical movement of the
poem is toward peace, its topological structure comes to rest
on that concentrated tumult which reverberates as well on the
agitated, gloomy quality (both in sound and meaning) of the
key rhyme words in the sextet: *fugge* (flies), *strugge* (con-
sumes), *rugge* (roars). They interlock with rhymes of comparably grave, dark phonic quality: *orme* (footsteps), *torme*
(herds), *dorme* (sleeps). This last rhyme word sets up a strong
semantic contrast with the immediately following one, the already discussed *rugge*; but on the whole, sound and tenor of
the sextet rhymes offset those of the octet, which are attuned
to one basic vowel key, the rather light (and long) *e* of *quïete*,
and to a concomitant node of soothing meanings (with the exception of *inquïete* in Line 5, which, however, fails to break
the lulling effect because it gravitates too strongly on its matrix, the decisive *quïete* of Line 1):

Forse perché della fatal *quïete*
tu sei l'immago a me sì cara *vieni*
o sera! E quando ti corteggian *liete*
le nubi estive e i zeffiri *sereni*,

e quando dal nevoso aere *inquïete*
tenebre e lunghe all'universo *meni*
sempre scendi invocata, e le *secrete*
vie del mio cor soavemente *tieni*.
Vagar mi fai co' miei pensier su *l'orme*
che vanno al nulla eterno; e intanto *fugge*
questo reo tempo, e van con lui le *torme*
delle cure onde meco egli si *strugge*;
e mentre io guardo la tua pace, *dorme*
quello spirto guerrier ch'entro mi *rugge*.

In a poem which manages to conjure an atmospheric image of spellbinding power without resorting to any word denoting color (a dominant trait in Foscolo's verse), color is translated into sound, and we can see that the octet hinges on chromatically light rhymes while the sextet rhymes have a dark quality, as if to underscore the final transition from day to night, from existence to nothingness—nothingness ("il nulla eterno") calling from the vast spaces beyond and within. Syntax conspires with sound to insinuate the psychic implications of the cosmic event, by flooding over the successive sluices of each major prosodic unit in rhythmic waves upon waves which counteract the strict definiteness of stanza and verse through enjambment and strategic pause. Thus the pause after the inward exclamation "o sera!" in Line 3 comes to reinforce the suspenseful effect of *quïete*'s dieresis—itself an opening on the infinite. And when Line 1 of Stanza 2 (fifth line in the octet) picks up the cue of Line 1 with the total rhyme "inquïete," dieresis and all, aided by the sigh of the word *"aere"* in the body of the line itself, we can no longer escape the spell: it is as if the sharp outlines of things were dissolving in the twilight, and as if the measured length of each eleven-syllable line were melting into pulses of measureless duration. Add the vowel and consonant chain "inquïete/ tenebre e lunghe . . . " bridging Line 5 and Line 6, and the insistent whispers of the sibilants in the whole octet, as compared to the tolling knell of *orme, eterno, intanto, tempo, torme, dorme, entro* in the sextet, and you will have realized some of the elements of the strange power at work in this unique voice.

Its airy effusiveness in the octet is balanced by the barely muted recall of life's self-consuming grief in the sextet, and once again we must note how resourcefully our poet can vary his use of the given sonnet pattern by finding each time a different proportion between syntax and meter. In the Zacynthos sonnet, syntax vehemently amalgamates the first three stanzas (two quatrains and one tercet) into one, pushing the last one (the second tercet) into lapidary isolation. In the sonnet addressed to the dead brother, no such forceful syntactical reorganization of the set metric mold occurs, yet a subtle subversion of meter does take place when we realize that the second quatrain and the first tercet coalesce into one sustained sentence, thus creating a syntactical mass at the center of the poem, neatly framed by an introductory stanza and an epitaph-like conclusion in the second tercet. The sonnet to Evening exhibits a still different tactic; it syntactically fuses the two quatrains into a compact octet, and the two tercets into a compact sextet, to underscore the complex inner balance of contrasting imagery and semantic tenor. It thus conveys, subliminally, an added sense of the contradictory impulses at work in a hypersensitive mind: the yearning for release and obliteration on the one hand, and the reassertion of existential identity on the other.

Verbal orchestration fits the theme, and the same holds of the sonnet to the dead brother, which stresses the fugal counterpoint of *gend-, gent*-rhymes (with internal echoes in the first quatrain) and mournful, dark *-uto, -lu-, nu-* sounds thickening in the second quatrain and in the first tercet, while the second tercet picks up the initial chromatic cue with the words *genti* and *rendete*. It works like a duo for piano and flute, considering the nasal resonance of the syllables *gen, gem, gend, gent* (end-stopped as they often are by a dental phoneme), and the wailing quality of the sustained *u* vowel. *U* is a naturally introverted sound and carries its own expressive connotation even before entering the structure of any articulate language. Somehow Foscolo's ear recaptures such pre-articulate qualities in the extremely articulate verbal matter at his disposal, and he thereby revives, within the time-worn linguistic constructs of post-Renaissance Italian, the primitive gestural elements that rescue important words from expressive inertia and make them musically new and individual.

As a consequence, his reliance on complex syntactical patterns avoids the pitfall of undue weightiness; the lines generally move along with snap and resilience, they do not march, for the expressive elements make themselves felt so as to mobilize each prosodic and syntactical structure. One could talk (borrowing Eliot's phrase apropos Milton) of a "Foscolian wave-length," and the phrase would be quite appropriate in view of Foscolo's avowed affinity for John Milton. This resourcefulness stands him in good stead even when the voice becomes overly loud, as happens with Sonnet VI, an outright cry of despair and fateful love which lacks the countervailing modulations we saw at work in Sonnets I, IX, and X—the acknowledged high points of this series. For the sonnet is phonically played out on chains of voiced or mute labials and of hissing sp-clusters:

> *Me*rita*me*nte, però ch'io *po*tei
> abbandonarti, or grido alle fre*men*ti
> onde che batton l'alpi, e i *pi*anti *mi*ei
> *sper*dono sordi del Tirreno i venti.

> Deservedly, since I found it in me
> to abandon you, am I now crying out to the wild
> breakers that crash against the cliffs, and my moans
> are lost in the unheeding Tyrrhenian winds.

The *m* and *p* alliterations interlock with the rhymes as if to shake the prosodic scheme from fixedness, and they convey a moaning effect, while the *sper-* of *sperdono* elicits a sequel of reiterated echoes in the following stanzas: *Sperai . . . sper-giure . . . sospirando . . . sperai . . . speme.* . . . The cry comes through, broken by convulsive pauses, in a mimesis which sins on the side of excess but not of mediocrity; the persona appropriately sees himself as a wild beast roaming the forests (line 11), and this time his "roar" cannot be muffled as in Sonnet I. The poem has its place within the tense harmony of the whole sequence, and as a landmark in the story the ten sonnets tell.

As such, it may aptly function as a foil to the dreamy sweetness of Sonnet IV (in the Petrarchan vein) and of Sonnet VIII, where love appears as an ecstatic remembrance and not as the tormenting, unexorcisable "spider love" of Twicken-ham Garden. The cry of the wolf sometimes subsides into the song of rapt contemplation; such are the vicissitudes of libido, and of literary language. Contemplation of time past and time future enables the haunted persona to face his des-tiny with stoic serenity, and for a moment relive the intact happiness of his island childhood, in the rapturously unfold-ing stanzas of Sonnet IX:

Né più mai toccherò le sacre sponde
ove il mio corpo fanciulletto giacque,
Zacinto mia, che te specchi nell'onde
del greco mar da cui vergine nacque

    Venere, e fea quell'isole feconde
    col suo primo sorriso, onde non tacque
    le tue limpide nubi e le tue fronde

    l'inclito verso di colui che l'acque
cantò fatali, ed il diverso esiglio
per cui bello di fama e di sventura
baciò la sua petrosa Itaca Ulisse.

    Tu non altro che il canto avrai del figlio,
    o materna mia terra; a noi prescrisse
    il fato illacrimata sepoltura.

Nor shall I touch again the sacred shores

wherein my body lay in blissful childhood,
O my Zacynthos, mirrored in the waves
of the Greek sea from which in virgin splendor
    Venus arose to make those islands fruitful
    with her first smile, so that your sunbright clouds
    and your groves found their proper celebration
    in the undying verse of the man who sang
the fatal waters and the manifold exile
that was Ulysses' lot, who, burdened with fame
and sorrow, finally kissed his stony Ithaca.
    Of your son, you will get nothing but the song,
    O my motherland; fate decreed for us
    only an unmourned burial in the end.

Needless to say, no translation can approximate the unique
musical effect Foscolo extracts from cumulative syntactical
progression coupled with the deftly exploited vocalic melody
and consonantal harmony of the Italian language. It is something else than commonplace *bel canto* mellifluousness. The
phrasing, overflowing metrical boundaries, has a wiry resilience which helps to create a kind of inexhaustible rhythm
within the absolute circumscription of the sonnet form. One
breathless sentence, in wave after wave of subordinate
clauses, sweeps through the first eleven lines of the sonnet,
subverting its classical structure—and indeed this imbalance
created by the Foscolian wave-length puzzled some early
readers, presumably the same kind of readers that resented
the Pindaric flights of *The Sepulchers*,[20] where narrative el-
lipse keeps short-circuiting the logic of ideas, to the advantage of dramatic imagery. The semantic space thus ranged
matches that noteworthy hypotactical cumulation whereby
clause generates clause (mostly in a straight descending order, but with some lateral ramification of syntax to avert

---

[20] See F.'s own report on certain strictures from friend and foe, chiefly
aimed at his compressed eloquence, in "Essay on the Present Literature of
Italy," *Edizione Nazionale*, XI, Part II, pp. 479-80.

monotony) and image sparks image. To be specific: the governing clause (line 1), after begetting one directly dependent
clause in Line 2, resumes with the pivotal vocative at Line 3,
which promptly sprouts into another directly dependent
clause overflowing into Line 4, and that clause in turn engen-
ders five more in quick succession. Of these, the first and the
second one (from the midst of line 4 to the midst of line 5)
stay on the same syntactical level, being mutually coordi-
nated, as if to suspend for a moment the relentless rush that
will come to a head in Line 11 with the finality of

baciò la sua petrosa Itaca Ulisse.

The headlong waters of eloquence spring at the outset from
a subterranean source (as indicated by the initial "*Né . . . ,*"
Nor . . . , which marks the transition from silent inner
monologue to open utterance) to cataract through five successive ledges of rock; but on the second ledge they deviate part
of their mass into a placid pool:

ove il mio corpo fanciulletto giacque,

and on the third ledge they find an even more spacious basin
to gather in:

. . . da cui vergine nacque
Venere, e fea quell'isole feconde
col suo primo sorriso, . . .

The first pool reflects the privileged image of the speaker's
own divinely favored childhood, Foscolo's equivalent of Hölderlin's "*Da ich ein Knabe war,/ Rettet'ein Gott mich oft*";[21]
the second, and larger, pool mirrors the correspondingly

[21] "In my boyhood days a god often saved me . . . ," from *Hölderlin—
Selected Verse*, with an introduction and prose translation by Michael Ham-
burger. Baltimore: The Penguin Poets, 1961, p. 26. See also "Der
Archipelagus," *ibid.*, p. 81.

privileged image of Venus-Aphrodite rising from the sea to quicken the Ionian archipelago (and implicitly the whole world) into verdant life. In other words, the tempo of the cumulative hypotactic movement—which allusively encompasses no less than the origins and fatal course of history, through the topical vicissitudes of Homeric Greece—relaxes twice in mid-course to let the voice longingly dwell on two mythical beginnings: the speaker's prehistorical innocence in his paradisal island, and Nature's intact origins, Aphrodite's "first smile," this side of history yet ushering history in with all its devastations as weathered by the typical hero, Ulysses.

What we have here is a cosmogony, poles apart from any mere rehash of classical commonplaces; Foscolo, as Mario Fubini has remarked, found his gods in himself rather than in books[22]—and in this he again paralleled or anticipated the mythopoeia of those two kindred spirits, John Keats and Friederich Hölderlin, for whom Hellas was the lost homeland, never actually known except through Lord Elgin's marbles or Homer's and Pindar's pages, and forever dreamed as the only possible release from the burden of history. To Foscolo, however, Hellas was both a never-never dreamland *and* a concrete personal experience, the unrenounceable bond of birth. As repeated exile pushed that experience farther and farther back into the recesses of memory, it blossomed into a myth whose nomenclature was naturally reappropriated from the seemingly worn-out stock of Greek fables once mandatory to the literary trade and now increasingly optional, or even suspect, with the advent of the Romantic dispensation. A cruel distance in time and space widened between Ugo Foscolo of Zante and his lost insular Eden, and then also between himself and his mother Diamantina, the living testimonial of his Hellenic identity. But once the Edenic origin receded to the threshold of dimness, individual memory could bridge the gap by broadening into racial memory, and the carnal beginnings of Ugo became consubstantial

[22] Fubini, *U. F.*, p. 124.

to the cosmic beginnings of Greece, that epitome of the whole meaningful world.

Zacynthos happens to be an island. In the poem, its earth and rock is retranslated into flesh and bone, its surrounding waters into the womb's amniotic fluid. Within its "sacred shores" the poetic persona's "body in his first childhood" "lay" safely sheltered. The mythical equation island-womb-bosom parallels the equation Zacynthos-Diamantina-Venus, to be sensed in the progression of images from "sacred shores" to "body in his first childhood" to Zacynthos "mirroring" herself in the "waves of the Greek sea" from which the birth of Venus is reenacted as if the goddess rising from those waters were the transfigured specular image of Zacynthos-Mother. And indeed Aphrodite appears as a sublimated mother figure, with the attributes of virgin fertility and beauty.[23] In this regard it pays to consider the syntactical bivalence of the epithet *"vergine"* (virgin) in Line 4. At first the reader may doubt whether it proleptically refers to Venus ("Venere," in the subsequent line) or postpositionally modifies "Greek sea" (*"greco mar,"* preceding "vergine" in the same line). Then the latter option is favored by semantic plausibility, since it seems pleonastic to emphasize the goddess' virginity at birth, and it makes sense to ascribe that inviolate quality to the living ocean that bore Aphrodite as the first of its creatures. On the other hand, excluding Venus in this context from the moot predicate, to the sole benefit of "the Greek sea," would force us to break the effortless line *del greco mar da cui vergine nacque* with a grating caesura between "vergine" and "nacque," thereby crippling the momentum of utterance, which also banks on a masterly enjambment. Beyond metric partitions and commonsense logic, the impulsion of the voice catapults "vergine" into the semantic field radiating from "Venere," a word that happens to echo "vergine" by initial alliteration, syllabic structure, stress

[23] The myth of Aphrodite Anadyomene, Venus rising from the sea, had a particular fascination for F., who used it also in his Odes.

placement, and vocalic color. It is another internal "mirroring," like the cosmic event connecting Zacynthos with Venus, and like the self-reflection of the exiled poet persona in bardic Homer and roaming Ulysses. Virginity, then, becomes a mystical quality enveloping Venus herself and permeating her cosmic matrix, as witness the goddess' "first smile." Since this is not the cold and hateful virginity of Herodiade, it does not surprise us to find it endowed with the magical power of fecundity:

> . . . vergine nacque
> Venere, e fea quell'isole feconde
> col suo primo sorriso, . . .

Whether we listen to the chant of Italian *e* vowels, a kind of bass counterpointed by the trilling Italian *i* of "*ì*sole," "*prì*mo," "so*rrì*so," or to the alliterative echoes whereby "*Vé*-nere" projects "*fe*a" (made), and "fea" generates "*fe*cónde," with a memorable etymological improvisation, we experience an expansion of breath and inner vision. This in turn is aided by the strong stress on the first syllable of the line in the word "*Vé*nere," which opens up a cosmogonic vista. The hendecasyllable prolongs itself, helped by strategic enjambments, into ecstatic duration.

The expansive movement of self-regenerating syntax which took over the two quatrains and the first tercet is brought up short by the strong pause after "Ulisse." Then what is left for the second tercet but to seal the whole exuberant utterance with a dry prophetic epitaph which sharply offsets the previous release of personal and mythic memory. The voice had expanded, now it contracts; so does the vision, which comes to rest, after so much exciting amplitude, on a derelict tombstone looming in the future. Yet from such shrinkage what liberation!

> . . . a noi prescrisse
> il fato illacrimata sepoltura.

The exile persona who had recognized a similarity between his fate and Ulysses' must now deny it, because his own "manifold exile" will not end up in a homecoming. His lot is exile outlasting death. And in that last line the poet sings his own dirge, with the fullness of vowels—all five of them—sustaining the voice in hieratic slowness (an Adagio after the Allegro of the first part) as it ranges the chromatic scale from the openness of luminous *ah* sounds down to the progressively occlusive, dark notes in *sepoltura*. Only the song will be left, nothing else; but it is already to be heard here, and we now understand the reason for the implicit claim of kinship with antonomastically introduced Homer. Foscolo the singer, last of a great lineage, will survive Ugo the wanderer; he has mirrored himself both in Ulysses and in Homer, no small feat of self-dramatization but no hybris either, since it really amounts to an act of allegiance toward the cultural source from which the validating types emerge for personal use. In a kindred spirit, Melville, another authority on exile, at least of the inner kind, was to speak of "reverence for archetype."

If the final line sounds like a matchless climax, the whole last tercet lays claim on our attention. It both contrasts and summarizes the long preceding part of the sonnet. Where the contrasting traits are, we have seen; we might actually add a further one, namely, the prevalence of the future tense, the tense of prophecy, as against the prevalence of the past, the tense of personal and ethnic memory. The *"prescrisse"* (prescribed, decreed) of the last line but one, though a grammatical past, works as a function of the future in *"Tu non altro che il canto avrai del figlio"* (Of your son, you will get nothing but the song); Karl Kroeber aptly spoke of "commemorative prophecy" apropos of Foscolo and other Romantic poets. The "pre-scribing" of Fate is, even etymologically, a future in the past, and a past prolonged into the actual future; moreover, not a datable past, like the milestones of individual and collective history, but an indefinite past, one and the same thing with the hidden force that actuates and consummates one's own existence. In using the classical word, Fate, the modern poet acknowledged his restlessness as the vocation of exile, and once again personalized the classical vocabulary. But to go on with the structural relationship of our sonnet's last tercet to the rest of the lyric, we must see how dialectical that relationship is, since the traits shared by the two syntactical units that make up the sonnet seem to counterbalance the striking difference in relative length and complexity between those units. Parataxis supersedes hypotaxis as prophecy supersedes reminiscence in this conclusive part, yet that negative prophecy had already loomed in the opening line of the sonnet,

Né più mai toccherò le sacre sponde,

Nor shall I touch again the sacred shores,

thus paving the way for a reiterated negation that brings out the elegiac essence of the tone. Just as in the first three lines of Quatrain 1 the dependent clause describing the persona's island-sheltered childhood is literally *cradled* between two segments of the governing clause which addresses the insular motherland, Venus-like Zacynthos, just so the clause addressing Motherland in the last tercet expressively encases the object of its verb, "the song . . . of your son" (*il canto . . . del figlio*), between the Thou (*Tu*) that replaces the direct name of the island as governing pronoun, and the vocative apposition that defines that pronoun to emphasize the maternal quality, "*o materna mia terra*" (O my motherland). In the quick review of his earthly destiny from remembered protection within the remote native shores to anticipated exposure and dereliction in exile-ridden death, the poet persona still expects one kind of return to the sheltering bosom of the island which is Mother—through his song, a posthumous gift, a disembodied visit. Analogously, though on a more literal level, he concludes the sonnet on his brother's death with the imploration to render his "bones" to "the sad bosom of Mother." There are ways and ways to go home again.

Yet one must lose home and mother and one's version of earthly paradise if one wants to find it all again—in memory and song. One must go forth from the enveloping bosom, into the threatening, enticing waters and wastes, into the pitiless light of the sun. Foscolo's vocation of exile, stronger than nostalgia, is the urge to grow, to know and see, to "experience the world and human vices and virtues," as Dante's Ulysses has it, a congenial figure no doubt. Insofar as this urge, aided by circumstance ("Fate"), takes on hyperbolic proportions with Foscolo, it marks his personal destiny as singular yet utterly representative of man's deep drives and conflicts; hence the poetry he wrung from his suffering can still speak to us, beyond any change of epochal styles.

No concession is made to the picturesque or the merely descriptive, as witness the lack of color modifiers, for one thing, in the sonnets. Green is suggested by the bare noun *"fronde"* (fronds); white as the color of unthreatening clouds is implied by *"limpide,"* an adjective which transcends color to catch the essence of light in a serene climate; and as for the sea, it is defined by its cultural, mythical connotations: "Greek"— rather than by a sensory epithet like "deep blue" or "wine-dark." Everything is caught in motion, or in some kind of essential action that pinpoints its identity; verbs carry the burden of expression. Rhymes enhance meaning, as the Zacynthos sonnet shows with its marked transition from the joyful resonance of the *-onde . . . -acque* pattern in the octet to the plaintive *-iglio*, the moaning *-ura* and the hissing *-isse* combination of the sextet; this chromatic transition underscores the shift from vocal diastole to systole I noticed before both in the global syntactical configuration and in the chromatic physiognomy of the last line. Furthermore, the amenable semantic implications of *-onde* (waves) and *-acque* (waters) are dominant in the octet, in contrast to the refractory

stoniness of *"petrosa Itaca,"* *"prescrisse,"* and *"sepoltura"* in
the sextet; sound, imagery, syntax, and connotative logic
conspire to effect the crucial passage from a liquid, generative, sheltering world to a hardened, sterile, ineluctable one.
The movement hinges on the semantic permutation of *"acque
fatali"* at Lines 3-9, which signals a change in the very quality of the so far trustworthy marine ambience: it was enveloping, protective, womblike; now it is estranging and fraught
with a dangerous challenge, a call to menacing openness.
The self is challenged to leave the indefiniteness of his matrix
for the ordeal of self-definition—a process entailing the confrontation of death, from which the root meaning of exile
emerges: the dying away from one's intact source, toward a
possible rebirth. If we experimentally isolate the rhyme words
we shall be sketching a skeletal diagram of the whole
poem's semantic itinerary along those very lines: *sponde-
giacque - onde - nacque - feconde - tacque - fronde - acque - esiglio
- sventura - Ulisse - figlio - prescrisse - sepoltura* (shores - lay -
waves - was born - fruitful - hushed - fronds - waters - exile -
calamity - Ulysses - son - prescribed - burial).

It is by now a commonplace of Italian criticism that Foscolo's best sonnets, and the only great ones, are the three to
which I have myself devoted special attention: No. I (To Evening), No. IX (To Zacynthos), and No. X (On the death of his
brother Giovanni). To them I would add a fourth, No. VIII,
which addresses Florence as a city hallowed by a significant
public history, by early literary accomplishment, and, for the
speaker of the poem, by singular private history—the revelation of love. This is one of the poems which lend support to
Mario Fubini's argument for a "Dolce Stil Nuovo" phase in
Foscolo's creative career.[24] The analogy holds not just because Foscolo intentionally drew on Dante's lyrical verse
(along with Petrarch's), but also in view of their common thematic development from passionate and sometimes subli-

---

[24] Actually, Fubini (in *U.F.*, Ch. III) says this of the two Odes; but the
sonnet under consideration is germane.

mated love to fierce political denunciation and prophecy, in
the context of final exile.

Certainly the paradisal vision of feminine beauty which
takes over in the sextet of Sonnet VIII to supersede the memory of bloody history as dramatized by the octet conjures
Dante's and Petrarch's lyrical best:

> E tu ne' carmi avrai perenne vita
> sponda che Arno saluta in suo cammino
> partendo la città che del latino
> nome accogliea finor l'ombra fuggita.
> > Già dal tuo ponte all'onda impaurita
> > il papale furore e il ghibellino
> > mescean gran sangue, ove oggi al pellegrino
> > del fero vate la magion s'addita.
> Per me cara, felice, inclita riva
> ove sovente i piè leggiadri mosse
> colei che vera al portamento Diva
> > in me volgeva sue luci beate,
> > mentr'io sentia dai crin d'oro commosse
> > spirar ambrosia l'aure innamorate.

> Yet you will have perennial life in songs
> o riverbank which Arno greets on its way
> as it divides the town that until now
> cherished its fading Latin ancestry.
> > Once from this bridge both Papal and Ghibelline
> > fury would pour much blood into the fear-struck
> > waves, where nowadays the traveller is shown
> > the house of a fierce poet. But to me
> forever dear, forever gladsome shore
> hallowed by the light-treading feet of one
> who walks like a true goddess—and when she turned
> her blissful eyes on me, I felt the wind
> > stirred into love by her long, golden hair
> > breathe an unearthly sweetness over me.

Only a master could so successfully steal Virgil's lines describing Venus' self-revelation to son Aeneas:[25]

> . . . et avertens rosea cervice refulsit,
> ambrosiaeque comae divinum vertice odorem
> spiravere; pedes vestis defluxit ad imos;
> et vera incessu patuit dea . . .

> . . . and turning around she shone with a rosy halo,
> and the ambrosial hair effused from the top
> a divine scent; the gown fluttered down to the feet;
> and she showed herself a true goddess at the gait . . .

The reader is not compelled to recognize the quote, for the Italian lines stand on their own merits; but if he does, he will discover a deeper resonance in the passage. In the *Aeneid*, when Venus appears in disguise to her son Aeneas she hears from him the story of his troubled exile and uncertainty about the future, then comforts him; then reveals herself to assure him that her information is reliable. The situation is somehow analogous in Foscolo's sonnet, where, in the octet, the landscape of history bespeaks loss of pride and memory of violence, and the apparition of the godlike girl is as incongruous to the scene as is Venus' to the African shore; both apparitions are consolatory, however, and if we place the sonnet within its context, we shall see that by importing the Virgilian passage into his lines the persona has insinuated once more his own condition as an exile facing an unknown future.

Dante, "fierce poet," looms behind the allusion to Alfieri's house on the Arno, since Alfieri—a man Foscolo revered—was himself a poet of high reputation and formidable pride, the kind that was trying in the latter half of the eighteenth century to give Italian poetry a new beginning, worthy of Dante's pioneering feat. Dante's house, it will be remem-

---

[25] Virgil, *Aeneid*, Book I, 402-405.

bered, is still shown in Florence, and it is impossible to refer to factional strife in medieval Florence without evoking him, the more so as the subsequent vision of beauty and love recalls, by force of context, Dante's apotheosizing devotion to Beatrice just as much as it does its obvious Virgilian source. Light, mostly thin sounds mark the rhymes, a violin solo; rhythmic composure, not tension, characterizes the sonnet, and if a remote vision of rage and cruelty emerges, it is immediately exorcized, as if the whole disaster of history could be momently bracketed to make way for the bliss of the Graces.

Foscolo's keyboard already has quite a range, and he is at no loss when it comes to finding effective variations on his versatile instrument. These twelve sonnets, though they are not all on the same level of mastery, do embody in sustained form the personal and ideological concerns of an exceptionally gifted, high-strung young man caught in an exceptional historical juncture. The only note missing from this autobiography in verse is humor, but even though the mask of Didymus is still to come, this is not enough to make the odes and sonnets a variation in verse on the novel, *Jacopo Ortis*. They actually purge the Ortis alternative, by immersion "in the destructive element" and by the slow exorcism of which only the sorcery of rhyme is capable. The artist as a conscious craftsman realizes he can master his dangerous turmoil through form, and he does so—witness the qualified, precarious statements of victory in Sonnets VIII, IX, and XII: there will be a survival through art, and life still has a purpose, no matter how hard the blows of fortune and how bleak the political prospects. The siren song of Nothingness has been heard, but our Ulysses took the trouble of having himself tied to the main mast, and survived to tell the story.

The Hellenizing odes and the almost Byronic sonnets trace the purgatorial itinerary of a mind struggling through ordeals and relapses toward an initiation of sorts. It is a mind incapable of compromise, addicted to absolutes: the absolute of passion, the absolute of justice, the absolute of beauty. It wants

either those non-negotiable values or the negative absolute of
annihilation; wisdom is hard. Poetry will save this mind as it
had saved Dante's in the face of comparable dilemmas, and
the salvation is enacted for us in the confessional pages of
Ortis—Foscolo's katabasis—and of the 1803 poems—his
purgatorial ascent. The initiation is accomplished when the
persona has faced his past and prospective losses in one, and
eaten or foretasted his bitter bread of exile; his only fulfillment remains in the act of writing. An investiture is still
needed, and it comes three years later with the vatic utterance of *The Sepulchers* in 1806.

For here, the persona's commitment is not just to himself,
as it was in the sonnets, or to the private worship of an Eternal Feminine ephemerally embodied. He now speaks to his
nation and to all mankind. And he speaks from the utter
destitution of a common fate which is annihilation without the
compensatory dream of a Beyond. He foresuffers his death
and the death of all, and from this zero point of experience
endeavors to salvage whatever values can survive the test.
The scope is Lucretian (and we have an interesting essay on
Lucretius[26] from the years preceding the composition of *The
Sepulchers* to support the link); a ruthless freedom has ac-
crued as reward to the disabused contemplator of the ceaseless apocalypse which Nature is, and it is that freedom, that
disenchantment beyond despair, that will make a new piety
possible:

> In the shadow of cypresses and within
> the urns solaced by tears is the sleep of death
> any softer? Once the sun for me no more
> fosters on earth this lovely family

---

[26] "Della poesia, dei tempi e della religione di Lucrezio" (On the poetry,
on the times and on the religion of Lucretius), in *Edizione Nazionale*, vol.
VI (*Scritti letterari e politici, dal 1796 al 1808*, a cura di Giovanni Gambarin). Florence: Le Monnier, 1972, pp. 239-50. The fragmentary essay is
preserved in MS at the Florence National Library, and dates from 1802-
1803.

of vegetal, of animal existences; and when
no more the dance of future hours will
dawn on my mind, and when from you, dear friend,
I shall no longer hear that subtle harmony
of melancholy verse, and when no more
the virgin soul of poetry and of love
will speak to me, my only inspiration
and sustenance along a roaming life,
what restoration can be to my lost days
a headstone placed to tell my bones apart
from the myriads death sows through land and sea?

It is true, Pindemonte! Hope itself,
last of godheads, deserts the tombs; oblivion
envelops everything in its night;
and a restless force drives all the elements
from motion on to motion; and man and his tombs
and the last images and relics of earth
and sky become only playthings of time.

The breathtaking conclusion of this tense hymn has
already engaged our attention in Chapter I, and yet the
ratiocinative eloquence of the beginning would hardly lead us
to expect such a conclusion. A son of the Enlightenment, Ugo
Foscolo here risks sacrificing his Muse on the altar of inflexible Reason. Actually, *The Sepulchers* is a triumph of poetry
over rhetoric, as I hope to show. The utterance takes shape as
a conversation with the friend and fellow poet, Ippolito Pindemonte, in accordance with Foscolo's predilection for the
epistolary or dramatic I-Thou form. The second-person address to the "sweet friend" in Line 8 (line 7 in my translation)
comes in time to focus existentially the avalanche of dependent negative clauses which are going to discharge their
cumulative tension on the governing clause. The latter is stra-
tegically withheld until the very end to create semantic sus-
pense, and once more we note Foscolo's deft use of prolepsis
to energize discourse. The unremitting sequence of negations

is thus projected beyond itself, to impart definitive momentum on the big syntactical conglomerate. The whole poem uses the reconnoitered past as a springboard toward the future, in a neat inversion of the customary epic attitude which banks on remembrance of things past.

The past is death, and death is taken for granted, as a physical inevitability; what is not taken for granted is life, life in progress, life as the sum of unique and shared experiences that demand renewal with each new human existence, each new people. History, the true subject of the poem, becomes expectation, rather than sheer memory of things remote; it is now prophecy, of the strictly immanent kind, because there is no transcendent Beyond to lure man's hope away from the unceasing struggle for physical and cultural survival; Locke, Helvétius, Hobbes, Vico have weaned our poet, and he looks ahead in time, not up into eternity. The horizon of discourse progressively widens to encompass these cosmic yet humanly accessible vistas. After the impersonal question of Lines 1-3, the "me" of the involved persona emerges into view as the focal object of the life-giving natural forces (the Sun) and as the sentient locus of anticipation (experiential time, lines 6-7). Then (lines 8-9) as the object becomes a grammatical subject, the speaking "I" evokes a correlative "Thee" to set up a first communal bond in the neutral vastness of the universe. At the same time, the active verbal voice *udrò* (I shall hear, line 8) marks the development of that "Me" from physical sentience in Nature's keep to articulate consciousness. The latter asserts itself by objectifying the enveloping scene—only to redescend to passive object status with "le mie ossa" (my bones, line 14), a complement governed by the final subject and agent, Death. Thus, grammar aiding, an individual life cycle is enacted; but as the stalwart voice resumes, after a marked pause, to qualify the triumph of death and time by asserting the continuity which personal memory of the dead can maintain, the social implications of that death-denying cult come to a head in the "Noi" (us) of Lines 33 and 50. Care for the dead is but a form of care for the

living, it establishes a communion in time to provide a ritual
foundation for the communion in space which the society of
the living involves.[27] An individual voice has become choral
and it will remain so throughout the elegiac hymn, without
surrendering, on the other hand, its own particular identity—conferred by the burden of exile and by the very vocation of poetry (lines 10-13, and again 226-29). The persona
speaks not privately, as it often did in the sonnets, but as a
choragus; and the choragus gradually dons the mask of the
shaman, conjurer and exorciser in one. There are specters to
be exorcised and heroes to be conjured; the song is a spell.

The spell works by sheer musical insinuation. From the
very start, this saves the freely philosophizing meditation
from the danger of flat discursiveness—versified didacticism
of the type the Age of Reason had cherished. The keynote is
already to be heard at the outset:

All'ombra dei cipressi e dentro l'urne
confortate di pianto è forse il sonno
della morte men duro?

In the shadow of cypresses and within
the urns solaced by tears is the sleep of death
any softer?

These lines cannot be declaimed, they have to be murmured,
as Hamlet's monologue has to. The consonantal quality of
words like *ombra* and *cipressi* suggests a sigh, not a shout; the
enjambments work against the limits imposed by metric

---

[27] The anthropologist Victor W. Turner has pointed out the importance
of such values in *The Ritual Process* (Chicago: Aldine Publishing Company, 1969), especially in the chapter entitled "Communitas: Model and
Process." Though Turner studies primitive societies, and incidentally mentions Dante and Aquinas, not F., his findings provide additional support for
my reading of F.'s vatic verse. Another aspect of Turner's research that can
throw further light on F.'s literary predicament is the emphasis on "limi-
nal" culture. F.'s poetry is essentially about cultural survival.

strictness, as so often happens with Foscolo, and we then hear a basso continuo lilt, loosely flowing, over and beyond the blank verse measure. In this, Foscolo shows a dramatist's vocation, as we may realize upon remembering that his first publicly acclaimed work was the Alfierian tragedy *Tieste* (Thyestes) of 1796, to be followed a decade and a half later by the ill-starred *Ajace* (Ajax)[28] of 1811 and by *Ricciarda* of 1812. *Ajace*'s dialogues and monologues in particular manage to spar, ratiocinate, and occasionally brood or dream without failing the dramatic requirements of directness and modulation. Here in *I Sepolcri*, where the occasion for poetic argument has been supplied by a controversial piece of sanitary legislation forbidding intramural burials (Edict of St. Cloud, 1804, extended to the Italian Cisalpine State, 1806), ratiocination is dramatically argumentative and it finds its suitable rhythmical embodiment in a versatile blank verse (*endecasillabi sciolti*) which manages to modulate all the way from prose-like relaxation to plaintive lilt to high-pitch singing.

Thus if one minds the rhetorical apparatus, with its insistent rhetorical questions (five in the first seventy-three lines) and the attendant panoply of emphatic particles like *forse* (perhaps), *Ma perché* (But why), *Pur* (Yet), *Se* (If), or adverbially used clauses like "Vero è ben" (Yes it's true) etc.; if one does find the rhetoric a bit too aggressive, one will be well advised to recite the poem inwardly, in muted key. In other words, oral performance has to be taken into account as an intrinsic dimension of the taxonomically intractable poem. And then we shall stop wondering whether it is best definable as elegy, hymn, dramatic monologue, miniature epic, or

---

[28] To be found at pp. 149-221 of *Opere di F*. The most eminent critics, from Croce to Fubini, have been unappreciative of F.'s tragedies, yet *Ajace* deserves a second look, for it is not devoid of stirring passages. Napoleonic censorship stopped its performance in Milan after a few evenings, believing the tyrant Agamemnon in the play to be a veiled counterpart of Napoleon. Ajax, the libertarian suicide, is a new version of Jacopo Ortis. Along with the two other tragedies by F., *Ajace* is now in *Edizione Nazionale (Tragedie e poesie minori*, a cura di G. Bézzola, 1961).

gnomic rhapsody; we shall instead enact and perceive it as a
sequence of logical, visual, and musical modulations in
which the circumstantial theme, and the attendant argumentative mode, are eventually transcended by the sheer power of
vision. One would also do well to listen to the recurrent lyrical eventuations:

> Non vive ei forse anche sotterra, quando
> gli sarà muta l'armonia del giorno,
> se può destarla con soavi cure
> nella mente dei suoi? Celeste è questa
> corrispondenza d'amorosi sensi,
> celeste dote è negli umani; e spesso
> per lei si vive con l'amico estinto,
> e l'estinto con noi, se pia la terra
> che lo raccolse infante e lo nutriva,
> nel suo grembo materno ultimo asilo
> porgendo, sacre le reliquie renda
> dall'insultar de' nembi e dal profano
> piede del volgo, e serbi un sasso il nome,
> e di fiori odorata arbore amica
> le ceneri di molli ombre consoli
>
> (Lines 26-40)

> Does he not live on even under thick earth
> when daylight's harmony is silent to him,
> if he can rouse it with delicate thoughts
> in the mind of his loved ones? It's heavenly,
> this correspondence of unbroken love,
> a heavenly gift in human beings; and often
> through it we live with our departed friend,
> and he with us, if only that piece of land
> which welcomed him at birth and nursed him on
> afford him the last shelter in its motherly
> womb, thereby protecting his remains
> from the assaults of the weather and the trampling
> populace; if but a stone do keep his name

and a friendly tree redolent with flowers
do but console his ashes with soft shadow.

The Italian music of these lines is not transposable, nor is,
to be sure, the poignant melody of the following passage, a
few lines later (46-50):

> . . . ma la sua polve
> lascia alle ortiche di deserta gleba
> ove né donna innamorata preghi,
> né *pass*eggier *sol*ingo oda il *sosp*iro
> che dal *tum*ulo a noi manda Na*tu*ra.

but his dust he will leave to a patch of nettles,
forlorn, with no woman to bring her prayer,
and no passerby to hear the gentle sigh
that Nature sends us from the burial place.

Even if the oratorical shape of the "argument" keeps the picture on the general level (the talk is about the general human
condition, about Everyman), poetry takes over by sheer force
of musical cadence and vivid imagery. The chiming vowels
with their transition from a trilling *ee* to a mournful *u* key, and
the concurrent rustling alliterations I have italicized in the
last two lines of this excerpt, recall similar effects in the sonnets, but here they operate with clearer emphasis because
rhymes are not there to compete with their charm. The loving
woman kneeling in prayer, the intent passerby and the sorcery of nature's vegetal sigh suddenly dominate the very
world from which they have been excluded, and capture our
memory forever. They are worthy of Virgil at his melodious
best.

Not accidentally, the rhetorical questions occur only in the
introductory part. Listening carefully, we realize they elicit
not just the answers which should be logically presupposed,
but a reiterated surge of passionate meditation encompassing
human destiny as experienced from one existential station

which provides an outlook on the whole. If so, they are more than just *rhetorical* questions, because the answers are not quite contained in them; the questions release a music and a gnomic perception that vastly exceed them, in fact the first question is finally answered by another question (lines 13-15). They are of course ironic questions, gadfly questions meant to arouse the *saeva indignatio*, the bitter wisdom and the epic vision waiting for a chance to break out and reassert themselves over the impoverished, constraining times that have been able to disregard certain essential values of human culture in the name of what (to the author and his persona) seems a crudely abstract principle of social engineering. Man cannot live by bread alone; he needs a cultural horizon to breathe in, whatever the contingent dictates of urban sanitation.

Just as the rhetorical questions merely serve to ignite the chain-reaction of thoughtful vision that ranges through all history, the reasoning behind the rhetoric is self-destructive and the protest against the St. Cloud edict (which was to be vindicated by subsequent town planning anyway) merely quixotic. The poem itself, in the course of its plea for ecological sepulture and the cultural significance of individualized funereal mementoes, at one point inadvertently espouses the basic view of the adversary by decrying the medieval custom of burying corpses under the pavement of churches:

> Sepulchral slabstones did not always pave
> temple floors; nor corpse stench mixed to incense
> contaminate the worshipers; nor cities gloom
> with sculpted skeletons . . .
>
> (Lines 104-108)

and then by opposing to this superstitious degeneracy the Elysian peace of verdant suburban graveyards as practiced by ancient Hellenes and modern Britons (lines 104-136). Of course the flagrant contradiction does not matter poetically, and it even fails to undermine the essential anthropological argument of *The Sepulchers* which aims its barbs, not at urban hygiene, but at the idea of nameless mass burial which the new regulations were rumored to entail. Not by hygiene alone, and not by geometry alone, says the son of the Enlightenment who, as happens, cannot forget the lesson of history as imparted to him by anti-Cartesian Vico. Undeniably the French Revolution, in order to make the desirable difference in a stale society, had momentarily to act as if history did not matter, and to "drive [its] plough and [its] cart over the bones of the dead. . . ." Still, certain intangibles (they actually are the anthropological tangibles) should be taken into account, if we do not want to confuse the vital work of revolution with the dreadful homogenization of society of which abstract reasoning is capable. Who but a poet should say that to Napoleon's men? and a poet who had fought in Napoleon's armies, at that. In *The Sepulchers*, the rhetorical questions hitting away at abstract rationalism as embodied in ruthless social politics are Beethovenian.

And it is a Beethovenian structure one overhears in the very alternation of questions and effusive statements which gets the poem under way. For the staccato phrases which each time release a dreamily or passionately flowing response from winds and strings in many a symphony or concerto by the composer who first acclaimed Napoleon as a liberating hero, and then sarcastically mourned with a dirge the liberator's turn to tyranny, may well remind Foscolo's reader how similar to that wordless dialectic is the verbal music that the author of *The Sepulchers* composed as a dialogue between himself and destiny. Poetry is made of words, not ideas, and music, of notes; but the focal ideas that stirred Europe at the dawn of the new century were the generating power behind notes and words alike. Beethoven's vatic and confessional music eventually sought a verbal complement in Schiller's *Hymn to Joy*, and Foscolo, in *The Graces*, wrote to such an ideal score that words and images at times seemed about to pass into pure unearthly music—as in the episode of the harpist, or of the "hermit virgin" at the piano.

That was Foscolo's moonlight sonata; it is, however, in *The
Sepulchers* and in *Ajax* (unlike *Fidelio*, a tragedy of freedom
defeated) that one can find verbal equivalents of Beethoven's
full orchestra. Take for instance the sudden transition from
celebration of Santa Croce's tombs (a holy memorial to Italian
civilization) to the necromantic conjuring of Marathon's battle
(the link being provided by the implied recognition that
Italy's Renaissance was a rebirth of Hellenic culture on new
soil, that both are the roots of Western tradition at large, and
that Greece's triumph was achieved against dreadful odds, for
civilization is a precarious conquest):

Con questi grandi abita eterno, e l'ossa
fremono amor di patria. Ah sì! da quella
religiosa pace un Nume parla:
e nutrìa contro a' Persi in Maratona
ove Atene sacrò tombe a' suoi prodi,
la virtù greca e l'ira. Il navigante
che veleggiò quel mar sotto l'Eubèa,
vedea per l'ampia oscurità scintille
balenar d'elmi e di cozzanti brandi,
fumar le pire igneo vapor, corrusche
d'armi ferree vedea larve guerriere
cercar la pugna; e all'orror de' notturni
silenzi si spandea lungo ne' campi
di falangi un tumulto e un suon di tube,
e un incalzar di cavalli accorrenti
scalpitanti su gli elmi a' moribondi,
e pianto, ed inni, e delle Parche il canto.
    Felice te che il regno ampio de' venti,
Ippolito, a' tuoi verdi anni correvi!
E se il piloto ti drizzò l'antenna
oltre l'isole egèe, d'antichi fatti
certo udisti suonar dell'Ellesponto
i liti, e la marea mugghiar portando
alle prode retèe l'armi d'Achille
sovra l'ossa d'Aiace: a' generosi

giusta di glorie dispensiera è morte;
né senno astuto né favor di regi
all'Itaco le spoglie ardue serbava,
ché alla poppa raminga le ritolse
l'onda incitata dagl'inferni Dei.

(Lines 196-225)

Now he [Alfieri] dwells here forever with these great
ancestors, his bones still shuddering with love
for the ravaged homeland. Yes, from this awe-filled
peace a godhead speaks: the same that once in Marathon,
made holy by all those Athenian graves,
aroused Greek fury against the Persian invaders.
Whoever sailed that sea off the Euboea
would see through the vast darkness sparks flash out
from clashing helmets and swords, pyres smoke ruddily,
and phantom warriors glittering with armor
rush into combat; and the awestruck night
would be flooded by a turmoil of phalanxes
and blaring bugles, and horses clattering upon
the helmets of the dying, and moans, and hymns,
and the weird threesome singing of the Fates.

O happy Ippolito, who in the years of your youth
freely ranged through the huge kingdom of wind
and water! and if your pilot steered the course
beyond the Aegean islands, you then heard
Hellespont's surf roar with ancient memories
and the high tide bellow to bring Achilles'
arms to the beach where rest the bones of Ajax:
death is just: not astuteness, not the favor
of kings secured the long coveted trophy
for Ulysses: his roaming ship soon lost it
to the waves that the nether gods let loose.

One thinks of *The Ruins of Athens*, of the *Leonora* overture;
but, most of all, of the dynamic pattern so central to Beethoven's symphonies, where often the orchestra works into a

crescendo scanned by the reiteration of accelerating phrases, echoed at the different timbric levels, interwoven, and then climaxing in the full volume colored by the cellos, horns, trombones, oboes, until that stormy joy subsides into thin andantes or adagios, and the tympanum yields to violins and clarinets. Comparably, Foscolo's verse here surges forward in a visionary crescendo of panting phrase upon phrase that exploits the clanging and howling sonorities available in the Italian language, until the climax is reached in the word *canto* (song). And immediately an antiphonal movement begins, a total release of the voice after all the tumult, and as the inner eye ranges over the free spaces "of wind and water" one senses the metric constant—the versatile hendecasyllable—has succeeded in expanding its duration to an unforeseen extent, yet without violating its statutory firmness. Much in the same way, Beethoven can make an *Allegretto* sound like an *Adagio*. As the composer handles his tempo, so does the poet use his meter—by refusing to be used. And both were an apt illustration of the statement of their contemporary Goethe, who said that freedom, poetically speaking, can only be found in limitation. Provided of course, both artists might possibly add, that those set limits function as heighteners of energy, to be potentially transgressed though never obliterated.

"Felice te che il regno ampio dei venti,/ Ippolito, a' tuoi verdi anni correvi!" "O happy Ippolito, who in the years of your youth/ freely ranged through the huge kingdom of wind/ and water!" The happiness, the spaciousness, heightened by contrast with the accelerating tempo of the crowded battle scene, inhere in the expansive quality of sound and sense in key words like *ampio* (ample), *venti* (winds), *verdi anni* (green years); these words must be pronounced by opening the mouth and then closing it after letting the fullness of each vowel shade into the nasal resonance to be concluded on the plosive dental or labial stop. They set up a chain of assonance within the two lines in question, and the phonic emphasis of each is thereby multiplied. Because the voice is compelled to dwell on each so as to fulfill its phonic and semantic value, a retardation effect occurs which prolongs the actual duration of each line; pauses help. The slowdown is inversely proportional to the faster and faster pace of the immediately preceding lines describing the phantom battle of Marathon. Foscolo's hendecasyllables, as he himself pointed out in *the Essay on the Present Literature of Italy*,[29] vary their pace according to their emotive tenor; they must be uttered with an ear for the respective tempo as suggested by the qualitative factors of basic component words and by their compounding mutual relations.

How rich those factors can be one will appreciate through careful listening to this whole sequence, with due attention to the driving rhythms of the battle scene; here the paratactic clauses, like serried ranks of advancing soldiers, crowd one another into the tensest syntactic space, and they dictate a fast staccato pronunciation with clashing stresses and pauses. Consequently the very sounds which make for release and amplitude of utterance in the following movement, as touched upon before, here thicken into metallic hardness: *cozzanti brandi . . . campi . . . falangi . . . accorrenti . . . scalpitanti . . . moribondi . . . pianto . . . canto.* These nasal and occlusive sonorities interlock with a chain of harsh alliterations to reinforce the metallic effect: *incalzar . . . cavalli accorrenti scalpitanti.* They also intersect a short but mimetically effective chain of syllables alliterating on *t* and "rhyming" on the dark, close *oo* sound: *notturni . . . lungo . . . tumulto . . . tube* (one does hear those bugles!). The orchestration modulates, as we saw, into the subsequent liberating cadence which even offers at one point an anomalously regular rhyme with one of the previous lines marking the very acme of battle:

[29] Originally written at the request of Mr. Hobhouse, as a commentary to be appended to Byron's *Childe Harold*'s Book IV, this essay is now included, with its Italian version, in *Edizione Nazionale*, XI, Part II (*Saggi di letteratura italiana*, Parte seconda, a cura di Cesare Foligno, 1958), pp. 399-455. In the essay, F. speaks of himself in the third person.

. . . incalzar di cavalli accorrenti
(Line 210)
. . . il regno ampio dei venti
(Line 213)

Sound mimesis, in Foscolo's verse, does not operate statically or naturalistically; it depends on close correlation with the particular rhythm and tenor, of which it constitutes a frequent though not inevitable function.

Thus we see a connotative permutation of meaning and rhythmic impact within what would remain, if taken in its physical absoluteness out of the qualifying context, one and the same chain of sounds: accor*renti*, scalpit*anti*, pi*anto*, c*anto*, amp*io*, *venti* (and the one perfect rhyme as above discussed stresses the essential change in the seeming identity of the two rhythmic-phonic series). We even find one identical keyword semantically and rhythmically transformed by the two syntactic segments descanting on each other: the adjective *ampio* (ample), which in Line 203 modifies (and is modified by) the noun *oscurità* (darkness), and in Line 213 attaches to *regno* (kingdom) but actually functions as a direct link between that noun and the next one, *venti* (winds). Because of its salient phonic physiognomy, it attracts to itself much energy from the two surrounding nouns it modifies and connects, so that it tends to usurp their grammatical status; it is as if they were the adjectives and it, the modifer *ampio*, were the real noun; for it concentrates and brings out their substance; it is in short, a *de facto* substantive. In the syntagm *ampia oscurità*, instead, there can be no doubt about the modifier's status; *ampia* gravitates on *oscurità* and the reverse is not true; *oscurità* is the semantically, rhythmically stronger word, privileged also by its placement in the line, which confers on it the most emphatic metrical stress of the three allotted to this particular hendecasyllable (*á*mpia . . . oscurità . . . scint*í*lle). *Ampia* waits to be fulfilled by *oscurità*, and the conglomerate sets the stage for the subsequent nightmare.

Ten lines later, the syntagm *regno ampio dei venti* marks
the release from constraining nightmare and the joy of unim-
peded ranging in free space. In this syntagm, as we saw, the
emphatic stress falls on *ampio*, with an effect of metric displacement vis-à-vis the preceding noun *regno*. Just as *regno*
surrenders its function to *ampio* and becomes a merely nominal substantive, it cannot retain metric dominance for its
tonic accent once the forceful vocal opening of *ám*pio inter-
venes to claim aural attention for itself. Two of the alternative
accentual patterns allowable in the Italian hendecasyllable
vie for supremacy in this unique line. One is the pattern hing-
ing on two major metric stresses respectively on the sixth and
tenth syllable, with a minor one on any of the first four. This
is the formula that would prevail if the word *regno* were to
retain unchallenged metric emphasis:

Felice *té*, che il *ré*gno ampio dei *vén*ti

Another standard accentual pattern distributes metric
stresses on the fourth, seventh and tenth syllables:

Felice *té*, che il regno *ám*pio dei *vén*ti

Neither of the two alternative patterns can prevail without
aural interference from the other in this line, because the
contiguous vowels *o* and *a* refuse to elide each other (the eli-
sion being demanded by the metric rule that forbids super-
numerary syllables in the body of the line). On the other
hand, the two crucial vowels merge into a kind of interverbal
diphthong *oa*, thereby creating an exceptionally long metric
syllable which carries one of the three main stresses in the
line. If so, the fourth-seventh-tenth syllable stress pattern
seems to take over, with an appropriate effect of retardation;
but the word *regno* still makes its tonic accent heard, and this
accent does not clash with the syllabically following one on
*ám*pio because of the dilated rhythmic space created by the

fusion of *o* and *a* into *oá*. The result is an anomalous, power-
fully stretched configuration of syllabic values and stresses
featuring four metric accents, i.e., on the fourth, sixth,
seventh, and tenth syllable:

Felice té, ‖ che il régnoámpio dei vénti

The strong caesura after *te* contributes to the rhythmic release
and prolongs the line, while the *oàmpio* conglomerate enacts
an expressive oral gesture: the mouth opens to pronounce the
two fused vowels in marked transition from a dark to a lighter
sound—a clear analogue, on the larger scale, of the transition from night to day, from oppressive hallucination to joyous freedom, from the crowded battlescene to the open spaces
of the sea as ranged by Pindemonte's ship. It is as if the careful interplay of sound and rhythm reconstituted an original
cry of relief, *oàh*! As a matter of fact, the whole clause where
this expressive event occurs happens to be exclamatory.

In Foscolo's Pindaric universe of words, "a restless force
drives all the elements/ from motion on to motion," one image
generates another, one scene touches off a different one,
often antithetical, and one rhythmic shape evokes new ones.
The voice does not dwell long on any climactic tumult or repose; it traverses huge narrative spaces, and here no sooner
does the liberating exclamation swell the sails of the envisaged ship to head for the open sea, away from Marathon's
haunted shores, than new memories and new rhythms meet
the ear of the stowaway listener. Having regained amplitude,
the lines now move on in a kind of stately groundswell, until
Pindemonte's eastbound ship sights Hellespont's shores and
conjures even remoter ghosts: the ancient wrong of Ajax, the
nemesis visited on his cheater Ulysses, the stern finality with
which divine (infernal) justice seals man's mischief. The operation of that justice is one and the same thing with the cosmic force on which prevaricating man intrudes; the restoring
action is the action of the impartial waves, and their majestic

rhythm echoes in the sustained measure of the concluding verses:

> . . . A' generosi   220
> giusta di glorie dispensiera è morte;
> né senno astuto, né favor di regi
> all'Itaco le spoglie ardue serbava,
> ché alla poppa raminga le ritolse
> l'onda incitata dagli inferni dei.   225

Here is the accentual skeleton:

```
                    ... ∪ ∪ ∪ _́ ∪
  _́ ∪ ∪ _́ ∪ ∪ ∪ _́ ∪ _́ ∪ ‖
  ∪ _́ ∪ _́ ∪ ‖ ∪ ∪ _́ ∪ _́ ∪
  ∪ _́ ∪ ∪ ∪ _́ _́ ∪ ∪ _́ ∪ ‖
  ∪ ∪ _́ ∪ ∪ _́ ∪ ∪ ∪ _́ ∪
  _́ ∪ ∪ _́ ∪ ∪ ∪ _́ ∪ _́
```

Falling and rising rhythms (depending on whether or not the line begins with a stressed syllable) resourcefully vary the overall movement. As happens, in the five and a half lines sampled here, the two falling (nearly dactylic) patterns govern Line 221 and Line 225. These are the lines referring to the justice meted out by cosmic powers (Death first, and the nether gods afterwards). By contrast, the three intervening lines have a rising, mostly iambic or anapestic pattern (though jerked midway by the clash of two contiguous stresses—one metrical and one tonic—in line 223). These lines dramatize the contrary push of prevaricating human effort (Ulysses' machinations to misappropriate Achilles' arms, driving valorous Ajax into despair and suicide, and the Ithacan sea rover's attempt to carry the unearned trophy all the

way home). Strong caesuras and syntactical pauses between
lines are marked in the above graph; it should be noticed,
however, that minor articulating pauses occur in the midst of
some lines, with an effect of binary subdivision and inner
balance; thus Line 221 and Line 222 sway like scales, sub-
divided as they are each into two fairly equal segments
(*giusta di glorie—dispensiera è morte*, respectively five and
six syllables, with two stresses on each segment; *né senno
astuto—né favor di regi*, again five syllables to six and two
stresses to two, plus the syntactical parallelism created by the
initial repetition of the disjunctive particle *né*, "neither").
The scales are tilted by Ulysses and his factional supporters
until a superior justice levels them back. The last line (225)
seals the whole action with its perfect equilibrium: the first
syllable, strongly stressed, is echoed by the equally strong
stress of the very last syllable, itself an entire word that may
be defined as a semantic culmination of the concise narrative—"*dèi*" (gods); similarly, the word containing the first
syllable and the first stress, "*onda*" (wave), is a major vehicle
of meaning. This significant symmetry extends to the
rhythmic and syntactical structure of the whole line: for the
latter neatly falls into two syllabically equal segments which
mirror each other accentually (*l'ónda incitáta—dagli inférni
déi*). The symmetry avoids mechanicalness because the last
word, strongly accented as it is, is far fròm abrupt, and actually prolongs itself into vocalic openness: *dèi*. The constancy of cosmic rhythm is reasserted; it is not a matter of
closure.

Indeed the corresponding constancy of meter, in the universe of the poem, has not constrained utterance in stiff,
monotonous measures; it has if anything made a rare resilience possible, and we have just seen the resulting versatility
at work. The strength of *The Sepulchers* lies not just in the
respective felicities of the several scenes or moments of evocation that go into the making of the total harmony, but even
more in the unpredictable transitions from scene to scene.
One of the most impressive of such transitions occurs, as we

saw, when the bardic voice suddenly seeks release from the mounting pressure of the lines evoking the ghostly melée and brings in the personal note, and the present reality of a responsive Thou, and in so doing finds exorcistic breath; yet the refreshing intervention only serves to delve into a more ancient layer of tribal memory, the war of Troy, which for our rhapsodist indelibly defines the vividly sketched landscape.

And as this further movement is concluded on the note of divine nemesis (the author himself has marked it off by paragraphing), another personal intervention takes place, the speaker of the poem bringing himself into the picture (lines 226-29) with his wandering destiny and his poetical mission—he now invokes the Muses, not through any repudiation of his disenchanted materialism as voiced at the outset, but because cultural, anthropological values have a claim on him, and he can accept the spell emanating from his communal investiture. After this last self-introduction, he will disappear from his poem and let "the Muses," and then Cassandra, speak. We saw in Chapter I to what a sublime pitch this last movement of *The Sepulchers* rises; a long way indeed has been travelled from the initial questioning and incidental topicality of treatment and satirical injections; the mood now can only be epic and prophetic in one. It is as if the autobiographical persona had purged himself in the process of surveying nature and history.

Now we also notice that the rhetorical, ratiocinating frame, so conspicuous in the first five movements until Line 150, has disappeared to make room for the restless chain of evocations: Italian Renaissance as focused in the Santa Croce memorials, Greek history as epitomized by Marathon, Greek history shading into legend and myth with the Trojan war's aftermath, and finally the cradle of all that history, Troy itself, prototype of the ever menaced city of man. The Pindaric transitions have effected a steady movement of the imagination backwards in time, toward the sources of human culture, from modern anonymous graveyards to the lost princely tombs of Troy, where the first of poets, Homer, goes to bring to light

the tragic past of mankind and make it a future memory.[30]
The discontinuities of metanarrative form have tapped the
source of this basic continuity that human culture is, however
threatened at every step by the relapse into barbarism and by
the impersonal forces of nature; and we are left with the
climactic image of the blind rhapsode groping his way into
the stony womb of a grave to seek there the rebirth of the forgotten.

From this vantage point it is easier to survey the whole
itinerary of the poem and appreciate how it succeeds in redeeming its own faults. Among these I would count the morbid mannerism of Lines 70-90 (Italian text), with its macabre
yet naive depiction of nocturnal horrors in abandoned
cemeteries (the hoopoe fluttering out of a skull, the scratching
bitch, and above all the rather irrelevant disgust at the idea
that Parini's anonymously buried remains may be contami-
nated by the gore of a beheaded criminal). Musical prowess
here fails to disguise the jarring note of mortuary fetishism
which, if it may serve as dark foil to the prevalently sunny
scene, nevertheless threatens to pull the central insight apart
at the seams. Ironically—and the author has been unaware of
this irony even while fustigating the oblivious city of Milan
(lines 72-75) along with its pampered patricians (lines
57-61) who did nothing to commemorate the poet that had so
effectively satirized their vices in *Il Giorno*—the horror scene
is wasted; what matters of Parini the poet is his poetry, not his
corpse. For Parini's presence is successfully evoked by the
very lines which claim *not* to sense it (62-69):

O lovely Muse, where are you? I don't feel
the breath of your divine presence among
those trees where I am sitting to sigh forth
my unabating homesickness. You came

---

[30] Octavio Paz, *The Bow and the Lyre*, tr. Ruth L. C. Simms. Austin and
London: University of Texas Press, 1973. At p. 51, in the chapter on
Rhythm, we find the following statement: "The myth is a past that is also a
future."

and smiled to him under that linden tree
which now shakes through and through in its lush foliage
missing forever the old man on whom
it once bestowed the gift of peace and shade.

The fine satirist's shade is also conjured by the lines which borrow his mode to attack the spoiled Milanese (lines 57-61); nor does the self-reference of the autobiographical persona mar this passage, in a poem which strives to focus the wide expanse of human culture and history on personal experience. We as innocent readers should respond even if we did not know from Foscolo's biography,[31] and from his memorable *Ortis* pages, that he actually met old Parini. But we could do without the charnel-house sequel, a logical and poetical nonsequitur which flatly retracts the grand Stoical statements of the outset (lines 1 to 22) and seems to portend complicity with the benighted customs so dramatically portrayed in the following movement (lines 104-114): the church burials and the nightmares attendant on such superstition as believing that the ghosts of the departed would appear to terrorize their surviving kinsfolk if money was not paid for a Requiem Mass.

The macabre scene of dereliction is, on the other hand, not without interest. Regardless of what may happen to Parini's physical remains there, the view of an abandoned graveyard with its nameless tombs sets up a contrast with the gentle cemeteries of Britain and of ancient Greece, then with the temple memorials of Santa Croce, and, in the end, with the Trojan necropolis that survives the ill-fated city and allows it to obtain resurrection in Homer's epos. The city of the dead is, as Italo Calvino would say now,[32] complementary to the

---

[31] For these and other details one can now refer to a recent and spirited biography of F.: Enzo Mandruzzato, *Foscolo*, Milan: Rizzoli, 1978. In Parini's adamant integrity and careful craftsmanship F. saw a lesson for himself and for Italy at large, his other literary and ethical model of comparable stature, among the contemporaries he met, being Vittorio Alfieri, the libertarian playwright.

[32] Italo Calvino, *Le città invisibili*. Turin: Einaudi, 1972.

city of the living, and its reflected image; man-made dereliction is incomparably worse than nature's impartiality, and to forget the dead is to forget ourselves. Neglect of the tombs signals neglect of the mansions of the living; and the opposite vice, fetishist superstition (as depicted in the lines already quoted on medieval church burials and venal prayer induced by fear of ghosts), is as stifling to us as the barbarism of carelessness. In Foscolo's verbal universe both degenerations find their iconic portrayal in dark imagery: night as blindness and hallucination, the stray bitch that is *heard*, not seen, to scratch among the graves and to howl, while the moon vanishes behind a cloud, the mother who jumps at night at the presumed moan of an avaricious ghost; the stinking gravestones in a church, so horribly unlike the sweet-smelling flowers that enable us to converse with our dead at a properly kept and properly situated tomb. Within the poem in progress, these images of a cultural antiworld serve to strengthen dialectically the image of the cultural cosmos which it is up to us humans to foster and defend, as darkness serves the drama of threatened, ever reappearing light.

Within the literary framework in which the poem itself operates, it is appropriate to remember that it recapitulates and in a way purges away the sepulchral poetry of which Foscolo, devout reader of Young, Blair, Gray, and Ossian, was consciously fond: his vatic persona in fact ends by exorcising this kind of poetry through the *in*- and *e*-voked figure of Homer, who supersedes all others. (In the same way, *The Sepulchers* recapitulates in foreshortening, and purges away, the eighteenth-century genre of didactic poetry and the genre of satire, and transforms the lyrical genre itself by disentangling it from the private context and raising it to public relevance.) In the existential key in which it is possible to read such a poetry, the macabre and fetishist note bespeaks a childhood fascination which the poet must dispel—and he will only be able to do so after voicing it in full. *The Sepulchers* rehearses the purgative itinerary of *Ortis*, and attains conversion (to a personally discovered communal value) only after risking perversion.

The speaking "I" undergoes a perceptible change through its several appearances in the writing. It is at first only a private, haunted, generally ratiocinating persona; then he validates the evoked cultural landscape by witnessing to personal experience of it (of the Santa Croce tombs he says "I saw . . ."); and finally he speaks chorally for mankind, through the masks of Cassandra and Homer, and after receiving the Muses' investiture. The rising tone of the utterance, from the initial Pianissimo to the final Fortissimo, reflects this inner metamorphosis of the persona. *The Sepulchers*, no less than *Ortis* and the sonnets, dramatizes the writer's initiation—on an altogether different register, for it is a ritual Foscolo had to undergo each time anew, and each time with a different, more advanced outcome. *Stirb und werde*. Ortis dies literally to himself and to the world, to reenter the "grembo materno" (maternal womb of Mother earth, cfr. *Sepulchers* 34-36); the persona of the sonnets dies to the world of action to reassert his commitment to a free, ethically responsible literature; the persona of *The Sepulchers* dies symbolically to himself, first by envisaging his future physical death, then by taking death and burial, the zero point of existence, as his point of departure, and finally by disappearing behind the masks and into the voices of Cassandra and Homer. He disappears, however, only after voicing his own expansive presence.

In the crowning image of Homer groping his way into the vaults of the Trojan necropolis much of the significant imagery that ran through the poem reaches its fusion and culmination. Not only does the bardic figure compound in his person all the poets and culture heroes that have variously been heard of or addressed in the course of the mercurial meditation: Dante, Petrarch, Alfieri, Foscolo himself as a mediating voice and pilgrim persona, Parini the satirist, Galileo and Newton who broadened our cosmic view, Machiavelli with his hard-won truth, Pindemonte who receives the earnest message and can answer in kind, Cassandra whose prophecy is fulfilled. Homer's act as such amounts to a creative violation of the tomb, a transgression of death, whose final silence can only yield to the poet's voice. Sepulchers are no longer final; they become a new start in the cycle of forgetfulness and memory which makes up the drama of tradition. After absorbing this intense poem on tombs, one is thus left with the scene of a tomb that is opened, and therefore denied as tomb, for the sake of life. The gesture is the essential gesture of Foscolo himself in the writing of the poem: poetry is a ceaseless recovery of what was lost, a resurrection of sorts. And the subterranean response of the old voices awakened by Homer's sacred violation seems to rehearse and purify all the ghostliness that had found an earlier, and morbid, embodiment in the nocturnal scenes of the graveyard, of the startled mother, and of Marathon's hallucination.

The vault is, though man-made, a chthonic womb finally penetrated by the life-engendering poet; one remembers the reference to earth's "maternal womb" which receives the properly cared-for bodies of our loved ones at lines 34-40. In this way the Apollonian, masculine, sunny note which also rang out at Lines 119-123

Rapian gli amici una favilla al Sole
a illuminar la sotterranea notte,

The friends would wrest a spark from the Sun
to illuminate the subterranean night,

converges into an integrating Gestalt with the chthonic, feminine, nocturnal note which made itself heard in the semantic tenor as well as in the recurrent music of the rich poetical score. The darksome, close, wailing echoes of alliterating -u- syllables characterized the chromatic make-up of passages like the one of the stray bitch and hoopoe in the graveyard, and contributed to the chordal effect of the

Marathon scene (as well as of the startled mother's episode at
Line 112, "il gemer *lu*ngo di persona morta," the long moaning of a dead person). These mournful sounds have alternated
in the course of the poem with the limpid notes of trilling or
singing open vowels, as they sometimes do in the sonnets:

> Lieta dell'aër tuo veste la Luna
> di luce candidissima i tuoi colli
> per vendemmia festanti, e le convalli
> popolate di case e d'oliveti
> mille di fiori al ciel mandano incensi . . .
> (Lines 168-72)

> The moon rejoicing in your air
> clothes with crystalline light your happy hills
> astir with vintage, and the farm-studded valleys
> thick with their olive groves exhale incense
> from myriad blossoms . . .

Now, in the concluding scene, a different harmony occurs,
dominated by the chromatic quality of *ra* and *ar* and *ann*,
ant, and syllables. They convey a frenzy of vision, and a conquered openness; yet the *i* (ee) of *antichissima* recalls the
Florence joy, while the contrapuntal *u* (oo) of *urne* (line 282)
brings a last purified echo of those earlier macabre sounds:

> Un dì vedrete
> mendico un cieco err*ar* sotto le vostre
> *ant*ichissime ombre, e *branc*o*lando*
> penet*rar* negli avelli, e abbra*cciar* l'*ur*ne,
> e interrog*ar*le. Gemer*anno* gli *antr*i
> secreti, e tutta n*ar*rer*à* la tomba.

It seems that the accumulated harmony of the poem resonates
in this final passage, which in perfect unison with the development of imagery makes good the momentary uncertainties of earlier passages. Even these, I think, can be vindi-

cated by the claim Guido Almansi and Guido Finzi recently
made in a different context, namely, that with some writers
"the force of style and syntax retains the text at the edge of
nothingness."[33]

The prophetic vehemence of *The Sepulchers*, while seemingly headed upstream against the grain of modern history,
finally pointed to certain developments in nineteenth-century
Europe—not just the Italian Risorgimento, or the political resurgence of Greece, but, more significantly and less obviously, the vast enterprise of archeological recovery which
brought to light so many buried worlds. Above all,
Schliemann's discovery of Troy and of the Mycenaean tombs.
I am not aware that Schliemann ever perused *The Sepulchers*,
but if he did, he could only sense there a shining confirmation
of what was to be his missionary lifework and of his belief that
Homer, the poet, told the truth. In this large yet specific historical perspective, Foscolo's grand epilogue takes its place
with the Helen episode of *Faust II*. It too said in its unique
manner that Western civilization could only progress in any
real sense by finding its way back to the ancestors—to the
lost beauty of Greece.

This was by no means the obsession of sophisticated esthetic pedants. It expressed the deep search for its origins in
which Western society at large was engaged at the time of
revolution, when the need to change its structures and make a
clean slate of the past aroused the complementary need to ob-
jectify that past, and to widen and deepen the historical space
of consciousness in which this objectification could happen.
Hence the Romantic quest for roots and origins, for the "*Ur*"
dimension of everything, and the apparently regressive orientation of the substantially progressive nineteenth-century
passion for history. The descent to the Mothers took many
forms, from archaeology of society, of art and language, to the
archaeology of life and nature at large. Anthropology superseded theology and metaphysics; a new kind of humanism

---

[33] Guido Almansi e Guido Fink, *Quasi come, parodia come letteratura,
letteratura come parodia*. Milan: Bompiani, 1976, p. 182.

was in the making because a new genealogy was being discovered, a new humility, a new vertigo, and a new pride. The
lofty lexicon in which Foscolo chose to embody his vision of
the new man in the act of unearthing the troubling truths
about himself only reflects the need to ritualize this blessed
violence. The passage of Homer entering the Trojan vaults is
all wiry verbs, and rings with the echoes of anguish and excitement attendant upon such an enterprise. *Gemeranno gli
antri. . . .* Once again, the highly articulate poet manages to
force an elemental cry out of his revered, and violently repos-
sessed, language.

CHAPTER IV

Vatic Conjuring: *The Graces*

Poring over the worksheets of Foscolo's unfinished long poem, *Le Grazie* (The Graces), at the National Library of Florence and at Leghorn's Biblioteca Labronica is a rare experience. It has engaged the wits, and the patience, of dedicated scholars like Giuseppe Chiarini, Francesco Pagliai, and now Saverio Orlando,[1] who has come up with the latest attempt at a critical edition (1974), while Pagliai's lifelong endeavor, so far known from the three sustained preliminary essays in textual criticism which he published between 1952 and 1966, has been cut short by his death in 1976. For the

---

[1] Giuseppe Chiarini, *Poesie di U.F.*, edizione critica. Livorno: Vigo, 1882. — *Appendice alle Opere edite e postume di U.F.* Florence: Le Monnier, 1890. — *Poesie di U.F.* Nuova edizione critica. Livorno: Giusti, 1904. Chiarini's steadily improved attempts at a reconstruction of the supposedly final text of *Le Grazie* are the first respectable critical edition of that poem, and Chiarini's 1904 textual version had remained normative until Pagliai's and Orlando's more rigorous work began to appear after the mid-century. Chiarini's edition, for instance, is reproduced with minor changes in Puppo's *Opere di F.*, *cit.* Then see: Francesco Pagliai, "I versi dei silvani nelle *Grazie* del F.," in *Studi di filologia italiana*, 1952, pp. 145-412; *ibid.*, "Prima redazione (fiorentina) dell'*Inno alle Grazie* di U. F.," in *Studi di filologia italiana*, 1961, pp. 45-442; Saverio Orlando, "La seconda redazione dell'*Inno alle Grazie* di U.F.," in *Paideia* XXVIII (1973), pp. 15-39; *ibid.*, U. F., *Le Grazie, carme ad Antonio Canova*, edizione critica. Brescia: Paideia editrice, 1974; *ibid.*, *Dall'Ortis alle Grazie*. Orlando's words at p. 196 of his critical edition of *Le Grazie* are worth quoting: "For a work in progress [*in fieri*], like *Le Grazie*, it is not possible to use the normal standards of philology, simply because the problems do not arise from the transmission and copies of the text, but from the autograph text itself."

critic who lacks that kind of philological ambition and exper-
tise, retracing Foscolo's steps through his dogged pursuit of
the crowning poetical dream in the troubled years of Napoleon's fall (1812-1815) is still, beyond the recurrent baffle-
ment, an awesome joy, not unlike what sustained the German
scholars engaged in deciphering Hölderlin's late manuscripts.[2] It is no mere question of philological guesswork with
the excitement and frustrations attendant upon such a complex puzzle game. It is in fact an education to poetry.

Through the tireless revisions, the prolonged weighing of
alternatives to a phrase, a line, a word, a word order, or a
narrative juncture, one sees an image emerge and take shape,
or undergo an unpredictable metamorphosis, or sprout into
more images, or fall into the limbo of discarded ideas. One
watches a poet's mind in action, the work in progress afford-
ing so much greater a challenge as that particular mind was
addicted at the same time to the sheer delight of proliferating
ideational associations and to the discipline of the most exacting craftsmanship. His ear was hard to please, as one better
realizes upon noticing how little there is in Italian poetry between Petrarch and Leopardi that can bear comparison with
Foscolo's verbal music—whether he captures it on the wing,
at the first dawning of sound and image, or through protracted
auscultation, after dozens or scores of attempts.

It takes many years—as Pagliai well knew—to make diachronic sense of this intricate wealth of notations and find the
plausible thread or threads that will combine the often inde-

[2] After the earlier editions (by Zinkernagel and by Hellingrath), F.
Beissner's had become the authoritative critical edition of Hölderlin's
work, but it is now being challenged by D. E. Sattler, whose "Frankfurter
Ausgabe" (Verlag Roter Stern) has begun to appear in 1975, in Frankfurt-
am-Main. I have at hand its latest volumes to date (*Elegien und Epigramme*, Bd. 6, 1976, and *Jambische und hexametrische Formen*. 3, 1977),
and the problems raised by the richness of variants (as well as by Hölderlin's increasingly stenographic handwriting) call to mind the even greater
difficulties confronting the editors of *Le Grazie*. The comparison is naturally
suggested by the shared Hellenic myth and vatic style, and by the similar
political orientation of the two mutually unknown poets.

pendently growing narrative or iconic units into an integrated rhapsody. Pagliai needed hundreds of pages in 1952 to put in chronological order the nearly endless elaborative stages of one seemingly minor motif, the passage of the Sylvan deities from Hymn II—and to discover in the process that it innervated, narratively as well as iconically, an expanding range of incidents and motifs in the whole projected poem. The same scholar again needed several hundreds of pages to sift and connect the relevant textual evidence into what could be reasonably called the first draft of *The Graces* as a whole. This admirable endeavor was published in 1961, and it in turn provided a younger scholar, Saverio Orlando, with the basis for a reconstruction of an acceptable "second draft," in 1973, and then of a final draft in 1974. Both men also went on less far-reaching trails in the Foscolian forest when they respectively worked on the diachronic order of extant manuscript drafts for individual motifs of limited scope: Pagliai (1966) studying the development of the short passage concerning Dante in Hymn II, and Orlando (1974) unraveling the sequence of the extant versions of the "Atlantis" passage in Hymn III;[3] yet even these more circumscribed ventures proved how rich and inextricable the thematic ramifications are, and how essential, therefore, each episode to the physiognomy of the whole. On the yellowing, porous paper of the packets Foscolo left in the care of a friend in Milan in spring 1815, when taking the way of exile, his unmistakable, nervously elegant handwriting runs on, hesitates, peoples the pages with blocks of lines, superseding itself, adding, deleting, superimposing new deletions and variants on the provisionally completed parts he had entrusted to the transcription of his Zantiote scribe, Andrea Calbo. One feels the restless yet firm hand move back and forth as it hunts for the definitive. The patina of time fails to blur the marks of that energy

<hr />

[3] Francesco Pagliai, "Versi a Dante nelle *Grazie* del F.," in *Studi Danteschi* XLIII (1966), pp. 135-92; Saverio Orlando, "Il mito di Atlantide nelle *Grazie* del F.," in *Italianistica* III, 1 (January-April 1974), pp. 33-53.

harnessed for the task of achieving the ultimate harmony, the encompassing vision.

The tentative solutions given by the best editors to date, beginning with Chiarini, who composed his version of the presumable whole much as a mosaic of sometimes freely juxtaposed or salvaged passages, attest both to the pretty high level of total definition that the design had reached when the poet abandoned it, and to the margin of indeterminacy we either cannot fill or have to leave to optional answers. The labyrinth of provisional drafts is not hopeless, and we have—at the Labronica library to which Foscolo's faithful friend Mrs. Magiotti bequeathed a sizable legacy of the poet's papers—a detailed summary in which the poet himself outlines the thematic distribution. Yet recent scholars, notably Orlando, have questioned the reliability of that elaborate summary (there had been others, clearly vaguer) and taken Chiarini to task for his absolute faith in that source.

One might—on the authority of Foscolo himself[4]—postulate a generally complete but unfinished work, and it would be enough to rescue *Le Grazie* from formal nonexistence. It is something else than an insecure project; comparison with Michelangelo's unfinished statues like the *Captives* and the *Pietà Rondanini* readily suggests itself once we realize the grandeur of the guiding idea, the strength of the many perfected parts, and the dynamism of their interaction even across whatever gaps of execution. As Kenneth Clark has said,[5] the modern sensibility has come to value the frag-

---

[4] Orlando, *Le Grazie, ed. crit.*, p. 22: "The *Grazie*, to say it with Foscolo, is 'completed, but not finished' [*terminate, ma non finite*]: the latter verb points to a formal *incompiutezza* [lack of final touch]," but Orlando adds that this is not to be understood as a flaw, and that F.'s "*non-finito*" work has its own power, far from being inchoate. (*Non-finito*, we remember, is the expression applied to Michelangelo's late work.) Passages in Foscolo's letters to his friends Pellico, the Countess of Albany, Pindemonte and Leoni, between 1814 and 1816, offer many variations on such motifs as concerns the work on *Le Grazie*. See also fn. 7, below.

[5] Kenneth Clark, *The Nude, a study in ideal form*. Garden City, N.Y.:

ments of antique masterpieces precisely as fragments, and
would probably be put off by the perfectly reconstructed
works of art if such a reconstruction were possible. That is
notoriously so since the era of Impressionism, when the artist
discarded narrative superstructures to aim for the fleeting
moment and the unselfcontained element of reality.

A critic like Orlando has ventured the hypothesis that if
Foscolo had managed to finish *Le Grazie*, the result would be
more dated and less interesting than it is. That compliment
should be possibly replaced by the recognition that with *The
Graces* Ugo Foscolo was anticipating much later ventures.
Though he kept his sights on classical perfection and harmony, a different harmony took over as the work, unfolding
through its feverish sequence of expanding and intertwining
motifs, ceaselessly revised in depth, began living its demonic
life. We talk of open poetry today, after Ezra Pound; and
Pound's *Cantos* are the twentieth-century equivalent of what
Foscolo achieved with *Le Grazie*. That is not static poetry,
regardless of the Neoclassical veneer Foscolo could not help
absorbing from his period, and from one occasional
inspiration—Antonio Canova's sculpture. The polished surfaces Foscolo attains reveal a wiry skeleton and break up into
overlapping, nearly disjointed, phases or moments of vision.
The status of his poem as a becoming stems also from this
structural basis, and not only from the accident of history that
compelled him to relinquish the project at a nearly complete
but still unfinished stage. If we try to grasp the unfolding
poem through the many variants, repentances, and eurekas,
we touch the idea in motion, an Anadyomene rising from the
sea-foam of its literary and personal materials, just as we
share with Michelangelo the shudder of form's birth when we
look at the Florence Accademia *Captives* in the act of emerging from their marble matrix.

1959, p. 303: "We have come to think of the fragment as more vivid, more
concentrated, and more authentic" [than the complete work of statuary].
Clark's book is also useful for the iconographic background it provides to a
poem like *The Graces*.

Such comparisons, such evaluations, would be impossible if the work in question did not bear the deep mark of individualization which makes it exist aesthetically even beyond marginal fluctuations of detail. "Unfinished" is not the same as "half-finished." One confirmation of this comes from Foscolo's own attempts to keep up with his fast-developing creation, whose first shape, as planned, was to consist of one hymn to the Graces, while as the diverse passages kept surfacing on the pages and twisting under the frequent surgery the author applied, the original plan made way for a tripartite composition ("Carme"), three hymns, each to one goddess. Even then the order of appearance of the women in the flesh who mirrored the Graces on earth underwent important changes, and one particularly stunning passage dedicated to Maddalena Bignami of Erba near Milan, which had materialized as a footnote to another sequence, gradually reached absolute definition and, contrary to the initial idea, ended by providing the climactic end to the third Hymn.

In the Biblioteca Nazionale we have the first sketches and tentative plans for the poem to be, but at the Labronica library of Leghorn we can read Foscolo's own final prospectus (the mentioned summary) and his notes toward a definition of the informing idea *(Ragion poetica del Carme*, in his own hand; then there are similar reports in Quirina Magiotti's hand, who had it from him viva voce and by letter). According to this "poetical rationale" the *Grazie* poem is to be understood "metaphysically" (as an investigation into the "arcane and undefinable" causes that may lead to a theory of fine arts), or "poetically" (as an allegorical personification of gentle passions), or "socially" (as an educational work, a paideia); and here one may be reminded of Schiller's *Letters on Aesthetic Education*. For the most part, these dated attempts at self-explanation are far from convincing, and they betray the author's preoccupation to find acceptable labels for his reluctant creation, which kept outgrowing his diagrams and definitions because it amounted to a taxonomically intractable experience. We laugh when Foscolo (a sharp, aw-

fully perceptive critic as a rule) solemnly explains to his
friend the poet Pindemonte (the one to whom he had addressed his *Sepulchers* eliciting a homonymous poem in response) that the point of the poem in progress was to combine
the lyrical with the didactic genre.

It was far more than a matter of genres, however fastidious
the Neoclassical readership might be with which our innovat-
ing poet had to reckon. It was, for one thing, the inner logic of
the poet's own development (as Aldo Vallone has seen)[6] from
the short lyrical piece reflecting a moment of perception to
ever wider compositions encompassing a personal, yet more
than personal experience, and coming to terms with history—history past and history in the making, that history to
which Foscolo happened to be both a pragmatic contributor
(as warrior, political deputy, and, briefly, educator) and a
fervent though increasingly disabused witness. All the genres
merge into this kind of undertaking, but it would be mislead-
ing to classify it as a mere academic experiment of fusion of
two genres. In the act of encompassing history from a
mythopoeic vantage point Foscolo was exploding the literary
genres as they were known.

Mythopoeia, not didacticism, was the point. From the bittersweet wisdom of Didymus, a fictional mask of the late man
who has seen too much and through everything and thus
learned to smile at everything, the poet was reaching all the
way back to Homer, the poet who had seen everything in the
virgin moment of sunrise. "I am reading . . . Homer, Homer,
and always Homer,"[7] Foscolo wrote in that creative phase to

[6] Aldo Vallone, *Interpretazione delle "Grazie" di F.* Lecce: Milella,
1970-71. Ibid., *Linea della poesia foscoliana*. Florence, La Nuova Italia,
1957.

[7] Letter No. 1587, to the Countess of Albany, dated October 12, 1814:
". . . da più mesi non leggo se non Omero, Omero, Omero, e alle volte tre
o quattro Latini, e quattro Italiani, tutti poeti, perch'io attendo, ed oggi
con tutte le forze, e in tutti i minuti, quando pur dovessi morire sotto il
lavoro, a una certa operetta in versi ch'Ella ha veduto nascere, consacrata
alle *Grazie*. La tela mi s'è allargata nel tessere; ma perché la troppa lar-
ghezza poteva forse nuocere al disegno, ho reciso molte parti già belle e

a friend. Homer, let us remember, was to him the poet he was
not and could not be, and therefore the poet he most wanted
to approximate—whether through simple reading, or through
thematic borrowing, or again through the acrobatics of translation, from the impressive "experiment" of 1807[8] with the
Iliad's first book to the further, fragmentary but insistent, experiments he protracted to the very end of his life. Homer was
the continuous, ample voice of epic narration, who was
privileged to see the world as a natural miracle, but he, "Didymus," "Ortis," could not be at home in innocent fable, because he had come too late for that. The veil of Maya had
been torn asunder by the irrevocable ruthlessness of science;
and his gift, understandably, was to seize the fleeting moment
of illumination only. He lacked the sustained breath and the
unquestioning belief of the epic poet, and that is why he tried
so hard to be one.

---

tessute, e la composizione, sì delle parti, sì dell'Architettura di tutto il
poema è pienamente perfetta secondo me; mi manca solamente la verseg-
giatura qua e là; e chi sa forse? mi sarei spicciato a quest'ora; e avrei, tutto
al più, la poca pena di *ridipingere* il tutto; se non che . . . alla fine di set-
tembre finiva il contratto della mia pigione, e m'è convenuto lasciare la mia
verdeggiante solitaria casetta . . ." (". . . for many a month I have been
reading but Homer, Homer, Homer, and at times three or four Latins, and
four Italians, all of them poets, because I attend, and today with all my
strength, and every minute, even if I had to die of the effort, to a certain
little work in verse which you saw taking shape, consecrated to the Graces.
The fabric has broadened in the process of weaving; but since excessive
breadth might have hurt the design, I have cut out many parts already completed, and the composition of the parts as such and of the poem's total
Architecture is fully perfect in my opinion; what's left for me to do is only
the versification here and there; and who knows? by now I'd have seen the
end of it; were it not that . . . at the end of September my lease expired, and
I had to leave my solitary, verdant little house . . ."). *Epistolario* v, in
Edizione Nazionale, *cit.*, p. 262. Shortly later (October 15, 1814, Letter
1590, *ibid.*, p. 270) the poet said to the Countess, his friend, that he was
"about to finish the *Grazie*," and that those who had heard him recite some
parts of it found them wonderful, though he was skeptical.

[8] See Note 8 to Chapter I, and *Edizione Nazionale*, III (*Esperimenti di
traduzione dell'Iliade*, a cura di Gennaro Barbarisi, in three parts). Florence: 1961, 1965, 1967.

He had to lean on the unattainable ideal of Homer for the same reason that, in the realm of fiction, he had to counteract and possibly exorcise Ortis with the anti-self of Didymus. If Didymus was the exorciser of demons, "Homer" held the magic key to the conjuring of the gods. And they had to be conjured. Ortis' passionate despair and Didymus' wise smile (no matter how adaptive) left a gaping Nothingness in the soul; the luring *"nulla eterno"* of the sonnet to Evening, the tolling *"nulla, nulla, nulla"* of a letter[9] to the Countess of Al-

---

[9] Letter No. 1434, in *Epistolario* V, pp. 8-10, passim: ". . . e per me non v'è più ragione: la mia ragione sì sdegnosa ed alta una volta, corre pericolo di smarrirsi: tutte le mie facoltà sono sovvertite: e intanto nell'amor mio non vedo che il freddo orrore del nulla: le mie speranze su l'avvenire s'annientano nell'idea perpetua del nulla; spesso in tutte le ventiquattr'ore d'un giorno, e giacendo febbricitante, e all'oscuro, non passa minuto che io non abbia innanzi a me quell'unica donna infelice, la lunga storia della mia passione, e quest'orribile nulla. . . . La vista di quel bambino uscito quasi dal sepolcro in que' giorni ch'io m'avvicinava per l'ultime volte a sua Madre mi ha illuso di mille folli e care illusioni che sono tosto tornate nella solita disperazione del *Nulla:* questo *Nulla* è pur prepotente addosso a me: mi circonda sempre, mi distrugge tutto, non mi lascia che il *passato* distrutto anch'esso nel tempo che non tornerà più; il nulla dell'avvenire, s'io vivo; il nulla del sepolcro m'inorridiscono sempre—non conosco me stesso! . . ." (and for me there is no reason any more: my reason once so disdainful and lofty, runs danger of losing itself: all my faculties are upset: and meanwhile in my love I see but the cold horror of nothingness: my hopes for the future are annihilated in the perpetual idea of nothingness; often in all the twenty-four hours of a day, and while I lie a prey to fever, and in the dark, no minute goes by without my having before me that one unhappy woman, the long story of my passion, and this horrible nothingness. . . . The sight of that child who had, almost, emerged from the grave in the days when I approached his Mother for the last times has beset me with a thousand crazy and dear delusions which have returned right away into the usual despair of *Nothingness*: this *Nothingness* is really overwhelming: it always surrounds me, destroys me utterly, leaves me but the *past* itself destroyed in the time which will return no more; the nothingness of the future, if I live; the nothingness of the grave always horrify me—I do not know myself! . . .) Such nihilist outlets on F.'s part are correlative to the negations in *The Graces*. Against the imputations of political escapism that *The Graces*'s denial of history had aroused, Vitilio Masiello has observed that F.'s poem implies a sharp judgment of history, for autonomous

bany, Alfieri's widow, whom Ugo had made a benevolent confidante of his worries and plans. If Nothingness yawned, and its psychic offspring, Ennui, la Noia, malady of an *enfant du siècle*, gnawed at his vitals, the indefatigable pen could become the wand of a conjurer, Helena could be resurrected, the beauty that never was could fill the gap left by the death of fable and belief. And in the moment of conjuring, the wizard who vainly tried to be Homer could believe in his ghostly creation. Venus appeared to him, and the world could begin again.

Venus, as Wallace Stevens would have put it, was a name for something that could not be named. But Foscolo, the poet that Foscolo was, needed names; he knew what was in a name, and the power of Adam. The name could conquer the "silence of a thousand ages," the vision could reassert itself against nihilist irony and despair. As the feverish pen keeps trying to capture the vanished, and the future worlds, in its methodic loops and jabs, we come across the adversary, right there in the fading pages of the Florence library manuscripts:

Dear Andrea:

Dreams! Beware of waking up. What are you now talking and prattling of fatherland of arms and of Greek valor? Greece is a corpse stripped to the bone, Italy for several centuries has been a fleshly corpse, but still a corpse: let us leave the dead in peace then, and try to live ourselves in peace. Farewell, farewell.[10]

Next to this, Andrea Calbo's letter to him; his scribe had

---

art can be even more polemically efficient than the obviously "committed" kind. See V. M., "Il mito e la storia. Analisi della struttura dialettica delle 'Grazie' foscoliane," in *Angelus Novus* 12-13 (1968), pp. 130-70.

[10] Foscolo MSS at the Biblioteca Nazionale in Florence, Vol. III, Fas. D. The letter to Andrea Calbo, his fellow islander to whom he dictated so many pages, follows the sketch of an Ode to the Ionians, while Calbo's letter is on the other side of the same sheet. In those days the Marshal De Bellegarde had occupied Milan in the name of the Austrian Emperor, and Viceroy Eugène de Beauharnais had left Italy for Bavaria.

looked for him in Florence and was writing from Fiesole on June 18, 1814. Much had happened to Italy, to Europe, and to Foscolo since the inception of the new poem; Napoleon had fallen, gone to Elba; Viceroy Eugène Beauharnais' Italian Kingdom was becoming a thing of the past, and the hopes of patriots like Foscolo and Calbo were shattered by the Austrian takeover. Foscolo had left Florence, the oasis that had sheltered his labor of love for the best part of two halcyon years, and that accordingly figured within the poem in the making as the appropriate locus for the Graces' ritual. Hymn I begins by an invitation to the sculptor Canova to join the celebration at Bellosguardo, a hill overlooking the Tuscan capital, and Hymn III ends on the note of leavetaking from Florence. If we pay attention to the precarious circumstances in which the poem was struggling to achieve itself, the way a convulsive history knocked at the door of the poet secluded with his vision, we shall be less inclined to dismiss the ritualistic apparatus of invention and the highly stylized diction as trappings of a dated taste. The adversary was knocking at the door, *Nulla, nulla, nulla*! Nothingness kept besieging the citadel of consciousness. An apotropaeic ritual was necessary, the dream could not be surrendered. Only if the incantatory formula was precise would it have the power to evoke the goddesses. Mankind was what it was: brutal, selfish, destructive, traitorous; therefore the thing to do was to invent Venus Anadyomene, and her daughters, the Graces, the intangibles of civilization springing from the very heart of Nature's bounty, and hold them up as a mirror to the nation that had harbored these deities after they left Greece; the nation that was struggling to be reborn, against many odds, even as the ancient poetry strove to rise again in the metamorphosed accents of the new.

And Venus took verbal shape. She had materialized several times in women Foscolo physically loved or just adored from a distance; she had been the world-wise Isabella Teotochi, the capricious Antonietta Arese, the pure and renounced Isabella Roncioni, the sisterly Quirina Magiotti, the

learned apiculturist Cornelia Martinetti of Bologna, the musical Eleonora Nencini of Florence, the sweet and fate-stricken
dancer Maddalena Bignami of Brianza in Lombardy. The last
three, unnamed but recognizable as embodiments of their respective arts, enter Hymn II of the poem as priestesses at the
altar of the Graces; the author of *Ode to his Lady on her recovery* has not quite forgotten his tenet that godheads are
merely apotheosized humans, and here in *The Graces* he sets
up an elaborate structure of humanization—an apotheosis in
reverse—whereby the three Italian beauties represent the
three Graces, and the Graces in turn are emanations of Venus
the mother goddess who animates the universe. The structure
rehearses an inner process, whereby in all the women our
poet met and found emotionally significant he recognized that
first theophany of his life, Venus risen from the Ionian sea at
Zante, and now properly enshrined as the personified force of
benevolent nature. Nature, to the native Mediterranean, was
a graspable totality, a cosmos of perceptible, generative
forces, and what else but feminine? No wonder then that Foscolo's theogony is feminine, whether anchored to the tactile
and visible shape of a woman in the flesh, or diffused in the
choir of chthonian and heavenly presences mother Nature
suggests. His poetical work is all a hymn to the Eternal
Feminine, and if its form necessarily leans on the venerable
literary tradition to make it new, the original stimulus came
from a personal revelation.

In the introductory passages to Hymn I, which Orlando expunges from his scrupulous edition while old Chiarini made
them part and parcel of his uninhibited reconstruction,
Venus brightens the universe with her sudden filial retinue of
three, and the apparition is immediately connected with
Zante and the writer's own childhood memories:

Una Diva scorrea lungo il creato
a fecondarlo, e di Natura avea
l'austero nome: fra' celesti or gode
di cento troni, e con più nomi ed are

le dan rito i mortali; e più le giova
l'inno che bella Citerea la invoca.

 Perché clemente a noi che mirò afflitti
travagliarci e adirati, un dì la santa
Diva, all'uscir de' flutti ove s'immerse
a ravvivar le gregge di Nerèo,
apparì con le Grazie; e le raccolse
l'onda Ionia primiera, onda che amica
del lito ameno e dell'ospite musco
da Citera ogni dì vien desiosa
a' materni miei colli: ivi fanciullo
la Deità di Venere adorai.
Salve, Zacinto! all'antenoree prode,
de' santi Lari Idei ultimo albergo
e de' miei padri, darò i carmi e l'ossa,
e a te il pensier: chè piamente a queste
Dee non favella chi la patria obblìa.

A Goddess was overrunning creation
to make it fruitful, and her austere name
was Nature: now she has a hundred thrones
among the gods, and mortals consecrate
many an altar and name to her; she favors
the hymn invoking her as Cytherea.

 For in her clemency to us whom she saw
self-tormented by wrath, one day the holy
Goddess, on rising from the surf she'd visited
to quicken Nereus' flock, appeared with the Graces;
and the pristine Ionian wave welcomed them,
the wave that cherishing the inviting shore
and hospitable moss comes daily desirous
from Cythera to my maternal hills:
there as a boy I worshiped Venus' deity.
All hail to you, Zante! to the Paduan land
which afforded the last shelter to Troy's
Lares and to my forefathers, I will
give my songs and my bones, and to you

my thought: for he who forgets his own homeland
cannot properly talk to these fair goddesses.[11]

It is true that Orlando appends the Leghorn library text of this
pivotal passage, since the so called *Quaderno* or *Quadernone*
is in his estimation a final redaction of the parts completed.
But before interfering with any commentary, let us resume direct quotation from the extended passage dealing with the apparition of Venus and the Graces:

> Splendea intorno tutto quel mar quando sostenne
> tutto
> su la conchiglia assise e vezzeggiate
> dalla Diva le Grazie: e a sommo il flutto,
> quante alla prima prima aura di Zefiro
> le frotte delle vaghe api prorompono,
> e piú e piú succedenti invide ronzano
> a far lunghi di sé aërei grappoli,
> van alïando su' nettarei calici
> e del mèle futuro in cor s'allegrano,
> tante a fior dell'immensa onda raggiante
> ardian mostrarsi a mezzo il petto ignude
> le amorose Nereidi oceanine;
> e a drappelli agilissime seguendo
> la Gioia alata, degli Dei foriera,
> gittavan perle, dell'ingenue Grazie
> il bacio le Nereidi sospirando.
>   Poi come l'orme della Diva e il riso
> delle vergini sue fêr di Citera
> sacro il lito, un'ignota violetta
> spuntò a' piè de' cipressi; e d'improvviso
> molte purpuree rose amabilmente
> si conversero in candide . . .

---

[11] *Le Grazie*, Hymn I (Venus), lines 32-52, p. 51 *Opere di F.*; lines
31-51, pp. 106-107, *Dall'Ortis alle Grazie*; lines 27-51, p. 166, *Le Grazie*,
ed crit. (from the Leghorn *Quaderno* draft). Translation mine.

The whole sea there shone all over as it upheld
on their seashell the Graces, sitting to receive
the parent Goddess' caress: and atop the wave,
such as at the very first breathing of Zephyrus
the honeybees swarm out in throngs, and pressing
one another in emulous zest, buzz
to pile up into long clusters airborne,
and hover here and there on nectar-filled
cups and already rejoice inside foretasting
the honey to come, as many ocean Nereids
surfacing through the immense radiance of waves
made bold to show themselves, bare-breasted,
astir with love; and following in nimble
schools the winged messenger of the gods,
Joy herself, the Nereids scattered pearls
all around, yearning for the Graces' kiss.

Then as the Goddess' step and the luminous
laughter of her daughters made holy the beach
of Cythera, an unknown violet blossomed
at the foot of the cypresses; and suddenly
many dark red roses lovingly changed
to white . . .[12]

As is to be expected, much of the expressive force gathers
in certain verbs on which syntax and semantics hinge; thus

---

[12] *Le Grazie*, Hymn I, lines 66-87, pp. 44-45 *Opere di F.*; lines 65-86,
pp. 107-108, *Dall'Ortis alle Grazie*; lines 65-86, p. 167, *Le Grazie, ed. crit.*
(Leghorn *Quaderno* draft, with variant at line 65. There [and I have the
facsimile under my eyes] the word *intorno* (all around) is penned above the
word *tutto* (all), but the latter is not crossed out. The alternative word is,
accordingly, not definitive. The whole *Quadernone* is in Foscolo's own
hand.) Tr. mine. The lovely honeybee simile is taken from Homer, and
Barbarisi (*Edizione Nazionale*, III, Part I, p. 353) reproduces a slightly
different version of it in the context of F.'s revised draft of a translation of
Iliad, Book II, dating from 1815-1816. In this context, the simile describes
the Greek army congregating on the plain of Troy at Agamemnon's call.
This is one revelatory proof of the creative exchange between the two experiments F. was conducting in those years. The honeybee simile engaged his
auditory imagination to an impressive extent.

one can trace Venus' action (for she is present here through her action chiefly) through the words or expressions *scorrea . . . a fecondarlo* (overran . . . to make fruitful) . . . *mirò* (gazed) . . . *s'immerse* (dived) . . . *a ravvivar* (to quicken) . . . *apparí* (appeared), and they carry the essential meaning in their very progression—from the diffuse dynamism of *scorrea*, with its generative correlate *a fecondarlo*, to *mirò's* focal intensity, to the consequent katabasis, *s'immerse . . . a ravvivar*, which repeats the sequence *scorrea . . . a fecondarlo* and finally resolves the whole series on the climactic act *apparí*. The progression goes from force to form, from diffused energy to concentration, as the cosmic power of "Nature" focuses into consciousness and then into individualized shape, "Venus," who does her utmost by simply *appearing*. Syntactical and semantic parallelism enacts a theogony articulated in two cycles, the second cycle rehearsing and enhancing the first to bring the whole process to completion; and in so doing all the central attributes of Venus-Aphrodite the earth goddess have emerged: fecundity, vitality, generosity, shapeliness.

But when the conclusive verb *apparí* precipitates the whole movement into visibility, converting theogony into theophany, it is only to open a new cycle in which Venus' attributes are, not "personified," but rather hypostasized as the Graces. Creation continues in a proliferation of energy made visible, and it is a wave of joy going through everything as the volcanic chaos (*Enosigeo*, etc., lines immediately preceding the first of our two quotes) becomes a cosmos, with life taking over the fearsome domain of formless matter and gradually transforming it into fecund beauty. Venus "appeared" *with* the Graces after her immersion in the watery deep, and it is in the realm of water, the element of life, that they manifest themselves in their full splendor: "*Splendea tutto quel mar. . . .*" The element partakes of the divine beauty it has brought forth, and very appropriately one verb focuses the process. "*Splendea*," shone, actually initiates the whole verbal sequence, as if it were from this splendor itself,

from this first culmination of Venus' beneficent power, that
the new phase of life began on earth. *Splendea* heightens the
appari that marked Venus' and the Graces' theophany a few
lines above, and once again we see how the functional and
semantic nexus between these two verbs, so essential to the
dynamics of the whole sequence in question, has an additional support in Foscolo's Greek background: his awareness
of the etymological correlation between *phos* (light) and
phainomai (to appear). In this regard one may profitably remember his insistence (in the essays, especially *Epochs of the
Italian Language*)[13] that ancient Greek was the musically
strongest of tongues, superior even to Italian, and his self-
investiture in the poems (end of *Ode all'Amica risanata*, beginning of the third *Hymn to the Graces*) as the reviver of Hellenic modes in the Italian medium. One should also keep in
mind his tireless practice as a translator of the *Iliad*, his
sharp linguistic footnotes to that work, and his essay on Zeus'
nod. This evidence corroborates the esthetic realization that
when Foscolo appropriated Greek mythology for his poetical
purposes he was far from indulging in the fashionable man-
nerisms of Neoclassical style; it was a true revival not a decorative affectation; and the three *Hymns to the Graces* could
well rank as a worthy addition, in the Italian language yet in
the authetic Hellenic spirit, to the lovely *Homeric Hymns* that
Foscolo knew and to some extent "imitated" here.[14]

---

[13] *Edizione Nazionale*, XI, Part I. In both English and Italian. The Italian text is also available in *Opere di F*. For illuminating discussions of the
circumstances of composition and publication of this work, which originally took shape as a series of public lectures in London, see C. Foligno's
Introduction to *Edizione Nazionale*, XI, and Vincent, U.F. The *Epochs of
the Italian Language* is a sustained endeavor to delineate a history of Italy's
literary language and national spirit.

[14] One handy and scholarly, but also generally useful edition of the
Homeric Hymns is the bilingual, annotated and prefaced *Inni omerici* a
cura di Filippo Càssola. Milan: Mondadori, 1975. A recent English translation is: *The Homeric Hymns*, translation, introduction and notes by Apos-
tolos N. Athanassakis. Baltimore and London: Johns Hopkins University
Press, 1976. For an edition with the Greek text and the English translation

In the specific context on hand, *splendea* functions above all to manifest Venus' power of irradiation. Her daughters the Graces, risen with her from the deep, embody and propagate this power to the world; their loveliness makes a new universal dawn, it actually reverberates as light from the surrounding-sustaining sea, which is itself now—grammatically as well as semantically—the source of that luminous radiation it had received from the goddesses harbored in its depths and born(e) to the surface:

Splendea tutto quel mar quando sostenne
su la conchiglia assise e vezzeggiate
dalla Diva le Grazie . . .

Syntactical structure and semantic tenor undergo a change here as the Graces take over. Their mother Venus had entered the poem much like Lucretius' nature goddess at the beginning of *De Rerum Natura*, as a restless fertilizing force, and grammar signalled this function by making her every time the subject of the active verbs we saw above. Moreover, these verbs repeatedly converged into syntagms of purposive import: *scorrea . . . a fecondarlo, s'immerse . . . a ravvivar.* Once the Graces emerge, however, they are grammatically defined as subjects of passive verbs and at the same time objects of active ones, the grammatical or at least semantic agents being, respectively, the sea that "sustained" them and Venus who "caressed" them. The Graces do not act, they can only *be*, and they have their purpose in themselves, not beyond themselves as their mother did who fulfilled her own nature in fecundating the world and procreating them in a kind of parthenogenesis. With their mother, they are the new cen-

---

en face, see: *Hesiod. The Homeric Hymns. Fragments of the Epic Cycle. Homerica.* Translated by Hugh G. Evelyn-White. London and Cambridge, Mass.: Heinemann Ltd. and Harvard University Press (The Loeb Classical Library), 1914; revised 1920 and 1936. References to other recent English translations to be found in Julia Haig Gaisser's review of the Athanassakis tr., in *The Classical World*, November 1977, pp. 191-92.

ter of the world, or better, they provide the world with a center, none having been there so far; they have thus given a
form to reality, they are even the center of the center, the
final cause so to speak: for everything, including their adoring mother, looks to them, tends to them, finds in them the
only reason for being.

And if they, the Graces, do not act, they of course generate
plentiful action in a universe in which they have introduced
meaning and purpose. It is as if the movement their mother
had enacted in going about her fecundating work were now
endlessly multiplied as the embodiments of marine life—the
Nereids—surface all around them to manifest their desire
and joy; and the seemingly incongruent simile of the busy
bees, which momentarily distracts us from the particular
oceanic scene, actually serves to compound the choral animation of which the newborn goddesses are the focus. What we
thus get, esthetically speaking, is the figuration of a blissful
plenitude of being such as Dante himself was envisaging in
his *Paradiso*—especially where he depicts the joyful motions
of the blessed spirits as bees swarming around flowers.[15] The
paradisal aspect of *Le Grazie* as a poem has not escaped Mario
Fubini, who also happens to single out for praise the honeybees passage I am discussing; and there is no need to emphasize Foscolo's addiction to Dante. "Paradise," in Foscolo's case, cannot obviously be what it ontologically was for
a man of Dante's transcendent faith; paradise is the fulfillment of nature's possibilities on the esthetic level, and when
these possibilities are realized it is because the Graces are
present, man's true creation and hope. At that rare juncture
in history, beauty is truth and truth is beauty, as Foscolo
shows in his elaborate attempts to follow the Graces in their
journey through Greece and then in their migration to Renaissance Italy after the Turkish invasion of their original Hellenic homeland.

This is no doubt the least successful part of the poem, nor

---

[15] Dante, *Divine Comedy*, Par. XXXI, 4-12.

does it help to have the bees narratively allegorized as the material carriers of poetry's honey from the Ionian to the Tyrrhenian shores, despite the outstanding moments of poetic achievement to be gleaned. But the first buzz of those bees in the gloriously Homeric simile we have been scanning has the surprise and the ex-post-facto inevitability of great poetry, as the careful listener can find out for himself by first taking in the total music of these lines and then singling out for analysis the notes and chords that go into the making of that rich harmony: whirring alliterations on *r* phonemes and *ro* syllables, proparoxytone verse endings (five in a row) that somehow prolong the "buzzing" effect and introduce a phantom rhyme into the blank verse poem, effective diereses and hiatuses that enhance the felt duration of some lines. Later on in the poem (Hymn II), in the very midst of some strenuous effort to provide allegorical support for the narrative framework already mentioned, this early felicity will be echoed by a similarly experimental passage which manages to transcend its allegorical functionalism for the sake of its words' intrinsic music:

Però che quando su la Grecia inerte
Marte sfrenò le tartare cavalle
Depredatrici, e coronò la schiatta
Barbara d'Ottomano, allor l'Italia
Fu giardino alle Muse; e qui lo stuolo
Fabro dell'aureo mel pose a sua prole
Il felice alvear. Né le divine
Api (sebben le altre api abbia crudeli)
Fuggono i lai dell'invisibil Ninfa
Che ognor del*usa* d' amo*rosa speme*
Pur *geme* per le quete aure *diffusa*
E il suo altero nemico *ama* e rich*iama*;
Tanta dolcezza infusero le Grazie
Per pieta' della Ninfa alle sue voci
Che le lor api immemori dell'opra
Ozïose in Italia odono l'eco

Che al par de'canti fe' dolce la rima.

For, when upon Greece's motionless body
Mars unleashed the Tartar mares eager for prey,
And gave her crown to Ottoman's barbarians,
Then Italy became the Muses' garden;
And here the swarm that makes the golden honey
Placed its plentiful hive for its own offspring.
Nor do the divine bees (unlike the others)
Cruelly flee from the laments of the unseen
Nymph who ever deluded by love's hope
Keeps effusing herself into the still
Air through her wails, and calls and again calls
Her haughty enemy; the Graces in their mercy
Infused such a sweetness into the Nymph's voice
That their bees, utterly mindless of their work,
Idling in Italy intently hear
The echo that, with song, made rhyme so sweet.[16]

Auditory craftsmanship, by interweaving internal rhymes
(in the words italicized by me), evokes the classical figure of
Ovidian Echo as the mythical source of that exclusively Romance, and conspicuously Italian prosodic phenomenon:
rhyme. By making words echo one another in intersecting
chains within and across the individual lines rather than at
line ends, Foscolo achieves several effects in one. He musically conjures the "invisible Nymph" Echo, who is sheer disembodied voice, and makes her part of a new myth of his invention to "explain" the transformation poetry underwent by
migrating from Hellas to Italy. Likewise Goethe, in the
Helena episode of *Faust* Part II, has Faust teach the Greek
beauty to talk and sing in rhyming couplets instead of
hexameters—a more extended case of the same dramatic
mimesis in the service of the historical imagination. At the

[16] *Le Grazie*, Hymn II (Vesta), lines 264-80, p. 60 *Opere di F.*; lines
182-98, pp. 125-26, *Dall'Ortis alle Grazie*; lines 478-94, pp. 182-84,
Le Grazie, ed. crit. (reproducing the Leghorn *Quadernone* draft).

The "divine" (or, in Chiarini's choice, "Phoebean") bees
are, as we saw, allegorical, a far cry from the sensuously perceived creatures of the first passage; the Florence manuscripts show endless revisions through which Foscolo tried to
reconcile the cultural burden imposed upon this image with
an iconic vividness that would rescue the lines from artistic
inertia. He ended by discarding any sensuous element and
banking on the spiritually and musically suggestive word
"immemori" (unmindful, forgetful) to the advantage of narrative precision: the "divine" insects immigrating from Greece
are spellbound by the new music they hear in Italy, as
Helena, in Goethe's graceful fantasy, was charmed by Faust's
troubadour rhymes to change her venerable metric mode. The
bravura piece testifies to Foscolo's rhythmical prowess; but a
look at some of the intermediate drafts may make us regret
the sacrifice of imagistic felicity his narrative structure
exacted. In one of the variants, the line "che le lor api immemori dell'opra" was "che le lor api immemori dell'*alba*," a
miracle of sound, image, and meaning. *Alba* (dawn) contains
all the needed semantic suggestiveness of *opra* (work), plus a
visual and aural power that makes the other choice sound flat

---

Chiarini integrated in his own critical edition but Orlando and Pagliai do
not, Tasso's madness is described at the end in four lines directly quoted
from Tasso's own *Aminta*, a pastoral play successfully performed at the
Ferrara court long before the unhappy author fell a prey to intermittent lu-
nacy. The three identical rhymes in *riso* (laughter) are of special interest
because they represent still another way of introducing rhyme into the
rhymeless poem without breaking the overall convention. A quote is
privileged but alien space within the prosodic space of the whole project,
and here it functions as the speaker's corner of rhyme. Since we know from
Foscolo's critical essays how highly he valued Tasso's poetry, which according to him was the last great flowering of Italian Renaissance literature,
followed by a huge historical gap, the deft insertion of perfect rhyme in this
floating passage acquires overtones of a final consummation of poetical
creativeness, rhyme clearly standing, in Foscolo's context, for Italian
poetry as such. While understanding Orlando's philological scruples, we
may view with some sympathy Chiarini's boldness in rescuing the passage
from its limbal status for the sake of the narrative and structural progression it set up if juxtaposed as a sequel to the Echo cum bees passage.

by comparison. Likewise, the following line, "ozïose in Italia odono l'eco," has superseded two alternative drafts which gave body to those honeybees:

Sovra l'ali sospese odono l'eco

Hovering on still wings they hear the echo

Alïando su l'alba odono l'eco

Winging around toward dawn they hear the echo

Foscolo's only excuse for sacrificing poetical life to overall design was his preoccupation with total coherence—a concern not to be silenced, after all, when the seminal nuclei of the poem in progress kept growing and interfering and he, the addict to Pindaric transitions, tried to turn from acrobat to architect.

Fortunately for the poetry, those ubiquitous bees do eventually make themselves heard and seen on their own in Hymn II in such a way as to make good the promise of that initial simile in Hymn I where they teemed with a life that for a moment threatened to invade the whole macrocosmic scene. When they function as mere narrative vehicles for a review, in bold foreshortening, of Greek and then Italian poetry from Petrarch and Dante to Tasso, the sleight of hand fails and the awkwardness is hardly redeemed by the incidental flashes of poetry about poetry; they do remain incidental. But when the bees buzz over the flowers that Cornelia Martinetti tends in her garden near Bologna, at the end of Part II of the second Hymn, they regain poetical status as her live aura and mysterious projection. We should sense this even if we did not know from Foscolo's letters and biography[18] how impressed

---

[18] For instance, the letter numbered 1207 by Plinio Carli in *Epistolario* IV. It was written from Florence between August 19 and 20, 1812, shortly after Foscolo's visit to Cornelia Martinetti in Bologna. It is so nobly passionate and self-descriptive that it takes its place with some of Foscolo's

he was by a visit to the lovely and learned Bolognese apiculturist right at the time *The Graces* entered gestation, Bologna
being for him a way station to his own Eden, Florence. Cornelia, unnamed but clearly identified, lives forever in this
terrestrial paradise of hers where, as a priestess of nature's
vegetal and minute animal presences, she has taught him and
us to listen to its secret voices. Literary stereotype—bees as
the makers of poetry's honey—thus melts into concrete esthetic experience as our poet recasts it into an original image
that both "means" and "is." The priestess of bees actualizes
that rare harmony between nature and culture which is the
perennially lost paradise of mankind. In her, rather than just
through her as the poem's design would have it, we come to
see what the Graces are; she is one of their incarnations, like
the two other women artists (musician Eleonora Nencini and
dancer Maddalena Bignami) who take turns at the altar of
Venus in a breathless interval of history.

The thematic ramifications of one image across narrative
boundaries have led us to digress from that early passage in
Hymn I where the joint theophany of the Graces and their
parent goddess seemed to have, poetically speaking, such an
arresting power. The digression was by no means arbitrary,
for to pursue close analysis of *The Graces*, in whatever direction, is to enter the workshop of poetry. But now let us return
to the theophany. Whether on the microcosmic scale of the
honeybees simile or on the oceanic scale in which the
Nereids move "surfacing through the immense radiance of
waves," the theme is teeming life, propagating joy. This propels the rhythm of sixteen hendecasyllables that sustain their
airy song without crowding their syntactical space—one

---

best lyrics as a poetical self-portrait, while also documenting a seminal
moment and motif of the creative process that will lead to the composition
of *The Graces* before long. In particular one should note the theme of conscious renunciation, already operative years before in Foscolo's relationship to Isabella Roncioni when completing *Ortis*. This theme pervades the
whole conception of *The Graces*. As for biographical studies relevant to this
phase of F.'s life, the most recent at this writing (1978) is Mandruzzato, E.

sweeping sentence, nimbly articulated into subordinate and coordinate units. Free erotic overtones arise, of particular importance in a poem that wavers between repression and sublimation of Eros. Apart from that, the passage curiously anticipates the fin-de-siècle paintings of Arnold Böcklin, an artist who knew Italy well but need not have derived his pagan mythology, whether of the joyously marine or of the funereal sort, from a reading of Foscolo's poem. But there it is: painting comes to mind, and the detail of the violet and of the dark red roses changing to white, like similar touches in the depiction of Cornelia's garden in Hymn II, makes us realize that color, the final mark of visual delight, has entered Foscolo's verbal cosmos in *The Graces*.

Nor is this newly found pleasure necessarily tied to symbolic functions, as happens in part of Hymn III; the brushwork connotes a richer poetics, and as such it is an integrating value of the whole picture, not a mere token of semantic values. In his endeavor to represent the possibility of existence as esthetic fruition, the poet put all his feelers out, in the musical as well as in the pictorial sphere, whereas the earlier affinity, for the author of the *Odes* and of the *Sepulchers*, had been to sculpture. A remarkable fact, when we consider that one direct stimulation for *The Graces* had come precisely from two statues Antonio Canova had just completed and, respectively, projected: a Venus put in the Uffizi gallery to replace the Venus de Milo that Napoleon had taken away to France, and a group of the three Graces, still in progress when Foscolo wrote his poem of the same title. Canova, besides, is addressed at the beginning of Hymn I and invited to join the propitiatory ritual for the Graces at Bellosguardo, Foscolo's Florentine *buen retiro*; further on, Hymn II encourages Canova to immortalize fleeting beauty in marble, while directly after addressing him at the outset the poet's persona has this to say to him in friendly emulation:

Forse (o ch'io spero!) artefice di numi
Nuovo meco darai spirto alle Grazie

Che or di tua man sorgon dal marmo: anch'io
Pingo e la vita a'miei fantasmi inspiro;
Sdegno il verso che suona e che non crea;
Perché Febo mi disse: io Fidia primo
Ed Apelle guidai con la mia lira.

Perhaps (it is my hope!) you, maker of gods,
With me will breathe new life into the Graces
That your hand is eliciting from the marble:
I, too, paint and infuse life into my phantoms;
I scorn the verse that rings and does not create;
For Phoebus told me: I first gave guidance
To Pheidias and to Apelles with my lyre.[19]

More than the claim for poetry's primacy over the visual
arts, which according to a diehard Neoclassic prejudice
needed to borrow their subjects from literature, what matters
here is the poet's choice of a verb like *pingo* (I paint) to describe his competition with the famous sculptor in tackling an
identical theme. A few lines above, at the very beginning,
Foscolo had prayed the three virgin goddesses to grant him
l'armoniosa melodia pittrice, the harmonious melody that
paints [their] beauty. The music of good verse should never
be an end unto itself but should create an image, which in
turn is envisaged as analogous to painterly, not sculptural
form. In *The Graces*, significantly, one long-wrought passage
referring to the musician lady of Florence mentions Raphael
as painter (as well as architect), and Apelles the Greek
painter represents his art in the quote under scrutiny. *The
Sepulchers* had no room for painters in its hall of fame, for
Michelangelo there appears strictly as the author of St. Pe-
ter's dome. More cogently, the Hymn I passage evoking the

[19] *Le Grazie*, Hymn I (to Venus), lines 21-27 in Chiarini's edition as followed by Puppo in *Opere di F.*, p. 43. The numbering is 20-26 in the most
advanced draft of the Leghorn MS (*Quadernone*), which Orlando reproduces
at pp. 165-66 of his critical edition; Orlando keeps the same numbering in
Dall'Ortis alle Grazie, p. 106.

appearance of Venus and the Graces in the ocean has the
younger threesome seated on a floating seashell. It is reasonable to infer that the visual cue for this stylization came from
Botticelli's *Birth of Venus* and *Spring*, which Foscolo could
hardly avoid seeing at the Uffizi. (The latter masterpiece contains the three Graces.)

Not that the poem's dedication to Canova, and the addresses to him in the completed parts of the text, should be
considered perfunctory, for at pages 5-6 of the manuscript
packet marked *Registro Mors* (or Fascicolo IV) in Florence's
National Library[20] we find three diary-like passages of prose
jotted down on August 31, and September 1, 1812, to record
Foscolo's response to Canova's Venus. They are lively in
themselves, and they document a contributory stimulation
toward the poem in the making, at the crucial first phase. I
translate the passages from my own reading:

August 31
The new Venus really is a wonderful thing! she does not
radiate divinity as the other one does, or that heavenly
harmony: but it looks as if Canova feared the awesome
confrontation of art with the Greek sculptor; so that he
did indeed grace his Venus with all those charms that
effuse a somewhat terrene aura but more easily move my
heart, itself made of clay: and I remember that in the
past years I worshiped that other Venus for several
weeks: but the second time I saw this one I have sat
down near her all alone sighing with a thousand desires
and a thousand memories in my soul —

September
The Venus de Medici was a most beautiful goddess; and
this one I'm looking and looking at again, is a most vo-

[20] The same MS packet also contains (pp. 7-10) a variant of the foreword
to F.'s translation of Sterne's *Sentimental Journey*, and eight pages (14-21)
of initial worksheets of *Le Grazie*, plus fragments of two tragedies (*Ajace* &
Ricciarda) partly coeval to that project.

luptuous woman: the former made me hope for paradise outside this world: and this one flatters me that I can grasp (contemplate) paradise even in this valley of tears—Canova seems to me to have excelled himself, in the voluptuous attitude of the neck, in the amorous modesty of the visage and above all of the eyes: and in the lovable turn of the head—O what! have I too become the kind that prattles of fine arts?

September 1

And last night as happens I had been in a short while nauseated with a certain company so magnificently distinguished of gentlemen and ladies—none of whom was beautiful, and most of them were old—and the gentlemen were agreeing with one another; and the women chatting less softly were malevolently pitying many women I did not know, and whom I don't care to know as worthy of pity and satire . . . But there was in a secluded corner of that hall the softest and most candid face in the world, and the most gracefully plaited hair, and a forehead bordering on the heavenly, and a pair of eyes bold and modest at the same time, and a virgin mouth on which I would have just sighed without daring to kiss it—and all those lovely things in one head that said no words; and she scarcely let me tell her a few nice words under my breath, and replied by nods so that nobody would hear us:—come, womanizer, come, and she might have let you kiss her: but my lips will get cold, for she is a woman sculpted by Canova, and purchased by the Queen of conversation, or placed I think to keep company to motionless and silent men, as I sometimes am in certain places—

In Foscolo's mind, the replacement of the ancient Hellenic statue by Canova's Neoclassic masterpiece became a mythical event: the translation of idea into flesh, of otherworldly beauty into tangible and seductive womanly shape, and the

intensity with which he experiences the event at a time when
Le Grazie is in full gestation contributes to rekindle his imagination for that comprehensive task. We remember the poetical process by which Venus, conceived at first as a diffuse
cosmic force in Lucretian vein, takes on a more definite
shape until she "appears" with her anthropomorphic emanations the Graces (Canova, in the first of the above diary entries, is said to have embellished his Venus with those *graces*
(grazie) that effuse a terrene aura etc). The barely contained
eroticism displayed in the writer's response to Canova's
statue will also find a counterpart all over the poem in progress, where the Graces' beauty is said to arouse human desire
and to be sheltered from it by the veil other goddesses will
weave. This esthetic balance whereby (as Sir Kenneth Clark
would gladly note) desire is both enhanced and suspended
characterizes human response to the pure image, and it is the
sublimation on which *Le Grazie* thematically thrives. Raw
Love, in that poem's mythology, is said to be a destructive
force, the equivalent of the Earthshaker Enosigaeus on the
psychic level. Eros and Thanatos seem to be in Foscolo's
conception the prime enemies of man, nestling in man, and
ever ready to break out on a rampage unless held in check—
by the civilizing, the sublimating agent, the "Graces." Much
as it might sound facile and modish to underline the nearly
Freudian character of Foscolo's cathartic mythology, we are
justified in seeing here an anticipation of sorts. In this regard
one has to take into account one of Foscolo's chief philosophical sources: the germane materialist anthropology of
Machiavelli, Hobbes and Vico.

Even in the diary jottings that were to prove so seminal to
the far-reaching poetical project, Foscolo is not seeing the
statue as a statue, but converting it into a live womanly presence, and with her he establishes a secret rapport in the very
midst of the frivolous, madding crowd. To our new Pygmalion
beauty thus becomes a religious experience, whose numinous
overtones make themselves heard all over the poem. Marble
has become flesh; the flesh, in turn, will become word. Cano-

va's sculpture has merely served as a cue for the poet's own "pictorial melody," and it will act in the poem as a spark, rather than as a ready-made object to be literally transposed into the verbal medium. The intensity of that religious tête-à-tête in mundane circumstances passes into the preliminary drafts for *Le Grazie*'s opening passage at pages 17 ff. of the *Registro Mors:*

Di così lieto carme al cor mi fea
Dono la Grazia che d'eterno riso
                    ~~ridente e altera~~
~~Invisibili a tutti e a noi splendenti~~
Con le nude sorelle inghirlandate
E invisibili ~~a tutti, e a noi splendenti~~
~~Vidi danzar~~ vid'io agli altri, intorno al marmo
della loro regina, io veggo spesso
Carolar mollemente, e del tuo nome
Fan lieta l'ara, o mio Canova, o questi
Mirteti, e il fiume, e il puro aer tranquillo,
di Bellosguardo onde già un dí guardando
l'immenso regno delle belle ~~(selve? belve?)~~

Of such a gladsome song the Grace made a gift
To my heart whom with eternal laughter
                    ~~laughing and proud~~
~~Invisible to all and to us shining~~
With her naked sisters crowned with their garlands
And invisibl~~e to all, and to us shining~~
~~Dancing I saw dance~~ to the others, around the marble
Of their queen, I often see
Dance in soft roundelays, and with your name
They brighten the altar, o my Canova, and these
Myrtle groves, and the river, and the pure calm air
of Bellosguardo from where once overlooking
the immense realm of the lovely? woods? beasts?

In the early fragments, clearly coeval to the diary pages,

Canova's statue becomes a mere occasion to arouse the creative contemplator's imagination into descrying the dancing
presences of the Graces, which are anything but sculptural:

> Al simulacro della lor regina
> Recan gigli e colombe, e di lor mano
> Le chiome della fresca onda stillanti
> Tergendo vanno . . .

> To the graven image of their queen
> They bring lilies and doves, and with their hands
> They rinse the hair dripping with the cool waters . . .

As the writer warms up to his subject, the evocation takes on
all those pictorially impalpable, sensuous yet atmospheric
traits which sculpture excludes; and the craftsman's ear
counsels the eager pen with ever more exacting insistence to
make sure that the evocation gains power through rhythmical
and iconic accuracy; yet individually perfect lines are jotted
down and crossed out before they manage to round themselves out in complete phrases, then tried again for variations:

> Invisibili agli altri, a me splendenti
> Veggo sovente carolar;—discorre
> ~~Fragranza soavissima dal crine;~~
> ~~E invisibile agli altri, a me splendenti~~
> ~~Scorre l'ambrosia, e degli eterni rai~~
> Da le lor membra l'armonia d'Amore,
> E del roseo splendor mite dell'alba
> ride l'aere a que'sguardi, e spira intorno
> D'ambrosia soavissima frangranza.

> Invisible to the others, to me shining
> I often see [them] dance roundelays; there issues forth
> ~~The sweetest fragrance from their hair;~~
> ~~And invisible to the others, to me shining~~

~~Ambrosia flows, and of the eternal eyes~~
From their limbs the harmony of Love,
And with the rosy mild splendor of the dawn
the air smiles at those glances, and effuses
The sweetest fragrance of ambrosia around.

As the experiment branches out, testing, discarding or
rearranging its incidental visual and rhythmical discoveries,
the persistent idea of the persona's exclusive communing with
the goddesses (which stems from the diary prose pages we
saw) broadens to include the fellow artist and rival, Canova,
whose very creation the poet is appropriating for his own purposes, like the verbal Pygmalion he is:

Pettine a ricomporle in lunghe anella
Mollemente le scevra; e un'altra ai vanni
Di Zefiro l'umore ond'è irrorato
Il verecondo sen [lesta?] consegna
acciò per le celesti aure il diffonda

La terza Grazia intanto il vel compone
Su le divine membra, ed a' profani
Occhi contende i vezzi onde piú cari
A noi Canova, a noi splendano intatti:
Ed io come dal mar tu la traesti
                    ~~ciel~~

                              ~~dea~~
Cosí conversi al ciel veggo la santa
Genitrice d'Amore. Scorre al velo
In quelle membra l'armonia d'Amore
E del vago splendor mite dell'alba
Ride l'aere a' suoi sguardi, e spicca intorno
D'ambrosia soavissima fragranza.

. . . Comb to recompose them into long curls
Softly parts them; and another to the wings

Of Zephyrus aptly entrusts the dew that wets
Her pure bosom, that he may spread in turn
The liquid essence into heaven's space

Meanwhile the third Grace adjusts the veil
On the divine limbs, thereby sheltering
From profane eyes the charms so that they may
Shine intact just for us, Canova: and I
Such as you brought her forth out of the ~~sky~~ sea

Thus her eyes turned to the sky I see the ~~goddess~~ holy
Mother of Love. There flows to the veil
In those limbs the very harmony of Love
And with the delicate splendor of dawn
The air smiles at her glances, and effuses
The sweetest fragrance of ambrosia around.[21]

Despite residual uncertainties of small account, something
like an organic moment of vision has now taken shape, provisional though it will turn out to be in the dynamics of *Le
Grazie*'s growth; the tireless prodding of Foscolo's taskmaster
ear has brought results, for the alternately compact and lissome lines succeed in delineating a lovely group in motion.
Those vague presences, the Graces, have now been caught in
midair and gathered as a chorus of individualized gestures
around their cynosure mother, who, with them, becomes the
focus of a sunrise. What we have been following as we re-
traced the inchoate poem's steps on the *Registro Mors'* porous
pages is more than the genesis of one good fragment, for this
fragment amounts to an essential theophany, and even more,
to the process of formal individuation whereby an artist's
mind can progressively define the liberating vision, through
fidelity to his craft, out of the first vague conjuring. The goddesses are seen as the eye of their creator captures them, as
his hand draws them out of the native element; of himself he

[21] These and all other translations of Foscolo's verse and prose, whether
taken from the manuscripts or from available editions, are mine.

can say, as Paul Valéry later would, "et mes yeux sont ouverts."[22]

In the final draft, which is to be taken from the Leghorn *Quadernone* and the marginal variants later published in the English *Dissertazione*, the artist's persona disappeared to let his objectified vision stand on its own as a fit climax to the whole sequence of Venus and the Graces rising from the sea to reanimate the elements of water, air, and earth. After a few lines telling the origin of the ritual offerings of milk, white roses and pearls for the advent of Spring, here is the final tableau:

> L'una tosto a la Dea col radïante
> Pettine asterge mollemente e intreccia
> Le chiome de l'azzurra onda stillanti.
> L'altra ancella a le pure aure concede
> A rifiorire i prati a primavera,
> L'ambrosio umore ond'è irrorato il petto
> De la figlia di Giove; vereconda
> La lor sorella ricompone il peplo
> Su le membra divine, e le contende
> Di que'mortali attoniti al desìo.

> One right away clears delicately and plaits
> With the gleaming comb the hair of the Goddess
> As it still drips with the ocean's blue wave.
> The other attendant dispenses to the air
> So that it may cause the meadows to blossom

---

[22] "Veille; ta forme veille, et mes yeux sont ouverts" (Wake, your form is awake, and my eyes are open). This is the last line of Paul Valéry's *La dormeuse* (The Sleeping Girl), in the section *Charmes* of his collected poems (P.V., *Poésies*: Paris, Gallimard, 1942, p. 104). In general, Valéry's cognitive interpretation of classical mythology, his love for the sun-filled Mediterranean scene, and his sensuous yet experimental imagery couched in strict measures, offer some pointed resemblance to Foscolo's. It would not be far-fetched to take Valéry as a touchstone of our claim that Foscolo, especially in *The Graces*, anticipates some aspects of *Symboliste* poetics.

Again in Spring, the ambrosial moisture bedewing
The bosom of Zeus' daughter; bashfully
Their sister rearranges then the peplum
On the divine limbs, and thereby shelters them
From the desire of those astonished mortals.

Evolving into its definitive shape and narrative juncture,
the theophanic tableau has heightened its pictorial quality by
adding color and light effects, though it has shed the sunrise
aura and the olfactory miracle, which inhere in so many other
parts of the total composition (but the initial *Splendea* with its
attendant marine and terrestrial effects already contained the
essence of dawn and its colors). A subtler touch supersedes
the earlier experiment when our poet at one stroke removes
himself, Canova, and the cosmic halo-cum-ambrosial-fra-
grance from his achieved vision to let it reverberate in the
astonishment of those primitive humans who have now become the witnesses of this miracle, and its intended bene-
ficiaries. The transition from privacy to communion is well on
its way; the artist is no longer concerned with his own exclusive enjoyment of the vision that remains inaccessible (*"in-
visibile"*) to the other men and that he has consciously brought
forth to share it with a few connoisseurs or fellow artists; he
instead tests that vision on mankind at large. Mankind, in
fact, at its rawest; for all of a sudden a feat of dramatic insight
has a chorus of Hobbesian savages, of Viconian "bestioni
tutti stupore e ferocia" (big beasts all stupor and ferociousness) confront the splendor they do not understand, the spectacle of grace made visible as if from above but actually from
the depths of their own unknowing hearts.

Grace, beauty, the values so aptly embodied by those Hellenic deities in the midst of a murderous struggle for survival
that leaves little room for them, are the revelation of human
possibilities beyond sheer subsistence, and as such they appear incommensurable to the human, but really not yet quite
human animal. This incommensurability between the civilizing force and its reluctant subject, aboriginal man, is not

glossed over by Foscolo, who accordingly manages to sustain the tragic tension of his "paradisal" vision. The revelation of form, a task entrusted to the artist but with human society as its constant destination, will never be achieved until society as a whole participates, and not just as recipients; and society has its endless relapses, as *Le Grazie* intermittently deplores with throwbacks to the ravages of contemporary history in Europe. Santayana will later say that the realm of essences, "spirit," has no material power yet it alone gives a worthy sense to human life; and no better comment could be devised for Foscolo's last poem, which comes very close to claiming for poets the role of unacknowledged legislators of mankind:

Non prieghi d'inni o danze d'imenei
Ma de'veltri perpetuo l'ululato
Tutta l'isola udía, e un suon di dardi
E gli uomini sul vinto orso rissosi,
E de'piagati cacciatori il grido.
Cerere invan donato avea l'aratro
A' quei feroci; invan d'oltre l'Eufrate
Chiamò un dí Bassareo, giovane dio,
A ingentilir di pampini le rupi.
Il pio strumento irruginia su' brevi
Solchi, sdegnato; divorata, innanzi
Che i grappoli recenti imporporasse
A'raj d'autunno, era la vite: e solo
Quando apparian le Grazie, i cacciatori
E le vergini squallide e i fanciulli
L'arco e il terror deponean, ammirando.

No hymning prayers and no nuptial dances
Did the whole island hear, but a perpetual
Howling of hounds instead, and whirring arrows
And men quarreling over the killed bear,
And the cry of the wounded hunters. Ceres
In vain had made a gift of the plough to those
Ferocious creatures; in vain from beyond

The Euphrates did she call one day Dionysus,
A young god, to adorn the rocks with the grapevine.
Rejected, the pious tool rusted on the short
Furrows; the grapes were devoured on the vine
Before the autumnal sun had any chance
To empurple them: and only when the Graces
Appeared, hunters and unkempt maidens and boys
Would let go of the bow and of their fear
By admiration's rapture overwhelmed.[23]

These lines immediately pick up the cue from the theophany climax, "from the desire of those astonished mortals," to make the island of Cythera an epitome of the whole world in its anthropological infancy. If it were not too pompous, one might conceivably coin the word "anthropogenesis" to denote the sense of the new evolutionary cycle that begins when the old one has just completed itself. Venus the earth goddess (and she is recurrently designated as "mother goddess" throughout the poem) had brought life to the chaotic world of Enosigaeus the earth-shaker; now through her emanations the Graces she begins to instill form into the violent, half-brutish humans of prehistoric times; the cycle moves, on each respective level, from formlessness to form, from dull violence to harmony. Harmony pervades Foscolo's poem as the comprehensive term for whatever higher integration of forces, and revelation of form, can occur in the universe at the cosmic or psychic level; it is the supreme value, manifested by those deities our poet envisages as so many embodiments of the Eternal Feminine, his true godhead, forever pitted against the destructive masculine principle which epitomizes aggressiveness. One should note how dominantly

---

[23] *Le Grazie*, Hymn I, lines 102-17 in Chiarini's edition as reproduced in *Opere di F.*, pp. 45-46; lines 101-15, with minor variants, in *Le Grazie, ed. crit.*, p. 168. The passage reached final form in Foscolo's *Dissertation on an ancient hymn to the Graces* (London: 1822), in "Outline, Engravings and Descriptions of the Woburn Abbey Marbles." For more details, see *Dall'Ortis alle Grazie*, pp. 135-36, footnote.

feminine Foscolo's pantheon is, and how self-contained in its
avatars; it does not even seem to need a masculine counterpart to express erotic attraction, for that attraction occurs entirely between Graces and Nereids, Nereids and Venus, and
so forth, and when male desire appears in the form of Cythera's "astonished mortals," it is held at bay. Foscolo recasts
the ancient mythology to create a personal myth of his own,
and this myth strangely recalls, and contrasts with, William
Blake's. There seems to be little chance for a marriage of
heaven and hell in the Foscolian universe; the poles of energy
and form, male and female principle, Yang and Yin, cannot
meet or merge, they can only sustain a tense antinomy, which
now and then may be suspended in moments of fleeting contact.

Harmony, civilization, is not inevitable and it is precarious
even when achieved, being forever threatened by the erup-
tions of aggressiveness and unchecked libido (what Foscolo
repeatedly indicates as disruptive Love). Hence the "miraculous" nature of the civilizing process at its outset: when the
Graces appear to the prehistoric barbarians, the latter stand
agape, wishing but not daring to reach out for the revealed
beauty that awes them like children, they are "astonished"
and later on they will suspend aggressive activity to take in
the marvel, by *admiring* ("ammirando"). The *miracle* happens through ad-*miration*, and it is beginning to change them
for the better. On the other hand, this development is only
possible, not necessary, as the poem shows by dramatizing its
catastrophic alternative in the narrative sequel to the Cythera
passage. Venus and the Graces leave the privileged island for
the Greek continent, and they come across the isthmus of
Laconia which is inhabited by a fierce race of cannibals. Instead of yielding to rapture at the divine apparition, they
react by viciously attacking, and they are accordingly
punished by annihilation:

. . . Ancor Citera
Del golfo intorno non sedea regina:

Dove or miri le vele alte su l'onda,
Pendea negra una selva, ed esiliato
N'era ogni dio da' figli della terra
Duellanti a predarsi; e i vincitori
D'umane carni s'imbandian convito.
Videro il cocchio e misero un ruggito
Palleggiando la clava. Al petto strinse
Sotto il suo manto accolte, le tremanti
Sue giovinette, e: Ti sommergi, o selva!
Venere disse, e fu sommersa . . .

. . . Cythera did not yet
Sit queenlike over the surrounding gulf:
Where one now sees the sails high on the waves,
A dark wood overhung, with no gods allowed
By earth's children perpetually intent
On fighting one another for prey's sake;
And the winners would banquet on human flesh.
They saw the chariot and broke into a roar
Wielding their clubs. Hugging her trembling
Girls to her bosom, Venus said: "Now sink,
O forest!" and it sank . . .

To make the point that this did not dispose of man's ever resurgent destructive instinct, and that actually our cannibal
ancestors still lurk within us, the poem goes on:

. . . . Ahi tali
Forse eran tutti i primi avi dell'uomo!
Quindi in noi serpe, ahi miseri, un natio
Delirar di battaglia; e se pietose
Nol placano le Dee, spesso riarde
Ostentando trofeo l'ossa fraterne.
Ch'io non le veggia almeno or che in Italia
Fra le messi biancheggiano insepolte![24]

---

[24] Lines 132-50 of the Chiarini edition as reproduced in *Opere di F.*, p.

. . . . Such, alas,
Were perhaps all of man's first ancestors!
Hence in us, poor wretches, there creeps a native
Frenzy of battle; and if the compassionate
Goddesses do not soothe it, often it flares up
To flaunt as trophy the fraternal bones.
Oh let me not see them now as they whiten,
Unburied among the wheat, the Italian fields!

With dramatic suddenness the poetic "I" breaks through
the epic fiction to reassert the urgency of present history as it
both spurs on and threatens the writing itself. From the im-
memorial past of the race he has been evoking, catastrophe
recalls catastrophe repeatedly to interrupt the vision of divine
serenity, and the rapt gaze of remote savages, subdued by
beauty, is lost in the turmoil of fury ancient and new. Contemplation is shattered by a cry of horror as the whiteness
dawning on the evoker's horizon is no longer that of
spellbound sails on a sea that seemed to have submerged the
dark wood of bestiality forever, but that of unburied bones
from recent battles on native soil: Moscow has burned, what
is left of the *Grande Armée* has retreated to the Elbe, Leipzig
soon relegates Napoleon to a Tuscan island, and the hostile
armies of Austria and Russia approach once again the Italian
homeland where they had left grisly traces of their intrusion
between Trafalgar and Marengo, at the start of the new century. We should note the gap between the fulfilled miracle of
timeless vision and the cry that rends it asunder to bring us
back, with the anguished persona, to the menacing present
he could only intermittently exorcize.

It is Jacopo Ortis rather than Didymus speaking here,
though in a letter to a friend, dating from those fateful years,
the poet said that he was no longer Ortis, nor Didymus, nor

46; and lines 130-48 in Orlando's edition at P. 110 of *Dall'Ortis alle
Grazie*. The text, in all these cases, conforms to the 1822 *Dissertation*, and
all editors assign the passage to Hymn i.

Ugo.[25] The impending catastrophe, and the sense of his own impotence to avert it, may have caused him to feel something like a temporary loss of identity, for if European history was about to enter a no-man's land, the passionate witness could hardly help being involved. The qualitative leap from mythic past to painful contemporary reality, and from objective vision to first person utterance, amounts to a formal break only if we adopt the restrictive convention of genre and forget that, like Dante in the *Comedy* and Pound in the *Cantos*, Foscolo is recasting mythic epos for confessional purposes; his transition from primordial beauty and terror to shared present-day anguish parallels Dante's powerful rhetorical shift from objective narration to personal invective, and Pound's deprecatory or prayerful outbreaks in the midst of the *Cantos'* vast tapestry, China or America, Italy or Provence or Greece, from the wreckage of Europe the "ego scriptor" pulling down his vanity. Ugo could do no less.

The verse sequence we have been surveying goes all the way from theogony and theophany to human history in its genesis and unfolding, to a *Goetterdaemmerung* of sorts. Thematic scope goes hand in hand with tonal modulation and rhythmic versatility in this exemplary part of the Hymn to Venus, what follows having remained, in Orlando's view, at a more or less unperfected stage. And the mythopoeic impulse keeps feeding imagery, existentially as well as topically significant. A mother goddess re-emerges from her native element the sea, enriched with offspring, and she submerges there the dark wood with its horrid inhabitants; islands repeatedly become the focus of scenery and action; the world's amniotic fluid brings out and reabsorbs life. Dante and Homer are part of the semantic resonance, since our poet openly acknowledges their normativeness; but they act as arousers of creativity, not as its constrainers. Seeking perfection, fulfilled form, paradise on the one hand, the poem con-

---

[25] Letter to Sigismondo Trechi, dated October 11, 1813 (in *Epistolario* IV, p. 389): "I make no verse, out of rage. . . . By now I am neither Ugo, nor Ortis, nor Didymus."

currently delves into the atavic darkness, and in so doing it
becomes prophetic much as *The Sepulchers* had done. In the
first two decades of the nineteenth century Ugo Foscolo is poetically voicing the European mind's growing concern with
collective genealogy; that century was going to be (among
other things) the century of anthropological history, of paleon-
tology and ethnology, and if *The Sepulchers* had prophesied
Schliemann, *The Graces* forecasts the coming of Darwin and
the discovery of the cavemen's relics.

In bringing to light the submerged atavistic monsters, the
poem of course relies on time-tested tools for that perilous
fathoming. We have mentioned Homer and Dante in this regard, but the Bible plays its part in the game. The confrontation between Venus the mother goddess and the man-eating
reprobates elicits a phrasing which in its graphic concision
recalls—and equals—that of the Old Testament depicting
Jahveh in the act of creation, "God said, Let there be light,
And there was light." Punitive destruction in the Bible is
likewise treated with a syntactic speed that abolishes all
causal intermediaries between sin and penalty, since God's
will acts instantaneously. In Foscolo's poem, Venus at the
same time shows a Madonna-like protectiveness for her
daughters, whom she shelters under her mantle, and a
numinous power quite unimpaired by the process of humanization which Foscolian deities have to undergo. But
when, at the outset, she overruns creation, it is hard to avoid
comparison with Jahveh hovering over the waters. The choral
animation around the seashell which carries her newborn
daughters on the ocean reminds one of the choiring angels
around Bethlehem's manger, and the primitive tribesmen
dumbstruck by the Graces into admiration likewise recall the
adoring shepherds in the evangelic legend. In the sequel to
this effective theophany and to the half-completed journey of
the divine foursome through Greece, when Venus rises to
Heaven leaving her daughters behind as uplifters of benighted mankind, we have a clear analogy to the Ascension,
an equivalent of Mount Tabor being also provided—and it is

the deity's earthly cycle; disappearance is an enhancing act, and the Italian verb tenses' sequence (as often happens in Dante) strengthens the focal effect by having *sparve*, a past expressing instantaneous action, followed by *si cingea*, an imperfect expressing duration; the latter reacts upon the former by contrast, and is semantically heightened in turn. The progressive duration of *si cingea* connotes an infinitesimal process of immersion in the element of light, neatly symmetrical to the earlier emersion from the element of water. The hesitation between such variants as *s'avvolgea* (she was enveloping herself) and *si cingea* (she was girding herself) reflects Foscolo's attentiveness to expressive intensity in the first case, and to the resonance of a mythic topos in the second, which calls readily to mind, for an Italian reader, the appurtenance known as *cinto di Venere* (Venus' girdle).

The Assumption of Venus aptly rounds out the myth of the mother goddess our modern poet has succeeded in reinventing for his own cathartic purposes as well as for the benefit of a rationally disabused yet myth-hungry generation. The embryonic formulation of that myth in Foscolo's work is to be found in *Ortis*, as we saw in the relevant chapter. But if in that novel the character-persona wavered between the deep wish to re-enter the womb of Mother Earth (variously worshipped in herself and through the unattainable beauty of Teresa) and the protesting invocations to a male godhead that one cannot help feeling mainly absent from Jacopo's world, here in the *Grazie* the residual masculine god has been totally reabsorbed by the triumphant mother figure who appropriates all his attributes and functions. She is creator, life-giver, punisher and comforter; she is merciful and just, and immensely powerful though infinitely attractive; Madonna and Cybele, Jahveh and Christ in one, she reshapes chaotic matter into life and rises to heaven to be etherialized while her creations, or emanations, the Graces, continue her work on earth, shaping the human clay into finer cultural forms. Thus while she removes herself from the difficult arena which "Mars" and "Love" (personifications of the masculine aggres-

incarnate who thereby become the necessary counterweight to those phantom goddesses—Vesta the keeper of the pure flame, Pallas the eternal artificer—who are supposed to preside over the second and third hymn. Foscolo's fondness for the number three recalls Dante's in its structural reverberations, but has different sources, and one of its motivations seems to be a deep wish to formalize the feminine bias of his pantheon by replacing the all-male Christian Trinity with an exclusive trinity of female godheads. There is no attempt to integrate the masculine trinity into a quatriad including the feminine principle, as medieval & Renaissance Mariolatry had done with some help from the painters, down to Raphael, or vice versa to round out the feminine trinity by injecting a suitable masculine figure for balance and good measure. The poet of the revolutionary age seemed to have little use for a patriarchal hypostasis; even Goethe's complacent God the Father who watches over the appointed order of the universe in *Faust*'s "Prologue in Heaven" will make room for Mary and Gretchen, twin embodiments of the Eternal Feminine, in that poem's epilogue. And in Foscolo's case, the matriarchal bias will have been strengthened no doubt by the experience of growing up with a widowed mother who had to become the head of the family in a difficult period of wandering and readjustment. His literary symbols, like the migration of Venus and the Graces from Greece to Italy, happened to be invested with historical as well as with a deep existential relevance.

The ritual to which the vatic persona leads the three lovely women at the beginning of Hymn II is likewise far from perfunctory. Against the ravages of war, in the very teeth of a newly impending threat which overshadows the hope for Italy's and Europe's resurgence, he summons the flower of the tribe, the youths who have not left their bones in the Russian snow and the girls who have been pining away in bereaved or delusory love, to propitiate the powers of tribal creativity by an offer of milk, roses, and doves—the ancient Cytherean custom—and to surround as a responsive chorus the three embodiments of that creativity—the harpist, the apiculturist, the dancer, themselves transient in the vicissitudes of flesh but apt to be immortalized by Canova's marble. What is being conjured is the intangible power of form, as a social not private epiphany; what is threatened is more than individual lives, it is the very values by which Mediterranean peoples can live and civilization itself subsist. The "pagan" *Veni creator spiritus*, sole antidote of chaotic violence, succeeds, and regardless of some negligible formal hesitancy which survived the elaborative fervor of many worksheets, the relentlessly wrought verse quickly soars into crystalline epiphany with the evocation of Galileo as part and parcel of the ancestral Tuscan landscape:

> Qui dov' io canto Galileo sedeva
> > a spiar l'astro
> Della loro regina, e il disviava
> Col notturno rumor l'acqua remota
> Che sotto a' pioppi delle rive d' Arno
> Furtiva e argentea gli volava al guardo.
> Qui a lui l'alba, la luna e il sol mostrava,
> Gareggiando di tinte, or le severe
> Nubi su la cerulea alpe sedenti,
> Or il piano che fugge alle tirrene
> Nereidi, immensa di città e di selve
> Scena e di templi, e d'arator beati,
> Or cento colli, onde Apennin corona
> D'ulivi e d'antri e di marmoree ville
> L'elegante città, dove con Flora
> Le Grazie han serti e amabile idioma.
>
> Date principio, o giovinetti, al rito . . .[28]

---

[28] *Le Grazie*, Hymn II, lines 12-27, pp. 53-54 *Opere di F.*; lines 12-28, p. 119 *Dall'Ortis alle Grazie*; lines 308-26, pp. 176-77 *Le Grazie, ed. crit* (following the Leghorn *Quadernone*). There are minor differences among these editions, especially in the initial lines of the passage, because of the several drafts extant at the Florence and at the Leghorn library. Orlando as usual prefers the Leghorn *Quadernone*, all in the poet's own hand and (in this passage) without deletions, though one line (*a spiar l'astro*) is left in-

Here where I sing Galileo would be sitting
Once to descry the star
Of their queen, and the nocturnal plashing
Of the faraway water would distract him
Which from behind the poplars of Arno's shores
Furtive and silvery flew to meet his eye.
Here dawn, moon and sun in turn would show him,
In a contest of hues, now the severe
Clouds poised upon the blue mountain, and now
The plain fleeing down toward the Tyrrhenian sea,
Huge scene of cities and of woods and temples,
And happy ploughmen, and now again a hundred
Hills whereby the Apennine makes a crown
Of olive trees and grottoes and marmoreal
Villas for the elegant city that provides
Wreaths and fair speech for Flora and the Graces.

Do start the ritual, my good youths . . .

Many factors converge into the vibrant transparency of this
scene: the intertwining melody of line after nimble line in effortless syntactic proliferation, the attention paid to vowel
tones and consonantal harmony, the painterly brushwork, the
cinematic mobility of vision which, firmly anchored as it is to
a stable point of view, ranges from one end to the other of the
landscape to take in its diversified amplitude along with its
hourly variations between night and day, finally to concentrate on Florence, the true center of the world that has been
so rapidly unfolding in this discovery of nature's benevolence
at one with man's harmonious work. And this cosmos is not
statically described, but progressively takes shape as it
exists,[29] or rather develops in the unsleeping eye of the star
gazer, as if by accident.

---

complete, thus postulating further plans for the finishing touch. The Florence MSS have a complete line instead.

[29] Karl Kroeber, in *The Artifice of Reality*, speaks of a "temporalization
of space" which differentiates Foscolo's (as well as Leopardi's, Words-

Something like the unpredictability of revelation inheres in the self-forgetfulness of the astronomer who lets the esthetic insinuations of the scene lure his attention away from his sky-scanning task to reconcile him to the musical and pictorial perspectives of earth. This is a different Galileo from the unswerving scientist of *The Sepulchers*, and he becomes part of the landscape he sees, just as that landscape, in Foscolo's poetical rendering, becomes for us one and the same thing with the focus and scope of Galileo's own vision. The esthetic experience is not what Brecht would later call a culinary pleasure, but a welcome digression from, and complement to, the severity of scientific analysis, because reality is more than a set of mathematical abstractions, and beauty has to do with the realization of reality. In the poem which celebrates menaced civilization we are undidactically given a concrete example of what civilization makes possible: the liberated activity of consciousness in and for the world. Such is the sense of contemplation as dramatized here by the Galilean persona, as later in the same hymn (in the fragments not definitively welded to the main completed body) by the figure of Homer. These contemplators climax the civilizing process which had started in the stupor of the primitive savages, surprised by "the Graces" in the midst of earthbound turmoil. We saw those cues in the theophany sequence of Hymn I, and we can catch a modified recurrence of the theme in the "stupefied fisherman" of the Como lake passage not long after the Galileo passage in Hymn II. In Foscolo's poem man grows "fostered alike by beauty and by fear."[30]

Structurally, the passage functions in a further way, by showing what heritage the youthful Italian chorus is called upon to keep alive, and what is meant by the harmony of man and nature, by culture in the perennial Hellenic sense. These are the Graces in action, the values to be recognized. They

worth's, and Keats') depiction of nature scenery from the more static Augustan kind.

[30] Wordsworth, *The Prelude*, I, 302.

have a way of happening unexpectedly, as they did to the
god-struck savages and (on a different level) to the intent
scanner of the skies; yet, paradoxically, they also exact hard
work from their devotee. Grace is gratuitous by definition, yet
it may reward persistent labor; it refuses to be taken for
granted. And the excerpt on hand proves it. The writing
underwent assiduous revisions, and one reward of the Graces
for their poet's unstinting labor can be seen to accrue to one
of the most advanced drafts in the Florence library MSS collection (Fasc. III, page 6), where Andrea Calbo's sedulous
hand is crossed out and interlinearly corrected by the nervous
hand of his employer and friend:

.notturno   onda remota
Col *tranquillo* rumor l' *acqua lontana*

A still more advanced draft restores the rich phonic effect of
acqua, with its unique oral dynamics of total vocalic openness followed by guttural closure and vocalic reopening. The
vibrant and liquid alliterations do the rest, aided by the dark
coloring of *o* and *u* vowels.

Not surprisingly, the momentous Galileo excerpt at one
stage of the overall elaboration had been attached as a sequel
to the invitation to Canova which I have discussed earlier,
and which has remained pretty definitely a part of the beginning of Hymn I. This is another instructive example of Foscolo's compositional dynamics, and of his fondness for independently working on several nuclei of vision and song which
could then be experimentally shifted around in the total structure without too much worry being wasted on narrative sequence. In the process, such seminal units could undergo
adaptive transformation or ramify into more units, or inter-
twine with other offshoots of developing creation, and finally
converge. It is hard to choose between the vegetal and the
physico-chemical metaphor for a useful analogical description of *Le Grazie*'s diachronic development, which at times
could also be alluded to in terms of molecular fusion, but the

implication of this compositional procedure seems to be that the poet tended to work synchronically rather than sequentially because this was the essential conception of his project. The poem, let us remember, evolved from a first stage (studied by Pagliai on the MSS) at which it had no subdivision to speak of, to a second stage (reconstructed by Orlando on Pagliai's footsteps) at which it could be described as a tripartite hymn, to be expanded into three separate Hymns in the final, still incomplete draft.

In the provisional, though fairly advanced draft that experimented with a convergence of the Canova and the Galileo units (Bibl. Naz. Fasc. III, p. 7, Calbo's handwriting), we see how the eight lines referring to Canova and the altar of the Graces being dedicated at Bellosguardo have already reached the form they will retain throughout, apart from two subsequent lines obviously serving as an ad-hoc link, while the sixteen lines referring to Galileo and the Florentine panorama have a quite different physiognomy from the one finally chosen by the author, and already given on the previous page of the same manuscript:

> . . . Amando gli ozi
> Le nostre dive aman la pace e l'arti.
> Qui Galileo sedeva a spiar l'astro
> Che la regina delle rosee Grazie
> Elesse albergo suo; qui sale al guardo
> Di sotto a' pioppi delle rive d'Arno
> Furtiva e argentea ad ora ad or quell'onda,
> Mentre alla Luna mormora da lungi.
> E qui la Luna e l'Alba e il sol colora
> Gareggiando da' cieli, or le severe
> Nubi su la remota alpe sedenti;
> Or il piano che sfugge alle Tirrene
> Nereidi, immenso di città e di vigne
> ~~felici~~
> Scena e di messi e d'arator beati;
> Or cento colli onde Esperia corona

D'ulivi e d'antri e di marmoree ville
L'eloquente città seggio di Flora
Dove le Grazie avean . . . sacello.

         . . . Loving leisure
Our goddesses love peace too and the arts.
Here Galileo sat to descry the star
Which the queen of the rosy-haloed Graces
Chose for her dwelling; here rises to our view
From under the poplars of Arno's shore
Furtive and silvery its persistent wave
While to the Moon it murmurs from afar.
And here the Moon and Dawn and the sun color
In turn, vying from the sky, now the severe clouds
Sitting on the remote mountain range; now
Instead the plain fleeing away toward the Tyrrhenian
Nereids, a huge scene of cities and of vineyards
And of harvests and of happy ploughmen; now
A hundred hills whereby Hesperia crowns
With olive-trees and grottoes and marble villas
The eloquent city that is Flora's throne,
Where the Graces used to have their lovely shrine.

In this less advanced version, Galileo is hardly more than a
stage-prop, and even the fact that he points his telescope toward the planet Venus seems a coy embellishment. The description of the surrounding landscape, for all its colorful
liveliness and incidental masterly lines, sounds externally
decorative, an insufficiently motivated set piece, while in the
version that makes Galileo the center of perception everything takes on a new life. This is reflected in the heightened
dynamism of some focal verbs: first of all *gli volava al guardo*
("flew to meet his eye," said of Arno's water glittering from
afar, instead of an impersonally framed *sale al guardo*, "rises
into view"). Then *a lui . . . mostrava* ("showed . . . him," said
of moon and dawn and full sunlight which in turn lit for
Galileo the rich scene, instead of the impersonal and static

colora, "colors," with its perfunctory appendage *gareggiando da' cieli*, "vying from the skies," which in the more accomplished version becomes *gareggiando di tinte*, "vying in colors," a functionally perfect solution that also absorbs the semantic indications of the earlier draft's *colora*). Finally, *fugge alle Tirrenel Nereidi* ("flees to the Tyrrhenian/Nereids," said of the Tuscan plain as it gradually recedes sloping toward the sea, a stronger expression than the *sfugge*, "escapes," of the earlier sketch). Furthermore, the coordination established between *sedeva a spiar* ("sat to descry"), *disviava* ("distracted") and *mostrava* ("showed") by the syntactical rearrangement that makes Galileo the focus of vision strengthens the verb initially predicated of Galileo, which ceases to be just episodic and incidental. Indeed the whole triadic sequence *spiava . . . disviava . . . mostrava* coheres into a dramatic rhythm: these verbs form the backbone of the poetic action, they are like a graph of the essential development in Galileo's consciousness and in the phenomenology of reality around him, for he gets distracted by an elvish being, the (happily unpersonified) Arno water, which then justifies its impish interruption of the sage's astronomic work by showing him another scene and another way of looking at it.

As so often happens in Foscolo's own poetry, a digression ends up by enriching the original vision which it had threatened to disrupt. When Galileo digresses from analytical science at the invitation of the very Nature he had been demystifying, he is not repudiating but simply suspending, in a phenomenological *epochè*, the hard-won way of truth to recover the esthetic experience as the audible and visible world unfolds around him to gather in his privileged eye. The dilemma of poetry and science, beauty and truth, which was going to excruciate Foscolo's follower, Leopardi, and which John Keats was defensively resolving by making truth the function of beauty at the expense of science, is voiced here with unique tact and honesty even as it provides a thematically structural articulation for the poem in progress and one of its artistic high points. This much would stand even if

Foscolo, and we after him, had been unaware of Galileo's keen interest in poetry as shown by the Florentine scientist's considerable work in literary criticism.[31] To be sure, in the lines that serve to introduce the perfected Galileo passage, Foscolo does make an unequivocal reference to the artistic merits of the author of *Il Saggiatore* and *Dialogo dei Massimi Sistemi* as an elegant and perspicuous prose writer. We may add that Galileo's championing of poetry as pure fiction vis-à-vis the stern requirements of the scientific method must have struck a responsive chord in Foscolo, who never ceased (in the essays and in *The Sepulchers*) to assert the life-enhancing value of illusion (=imagination) in the face of a reality stripped bare by modern science. Blake's and Goethe's notorious reaction against Newtonian science come here to mind, though unlike them, their Italian contemporary was not prepared to deny the cognitive value of the analytical, quantitative approach to experience. Neither was he going to make poetry ancillary to science, as a Cartesian *philosophe* might have.

Poetry (all of art, including those so aptly celebrated in *The Graces*) provides a viable alternative to quantitative physics because it does not claim to measure and verify; it instead makes reality present in its perceptible fullness, an alternative and complement to the dissecting operations science performs. It is therefore legitimate for the poet to "suspend" exact science and scientifically dissected reality, even though on another level he may find imaginative nourishment in some of modern science's insights. Actually *The Graces* tries to bracket or suspend in a poetical *epochè*, which is Foscolo's new myth, the negative or threatening and inharmonious aspects of contemporary reality *in toto*. Among these, chiefly the disturbing prospect of imminent war on Italian soil as French and Cisalpine armies lose ground to the reactionary alliance that will soon close the Napoleonic parenthesis and

---

[31] This aspect of Galileo's work is studied by Tibor Wlassics, in *Galilei critico letterario*. Ravenna: Longo editore, 1974.

try to turn the historical clock all the way back to pre-
revolutionary times. If history seems to be going downhill, the
poet can shift our perspective to what is timeless even if
precarious—the intangibles of contemplation, of knowledge
in its broadest sense, the heaven-girt Atlantis of Hymn III[32]
where Pallas and the arts find their ultimate shelter.

Before that, however, in Hymn II, he rallies the forces of
life (the surviving young men, the shy girls) to the ritual of
art, and in so doing the sensuous richness of the universe—or
of what the universe can be if properly tended by human
care—is displayed. Thus in a way all of Hymn II, the perfected as well as the provisional, floating parts, makes up a
sequel to Galileo's piece. In that piece, the knowing poet's
eye, the eye of the man who comes back from abstraction to
concrete experience, reorganizes reality on the esthetic level,
and thereby functions as the norm of the poem. Eye and ear,
in fact, become the center of the universe, since a universe
can only exist in a definite existential perspective; an emphatic repetition of the adverb *Qui* (Here) in the Galileo
passage pinpoints that placement and in so doing connects,
on the verge of identification, the astronomer of time past with
the poet persona that, in the present, is enacting the rite of
cultural survival: "Here where I sing Galileo would descry.
. . ." "Here moon and dawn and sun showed him in turn etc.
. . ." We are on privileged ground, on sacred ground in a way,
but sacred only because consecrated by human culture, by
continuity with the creative past that the memory of the poet
(as in *The Sepulchers*) restores; and it is no private memory
either, but the vehicle of a communal perspective on cultural
time. That perspective is not given once for all, but must be
periodically recovered if the collective identity of the tribe
has to be preserved; and in this case to preserve is to renew,
as the ritual enacted by the persona on the shrine-like hill
that affords such a vantage point on nature and history makes

---

[32] For a close analysis of the Atlantis motif's development, see article
quoted in fn. 3.

clear. The ritual renews the ancient Hellenic custom and
points to a future reenactment for the nation that in the poet's
view has inherited the Hellenic values. The poet-priest recovers and renews the solitary experience of Galileo the contemplator of new truths and ancient beauties, just as, in the
parts of this hymn that Chiarini integrates into his reconstruction and Orlando expunges, other creative figures from the
Greek and the Italian past, the outstanding poets, will be
evoked to complete the cultural revival.

And it is here and now, the perspective is not exchange-
able, the persona is instructing his chorus at this specific
juncture of space and time, and the act of writing merges with
the ritual act. They are one and the same thing; Foscolo's
writing, no matter how lofty in style and literary, does not
take place in an abstractly "universal" sphere, it reaches out
for timelessness from the contingent station in time and space
which the writer accepts. It is highly experiential writing. It
is in a kind of dramatic staging that the writer choreographs
the sequence of his three lovely priestesses at the altar in Bellosguardo. Here is the first one:

> Leggiadramente d'un ornato ostello
> Che a lei d'Arno futura abitatrice
> I pennelli posando edificava
> Il bel fabbro d'Urbino, esce la prima
> Vaga mortale, e siede all'ara; e il bisso
> Liberale acconsente ogni contorno
> Di sue forme eleganti, e fra il candore
> Delle dita s'avvivano le rose
> Mentre accanto al suo petto agita l'arpa.[33]

> Gracefully out of a palace of rare style
> Which for her as a future dweller of the Arno
> The artificer from Urbino built in a pause
> Of his brushwork, comes the first lovely woman

[33] *Le Grazie*, Hymn II, lines 53-61, p. 54 *Opere di F.*; lines 54-62, pp.
120-21 *Dall'Ortis alle Grazie*; lines 350-58, p. 178 *Le Grazie, ed. crit.*

And sits at the altar; and the generous byssus
Complies with all the outlines of her lissome
Shape, and among the whiteness of her fingers
Roses glow while close to her bosom she strikes the harp.

The experiential present which sets the dramatic tone for this
passage introducing the musician, first of the three Grace-
like priestesses of art, springs directly from the phrase "Here
where I sing" that started the Galileo passage. Likewise, the
local and historical definition that decisively contributes to
the poetical vitality of the mysterious, yet very specific figure, picks up the cues already discussed apropos the earlier
excerpt.

Another intrinsic link between the two passages can be
seen in their common emphasis on visual and auditory imagery, ear and eye providing distinctive avenues of discovery
for the intent listener-and-contemplator. Nature surrepti-
tiously revealed herself to astronomer Galileo, whose eyes
and ears the poet borrowed to evoke the viable cosmos that
set the stage for the whole ritual action to be unfolded; Art
now displays her power of sight and sound as the harp player
captures our eye through the elegance of her form in motion
and through the splendor of color in the act of eliciting from
her instrument the music that is pure sound and yet more
than sound: Harmony. We see her emerge from the portal of a
Florentine palace supposedly built by Raphael as if in anticipation of her coming into the world, and she does come into
the world at this moment, for us, fulfilling the unconscious
prophecy of an artist who made the stone womb that would
carry her. She is going through a formal birth, and it is the
rebirth of a whole past that lay dormant in the stones and in
the instrument, waiting for her to reawaken it. There is a
whole history to redeem, and only grace can do it.

The poet earned that grace with ascetic labor. He was as
stylistically scrupulous as Hölderlin avowedly was, and it was
no cramping scruple that made him ceaselessly rewrite this
passage until it seemed to have acquired the hallucinatory

clarity of rhythm and vision that alone would satisfy the requirements of his demanding project. The *Biblioteca Nazionale* worksheets are particularly numerous, and besides trying out several possible combinations with other motifs (the bees, Canova, Harmony), they keep testing specific words, phrases, and images. Raphael was present from the start (Registro Mors, pages 14-15), and at one point he was invading the scene, until syntactical compactness articulated his intervention into a quick picture which is all motion and does not narratively interrupt the dominant theme; not only so, but the foreshortening effect in the final draft, as quoted above, brings out the magical implications that no amount of discursive detail could have accounted for.

The harpist at one point (pages 9-10, Fasc. III) was called "L'altra ministra delle Grazie," the other minister of the Graces, with the word *ministra* interlinearly added over the cancelled *alunna* (pupil), but the *prima/ Vaga mortale* (the first/ Lovely mortal) of the final draft is less circumlocutory and more suggestively resonant with the motif set forth in an immediately preceding passage where the poet asks Canova to immortalize the three priestesses "pria che all'Eliso/ su l'ali occulte fuggano degli anni" (before they flee to the Elysian fields on the hidden wings of the years"). Moreover, in that fairly early version the musician was presented statically, sitting in the garden of her ancestral palace; then a later improved version gave her movement by using in her regard the verb *viene* (she comes), until the final text found the functionally perfect solution *Esce* (she comes out)—and syntax helps by placing that decisive verb after the expressions denoting respectively the source of her movement (palace) and the maker of that source (Raphael). The inversion causes us to see the harpist as historically and actually emerging from her cultural matrix, and at the same time it enables the subject to function as a hinge between that verbal predicate and the subsequent ones which describe the musician's ritual actions: *e siede* (and sits), etc. With typically Foscolian prolepsis, the adverb *leggiadramente* (gracefully), which materialized eventually in the chain of revisions, was finally moved to first place in its line and phrase, indeed in the whole isolable passage. As a consequence, the adverb ceases to be a purely decorative item, and foreshadows the appearance of the girl, whose essence it connotes. Another interesting emendation over the earlier drafts can be seen in the replacement of the adverb *quando* (when) by *mentre* (as, while). "When she plays the harp" would have denoted a repetitive action detracting from the uniqueness of the scene being evoked; "while she plays the harp" intensifies the sense of present, dramatic action which we have seen to be essential to the whole.

Finally, the choice of *s'avvivano* (come to life, glow) over the earlier *serpeggiano* (creep) for the roses enhancing by contrast the fingers' whiteness amounts to a discovery. It was a comparatively late variant in the evolution of the manuscripts according to Pagliai[34], and in the Bibl. Naz. Fasc. III version at pages 9-10, discussed above, it is merely weighed as an alternative to *serpeggiano*; a later draft restores the latter option, then *s'avvivano* returns for good. The reasons are to be inferred. "Serpeggiano" recalls etymologically the movement of the snake, *serpe*, and the contrapuntal hiss of Yeatsian fame is unwelcome in this context. Elsewhere in *The Graces* the verb recurs with sinister connotations, as in the explanatory coda to the cannibal episode in Hymn I, where anthropophagy is said to be atavistic and thus to account for the wretched aggressive lust that "creeps" (*serpe*) in us all, while in the floating Erinys passage which the poet had planned to hitch on to a particularly tormented part in Hymn I, and which did achieve formal completion by itself anyway (inducing Chiarini to include it in his text), phantom snakes loom in the Icelandic sky as part of the Northern Lights phantasmagoria—an evil pageant in Foscolo's universe. On the other hand, in the introductory lines of Hymn I, the grapevine is said to "creep" (*serpeggia*, as a creeper should)

---

[34] Pagliai, "Prima redazione dell'Inno alle Grazie," esp. pp. 310-13.

among the bay laurel trees of Bellosguardo where the altar of
the Graces is being set up, and here there can be no sinister
connotations. Perhaps a concurrent reason for Foscolo's final
choice of *s'avvivano* over *serpeggiano* in the harpist excerpt
was the incomparably more vivid pictorial implication of the
former verb in this context, versus the possibly disturbing
tactile connotations of the latter, in proximity to "fingers."
His verbal sensitiveness responded in this case to the
etymological aura as well as to the direct semantic charge of
those words. "*S'avvivano*" brought in a welcome idea—life,
or liveliness—as a metonymic summation of the musician's
nature.

What is in question is nothing less than a cosmogonic
myth, the power of Harmony that shaped the world, and the
harp tells the story in its wordless way. And besides *telling*
that story, the harp reenacts it in the psychic sphere, by
bringing the harmony of consolation into the afflicted or upset
human soul:

> Scoppian dall'inquiete aeree fila
> Quasi raggi di sol rotti dal nembo
> Gioja insieme e pietà, poi che sonanti
> Rimembran come il ciel l'uomo concesse
> Al diletto e agli affanni, onde gli sia
> Librato e vario di sua vita il volo, . . . [35]

> From the restless airy strings there burst forth
> Like rays of sunlight broken by a stormcloud
> Joy and compassion in one—for ringing out
> They remember how heaven gave man up
> To delight and to anguish, so that life's
> Flight may be sustained and withal various . . .

Because music is a mimesis of the emotions, it has cathartic
power, as exemplified by Socrates who, listening to Aspasia's

[35] *Le Grazie*, Hymn II, lines 62-67, pp. 54-55 *Opere di F*.; lines 63-68,
p. 121, *Dall'Ortis alle Grazie*; lines 359-64, p. 178 *Le Grazie, ed. crit.*

concert, holds up his smiling serenity as a mirror to mankind's possibility for wisdom and as a warning against the
hectic pursuit of fortune. This is another variation on the
theme of Galileo's contemplativeness in esthetic key—and it
should be remembered that Foscolo eventually chose Socrates to embody this Didymean ideal instead of leaving it in
the abstract as "Sophia," the version extant in the early drafts
of this passage which has come to take up an intermediate
position between the initial lines on music, as quoted above,
and their originally immediate sequel, the myth of Harmony
proper:

Già del piè delle dita e dell'errante
Estro, e degli occhi vigili alle corde
Ispirata sollecita le note
Che pingon come l'Armonia diè moto
Agli astri, all'onda eterea e alla natante
Terra per l'Oceano, e come franse
L'uniforme creato in mille volti
Co' raggi e l'ombre e il ricongiunse in uno,
E i suoni all'aere, e diè i colori al sole
E l'alterno continuo tenore
Alla fortuna agitatrice e al tempo;
Sí che le cose dissonanti insieme
Rendan concento d'armonia divina
E innalzino le menti oltre la terra.[36]

Already with foot and fingers and with fitful
Talent, and with eyes that keep watching the strings
Seized by inspiration she elicits the notes
Which depict Harmony as it imparted motion
To stars, to ethereal wave and to the Earth
Floating in the Ocean, and how it shattered
Monotonous creation into myriad aspects

[36] *Le Grazie*, Hymn II, lines 107-120, p. 56 *Opere di F*.; lines 97-110,
p. 122 *Dall'Ortis alle Grazie*; lines 393-406 (with line 396 left incomplete
as in the Leghorn *Quadernone*), pp. 179-80 *Le Grazie, ed. crit.*

By rays and shadows and made it one again,
And gave sounds to the air, and colors to the sun
And continuous vicissitudes to fortune
The perennial upsetter, and to time;
So that all things discordant may together
Yield orchestration of divine harmony
And elevate our minds beyond the earth.

With Pythagorean zest, the verse soars to encompass the cosmic law, which insures significant order in the universe through a dramatic diversification of the original undifferentiated unity ("l'uniforme creato") and a tempering of the consequent contrasts into a higher, articulated unity that allows the manifold to subsist within its scope the way a musical chord makes harmony out of dissonance. The throwback to Pythagoras' ideas on the music of the spheres and above all on the perfect correspondence between the order of things at large and the mathematical order of music, which is not just man-made, fits the specific context no less than did the previous reference to Didymean Socrates in the wake of the Galileo idyll. Contemplation of life's turbulence from a cosmic perspective enables man to make sense of that turbulence, and to accept his earthly lot in the assurance that the ups and downs of fortune tend to a resolution of sorts. Harmony is mythified as the beginning of everything because it is really the perennial goal, therefore the becoming of the world. As such, it can be both the object of philosophical or scientific speculation, and of esthetic perception; the latter appeared as incidental to Galileo's thinking, while for Socrates it is the occasion of ethical meditation, and in the subsequent Platonic-Pythagorean effusion esthetic and philosophical thought is one and the same act.

Accordingly, the privileged organs of perception, ear and eye, never cease contributing their part to Foscolo's "melodia pittrice" (painterly or depicting melody). They permeate the imagery ("from the restless airy strings there burst forth/ Like rays of sunlight broken by a stormcloud . . .") and provide the conceptual vehicles for the philosophical rapture (". . . it shattered/ Monotonous creation into myriad aspects/ By rays and shadows . . . / And gave sounds to the air, and colors to the sun . . ."). And just as ear and eye lured star-gazing Galileo away from his stern observation of the skies into the delight of sensuous perception on earth, here again they claim their poetical right by following up the highly philosophical passage of Harmony with a concrete example of its power when it becomes audible and visible in the terrestrial scene. This is the famous simile of Lake Como, illustrating at once the magic of Harmony on earth and the power of Foscolo's *melodia pittrice* at its best:

> Come quando piú gaio Euro provòca
> Su l'alba il queto Lario, e a quel sussurro
> Canta il nocchiero, e allegransi i propinqui
> Lïuti, e molle il fläuto si duole
> D'innamorati giovani e di ninfe
> Su le gondole erranti; e dalle sponde
> Risponde il pastorel con la sua piva:
> Per entro i colli rintronano i corni
> Terror del cavriol, mentre in cadenza
> Di Lecco il malleo domator del bronzo
> Tuona dagli antri ardenti; stupefatto
> Perde le reti il pescatore ed ode.
> Tal dell'arpa diffuso erra il concento
> Per la nostra convalle; e mentre posa
> La sonatrice, ancora odono i colli.[37]

---

[37] *Le Grazie*, Hymn II, lines 121-35, p. 56 *Opere di F.*; lines 111-25, pp. 122-23 *Dall'Ortis alle Grazie*; lines 407-21, p. 180 *Le Grazie, ed. crit.* All these texts conform to the Leghorn *Quadernone* elaboration, which appears in Sheet 6, third column, in smaller handwriting, right above the Harmony passage as quoted. But there can be no doubt that the author intended to have the Harmony passage precede the Lake Como one, since he marked the former with the number 1 between brackets, and the latter with the number 2, same way. This is another instance of his compositional pro-

As when with greater mirth the East wind arouses
Lake Como in the peace of dawn, and at that whisper
The sailor sings, and joy seizes the nearby
Lutes, and softly descants the plaintive flute
Of lovesick youths and maidens that drift by
In their gondolas; and from the lake shores
The shepherd boy replies with his bagpipe:
Among the hills boisterously echo the hunting
Horns to frighten the roe, while Lecco's sledge
Hammer thumps rhythmically on the bronze
From the factory furnaces; spellbound
The fisherman lets go of his nets and listens.
Just so the spreading sound of the harp roams
Throughout our valley; and while the player rests
The hills still hear all over and around.

Barbarisi reminds us of the Homeric pattern this simile follows, and Orlando[38] adds the Catullan reminiscences that
concur in shaping the structurally integral digression; he also
points out how memories of Lake Como and the Brianza hills
lingered on during Foscolo's Florentine period. Actually this
personal motivation for the sophisticated literary piece is to
be felt in the poem itself, even without resorting to external
biographical information. The conclusion of Hymn III unites
Florence and Brianza in an elegiac farewell centered on the
mourning figure of the dancer (Maddalena Bignami), to whom
the poet proclaims his love without mentioning her by name,
but sufficiently identifying her—she is set in her familiar
scene of idyllic Lake Pusiano, among the Brianza hills, in the
region of Lake Como. Once again we see how it is personal
utterance that makes creative use of literary sources; the
"Here where I sing" of the Galileo passage sets the keynote
also in this regard.

---

cedure by independently elaborated and experimentally shifted passages or
motifs. The *Quadernone* text of the Lake Como simile has only one word
corrected, in the last line but one.

[38] See *Dall'Ortis alle Grazie*, footnote pp. 122-23.

The Lake Como simile can be enjoyed as a self-contained poem (provided of course one excises the "As when" link), but it gains by contextual integration, for the thematic reasons we have partly discussed. It culminates the harpist movement in the unfinished symphony of Hymn II; it particularizes the vision which had soared into the abstract sphere of cosmic speculation, and once more brings thought down to earth; it brings to consummation the theme of music's creative power, not by simply talking of it, but by embodying that power in the resources of verbal language itself. What we have here could be called a musical cosmogony. The power of sound evokes, at one remove, a world taking gradually shape in our visual perception as music progressively defines the space that contains that world; and we remember how it was the seduction of ear that attracted Galileo's attention to the loveliness of the Bellosguardo panorama, for that, too, was an esthetic cosmogony. The dynamic pattern whereby the dawn wind awakens the whole lake and environs to a crescendo of man-made sounds was already present in the early drafts of the Como passage, though it reached completion only in the final version given above. As in the Bellosguardo sequence featuring Galileo, all the elements of the scene call one another forth in an expanding progression which keeps reality in motion; and the climax of it all is in the verb *ode* (hears), echoed by *odono* (hear), which seals all that aural motion in the fisherman's intent stillness: a world unfolds in the phenomenology of sound to achieve itself in a still point of consciousness.

To turn back to the scene on hand (the altar at Bellosguardo), which had occasioned the Lake Como simile, the last three lines echo the lake-bound effect with one important variation: the key verb *odono* is predicated, not of a human subject, but of the hilly scene itself. The chain of man-made sounds was elicited by a natural sound (the wind's whisper) and ends in an animistically receptive silence of Nature herself. Esthetically speaking, the Bellosguardo cosmos emanated from Galileo's consciousness, while the Lake Como cosmos emanates from a gentle yet powerful natural force to come to its focus in the wonderment of the fisherman, and to reverberate again in the Bellosguardo scene in such a way as to naturalize that wondering consciousness and at the same time humanize the natural elements (the listening hills). Harmony prevails between man and nature.

And that harmony is signalled also by the phonic quality and rhythmic arrangement of words. A network of alliterations, now liquid now occlusive, interplays with disguised internal rhymes or assonances to evoke the spellbinding effect of those various sounds as they gather in the ear of the fisherman. The onomatopoeia of Line 4, banking on two diereses, prolongs the duration of the syllables into a sinuous vocalization that expands the hendecasyllable to make us hear the flute:

Lïuti, e molle il fläuto si duole

The reiteration of liquid consonants, and the internal echo of *molle-duole*, contribute to the spell. An exact echo—in fact a perfect internal rhyme—occurs two lines down between *sponde* (shores) and *risponde* (replies), attracting the nearby *gondole* in its field of resonance to set up an alternative phonic series on the same vocalic key (the rich, mellow *O*) with a different consonantal timbre (the nasal -*nd*- which acts like a piano pedal on the vowel *o* to make it ring deeply and give it a darker color than the open, frontally pronounced *o* of *molle* and *duole*). But if the vowel key connects this rhyme series with the coloratura effects of the flute line, the *p* alliteration links *sponde* and *risponde* to the contiguous *pastorel* (shepherd boy) and *piva* (bagpipe) of Line 7, and in so doing emphasizes another vocalic modulation climaxing in the trill of *piva* that clearly offsets the long, dark *o* series before and after. The latter indeed resumes right away, reinforced by a plosive *c* alliteration and some nasal effects, in Line 8:

Per entro i colli rintronano i corni
Terror del cavriol . . .

The vowel *o* (open or closed) dominates, and will recur, with recapitulating force, in the last line of the sequence on hand:

> . . . e mentre *po*sa
> La s*o*natrice, anc*o*ra *odono* i *co*lli.

Chromatic significance accordingly accrues to the climactic verb forms *ode* and *odono*: perceived phenomenon and perceiving agent interpenetrate, so pervasive is the vibration.

Throughout the piece, then, the running interplay of vocalic and consonantal series extends all internal rhymes, assonances, and alliterations beyond their respective local range: instead of remaining more or less isolated phonic events, they interlock and coalesce into a system of modulation charged with semantic value. In this regard it helps to know[39] that an earlier draft of this passage had the shepherd boy mirror himself in the lake; in the definitive version we have been analyzing, the mirroring effect has been transposed from the visual to the auditory sphere, to the advantage of overall formal coherence, since sound, not sight, governs perception here. The *sponde-risponde* internal rhyme is an aural mirroring, and we have seen Foscolo turn the same device to account in the fable of Echo which is supposed to explain the origin of rhyme. Through these and other phonosymbolic ganglia, rhyme, felt as the characterizing trait of Italian poetry, informally permeates the blank verse poem; the sleight of hand is no mere virtuoso skill, for it contributes to the total structuring.

Sound never ceases to count in *Le Grazie*, and the sequel to the Lake Como passage abounds in melodic lines and harmonic effects which include internal rhyme and assonance; but now color comes into its own again as the poetical hierophant asks the maiden chorus to come forth with a ritual offer of flowers for the harp player who has just done her part. They are flowers of many kinds: roses, jasmines, violets,

---

[39] *Dall'Ortis alle Grazie*, footnote p. 123.

amaranths, hyacinths, lilies, daffodils, carnations (the player's favorites); and along with the brilliance of their several colors, they bring their heady perfume to enrich the sensuousness of these lines, which celebrate the outspoken charm of Tuscan girls and the conjugal bliss of musician Eleonora Nencini, a gardener of sorts. The joyous, life-affirming tenor echoes and develops the rapturous Yea of the Lake Como simile, which evoked a happy world populated by men and women at work or at leisure; it looks as if paradise were possible on earth, in the teeth of armed menace; and for a change, there is no coyness about Eros, no warning against the danger of love. Because a paradisal vision takes shape, the senses are laid under contribution; fruition is not bodiless; and the pleasures of ear, eye, and nostril converge into a kind of ecstasy oddly reminiscent of certain Dantesque raptures in *Paradiso*. Synaesthesia occurs there as it does here, and it marks plenitude, the heightening of perceptual powers:

> Spira indistinto e armonioso agli occhi
> Quanto agli orecchi il suon, splende il concento
> Che di tanti color mesce e d'odori,
> E il fior che altero del lor nome han fatto
> Dodici dei ne scevra e su l'altare
> Vel reca o dive, e in cor tacita prega.[40]

> Vague wafts the sound and harmonious to the eyes
> As well as to the ears, the concert shines
> That blends so many colors and rare smells,
> And the flower that twelve gods dignified
> With their name, she selects and on your altar,
> Goddesses, she places with a hushed prayer.

[40] *Le Grazie*, Hymn II, lines 158-63, p. 124 *Dall'Ortis alle Grazie*; lines 454-59, pp. 181-82 *Le Grazie, ed. crit.* The corresponding passage in *Opere di F.* (lines 168-73, p. 57) differs significantly in the first two lines, and I concur with Orlando in accepting the far bolder final version of the Leghorn *Quadernone*.

This is still another triumph of Harmony, as the *armoniosa melodia pittrice* grasps the visual, auditory, and olfactory perceptions into a unity which remains inaccessible to the ordinary dimensions of language and senses. Neoclassical stylization, so evident in the lexical choices of strongly Latinate flavor like *propinqui* for the current *vicini* (near) and *ninfe* (nymphs) for *fanciulle* or *ragazze* or *donne* (in the Lake Como excerpt), does not prevent Foscolo from experimenting on language to the point where no conventional Neoclassicist would have followed him. Only some of his Romantic contemporaries in Germany, and of his *Symboliste* successors in France, could score such breakthroughs into the inner sanctum of *correspondances*.

It pays to notice that the bold version here given is based on the Leghorn MS of the Labronica library, which shows evidence of elaboration; Chiarini instead accepted a less advanced version,[41] which moderates the synaesthetic effect by having *anima* instead of *orecchi* and *splendono i serti* (the wreaths shine) instead of *splende il concento* (the concert shines). In my translation, which I try to keep as faithful as possible to the Italian text but also rhythmically viable, I have made "concert" (through the pronoun *that*) the subject of "blends" (*mesce*), while the grammar of the original postulates an implied "she" (the musician who chooses the carnation among the flowers offered) as the subject of that verb. This, however, does not alter the essential semantics of the passage because the musician, Eleonora Nencini, remains the unequivocal agent and source of the total harmony released by her instrument in synaesthetic chords with colors and perfumes of the flowers.

In this way, when the second priestess of art, Cornelia Martinetti of Bologna, takes over the scene, the master of ceremonies has no trouble with the transition. Theme and tone are germane; more than a change, it is a variation on the

---

[41] To be found in *Opere di F.* See Note 40.

basic theme we have here, for the lady of the bees has a
luxuriant garden to tend, with real flowers and real hon-
eymakers in it (toads being discreetly passed over):

> La bella donna di sua mano i lattei
> Calici del limone, e la pudica
> Delle viole, e il timo amor dell'api,
> Innaffia, e il fior della rugiada invoca
> Dalle stelle tranquille e impetra i favi
> Che vi consacra e in cor tacita prega.[42]

> With her own hand the lovely lady waters
> The lemon tree's milky blossoms, and the shyest
> Of violets, and the thyme beloved of bees,
> And she invokes the blessing of much dew
> From the tranquil stars and cherishes the hives
> Consecrated to you, and silently she prays.

The preceding lines mention some of the exotic plants in that
garden, and situate it near Bologna, just as the part introducing Eleonora the harp player had stressed her close links to
native Florence; with like accuracy the subsequent part will
dwell on the Lombard ecology of the dancer, third of the three
priestesses in the order of appearance Foscolo finally settled
upon after some reshuffling. Each woman therefore becomes
an expression, a flowering of her own natural and historical
locale, and the celebration of their beauty and of the arts they
respectively cultivate is also a celebration of Italy as a country epitomized by three of its finest and historically richest
cities and regions. They happen to be three cities with which
Foscolo had much to do in the course of his Italian career,
and as with Eleonora Nencini, so with Cornelia Martinetti the
apiculturist and Maddalena Bignami the (unprofessional)
dancer the poem commemorates a personal connection.

---

[42] *Le Grazie*, Hymn II, lines 453-58, pp. 64-65 *Opere di F*.; lines 211-
16, p. 126 *Dall'Ortis alle Grazie*; lines 507-12, p. 186 *Le Grazie, ed. crit.*

Unless we keep in mind that the scenes envisioned here spring from biographically documented experiences, we might miss the delicate balance prevailing between the origin of the vision, firmly moored in space and time, and the timeless and cosmic essence of that vision, which is tragically heightened by the threat that history, revengeful Time, poses to it even while it is being achieved. To this effect Foscolo intertwines the episode of the dancer with an homage to the Queen of Italy, Augusta Amalia of Bavaria, wife of Viceroy Eugène de Beauharnais who, in 1813, had made a successful last stand at the Elbe against the Russian army pressing its advantage on the retreating remnants of Napoleon's *Grande Armée*. In keeping with the highly stylized treatment of the complex theme, a stylization clearly germane to the exorcistic and conjuring ritual the poem embodies, the Queen is shown in the act of consecrating a swan to the Graces as she thanks the gods for granting safe return to a husband for whose life she had had every reason to fear. And Eugène himself is portrayed as Homeric Ajax stopping the surging Trojan army at the wall. Ugo Foscolo had completed a tragedy on Ajax, the suicidal hero, and after a few evenings in Milan the performance had been stopped (1811) by the censors who, rightly or wrongly, but in any case at the instigation of Foscolo's enemies, had seen in the play a veiled attack on Napoleon the manipulating tyrant. Foscolo's criticism of Bonaparte's arrogance was no news, and it had already cost him the Pavia chair of eloquence in 1809, but his loyalty to gracious Amalia and his admiration of Beauharnais's valiant behavior in times of trouble were just as genuine, and they openly enter the poem, which both uses and transcends the personal motivations in question. The royal couple are portrayed as humanly vulnerable in their fortitude, and they are being threatened by fate as Italy, civilization itself (the "Graces"), and the poet's vision, are threatened. Augusta Amalia appears as mother and bride, not as a creature of power; as such she can stand for the many less privileged mothers that have seen

their sons depart for the disastrous Russian campaign, and
for the wives who have been bereaved. The *Grande Armée*
included a strong Italian contingent.

Lest external biographical information be suspected of irrelevant intrusion on the analysis of the poem itself, let us
add that the convergence of part of a completed tragedy with
the work in progress resulted from the tragic awareness that
impelled our poet to write under the shadow of impending
catastrophe. On July 21, 1813, he had submitted for approval
to the Viceregal censorship a "Fragment of Hymn III" of the
"Ritual of the Graces," which begins with the passage of the
bereaved dancer in her Brianza scene and ends with a subsequently excised passage of Tiresias blinded for having seen
the celestial beauty of Pallas; it contains the episode of the
swan offering, the celebration of the Queen's fortitude, and of
Eugène's Ajax-like valor in repulsing the Russian attacks. In
an accompanying notice the poet summarily describes the
theme and subdivision of his poem in progress, and says that
part of the present excerpt comes from his tragedy, *Ajax*,
which he hopes can be published with the emendations dictated by that extrapolation. The homage is ad hoc, yet not a
matter of adulation; it is in fact a sanction of shared misfortune and a vindication of the earlier insight, for the censors of
1811 had sensed something authentic in Foscolo's depiction
of Agamemnon as a Napoleon-like tyrant obsessed by power
and cut off from any personal loyalty, and the likening of
Beauharnais to Ajax the victim of Agamemnon was an act of
solidarity, not flattery. If the ad hoc drafting of the *Rito delle
Grazie* (which is conserved at the Milan State Archive in
Andrea Calbo's handwriting) had been just a political ma-
neuver devoid of permanent significance in the development
of *Le Grazie*, Foscolo would not have retained the Ajax-
Beauharnais passage in the more advanced versions. The
Rito obviously represents a still very fluctuating stage of com-
position, with structural alternatives being weighed and
tested; for instance, though it is described as a fragment of
Hymn III, most of its material will actually go into Hymn II,

and this hymn will conclude on the felicitous note of the vanishing dancer, not on that of Tiresias blinded by celestial
beauty, while the beginning of this *Rito* will find its stable
collocation at the end of Hymn III, though as a passage in itself it is already perfect. I have already brought the dancer
finale of Hymn II into the discussion in Chapter II, but now I
want to add how it functions at the same time as a coun-
terstatement to the earlier address to Canova and as a dialectical resolution of the Ajax theme so unexpectedly introduced
at the very climax of the possible paradise-on-earth vision.
Canova was asked to immortalize in marble the fleeting
beauties of the three lady celebrants, but marble freezes the
living form, and that is what Foscolo wants to seize—the living form in its transience, as dramatized by the dancer's re-
cessional acceleration. The Emperor had wanted to immortalize his power, but his empire is vanishing under the blows
of Fortune, as Socrates might have warned him, and the poet
seizes that experience. Then on a different level his persona
watches the vanishing figure that seems to defy his verbal
powers of portrayal, and he ponders the precariousness of all
values, including those particularly cherished by him—the
Italian language, the Graces of an old culture that can still
sustain life above chaos and barbarism. For a moment, in the
awareness of disaster, the unattainable is attained, and
paradise lost returns in pure vision alone.

But it is only momentary, always regained and always lost;
and through the phantasmagoria it is the viewer, the evoking
self that persists, scarcely glimpsing the dancer's veil as it
vanishes, white, among the bushes. Another whiteness,
equally sacred but haloed by horror not charm, had gleamed
to the viewer's eyes at a climactic point of Hymn I: the bones
unburied among the wheat. In that scene the viewing persona
was trying to avert the white horror of death, a mental apparition coming to disrupt his mythic meditation on man's fate
with sinister proof from contemporary reality. In the scene on
hand the viewer is endeavoring to capture the fleeting apparition of live beauty, which is rehearsing in a dance movement

its entire earthly trajectory: beauty is life and life unfolds in time, therefore it exists in the very act of vanishing. Both are realizations of a perceiving self, the priestly celebrant of the Graces' ritual, and not belabored allegories or abstract axioms; Foscolo's writing, here as well as in *Ortis*, is nothing if not experiential, and this redeems any incidental sententiousness, aesthetic complacency being also out of the question. In an organic reading, the self dispelling with a horrified gesture the sudden white vision of death and the self fascinated by the white motions of dancing life merge into a chord; the bones gleam among the wheat, life resurgent all over, and the dance of disappearing life is also a dance of death; whiteness is the fusion of all colors, and in each sequence it climaxes a rich pageantry of colors that the "painterly melody" had been lavishing on us.

And from climax to visionary climax, that self keeps resurfacing from the vision in which it tended momentarily to lose himself, and of which he will be the avowed spinner in Hymn III (Pallas). Since he repeatedly appears as contemplator or artificer persona in the "veil" he is spinning, it pays to give him a closer look as a constitutive element of the work in progress. To do this, we are not compelled to leave the level of objective analysis and take the plunge into speculative psychological depths or backgrounds; that self we are concerned with is *in*, not behind, the work itself. The work—the veil—both veils and betrays him. So if on the one hand the poem (especially Hymn II in the shorter version as edited by Orlando) projects a Didymean persona who, Galileo-like, acts as a star gazer above and beyond the bloody tumult of history, on the other hand a contrary pull makes itself felt and the Grace-filled mask of Socrates fails to hide the faun and the wolf under its distant smile. That smile, that detachment, do not come easily; they are only a strenuous act of self-transcendence on the part of the passionate persona who would rather be Didymus than Ortis or Ajax. Didymus is the anti-self of Ortis, because, as an existential stance, he is the alternative to crime, whether suicidal or homicidal. Detach-

ment protects from involvement, contemplation sublimates
the (repeatedly decried) urges of Eros and Thanatos. Sublimation, or "bracketing," suspension of desire and fear; the
operation intermittently eventuates in the vast act of knowledge which re-creates the world in the inner eye of Galileo, of
Socrates, of Dante, scrutinizer of heaven and abyss, and of
Homer, the "blind man" who

> . . . sullo scudo
> di Vulcano mirò moversi il mondo,
> e l'alto Ilio diruto, e per l'ignoto
> pelago la solinga itaca vela,
> e tutto Olimpo gli s'aprì alla mente
> e Cipria vide e delle Grazie il cinto . . .[43]

> . . . on the shield
> of Vulcan beheld the world turning around,
> and high Ilion demolished, and through the unknown
> ocean the solitary Ithacan sail,
> and all Olympus opened to his mind
> and he saw Venus and the Graces' girdle . . .

Both Dante and Homer inhabit those floating passages of
the *Carme*'s Hymn II that Chiarini salvaged in his edition;
and their high poetical quality explains his editorial decision
even if Orlando's purist philology calls it into question. At
any rate they can hardly be ignored in a thematic investigation of the poem as poem in progress, and for one thing they
invite comparison with those passages in *The Sepulchers*
which sketch a portrait of the Hellenic and of the Italian
bard. In the earlier poem, the portraits are strongly kinetic:
we get Dante's Ghibelline anger and restless wandering; we
catch Homer in the very act of entering Troy's sepulchral
vaults, a kind of creative violation. In *The Graces*, on the contrary, Foscolo's writing captures the intent peace of contemplation, the act of poetic vision as such; we have gone

[43] *Le Grazie*, Hymn II, lines 242-47, p. 59 *Opere di F*.

from purgatory to paradise, and the eventually chosen finale
seals it with the unique lines depicting the poet himself as he
gazes at the vanishing dancer. At the same time, the Galileo
of *The Graces* (unlike the *Sepulchers'* Galileo) is in a way se-
duced from astronomy by aesthetics, sensuous perception
displacing rigorous mathematical cognition. Underneath it
all, we have here a case of creative transgression, the scientist forsaking the abstract purity of his cognitive vocation to
indulge momentarily in the scientifically irrelevant pleasure
of aesthetic fruition. Even the fact that he was supposed to be
pointing his telescope on the planet Venus adds to the poignancy of these implications.

But there are far more explicit instances of sensuous involvement or transgression on the part of the supposedly Didymean persona (or personae) that underlies the paradisally
detached world of *The Graces*. They are, specifically, in the
long elaborated passage of the "sylvan god," which Chiarini
incorporated in Hymn II while Orlando assigns it to Hymn I,
and to which Pagliai devoted his painstaking diachronic
analysis; and in the Tiresias passage, which underwent far
fewer redactional transformations (five, according to Orlando)
but materialized much earlier, in fact before the entire *Le
Grazie* project itself, since we find it in Foscolo's commentary
to his 1803 translation of *Coma Berenices*.[44] At one point during the evolution of *Le Grazie* it came to be included in the
sylvan god episode, in juxtaposition to the scene of Boccac-
cian character Dioneo, who espies lovely Fiammetta naked at
the bath. In its final form we find it at the end of that "Frag-

---

[44] *Edizione Nazionale*, VI (Scritti letterari e politici dal 1796 al 1808, a
cura di Giovanni Gambarin). Florence: 1972, "La chioma di Berenice,"
pp. 269-444. The erudite commentaries precede the translation itself, from
Catullus' own version of a Greek poem by Callimachos. In these commentaries F. lavishes his ideas on mythology and poetics, while in the translation itself the critics have identified the germinal nucleus of the whole
Grazie project. But the translation of Catullus' Callimachean rendition appeared in 1803, in Milan, roughly nine years before the *Grazie* project
began taking shape in Florence.

ment" which Foscolo called *Rito delle Grazie* and sent personally to Viceroy Beauharnais.

Here (and the Milan manuscript, a transcription by the faithful scribe Andrea Calbo, has no revisions), the Tiresias mask comes in to make a delicate point, in the form of a classical apologue, about the poet persona who has just confessed to his ambitious attempt to capture in his verses the beauty of the Queen in terms which blend aesthetic rapture with voyeurism:

> Tentai ritrar ne' miei versi l'immago
> Della sposa regale. E quando in lei
> Posi industre lo sguardo, arieggiava
> Deità manifesta. Onde il mio Genio
> Diemmi un avviso, ch'ei da Febo un giorno
> Sotto le palme di Cirene udiva.
>   Involontario nel Pierio fonte
> Vide Tiresia giovinetto i fulvi
> Capei di Palla liberi dell'elmo
> Coprir le rosee disarmate spalle;
> Sentì l'aura celeste, e mirò le onde
> Lambir a gara della diva i piedi
> E spruzzar affrettando paurose
> La sudata cervice e il casto petto:
> Ma non più rimirò dalle natie
> Cime Eliconie il cocchio aureo del Sole;
> Né per la Coronea selva di pioppi
> Guidò a' ludi i garzoni e alle carole
> L'Amfionie fanciulle; e i capri e i cervi
> Tenean arditi le Beote valli,
> Chè non più il dardo suo dritto fischiava.
> Però che la divina ira di Palla
> Al cacciator col cenno onnipossente
> Avvinse i lumi di perpetua notte.
> Tal decreto è ne' fati. Ahi senza pianto
> L'uomo non mira la beltà celeste.

I tried in my verse to portray the image
Of the royal bride. And when on her
I set my eager eyes, she effused an aura
Of manifest divinity. At that my Genius
Gave me advice that he had heard one day
From Phoebus under the palmtrees of Cyrene.
    Unintentionally in the Pierian fountain
Tiresias adolescent saw the tawny
Hair of Pallas, released from the helmet,
Cover her rosy shoulder free of armor;
He felt the heavenly air, and saw the waves
Vie in licking the feet of the goddess
And in fearful haste spray the sweat-bedewed
Nape of her neck and her chaste bosom: but
Never again did he gaze at the Sun's
Golden chariot from Helicon's native summits;
Nor through the Coronean poplar grove
Did he ever lead the youths to their games
And the Amphionian girls to their dance, and now
Goats and deer would boldly range the valleys
Of Boeotia, for his dart whirred no longer
Straight to the target. For Pallas' anger
At one nod enveloped the Hunter's eyes
In perpetual night. Such is fate's decree.
Alas, without heavy penalty of sorrow
Man cannot look upon celestial beauty.

An erotic undercurrent streams under the courtly surface of
these firm lines, which bring to a head the impulsions of the
preceding part. There, the Queen was mythicized as the archetypal mother, and thus implicitly linked to Venus, whose
dominant epithet in *Le Grazie* happens to be "Madre." Of
course the erotic charge of the dancer and swan episode is
less evident in this *Rito delle Grazie* version, and the same is
true of some intermediate drafts of Hymn II in the Leghorn
Quadernone, page 8. Eroticism does intensify, instead, in the
ampler redaction which the twentieth-century editors have

considered more advanced than the one we are now examin-
ing, and which on the strength of Foscolo's own indications
has been definitively assigned to Hymn II rather than to
Hymn III as the *Rito delle Grazie* had it. In the last sheet the
Leghorn *Quadernone* MS devotes to Hymn II we see the votive
offering of the white swan to the Graces, as delegated by the
Queen to the dancer, develop into erotic overtones (of rare
poetic intensity) beyond the drafts of earlier Leghorn sheets
and of the Milan *Rito* itself:

> Ma udì il canto, udì l'arpa, e a noi move
> Agile come in cielo Ebe succinta.
> Sostien del braccio un giovinetto cigno
> E togliesi di fronte una catena
> Vaga di perle, poi ne orna l'augello;
> *Quei lento al collo suo del flessuoso*
> *Collo s'attorce, e di lei sente a ciocche*
> *Neri su le sue lattee piume i crini*
> *Scorrer disciolti, e più lieto la mira*
> Mentr'ella a questi detti scioglie il labbro.[45]

> But she heard the song, heard the harp, and toward us
> She comes as nimbly as in Heaven high-girt
> Hebe. With an arm she holds a young swan
> And she takes off a diadem of pearls
> From her forehead to adorn with it the bird;
> *He slowly twines his lissome neck around*
> *Her neck, and feels her hair in copious locks*
> *Cascade, black and loose, over his milkwhite*
> *Plumage, and then more gladly looks at her*
> While she opens her lips to utter these words.

The lines italicized by me go far beyond the limits of the
Neoclassical convention in hypersensitizing their object. Just

---

[45] *Le Grazie*, Hymn II, lines 490-99, pp. 65-66 *Opere di F.*; lines 248-
57, pp. 127-28 *Dall'Ortis alle Grazie*; lines 544-53, p. 187 *Le Grazie*, ed.
crit.; lines 11-18, p. 4, *Rito delle Grazie* (shorter and less innovative).

as in the *Rito delle Grazie* passage the waves licking the feet
of the goddess and spraying her nape and bosom, under
Tiresias' intrusive eyes, are a clear counterpart of his pent-up
erotic desire, here the amorous neck-twining of the swan
evokes phallic overtones. It would not be too far-fetched to
recognize in the bird's longing gaze an equivalent of Tiresias'
ogling. Tiresias besides is but a mask of the poet persona,
and so is, at a farther remove, the swan itself, whose behavior
verges on the human.

The overall effect is one of barely contained erotic energy,
with a side discharge in the marvelous synaesthesia (the swan
that "feels" the dancer's hair fall "black" over his "milk-
white" plumage). Word order, through inversions, enjambment, and juxtaposition not easy to duplicate in English without incurring awkwardness, enhances the power of imagery in
the Italian text to the point of inviting comparison with
Yeats's "Leda and the Swan." In both poems the electrical
terseness of language evokes a demonic creature of libido,
wholly "other" yet strangely familiar, to release a shock of
unknowing and re-cognition, man mirroring himself in the
non-human, whether divine or ferine. In Foscolo's lines, the
final choice of "milk-white" (*lattee*) over "snow-white" (*nivee*)
for a chromatic modifier of the swan's perceptual shape testifies to the poet's deliberate heightening of the sensual aura
in the image that, from draft to draft, had outgrown his initial
conscious intentions and thereby transformed a decorative
detail into a dramatic motif.

The motherly Queen is replaced by the dancer in the most
advanced drafts, where, as we saw, that third priestess at the
altar of the Graces becomes the elusive object of the intent
gazer and portrayer to conclude Hymn II on a note of sublimated ecstasy. The replacement occasions the falling off of
the erotically eloquent Tiresias sequel. Instead of being vi-
cariously punished by blindness—a symbolic castration in a
còntext characterized by repeated emphasis on the voyeur-
like activity of the eye—the speaker persona will now keep
his eyes open on the fleeting image that eludes his grasp,

while the erotic charge shifts to the earlier part of the poem, with the voluptuous swan taking on more and more of the poet's own attributes in disguise. The zoomorphic impersonation goes to the extent of having the sweet swan of Zante proclaim his suzerainty over fish and fowl, and his submission to the "sublime Eagle"; here obviously sexual implications merge with political ones, and the poet's devotion to Viceroy and Queen patterns itself on filial-oedipal modes. The substitution of dancer for Queen, tactful though it may be, deepens those implications; the dancer represents the Queen not just in the ritual offering of the swan, but in her own person as object of sublimated desire. We even hear the Queen invoking a delay of death for her warrior husband engaged in a desperate rearguard battle on the Elbe. Empathy and envy go hand in hand on the part of the "swan," who both wants to die and to take the place of the symbolic father in the Queen's intimacy.

The symptomatic displacement of Tiresias from the conclusive elaboration of Hymn II's end does not imply a final rejection of that well-wrought passage, which at one point had found its way into the sylvan god-Dioneo sequence, as we saw. When the further development of that much reworked episode brought about the shedding of Tiresias, Tiresias remained available and floating, and on the basis of Foscolo's summaries Chiarini included it, nonsequentially, in his reconstruction of Hymn III. It is a much too significant passage, both thematically and artistically, to be ignored, and its vicissitudes confirm the nature of Foscolo's compositional strategy, which subordinated narrative structure to evolving nuclear themes to be experimentally combined and rearranged at the bidding of a restless imagination. During its brief marriage to the sylvan god episode, the Tiresias passage had functioned as it did later in the *Rito delle Grazie* context, to express punishment of an erotic crime; and its removal made way for an altogether different solution that acquires equal significance in the total framework. The solution is, not punishment, but literary sublimation; Love's peeping on

Fiammetta at her bath, and then Dioneo's transgression in
chasing and wounding the guardian pigeons at the entry of the
grotto where a Faun and a Dryad are to be surprised in sexual
embrace, results in the "divine" Decameron, a book explicitly defined as dangerous to the virtue of well-bred girls.

If we overlook the quantum of dated, quasi-Victorian coyness on the part of a writer like Foscolo, who could not be
accused of feminist leanings, we shall not miss the encoded
message: creative literature is *dangerous*, is demonic ("the
work of the gods," of the sylvan gods of course, like Satyrs
and Fauns and Pan—it is also known that the Homeric hymn
to Pan contributed to the theme here).[46] Literature springs
from transgression, from "crime," from "immoral" instinct:

> Non son genii mentiti. Io dal mio poggio
> Quando tacciono i venti fra le torri
> Della vaga Firenze odo un Silvano
> Ospite ignoto a' taciti eremiti
> Del vicino Oliveto: ei sul meriggio
> Fa sua casa un frascato, e a suon d'avena
> Le pecorelle sue chiama alla fonte.
> Chiama due brune giovani la sera
> Né piegar erba mi parean ballando;
> Esso mena la danza. N'eran molte
> Sotto l'alpe di Fiesole a una valle
> Che da sei montagnette ond'è ricinta
> Scende a sembianza di teatro acheo.
> Affrico allegro ruscelletto accorse
> A' lor prieghi dal monte e fè la valle
> Limpida d'un freschissimo laghetto.
> Nulla pur anco delle ninfe inteso
> Avea Fiammetta allor ch'ivi a diporto
> Novellando d'amori e cortesia
> Con le amiche sedeva e s'immergea

[46] See *Inni omerici*, ed. Càssola, pp. 361-71, for Greek text, *en face*
translation, and historical commentary.

Te Amor fuggendo, e tu ve la spiavi
Dentro le cristalline onde più bella.
Fur poi svelati in que' diporti i vaghi
Misteri, e Dioneo re del drappello
Le Grazie afflisse. Perseguì i colombi
Che stavan su le dense ali sospesi
A guardia di una grotta; invan gementi
Sotto il flagel del mirto onde gl'incalza
Gli fan ombra dattorno e gli fan preghi
Che non s'accosti; sanguinanti e inermi
Sgombran con penne trepidanti al ciclo.
Della grotta i recessi empie la luna
E fra un mucchio di gigli addormentata
Svela a un Fauno confusa una Napea.
Gioì il protervo dell'esempio, e spera
Allettarne Fiammetta, e pregò tutti
Allor d'aita i Satiri canuti
E quante emule ninfe eran da' giochi
E da' misteri escluse; e quegli arguti
Oziando ogni notte a Dioneo
Di scherzi, e d'antri, e talami di fiori
Ridissero novelle. Or vive il libro
Dettato dagli dei; ma sfortunata
La damigella che mai tocchi il libro.
Tosto smarrita del natìo pudore
Avrà la rosa; né il rossore ad arte
Può innamorar chi sol le Grazie ha in core.[47]

---

[47] *Le Grazie*, Hymn II, lines 395-441, pp. 63-64 *Opere di F*.; Hymn I,
lines 176-222, pp. 113-15 *Dall'Ortis alle Grazie*; Hymn I, lines 176-222,
pp. 171-72 *Le Grazie, ed. crit.* conforming to the Leghorn *Quadernone*, also,
ibid., pp. 78-79, lines 150-90 (with variations in the last lines), as reconstructed on a broader textual basis. See also Pagliai, "I versi dei silvani
etc.," *cit*. This is one of the seminal motifs, and one of the most assiduously
reworked, as a look at the Florence and Leghorn MSS shows. There is a
structural difference between the Chiarini edition (reproduced by Puppo)
and Orlando's edition, which assigns the passage to Hymn I instead of
Hymn II, following F.'s summary and text in the Leghorn *Quadernone*.

They are no false gods. From my hilltop, I
When winds are hushed up all among the towers
Of lovely Florence, hear a sylvan god
The unknown guest of the silence-loving hermits
Of nearby Oliveto: toward noon
He makes a bower his home, and plays the pipe
To summon his flock of sheep to the spring.
At eventide he calls two young brunettes
Nor did they seem to bend the grass in dancing;
He leads the dance. There were once many
Under Fiesole's mountain in a valley
Which slopes down from its six surrounding knolls
After the fashion of an old Greek theater.
Affrico the merry rivulet ran down
At their entreaties from the mountain, and
Made the valley glitter with the freshest lake.
Yet Fiammetta had heard nothing of those nymphs
When seeking recreation with her friends
She sat there to tell stories of courtly love
And took a dip to escape you, god of Love,
And you saw her fairer in the crystal waves.
Then it was that these lovely secrets were
Bruited around, and Dioneo the leader
Of the company did offend the Graces.
He pursued the doves that hovered on thick wings
To guard a cave; to no avail did they
Moaning at his myrtle's relentless lash
Crowd around him to ask that he keep off;
Bleeding and helpless they flutter toward the sky.
The moon floods the innermost recesses
Of the cave, and there reveals asleep upon
Heaped lilies a Dryad entangled with a Faun.
The rascal rejoiced in this example, and hopes
To lure Fiammetta with it, and then begged
All the hoary Satyrs to help him and
Whatever nymphs were left out of the games
And of the secrets; and those witty creatures

Through many a night's idle hours told Dioneo
Stories of pranks, and of grottoes, and love beds
Made of flowers. Now lives the book dictated
By the gods; but woe to the unlucky girl
That will ever set hand to such a book.
Right away will she lose her native modesty's
Rose; nor can a blush artfully contrived
Inspire love in him who cherishes the Graces.

These lines, where Foscolo emulates Boccaccio by stealing madcap storyteller Dioneo from the *Decameron* and thereby fashioning his own myth of literature's genesis, are very much their own commentary, and perhaps in the shifting structure of *The Graces* it does not matter too terribly whether they more properly belong in Hymn II (as Chiarini thought) or in Hymn I (as Orlando concludes on the strength of some hard manuscript perusal). What matters is, rather, the grace of versification, sustaining narrative description on the level of mythic wonder, in a vein strongly reminiscent of Poliziano and Lorenzo de Medici. What matters is, moreover, the miracle by which a celebration of nature in pagan key (or, to be more accurate, of the harmony prevailing between man and nature when man accepts to be a part of it) becomes an account of literature's origin, without a perceptible break of style.

It was not easy, at this late stage of the game in Western literature, and in Western society, to make fauns and nymphs as credible as they had once been to readers of the Homeric hymns. One had to be Keats, or Hoelderlin, or Foscolo, to bring it off. And the way Foscolo does it at the very start in the passage under consideration is truly remarkable. To hear the "melodia pittrice" of those opening lines which establish the miraculous event as part of nature's rhythm, one would never think how many times our poet went over them, hunting for the decisive word, for the unquestionable pause, for the authentic word order, or just testing a choice by repetition. Whoever has taken the trouble of looking at the Florence and Leghorn manuscripts knows how painstakingly the poet attained that ease. The faun's music the persona hears (*"odo"*) during noon's interval of silence in the Florentine hills finds a counterpart in that verbal music the poet has to perfect within his own inner hearing until it becomes as inevitable, by dint of relentless artifice, as nature itself.

The definitive diachronic study of this passage's development has been done by Pagliai in his detailed monograph of 1952, and there one can see how insistently and freely the poet played on his keyboard, sifting numberless alternatives, until this very early *Le Grazie* theme took the desired form. Even the fact that in the first drafts the initial perceptual datum had to do with seeing nymphs and not with hearing the sylvan god(s), throws light on the working of Foscolo's imagination. When, shortly after the beginning of the motif's evolutionary cycle, the sylvan god materialized within the silence-struck circle of the tower-studded Florentine scene, he and his privileged milieu, the outcome of loving observation, became the constant of compositional experiments, the thematic cue to all successive variations. Once again, as with the Galileo motif and the Lake Como scene, instinct has suggested the right choice in the long process of exacting revisions. By changing the sensory tenor from sight to hearing, and by making the faun with his flute or pipe the object of that hearing, which in turn conveys through spontaneous association an expanding wealth of auditory and visual phenomena, our poet paralleled the feat of his Galileo passage: an aesthetic cosmogony occurs, anchored to the perceiving self,

> They are no false gods. From my hilltop, I
> When winds are hushed up all among the towers
> Of lovely Florence, hear a sylvan god . . .

and the dramatis persona bears witness to reality as it unfolds anew in his perception. Poetic reality thus is reality *tout court*, it is a function of existential perspective, not an abstract universal to be taken for granted; even though the literary sources to be reckoned with include Boccaccio's narrative poetry, Propertius, and the Homeric hymn to Pan, they become materials of a new vision. The poet subverts his own mythology by planting the relativizing clues in the midst of the achieved vision; but in this case to relativize is also to verify, and poetry becomes once more the re-creation of the world.

Needless to say, this re-creative function seems contingent on a violent, "criminal," act: the *transgression* of Dioneo who, physically and morally, violates a sacred threshold, a sexual taboo in the form of the cave guarded by Venus' pigeons. The apologue amounts to a mythical invention because it speaks for itself and well beyond the author's moral intentions as they are to be inferred from his pointedly cautionary lines against Eros the wicked, the disturbing god (especially in Hymn I). Realizing the apologue's subversive implications, Foscolo tried to counteract them by adding the older apologue of Tiresias as a sequel, then reconsidered. Dioneo's naughtiness after all had had, if not the originally desired result of seducing Fiammetta by exposing her to the free sexual mores of satyrs and nymphs, the unplanned triumphal outcome of bringing about the *Decameron*, book of the gods; and it would have sounded insufferably censorious to slap a symbolic punishment of Tiresias-like blindness on that kind of creative voyeurism. The replacement of Tiresias by the unwittingly comical warning to well-bred damsels against the *Decameron* (a warning, by the way, repeated by Foscolo in one of his subsequently indited, and only posthumously published *Letters from England*[48]) springs from the author's residual scruple about the upsetting revelation his poetical instinct had afforded. The poet fights on both sides of the taboo line, but it is his vital self, "Dioneo," that batters away at that line and successfully crosses it, whatever crocodile tears his constructed, bourgeois self may then shed on the wounded pigeons and on the flustered feminine readers of the *Decameron*.

[48] *Lettere scritte dall'Inghilterra*, cit., "Gazzettino del bel mondo No. 12," pp. 443-54 *Edizione Nazionale*, V; pp. 639-45 *Opere di F*.

The incidental information Quirina Magiotti[49] conveys about the external occasion for Foscolo's insertion of this episode helps us to gain an additional insight in the working of his imagination. Strolling through Florence while he mulled over his poem in progress, he had seen a painting with Dioneo at the grotto for a subject. In the same way, his reading of a travel book by Antonio Conti on *Aurora Borealis* had fired his poetic faculties into writing the Erinyes episode. His mind, or rather, the *Le Grazie* project, voraciously incorporated whatever experience came his way, and this perennial tendency to creative conflation could only make things harder for the discriminating aesthetic selector in him. The poet and the critic in him did not have a peaceful coexistence. The whole *Grazie* project bears witness to this, with its greatness and its failures, its incredibly perfect parts and its unresolved ambivalences.

Some of those ambivalences Ugo Foscolo could not solve, given his ambition and the constrictive pressures his social context still applied on a talent like his in the age of the aborted revolution. It is because of this that his attempted symbolic solution had been suicide in the case of *Ortis* and what Orlando calls "negative poetry" in the case of *Le Grazie*. We should note that, during his English period, Foscolo voiced stern criticism of Marquis De Sade's work, and, in the same breath, of his own *Jacopo Ortis*, which he sees as a sin of youth, really a dangerous book to be handled with care.[50] And yet he never repudiated it, to judge from the frequent identification of Ugo with Ortis in his epistolary style and from the care he devoted to new editions of the novel in 1816 and 1817. Perhaps we should add the Dioneo-Tiresias mask to those of Ortis and Didymus if we want to understand more closely the inner economy of Foscolo's work (*Le Grazie* in particular) and of the psychological dynamism that went into it. In that case it would help to situate Dioneo-Tiresias between

[49] Pagliai, "I versi dei silvani etc.," p. 251

[50] *Lettere scritte dall'Inghilterra*, "Al lettore" (To the Reader), p. 544, *Opere di F*.; p. 243 *Edizione Nazionale*, v.

the two extremes, namely tragical, passionate, self-destructive Ortis and detached, contemplative, humorous Didymus.
If Jacopo ends up killing himself out of too much uncontaina-
ble vitality, which the social conventions of the time cannot
accommodate, Didymus survives by placing himself at one
remove from that passionate urge, by "suspending" the
tumult of life in a perspective which affords immunity along
with knowledge; but Dioneo dares what Ortis did not, and he
carries out his transgression, not against himself, but against
those very taboos that were the ultimate defeat of the suicidal
character.

The only blood spilled happens to be pigeon blood, an
eloquent symbol of defloration, just as the "violated" cave
aptly represents vagina and uterus in one, with the result that
the vision of life in the making—Faun and Dryad sleeping
together—rewards the vital intruder, and a different conception of values, of what is really "sacred," dawns on him or at
least on us, the readers admitted backstage to this pagan mys-
tery of initiation. The pagan demons and godheads evoked
here are certainly no mere Neoclassical stage props; they
happen to fit the revolutionary context and its implications. If
satyrs and fauns and dryads, because of their free sexuality,
had been demonized by Christianity and relegated to the
dungeons of hell, Foscolo's poetry, in harking back to pre-
Christian Hellas and to the Hellenizing Renaissance, rescues
those sylvan demons from their underground jail. They are in
his rewriting of myth truly de-christianized devils just as
Venus Mother is a de-christianized Madonna, and they embody a new (and ancient) innocence, Blake's liberated energy
which is eternal delight.

But Foscolo cannot completely free himself of christian
and bourgeois puritanism—how could he, when he is committed to a bourgeois revolution? So he, and his delegate in
the poem, the persona, cannot entirely accept the revolutionary consequences of his troublesome revelation, and, as
we saw, Tiresias is blinded, while the *Decameron*, fruit of
"Dioneo" 's erotic aggressiveness and voyeur-like enterprise,

is coyly and hypocritically put on a bourgeois *Index Librorum Prohibitorum*—at least as far as young ladies are concerned. What's more, Tiresias and Dioneo's enterprise in unmasking reality is presented, retrospectively, as lewdness. If sex is innocent, there should be no stigma attached to it, and the voyeur should be just a seer. But that would topple the moral structure on which *Le Grazie* leans; we read, in fact, how Dioneo "offended the Graces." That this supposed offense results in his creative familiarity with the benevolent demons of the wilderness, and thus in Boccaccio's literary masterpiece, seems not to trouble the intermittently scrupulous author; he fails to see the poetical incongruence which mirrors a basic contradiction in his own conscious values. No sooner does his exuberant instinct well up with a liberated vision of life than he has to curb and repudiate it, to the detriment of artistic coherence. At this point Didymus comes in to save the situation; and he will interpose aesthetic distance between himself and the troubling experience, and convert perplexity into irony, humor, resignation. In this way the contradictions in the persona and in the author behind the persona are projected onto reality, and artistically exploited. But the truthful message of instinct, the liberating vision, has been betrayed, denied, or at least hedged in; the Graces become bourgeois snobs, whereas they were first conceived of as uninhibited deities, emanations of primal Nature (daughters of Venus).

Sublimation and distancing, as evasive tactics, do bear aesthetic fruit in the form of what I should call erotic suspension. It is abundantly exemplified by the rich passages in Hymn I and Hymn II where either the Graces themselves appear as luscious if veiled nudes, or their mortal priestesses move around in a very sensuous ambience, mostly floreal. The correlative attitude of the speaker persona, or viewer in the poem, is of course that caressing sight, that erotically charged viewing which however refrains from consummation, which I have ventured above to call voyeurlike, and which—in Tiresias' case—may itself become the object of repression or censorship because it comes occasionally to be felt as a form of substitutive possession or violation. The basic uncertainty of *Le Grazie*, along with the formal accomplishment, stems from this inner oscillation of the speaker. Furthermore, the difficulty of maintaining the delicate balance of erotic suspension combines with the awareness of impending disaster—Napoleon's betrayal of the democratic revolution, followed by Napoleon's defeat at the very hands of the absolutist monarchies that had been the prime obstacle and target of the revolution—to foster, in the *Le Grazie*'s persona, the extreme withdrawal manifested by "Atlantis," the third hymn.

There is no question here of "going the poet one better," so to speak, namely of treating his text as a symptom, as a disguised and unintentional confession of the psychic troubles he would rather keep to himself. We do not have to approach the poem extrinsically in order to hear its existential revelation. "Negative poetry," as Saverio Orlando has aptly defined the eventually dominant tenor of *Le Grazie*, springs from the avowed defeat the persona has to face; and the defeat is cumulative, for it involves a sexual, personal level, along with a collective, historical one. The historical defeat is the failure of the French Revolution to live up to its proclaimed ideals and ultimately to hold out against its external enemies, with the consequence that Italian hopes for permanent national unification and independence seem utterly forlorn. More broadly, the failure of this particular revolution becomes the expected failure of all such attempts at self-renewal on the part of society, and all wars seem accordingly wasteful to the point of madness, a matter of useless bloodshed, just as love, in the personal as well as social domain, seems a destructive force because it threatens the psyche's inner balance and impedes contemplation—the only redress of historical disaster.

Such are the roots of the negative myth that takes final, if fragmentary shape in Hymn III, "Pallas," to which I have often made anticipatory reference because it envisages the imaginative solution for the antinomies that had emerged to

stir and occasionally disturb the vision in progress. By now
the underlying view of reality has ceased wavering. And as it
definitely shifts to the negative pole, it achieves itself as
poetry with a far more unified tone, despite the desultory
genesis of the embodying verse. This Hymn is actually even
farther away from final form than the two previous ones, as
witness the fact that only its initial twenty-four lines, a kind
of protasis, appear in the *Quadernone* draft of Leghorn, which
on the other hand gives a sustained transcription of most of
Hymns I and II. Yet the fragments independently elaborated
for this third Hymn do cohere and, individually taken, ex-
hibit a rare formal finish. They include some of the finest
poetry Ugo Foscolo ever wrote, and if we have cause to de-
plore the impingement of adverse political circumstances on
the composition of his crowning song, which had perforce to
remain this side of absolute completion, we may also recognize the catalytic effect of those inimical circumstances. It
was after all the consciousness of debacle that pushed our
poet to the limit of invention and made him conjure the
apotropaic myth of Atlantis against the impending ruin of his
world.

A desperate fidelity to art, to the dream of harmony that
can never find fulfillment in the war-ravaged human polity,
this is what powers the vision that the defeated soldier and
patriot opposes to the devastations visited on Europe by his
stormy age. His response to what seemed to him a *goetterdaemmerung* is not negative *tout court*; it is a denial of
negation itself, negation being, at this point, equatable with
historical reality as such. Here, the lust for power and destruction possesses both fighting sides: Napoleon the prospective loser and the by now victorious Russians. But Pallas and
the Graces have their invulnerable domain in the island surrounded by sea and sky, and there they weave the splendid
veil which tells the story of mankind, safe from mankind's
blind fury. One thinks of Dante's backward glance from
Paradise's luminous heights to the "threshing floor that makes

us so ferocious." Atlantis is Foscolo's Paradise, devoid of on-
tological status; it actually arose as an anti-world, and—like
Dante's paradise—it ends by becoming the only true world,
beyond reality, while the real world, the domain of the She-
wolf, loses significance, to become the mere shadow of the
imagined one.

But in Foscolo's poem something else happens to mark
it as the unmistakably modern work it is vis-à-vis Dante's
faith-sustained accomplishment. From among the sunbursts
of vision the craftsman emerges as their conscious creator,
and if everything has been for nothing, if so much hope and
action and sorrow have been wasted in the maelstrom of history, this much at least will not be wasted: that a man has
seen through the vortex, and has translated those hopes,
those sufferings, into an intangible world of song. He knows
that he is weaving the tapestry of vision at the very moment he
lets himself go to its charm. Craft is witchcraft; the poet himself is the weaver of the Graces' veil, which will appear in the
central part of the surviving fragments as the objectified vision of his own dedicated, if disconsolate work in progress.
He thus becomes both the survivor of a communal disaster,
"from the ruins of Europe [Hugo] scriptor," and the evoker of
a supra-reality in the guise of irreality. The fruits of radical
negation are visible: the poet joins in his person the function
of existential witness and that of incantatory artificer, exorcist
and conjurer in one.

Out of defeat, victory; and the craftsman pulls his threads
together. The beginning of his hymn to Pallas, formally cer-
tified by the Leghorn manuscript, invokes the terrene, yet
etherialized trinity of the three languages in which Foscolo
sees civilization's order of succession: Greek, Latin, Tuscan;
and at the same time that ascendancy, now recapitulated in
the language to which these lines are committed, is the poet's
own lineage. Things may fall apart in the world of political
and military reversals, but he reintegrates his own cultural
being in the alternative world he is weaving; and he proclaims

himself (lines 12-24) the inheritor of Greek Pindar and of
Latin Catullus, in the triune harmony of the respective languages (lines 1-4):

> Pari al numero lor volino gl'inni
> Alle vergini sante, armoniosi
> Del peregrino suono uno e diverso
> Di tre favelle . . .

> Identical in number to the holy
> Virgins let my hymns fly, harmonizing
> The utterly rare sound, one and yet different,
> Of three languages . . .

In this way a continuity asserts itself over the breakdowns of
pragmatic history, past and present, and—as happened in
The Sepulchers—it is the poet who sustains that continuity, in
the realm of values, of essences. As in a play of mirrors, the
artificer multiplies his immanent trinities: three hymns for
three goddesses, three poets, three languages, and again
three women mirroring those goddesses and—inevitable in
the ethereally negative context—the three Fates, to preside
over the island-sheltered transcendental work, since spinning
precedes weaving.

In this metahistorical realm of the mind's own conscious
making, even the neoclassical-rococo fable of Eros frightening the Graces (as sketched in the thirteen elegant lines Orlando[51] assembles from two worksheet jottings) can have its
place, nor does the coyness disturb the basic tone. Eros is
sublimated and consummation denied in this myth of ultimate
withdrawal from history and life—a myth, of course, still utterly untainted by what will be, in some later European literature, a complacent decadentism, a savoring of morbidity and
preciousness for their own sake. Foscolo's aesthetic rapture
comes from a deep-seated yearning for the idea made

---

[51] *Dall'Ortis alle Grazie*, pp. 132-33.

flesh—but here it would be flesh retranslated into pure idea—in the teeth of history's brutality, whose counterpoint recurrently makes itself heard in the difficult harmony of the envisaged poetical whole. The greater the polish, the stronger his implied gesture of negation and affirmation; and the polish itself is Homeric, Homer having kept life-long company to his latter day translator:

E i chiusi strali presagian frementi
Quell'invisibil dio che pari a notte
Sovrastò su le Grazie, e sfrenò il *dar*do
De*li'arco* ar*gèn*teo un suon *lu*ngo per *l'ae*re.
Come se a' raggi d'Espero a*mo*rosi
Fuor d'una *mi*rtea *ma*cchia escon secrete
Le *tortor*elle *m*ormorando ai baci;
Guata d*all'o*mbra *l'u*pupa e sen du*ole*;
Fuggono quelle paurose al bosco
Così le Grazie si fuggìan tremando.[52]

And the locked arrows quivered at the feeling
Of the invisible god who like night itself
Hovered over the Graces, and the released
Dart roused a long whir from the silver bow
Through the air. Just as at Hesperus' rays
Instinct with love, the turtledoves come furtively
Out of a myrtle thicket, cooing between kisses;
The hoopoe stares from the shade and screeches
At them, frightening them back into the wood
Just so the Graces fled trembling all over.

Decorativeness is redeemed by a supreme musical craft, as any reader can verify for himself by listening closely to the alliterative interplay of liquid, vibratory, and plosive consonants, of open and close vowels, and of echoing syllables which set up furtive rhymes within the lines themselves; I

[52] Ibidem, and *Opere di F.*, p. 70.

have marked some such phonic-expressive occurrences in the
Italian quote above, though attention should also be paid to
the incidental rhythmic consequences, since a line like

Dell'arco argenteo un suon lungo per l'aere

seems to prolong its pronounceable duration with mimetic
wizardry, while the two last lines rush compactly along like
the Graces' flight they are embodying. The remarkable fragment, however, serves also a narrative function by providing
a transitional link to the Pallas-Atlantis-Veil passages which
were obviously intended as the central part of this Hymn.

The requirements of fabulation at this point have Pallas,
the Hymn's titular goddess, come to the rescue of her
frightened threesome (*Ins.* XIII, f. 2, p. 2) and take them to
the inaccessible island of Atlantis (Ibid., fas. II, p. 3), so that
the pure work of the veil may get started (*Dissertazione* of
1822; see Orlando and Chiarini). The first of these discrete
but easily conjoined passages matters both ideologically and
aesthetically. It, too, could have remained at the limbal stage
of a mere link in the story, to be totally superseded in our
consciousness by the advent of the focal *Atlantis* and *Veil of
the Graces* vision which it serves to introduce, if the poet's
hand had not dwelt on it with the relentless formative grip we
know from so many other instances. Pallas Athena appears as
the war goddess who is about to withdraw her support from
the so far victorious Russians ("Scythians") because they
have become reckless marauders in turn, after rightfully repulsing the foreign invaders (Napoleon's armies, obviously,
as the following fragment seems to imply). When she accidentally meets the fugitive Graces, she bares herself of her
armor:

e inerme agli occhi delle Grazie apparve

and weaponless shone in the Graces' eyes

Then she mothers them, taking over Venus' role, in whose
honor she advises them to celebrate anew the aboriginal
marine ritual:

> Scendete, disse, o vergini scendete
> Al mar, e venerate ivi la Madre . . .[53]

> Go down, she said, virgins, go down
> To the sea, and there venerate your Mother . . .

The three lines I have just quoted form a perfect nucleus of
vision in their own right; a miracle happens in the midst of
war's turmoil, and we forget that the modern poet has attempted an impossible tour de force by rhapsodizing about
contemporary events in terms of that classical mythology
which to many can only sound like a worn-out convention. If
the cue comes from Homer and Pindar, the fairytale spell is
all of Foscolo's own making; and once again it is advisable to
listen to his musical handling of the language which in his
opinion was heir to the splendors of Greek and Latin. *Mar*
(sea) and *Madre* (Mother) enhance each other's sound and
sense; they both carry strong metric stresses, one at the outset, the other at the end of the line, and the alliterating tonic
syllable makes *Madre* an echo of *mar*, as if to rehearse,
through the mimesis of sound, Venus-Aphrodite's seabirth,
while the use of the verb *venerare* for "worship" irresistibly
suggests the name of Venus (Italian *Venere*) to focus from the
subliminal depths the individual identity of that "Mother"
who in Hymn I was celebrated as the animator of the universe, subsequently withdrawn to her elemental matrix. I
sense a religious reticence here, as if the poet wanted to name
the (for him) supreme goddess without directly naming her.

Venus' withdrawal is thus directly echoed at this point by

---

[53] *Le Grazie*, Hymn III, lines 50-51, *Opere di F.*; lines 51-52, p. 133
Dall'Ortis alle Grazie; lines 57-58, p. 132 *Le Grazie, ed. crit.*

the withdrawal of her sister Athena and of her three daughters
to the heaven-girt island, Atlantis:

Isola è in mezzo all'Ocean là dove
Sorge più curvo agli astri, immensa terra
Come è grido vetusto, un dì beata
D'eterne messi e di mortali altrice.
Invan la chiede all'onde oggi il nocchiero,
Or i nostri invocando or dell'avverso
Polo gli astri; e se illuso è dal desio
Mira albeggiar i suoi monti da lunge
E affretta i venti, e per l'antico grido
Atlantide l'appella. Ma da Febo
Detta è Palladio ciel, da che la santa
Palla Minerva agli abitanti irata
Cui il ricco suolo e gl'imenei lascivi
Fean pigri alle arti, e sconoscenti a Giove
Dentro l'Asia gli espulse, e l'aurea terra
Cinse di ciel pervio soltanto ai Numi.
. . .
Poi nell'isola sua fugge Minerva
E tutte dee minori a cui diè Giove
D'esserle care alunne, a ogni gentile
Studio ammaestra: e quivi casti i balli
Quivi son puri i canti, e senza brina
I fiori e verdi i prati, ed aureo il giorno
Sempre, e stellate e limpide le notti.[54]

An island stands in the Ocean's midst where
It bulges toward the stars more markedly,
An immense land it is, by ancient fame,
And once nurtured ceaseless harvests and men.
Today vainly the sailor searches the waves

[54] *Le Grazie*, Hymn III (Pallas), lines 85-119, pp. 71-72 *Opere di F.*;
lines 61-95, pp. 134-35 *Dall'Ortis alle Grazie*; lines 57-58, p. 132 *Le
Grazie, ed. crit.* For this passage see Orlando's article on "Il Mito di Atlantide."

To find it, and vainly beseeches the stars
Of either hemisphere; and if desire deludes him
He sees its mountains dawn from far away
And urges then the winds, and calls it Atlantis,
By ancient fame. But Phoebus calls it instead
Palladian heaven, since holy Pallas,
Angered by its inhabitants' indulgence
In the soil's bounty and in lasciviousness
Which made them neglect the arts and deny Jupiter,
Drove them into Asia and girt the golden land
With sky that only godheads could traverse.
. . .

Then to her island flees Pallas Athena
And instructs in every gentle occupation
All the minor goddesses whom Jupiter
Inspired to be her pupils: and there chaste
Are the dances, pure the songs, and without hoarfrost
The flowers and green the meadows, and forever golden
The daylight, and starry and terse are the nights.

One notices allegorical pointers in the fable, particularly in the part my quotation skips: Pallas abandoning the field to ruthless and purely destructive Mars once both Napoleon (unnamed but evident) and his opponents have proven themselves unworthy of her enlightened support, for she is a warrior of justice; and then she becomes, in her island paradise, the goddess of wisdom and the arts. These pointers sustain whatever narrative thread may serve the purposes of the poem, i.e., rescue it from a merely inchoate stage, and thus do not interfere with the poetry, to which actually they provide an additional dimension, a contrapuntal strengthening of its fabulating, utopian bent. Likewise, it does not hurt the poem to remember that the Atlantis myth comes from Plato and from his Renaissance imitators. It is in fact very much in Foscolo's mode to descant on the ancient sources and thereby reaffirm their perennial viability and his power to meet their challenge; imitation with him becomes sheer invention, and erudition feeds mythopoeia. Notice how he changes the Platonic myth to suit his own fable: Plato's Atlantis was submerged in the ocean, and its inhabitants drowned, but Foscolo's is insulated in the sky, without any need for cataclysm or punitive holocaust. Submersion and total destruction at Venus' command, death by water, is what befell the bestial natives of the wooded Greek isthmus who threatened the Graces (in Hymn I). A repetition of the same catastrophe would have proved grossly mechanical, to the detriment of the poetical Gestalt that does inform the whole poem, regardless of its incidental waverings. But a substantial variation on the theme, such as we have it here, enriches the whole and reverberates favorably on the earlier episode; it makes for internal growth, and keeps the poem going through dialectical modulation.

We descry one archetypal image through these apposite changes, from Zacynthos, the openly celebrated native island (Hymn I, outset), through the cannibal-infested isthmus between Cythera and Laconia (ibidem, further on), to the continent forever subtracted from human greed and corruption to provide a seat for the divine weavers of art's veil (Atlantis). The iconic constant is the same as in the sonnet to Zante, which I have discussed earlier; it is the *island* theme, a central image, with its easily discernible correlates: safety, envelopment in the amniotic fluid, motherly protection or, as in the case of the Cythera-Laconia isthmus, motherly reabsorption—with a basic ambivalence of death and life. Birth is what consecrates the memories, individual or ancestral, that substantiate the Zante sonnet and Hymn I (to Venus); death or rather "death" seems to inform the mythopoeic fantasy of Hymn III, the Atlantis hymn. But even Hymn II, the hymn to Vesta, revolves around an island theme, with the protective existential implications we saw: Florence, or better, Bellosguardo as the *oasis* in time and space within which the nation's propitiatory ritual can take place. And if communal as well as personal remembrances of time past—of the world's infancy—provide the substance for Hymn I, while time present affords dramatic enactment for the ritual to be celebrated in Hymn II, Hymn III moves between a rejected future and a precarious timelessness, the timelessness of pure image, or, to say it with Plato but without Plato's underlying ontology, pure idea.

The infinite distance between image and existence, history and idea, measures the tension of Foscolo's negative Platonism in this third Hymn. From just such a distance life is to be contemplated, contemplation itself being a form of denial; the trajectory from Hymn I has been one from affirmation to withdrawal, from expansion to insulation, from procreative energy (Venus animating the universe and then bestowing the Graces upon it) to a retreat into what is purely potential form. Such is the immunity that the womb of Atlantis, the skygirt island, can offer; denial as "death," an overcoming of death and life at the same time. Comparison with Goethe's myth of the Mothers suggests itself; for they, like Foscolo's variously refracted feminine trinities (Graces, artist priestesses, Fates, Hours, Goddesses . . .), inhabit a secluded, inaccessible space—the womb of timelessness—to guard the pure forms of life, "nur Schemen. . . ." On the other hand, the sheltered activity over which Pallas presides in Atlantis, and the immunity gained at the price of existence in the flesh, call to mind Keats's *Ode to a Grecian Urn*.

And yet, Foscolo is most like himself. His Atlantis is a poetically more concrete place than the Mothers' underground den in *Faust II*; it shelters a creative fervor of which we can see both process and iridescent result. It also embodies the timeless dimension of art in a less funereal way than Keats's *Urn*, for it banks on airy mobility instead of on frozen motionlessness. It is, in short, mythically and esthetically richer than its two cognate creations, with which, to be sure, it shares the component of a style that transposes the variegated elements of the given language into vibrant composure. It is an islanded language: a language twice removed from everyday speech as Atlantis is twice removed from everyday life and history's ruinous contingencies. And it is Atlantis alone, the intangible idea, the island of the mind, that can make sense of that life, of that history. In Atlantis, island and mirage, the synaesthetic veil of art is spun. It is made of sunlight and cloud and moonlight, and it effuses an inconceivable perfume and music in the cosmos when completed:

> spellbound in astonishment islands and
> continents hear it,[55]

for the world as essence, the world as idea, has been revealed to the world of existence. The veil will envelop the Graces' nudity in its fiery transparence, a suspended Eros, a sheltering of pure form from destructive possessiveness, so that the eye alone may enjoy it.

The veil is embroidered with scenes of human existence, and they are all instinct with the sadness of impermanence: youth dancing itself away down a slope from which there will be no return, at the music of Time; the faraway warrior dreaming of father and mother, then looking at his prisoners with a sigh of recognition; a group of exiles gathered around a festive table to exchange free words that would not be allowed elsewhere; a mother anxiously watching over her baby's cradle as he cries and fearing for his life, not knowing that life, not death, is the pain he will have to suffer:

> Mesci cerulee, Dea, mesci le fila;
> E pinta il lembo estremo abbia una donna
> Che con l'ombre i silenzi unica veglia;
> Nutre una lampa su la culla, e teme
> Non i vagiti del suo primo infante
> Sien presagi di morte; e in quell'errore

---

[55] The floating passage of the completed veil of the Graces, one of the poetically intensest, is variously reconstructed from the available textual cues; see *Opere di F.*, p. 74, for Chiarini's version, while Orlando has a different ending (*Dall'Ortis alle Grazie*, Hymn III, lines 205-14, p. 141). My quotation is from Chiarini's reconstruction, last line.

Non manda a tutto il cielo altro che pianti.
Beata! Ancor non sa come agli infanti
Provvido è il sonno eterno, e que' vagiti
Presagi son di dolorosa vita.[56]

Skyblue, o Goddess, skyblue entwine the yarns;
And let the veil's hem figure forth a woman
Who keeps watch among silences and shadows
Alone; she feeds a lamp over the cradle,
And fears the cries of her first born may be
Omens of death; and in such misconception
She fills the sky with weeping and lament.
O lucky one! who not yet knows a child's
Best lot is sleep eternal, while those cries
Right now are omens of grief-ridden life.

The ancient Hellenic deploration (by Theognis) echoes in
these hendecasyllables: "to mankind the very best thing
would have been not to be born"; but it resounds with a modern accent, coming from one who had Greek beauty and
Greek stoicism in his blood, along with eyes open on the
modern world as it was seismically taking shape at the cost of
too much suffering and destruction. The mournful, Schopen-

---

[56] *Le Grazie*, Hymn III, lines 187-96, p. 74 *Opere di F* .; lines 164-73, p.
139 *Dall'Ortis alle Grazie*; lines 174-80, pp. 140-41 *Le Grazie, ed. crit.*
The latter text differs from the Chiarini-Puppo version, as well as from the
one to be found in *Dall'Ortis alle Grazie*, which relies (like Chiarini) on the
published text of the 1822 *Dissertation on an ancient hymn to the Graces* (in
"Outline, Engravings and Descriptions of the Woburn Abbey Marbles,"
London). In this publication F. presented his own verse as a translation
from the Greek, while it was actually the most advanced, and by now final,
draft of that part of *Le Grazie*; a part not included in the Leghorn *Quadernone*, which explains why Orlando, in his critical edition of the *Carme
tripartito* phase of *Le Grazie*, uses MSS from the Florence library. For an
illuminating commentary on the changes introduced by the 1822 text, see
U.F., *Opere*, Tomo I, ed. Franco Gavazzeni, Milano-Napoli: Riccardo,
Ricciardi, 1974, which includes an Italian translation of the *Dissertation*.

hauerian harmony is also woven with Catullan strands, in keeping with the invocation at the hymn's outset, and they come from the epithalamion for Thetis and Peleus.[57]

That masterpiece, itself harking back to a Greek Alexandrian model, has supplied two formal cues: the device of a story within the poem's story, in the guise of Theseus' and Ariadne's vicissitudes as embroidered on the coverlet of Peleus' marriage bed, and the refrain sung by the three Fates as they spin and weave:

Currite ducentes subtegmina, currite, fusi

Run, drawing the woof-threads, you spindles, run

Compare that with the refrain-like line the Foscolian persona recurrently interjects, with appropriate variations, in the veil-weaving section of Hymn II:

Mesci, odorosa Dea, rosee le fila;

Inweave, sweet-smelling Goddess, roseate yarns;
• • •
Or mesci, amabil Dea, nivee le fila;

Now inweave, loveable Goddess, snowwhite yarns;
• • •
Mesci, Madre dei fior, lauri alle fila;

Inweave, Mother of flowers, green laurels to the yarns;
• • •
Mesci, o Flora gentil, oro alle fila;

[57] For this poem, numbered LXIV and with English translation *en face* by F. W. Cornish, see The Loeb Classical Library Vol. No. 6 (Catullus, Tibullus, Pervigilium Veneris), London: Heinemann, and Cambridge, Mass.: Harvard University Press, 1966, pp. 98-126.

Inweave, o gentle Flora, gold into the yarns;

. . .

Mesci cerulee, Dea, mesci le fila;

Skyblue, o Goddess, skyblue entwine the yarns;

. . .

In this way the poem fulfills the expectation raised at the beginning of Hymn III where it invoked the triune harmony of
Greek, Latin and Italian as embodied respectively in Pindar,
Catullus, and their latter-day inheritor who is inditing the
present rhapsody against the background of his available cultural past the better to deal with the threatening uncertainties
of his troubled time. The yarn poets spin is perennial, for it
survives (and anticipates) time's reverses. There is a direct
lineage of cultures, and it coincides—as *The Sepulchers* also
stated—with the lineage of poetry.

But the variations Foscolo managed on the Catullan cue
are just as telling as his adoption of a Catullan-Alexandrian
mode for the poem in progress. He has, for example, unified
the two phases of Catullus' epithalamion—the past as tapestry and the future as spinning—into one phase which supersedes both future and past because it unfolds timeless images. (Timeless and general, semantically speaking, rather
than tied to one particular figure or name like Catullus'
Ariadne.) Accordingly, the epic (or narrative) and the
prophetic dimension of poetry, which Catullus kept separate,
fuse into one, just as the several particularized destinies become each time one with each omnivalent image of human
life. And we see these images as they unfold, as they are
called into being by the conjuring voice of the poetical persona; we witness the very act of weaving and not, as in Catullus' poem, first the finished product of that art and then the
act of spinning (on the part of the Fates) which prophesies
events not yet translated into definite image. This enables us
to see the making of the Veil, in Foscolo's version, as an

epitome of art—art as process, the spinning of a yarn, the weaving of a pattern, the conjuring of a timeless past and of a timeless future. By the same token, this transcendental weaving of images in which many godheads take a hand well fits that withdrawal into the sphere of purely potential reality which motivates the whole Atlantis myth and invests even the fantasy of erotic sublimation that has the Veil flutter enticingly but inaccessibly around the Graces' nudity.

There is meaning—and it is a meaning entirely of Foscolo's making—also in the kind of images the Veil is supposed to carry and in their order of poetic presentation. The color of the yarn inwoven to embroider each scene goes from pink (when Flora creates the image of youth dancing down the one-way slope) to white when Flora's work figures forth turtledoves cooing with love in a woodland clearing suffused by the light of the evening star (a wedding scene alluding to the epithalamion that provided the cue) to laurel green when the scene features the warrior far from home, to gold when the exiles commune in convivial safety, to sky-blue when the watching mother cries over her baby at night. Iris is among the goddesses who collaborate in the creation of the veil, and so it is no surprise that a rainbow of hues should adorn it, particularly if we consider the chromatic richness that characterizes *Le Grazie* as a whole vis-à-vis the rest of Foscolo's opus; we have seen how *Le Grazie*, despite its dedication to sculptor Canova, banks on painting and music and, at the limit, on a synaesthetic fusion of both arts—a fusion enacted by the veil of the Graces, which is woven and embroidered at the choral singing and dancing of many a goddess, emits celestial music when completed, and simultaneously effuses a scent of roses along with vivid color. A pertinent structural trait, of non-discursive import, can be seen in the way this polychrome display parallels the descending tone of the images as they succeed one another in the rhapsody. The first two are scenes of gaiety and promise—dancing youth in a triumph of flowers, turtledoves and a nightingale at eventide; then comes the grieving warrior, and the bittersweet banquet of exiles, and the anguished mother who evokes the desolate gnomic comment that death is better than life. The pink of the dawn sky modulates into the colors of full daylight and finally into the gold of sunset and the deep blue of night. Light gradually blooms and yields to darkness; the variegated splendor of life sinks into the grave, and the image of birth—another epithalamion pointer—is counterpointed by the yearning for death. The harmony presiding over Foscolo's poem, his *Kunstwerk der Zukunft*, includes the joyful notes but settles on a lullaby that is really a dirge. Life retreats from actuality into potentiality alone.

And the withdrawal movement which propels all of Hymn III informs its final sequence as well, though on a changed register. There can be no doubt, as Orlando notices, on the intentional placement of this envoi passage as a conclusion to the whole, even though its author never came around to transcribing it in a final draft along with the rest of the Hymn, for it and the Veil passage just examined are not to be found in the Leghorn *Quadernone*. The care testified by the assiduous revisions, and the resulting poignancy of the verse, compel us to include this moving sample of confession and craftsmanship in the perfect canon of Foscolo's art. Its significance is further enhanced by the position we have to give it in the context of *Le Grazie*; it is a farewell to the Graces, a farewell to Florence, a farewell to one of the most purely beloved girls, Maddalena Bignami, and as it were a farewell to youth and poetry itself in the shadow of impending disaster and exile. It thus symmetrically seals the mythological poem with a very personal note, just as a memory of his island childhood prefaced the description of the Graces' theophany in the Hymn to Venus:

> Addio, Grazie: son vostri e non verranno
> Soli quest'inni a voi, né il vago rito
> Obblieremo di Firenze ai poggi
> Quando ritorni april. L'arpa dorata
> Di novello concento adorneranno

Disegneran più amabili carole
E più beato manderanno il carme
Le tre avvenenti ancelle vostre all'ara.
E il fonte, la frondosa ara e i cipressi
E i serti e i favi vi fien sacri, e i cigni
Votivi e sacri i giovanili canti
E il sospir delle Ninfe; intanto, o belle
O dell'arcano vergini custodi
Celesti, un voto del mio core udite:
Date candidi giorni a lei che sola
Da che più lieti mi fioriano gli anni
M'arse divina d'immortale amore.
Sola vive al cor mio cura soave
Sola e secreta spargerà le chiome
Sovra il sepolcro mio, quando lontano
Non prescrivano i fati anche il sepolcro.
Vaga e felice i balli e le fanciulle
Di nera treccia insigni e di sen colmo
Sul molle clivo di Brianza un giorno
Guidar la vidi; oggi le vesti allegre
Obbliò lenta e il suo vedovo coro.
E se alla luna e all'etere stellato
Più azzurro il scintillante Eupili ondeggia
Il guarda avvolta in lungo velo e plora
Col rosignuol finché l'aurora il chiami
A men soave tacito lamento.
A lei da presso il piè volgete, o Grazie,
E nel mirarvi o dee, tornino i grandi
Occhi fatali al lor natio sorriso.[58]

Farewell, Graces: these hymns are yours, nor will they
come alone to you, nor shall we forget

[58] *Le Grazie*, Hymn III, 224-77, pp. 74-75 ed. Puppo, and 215-47, pp.
141-42 *Dall'Ortis alle Grazie*; 226-59, pp. 147-50 *Le Grazie, ed. crit.*;
204-37, pp. 475-76 U. F., *Opere*, Tomo I, ed. Gavazzeni. The latter edition is to be recommended for its useful notes and the inclusion of several
variant drafts of *Le Grazie*.

the lovely ritual on the hills of Florence
when April is back. Your three handsome priestesses
will draw new music from the golden harp,
will turn ever more beautiful roundels, will
sing ever so blissfully at your altar:
and the spring, and the altar nestling in foliage
and cypresses and wreaths, and the beehives
will be sacred to you, and the votive swans,
and the merry songs of youth and the long sigh
of the Nymphs. Meanwhile, o fair, o heavenly
virgins, keepers of secrets, hear my deep
heart's wish. Give limpid days to her who alone,
since my years blossomed into their full prime,
divinely burned me with immortal love.
Alone she lives in my heart, a sweet care,
alone and secretly she will loosen her hair
over my grave, unless destiny will
have my grave too in a far away land.
Once I did see her, shining with happiness,
on Brianza's soft hill lead in a dance
the dark-haired, buxom girls; today she has
forgotten the clothes of joy and her fair choir.
And if Eupili lake ever bluer undulates
glittering at the moon and at the stars,
she gazes at it wrapped in a long veil,
and mourns with the nightingale, until Dawn
call it to unsoothed silence. To her do turn
your steps, O Graces, and contemplating you
may her big, fatal eyes regain their smile.

The narrative placement of these concluding lines about
Maddalena Bignami, the dancer, changed twice, drastically,
during the elaborative process of the whole poem from what
Pagliai calls "the first [Florentine] draft of the Hymn to the
Graces"; and with the placement, the very texture of the lines
also changed considerably until it reached the firm and sensitive shape preserved in the more advanced Florence Library

MSS (the Leghorn Library *Quadernone* gives only the protasis
of Hymn III). Such interaction between overall structure and
microstructure, between design and fiber, pervades the entire
Le Grazie project, as we saw, but seldom did it eventuate in
this kind of perfection. As Pagliai confirms (p. 253, p. 352,
art.cit.), the elegiac lines on Maddalena in her native scene
of Lake Pusiano ("Eupili") in Lombardy first emerged as an
addition to the protasis of the Hymn in its early genetic
phase. Subsequently, the Hymn became tripartite, and the
dancer motif shifted to the beginning of its second part (later
to become Hymn II) along with the musician and the apiculturist episodes. At this stage, the conjuring choreographer
persona is calling the three priestesses of art to the Bellosguardo altar in an order which will be reshuffled later on:
musician, dancer, apiculturist. At a still more advanced
stage of elaboration, to be considered final, the dancer comes
last in the choreographic order of Bellosguardo's ritual, and
she seals the movement of Hymn II in the magical way we
saw. Meanwhile her motif has intertwined with the Queen and
Viceroy theme (the offer of the swan). But now a part of the
original dancer passage—the part envisaging her sleepless
night at the window on the lake—splits off from the proliferating bulk that has so well contributed to articulating much of
Hymn II, and finds its definitive place and function at the
very end of Hymn III. To say it in the words of Eugenio Montale, hymn turns to elegy.

This truly provides the deeper sounding board for the
whole music of *Le Grazie* and, with it, the revealing counterpoint to its initially planned melody of affirmation; the
negative insight takes over, as if the hymnic utterance had
gradually undercut itself to change into a disconsolate song of
unprotected transience, for which only "Atlantis," the un-
real, can afford shelter. The narrative transplant of the
Pusiano lake excerpt has enabled the dancer motif to develop
in Hymn II in ways more precisely consonant with that hymn's
ritual theme, while also purifying the tone of the lake passage
itself. The latter indeed has focally come to rest on contem-

plative stillness—in revelatory contrast to the accelerating
motion and fadeout effect of Hymn II's conclusion, where the
same dancer enacts her craft. A structural chord can be overheard in the thematic connection of the two finales, one of
which recalls and transforms the earlier one. Likewise, the
inner memory of the poem will alert us to the verbal consonance between "sorriso" (smile), the clearly intended last
word of the whole poem, and "sorriso" the last word of Hymn
I. Even if not quite so systematically as Dante, who pointedly
ends each of the *Comedy*'s three canticles on the climactic
word "stelle" (stars), Foscolo does rely on structural echoes.
Each time the poem returns upon itself, it seals a cycle, and
long-distance rhyme—a correlative of the poem's memory—
marks that event. A poem essentially achieved however unfinished it may be, *Le Grazie* lends itself to such scanning, not
unlike a Michelangelo *Captive* who is so totally realized in his
struggle to emerge from the marble block.

The process of formal individualization has been enhanced
by the simultaneous process of structural integration. The latter becomes apparent upon large-scale inspection; the former
shows in the insistent revisions that the Pusiano lake lines
underwent from worksheet to worksheet in the sometimes
jumbled jottings of the Florence Library MSS. Once again,
Francesco Pagliai can best guide us through this luxuriant
wilderness. At page 253 of his 1961 essay he gives a reliable
reading of the first textual embodiment of the Lake Pusiano
motif in the early phase of the Hymn's genesis. It appears as
"Fragment No. 16," Lines 872-880, vol. 3 NF 21 r ins. A
IInd column, table VII:

Poi che alla luna e allo stellato Olimpo
Più azzurro il risplendente Eupili ondeggia
Siede r[avvolta] in lungo velo, e plora
Col rosignuol finché l'aurora il chiami
A men soave tacito lamento.
Ma udrà l'amica delle Grazie e mia
Anche il mio canto; e moverà danzante

Con l'altre [dee]; perch'io lungo l'Italia
Di casti mirti adornerò i lor passi.

When at the moon and at the starry Olympus
Bluer the resplendent Eupili undulates
She sits wrapped in a long veil, and she mourns
Along with the nightingale until dawn
Call it to unsoothed lamenting silence.
But my friend, and friend of the Graces too,
Will hear my song as well; and will come dancing
With the other goddesses; for I throughout Italy
Will scatter myrtles all along their footsteps.

Comparison of this first version with the final one shows how
the shift in narrative positioning led to eliminate intrusive
ornament. Instead of fatuously scattering myrtles in the
dancer's footsteps, the persona lets her concentrate on her
sorrowing vigil and become one with the lovely scene, as
happened with Galileo. Colors, sounds, and silences of the
landscape coalesce into a sensory counterpart of her lonely
consciousness. She is alone with an inviolate world that mys-
teriously responds to her sorrow and thereby eases her pain.
The idyll where the silent starlit lake mirrors her pure mind
and the nightingale echoes her inner lament rivals the best of
Wordsworth, Keats, and Leopardi in their cognate vein. The
plaintive note modulates into catharsis, and we are left with
an indelible glimpse of the mourner's eyes, lake-like and
ready to brighten with the dawn of a smile to be.
　　As in the Lake Como passage from Hymn II, the spell
arises from the conversion of vision into sound. Key words
connect through alliterative chains or vocalic echoes. Liquid
syllables recur in the last ten lines, with emphasis on the *le*
combination: al*lé*gre . . . *lé*nta . . . *Lù*na . . . al*l'é*tere stel*là*to
. . . scintil*là*nte Eupi*li* . . . *lù*ngo ve*lo* . . . *l'Au*rora . . .
*la*mento . . . A *léi*. . . . An isolated internal rhyme occurs
between *plora* at the end of Line 6 from the bottom and *Au-*

rora in the midst of Line 5. This is a semantic chord, since the word for "sunrise" chimes consolingly with the word for "mourns" or "weeps"—and the strategic rhyme attracts to its field of resonance the word *coro* (choir) at the end of Line 9 from the bottom. The alliterative phenomena gravitate on rhyme as such, disguised though rhyme and assonance may be. The effect would not be the same if both consonantal and vocalic echoes were formalized and assigned to predictable positions. Alliteration, assonance, and rhyme constellate these lines (and, to a lesser extent, those of *The Sepulchers*) very unpredictably, as if spontaneously rising from the thematic cues of the text. It is Foscolo's way of de-formalizing the established phonic devices and bringing them back to the source, so that we can experience them, with him, as nascent form.

The chimes accordingly take on a semantic function. The liquid chain suggests softly lapping waves on the lakeshore, the prolonged vowels (sometimes combined with nasals) are attuned to the solemn tone, and the frequency of so many phonic echoes points in itself to a "rhyming" of figures and events within the conjured scene. For lake, sky, and nightingale, which at that juncture of space and time are all of Nature for the poet, answer the mourner in kind, *respond* to her as sound responds to sound in the poem, and the response is a true *correspondence*—in Foscolo's own words (from *I Sepolcri*) a *corrispondenza d'amorosi sensi*, correspondence of loving senses. The goddess Harmony makes herself heard—and felt—and seen.

We know from the many intermediate drafts of this passage that it was no instant theophany. To manifest herself in full splendor, the goddess exacted long labor from her devotee. Once the adventitious lines discussed above have fallen, the seminal ones grow, both in number and in quality. But even before the vital pruning occurs, some interesting alternatives do come up, to be weighed and discarded and revived in turn. The draft immediately following the first one, a garbled work-

sheet labeled by Pagliai "Fragment No. 17" (*op.cit.*, pp.
254-58), already contains, for the Pusiano lake part, some of
the definitive lines, interspersed with further variants:

> *E se alla luna e all'etere stellato*
> *Più azzurro il scintillante*
> > Scintillando più azzurro
> > > > *Eupili ondeggia*
> > Siede ravvolta
> *Il guarda avvolta*
> > *in lungo velo, e plora*
> *Col rosignuol finché l'aurora il chiami*
> *A men soave tacito lamento.*
> > Ma udrà etc.

The lines and hemistichs I italicized are those that will
remain (or reappear) in the final version. The important
changes are: the dropping of a pretentious "Olympus" for the
simpler, if still lofty, "etere" (sky); the choice of a sharper
brushstroke like "scintillante" (sparkling) over "risplendente" (shining), after the provisional pondering of still
another possibility; and the capital replacement of "siede
ravvolta" (she sits wrapped) by "il guarda avvolta" (she gazes
at it, wrapped). The subsequent draft (classified by Pagliai as
"Fragment 18," *op.cit.*, p. 268) retains these improvements,
which will pass muster through several further tests (*op.cit.*,
pp. 330-34). Then at later stages of textual evolution (*op.cit.*,
pp. 335-36, Fragments 25 through 27 et al.) we see the final
solution dawning when the importunate, myrtle-scattering
persona gives way to the dancer's "big, fatal eyes" regaining
their "smile."

But for a while, as they undergo some minor lexical and
syntactical changes, even these promising lines hover this
side of perfection. At first they are couched in the indicative
mood, as if the miracle of serenity and joy supervening on
grief could be taken for granted simply by summoning the
dancer to the Bellosguardo altar and dressing her up in Neo-

classical decor "like Hebe in Heaven"; then a more tactful option makes its way into the apparently hopeless context: the poet lets go of Hebe and weighs in turn a subjunctive and a future indicative for the "return" of those eyes to "their native smile." It is, happily, the subjunctive that will prevail, sealing the whole Hymn with a prayer that is answered in several ways at once on the very page. For the Graces are evoked as a numinous presence, as, indeed, the emanation of blessed Nature itself; but they become one and the same thing with the mourner who imperceptibly goes from grieving pensiveness to contemplative rapture, and with the invisible poet-persona who has disappeared in his creation. In this regard, the early substitution of "guarda" (gazes) for "siede" (sits) has been decisive. It has mobilized a basic resource by centering the scene on what repeatedly emerged, beyond any narrative scaffolding, as the ultimate focus of the whole poem: the act of contemplation, "mirare," miracle.

Exploring *Le Grazie* both as work in progress and as a simultaneous, if incomplete, formal structure, we certainly notice the significance of the *gazing* or *listening* motif, with its connotations of wonder, awe, erotic or ecstatic rapture. In Hymn I we found the hunters, girls and boys who let go of their weapons in wonder ("ammirando") at the occasional appearance of the Graces, while an antiphonal use of the cognate verb *mirare* occurred in the remarkable floating fragment of the Erinyes, which some textual clues (Foscolo's marginal jotting on one worksheet, "And put the Erinyes here") loosely relate to the unfinished part of Hymn I having to do with the Graces' journey in Arcadia. Still in one of the most insistently reworked parts of Hymn I, the Sylvan god episode, the speaker's intent listening calls forth the faun from the noontide-charmed hills of Florence, then the same speaker projects a double of himself, madcap Dioneo, into the twice-told story of the *Decameron*'s origin, to "espy" coy Fiammetta at her bath and then surprise a Faun and a Maenad locked in each other's arms after love's physical consummation. As an eventually discarded coda, this episode for a while included

the passage of voyeur Tiresias who is blinded for catching a
glimpse of Athena undressed. Voyeurism changes to sublimated love when the Graces take in their tear-filled eyes the
last vision of their departing-ascending mother toward the
end of this first Hymn, the Hymn to Venus.

In Hymn II, devoted to Vesta, Galileo looking at the
Florentine landscape provides a high point for the thematics
of *gazing*, vision. Galileo sublimates Dioneo's voyeur attitude
("spiar," to espy, is the verb used for both), while redirecting
vision from the rarefied sphere of pure science to the aesthetic seductions of earth. Then comes Socrates, who listens
to Aspasia's harmony and rises to Olympian heights with his
thought, to see ("mirò") from up there the dire vicissitudes of
human life (Fortune's chariot). Harmony finds auditory expression in the Lake Como scene, which is ingathered in the
listening fisherman's ecstasy. Among the present or imagined
chorus of the first priestess of art, the harp player, we then
find the traveler overwhelmed by the beauty of Tuscan girls in
the theater as he gazes ("mira") at them. As he gazes and listens, the spell of color and sound (and perfume too) fuse into
one when the harpist is honored by an offering of carnations.
The second priestess, tending her bees, is outlined as a cynosure for the rapt eyes of the young chorus ("miratela"). She in
turn looks ("guarda") at the third priestess, the dancer, as she
joins the ritual scene of Bellosguardo, and the votive swan
gazes ("mira") at the latter while enjoying his privilege of
being admired in turn as the symbol and embodiment of
beauty ("a chi lo mira . . ."). The swan also admires ("am-
mira") the eagle, with a touch of dated allegory.

The whole verbal and iconic series comes finally to a head
at the end of Hymn II when the poet-persona focuses eyes and
ears on the elusive beauty of the dancer he is trying to capture
in his verse. Here the sensuous, erotically transgressive elements converge with the sublimating ones into the concrete
act of artistic representation; it is the final possession of what
remains unpossessed, full body become pure image; and the
confluence of the senses into synaesthesia marks the imma-

nence of this act, both passive and active, saintly and satyresque. Ugo Foscolo has become his own sylvan god as well as Galileo and Socrates; his eyes and ears have become his hands, to capture the intangible. In Hymn III, whose *disiecta membra* still compose a recognizable intentional structure, sublimation takes over, as we saw; and its mythos is Atlantis, the intangible, twice removed from human reach. The veil of the Graces is a restatement of the theme that concluded Hymn II, art as the grasping of the elusive; and it is constellated by the gazing motif (Terpsichore looking at Psyche as she dances, the faraway warrior looking at his prisoners, the mother watching over her sleeping infant). The sublimating emphasis culminates in the Pusiano lake scene, which leaves behind whatever faun-like sensuality had erupted in the restless vein of this poetry. Consciousness is by now its own theme.

CHAPTER V

The Act of Writing

The Graces had stood momently poised between the Moscow fire and Leipzig's protracted aftermath. Napoleon had barely set foot on French soil once again, to launch on his last venture, when Foscolo solved a personal dilemma by choosing exile over a more or less honorable capitulation to the reinstated Hapsburg authorities in Lombardy and Venetia. Was not this another rehearsing of the first exile—of the farewell to his native island? Seventeen years before he had also had to leave Venice behind, the expanded mother island; and just as the first departure had been occasioned by the unwitting betrayal his father perpetrated by dying, the second one was brought about by another betrayal, Napoleon's. The third leavetaking compounded all the previous losses into a far greater one, foresuffered in verse, then enacted in spring 1815.[1] Goodby to Zante, then to Venice, then to Italy herself

---

[1] See Letter No. 1663, dated March 31, 1815, from Milan to F.'s family in Venice. On that very day he left for Switzerland. The letter in question is in *Epistolario* v, p. 372. See also the letter of an unidentified friend from Milan to F., dated April 1, 1815, numbered 1673, in *Epistolario* vi, p. 3. But on the actual, complex motivation of F. in this drastic step he took well before Waterloo, one should now see Giuseppe Nicoletti, *Il "metodo" dell' "Ortis" e altri studi foscoliani*, Florence: La Nuova Italia, 1978, Ch. iv, pp. 107-45. On the strength of available sources, Nicoletti demystifies the heroic halo surrounding F.'s sudden departure for Switzerland, for it seems certain that since February 1815 F. had been negotiating with the Austrian authorities on the project of a literary journal he was supposed to edit with their support. F. changed his mind when he saw that these dealings were

and to her hope for democracy, unity, and independence. And Ugo knows he will never see mother and siblings again.

But what about poetry, and the plenitude it captured, the glimpsed terrestrial paradise—even if that plenitude, after its sensuous epiphany in Bellosguardo, recedes into the infinite distance of Atlantis? Will it be granted again, will it make it possible for the erstwhile Napoleonic soldier to bear his exile, just as poetry had made it possible for his White Guelf—no, "Ghibelline"—ancestor?

To ask this question is like asking whether Dante would have written another line of verse had death not overtaken him shortly after completion of *Paradiso*. And *The Graces*, within Ugo Foscolo's narrower compass, are an equivalent of Dante's Paradise—a work of the "high imagination" bent on self-transcendence and therefore doomed to see its "power" ultimately "fail." Dante's reward for the long fidelity to his vision was a timely death. It came to crown a life inured to further growth after each loss and finally stilled by the harmony that the Love imparted "which moves the sun and the other stars"; and in that last interval of stillness no human song was needed for the spirit at one with the revolving spheres. Foscolo instead had a long way to go after reaching the high point of his poetical accomplishment, another portion of exile until he could earn, in death, his homecoming. The climactic poem could not be duplicated; the indwelling Harmony that poem had deified beyond personification would no longer be transcribed into sustained verbal rhythms,

---

alienating several fellow liberals from him. On the other hand, as Nicoletti observes, at that particular time the Austrian power was still pursuing a fairly "liberal" policy of conciliation, quite different from the repressive authoritarianism to come. And, one can add, it was precisely from the pages of such journals eventually published under Austrian rule, like *Il Conciliatore*, that F.'s friends (Silvio Pellico, for instance) were able to launch the Romantic program, whose political implications soon came to disturb the uneasy peace. Nicoletti's book also has valuable insights into the composition of *Ortis*.

though it would distantly reverberate in the prose writings that, along with the endlessly revised sample translations from Homer, make up the exilic aftermath to *The Graces*.

And so it is not quite a case of the man surviving the poet, as happened to Rimbaud. Nor is it a case of the poet repeating himself out of a refusal to die as poet; Eugenio Montale in our time has paid the handsomest tribute to Foscolo by defining him "un poeta che non s'è ripetuto mai."[2] It is rather a case of *Stirb und werde*; the Goethean imperative can serve as a symbolic description of Foscolo's career. Die and become; die to your past, to *The Graces*, to Florence, to Venice, to everything you have been—so that you may live by it, and accept the new horizon. Die that you may continue to live. But to live is to write; say farewell to poetry, to the supreme moment of imaged wholeness, and re-descend from that total unity to the particular, to prose, to the humbler craft; leave Atlantis and Bellosguardo, return to history. Reorder your thoughts; write analytically; pursue the vicissitudes of time; describe the accidental, this side of paradise. Come back from the one to the manifold.

The essays Foscolo wrote in London—the city where he was to end his life in poverty at forty-nine years of age—are far from anticlimactic to the poetry he had written in Italy during the fifteen years of the Napoleonic dispensation. They insure a considerable place for him in Italian letters as literary critic and historian, for as such he ranks as a pioneer, and he is the first to apply Vico's ideas to literary criticism. But they also count as writing, even though the accessible Italian text of some is due to the pen of a translator, Camillo Ugoni, and the English text required for publication in the English quarterlies is mainly the work of local scribes Foscolo had to hire.

---

[2] In "Intenzioni, intervista immaginaria" (Intentions, an imaginary interview), originally published by the Milan magazine *La Rassegna d'Italia* in January 1946, and now included in Montale's collected essays on poetry and poets, *Sulla poesia*, Milan: Mondadori, 1976, p. 561 ff. The reference to Foscolo as "a poet who never repeated himself" occurs at p. 563, and M. also remarks there that this is a "prodigious lesson."

What Vico would have called the "mental language," namely the inner articulation of thought impulses, makes itself unmistakably heard in his Italian texts as well as in the French drafts he submitted to journal translators and in the English elaborations resulting from the shared editing. Reading his admirable essays on Petrarch, which in their earliest form date from 1819 although they came out in book form in 1823,[3] one recognizes his nimble, vigorous style all over, whether in the English text that was published in London or in Ugoni's Italian version which appeared in Lugano, Switzerland, in 1824 (it does not lose by comparison with Foscolo's usual Italian). There is a syntax which bears his unique stamp, and it also has to do with the progression of imagery. If we want to bring into the picture an analogy from the visual arts, we can compare this procedure to the accepted practice of Renaissance masters who designed their big frescoes and then left the execution of many parts, under their own supervision, to their workshop apprentices. The finished product was still considered the authentic work of Raphael, or Titian, or Tintoretto. And we have seen a contemporary sculptor like Jacques Lipschitz put Carrara marble chiselers to work on his grandiose Philadelphia monument.

But there is another dimension to be taken into account for a proper appraisal of Foscolo's work in his English phase, and it is specifically literary. It is, quite simply, the predicament of the writer between two languages. Foscolo could never contemplate the solution that a Joseph Conrad gave to the dilemma by adopting English and forsaking his native language for literary purposes. Neither could he, on the other

---

[3] *Edizione Nazionale*, x (*Saggi e Discorsi Critici*, ed. Cesare Foligno. Florence: 1953), pp. 5-297. In English, the essays are: "An Essay on the Love of Petrarch"; "An Essay on the Poetry of Petrarch"; "An Essay on the Character of Petrarch"; "A Parallel Between Dante and Petrarch." The same volume of *Edizione Nazionale* contains the Italian translation by Ugoni and the first draft of an article on Petrarch. (The *Opere di F.* contains only the Italian text of the final redaction, pp. 829-927.) See Foligno's Introduction for details, in *Edizione Nazionale, cit.*

hand, make English as much his own as the native idiom was and thus become an accomplished bilingual writer, as Isak Dinesen (*saeculo* Karen Blixen) of Denmark and Vladimir Nabokov of Russia were later to do. Rather than a question of inadequate linguistic versatility—for that skill is abundantly attested by Foscolo's Vulgate Latin satire called *Hypercalypseos Libri*,[4] and by his nearly faultless French letters, as well as by his canny reading of Homer—his failure to achieve effective literary bilingualism is probably a deliberate abstinence, an expression of his will to keep Italian at the center of his creative work. One only has to peruse the *Epochs of the Italian Language* (1818),[5] with its utterly Dantean and Vichian emphasis on the historical problem of Italy's literary language, to realize how close this concern was to Foscolo's heart.

And yet this understandable fidelity of the Italian exile to his own national language (Greek having been to him a mother tongue but not the medium of his literary opus or of his adult social intercourse) did not harden into cultural defensiveness. He stayed in touch with developments at home, received literary or political visitors from there, and through the good offices of one of them, Marquis Gino Capponi, published a sample translation from the *Iliad*[6] in the Florentine journal, *L'Antologia* (1821, Book III; other passages would be

---

[4] The complete title is *Didymi Clerici Prophetae Minimi Hypercalypseos Liber Singularis*, and it was published in Switzerland, in 1816. Dedicated to F.'s English friend, William Stewart Rose, who was an accomplished translator of Italian Renaissance poetry and helped F. to make his way to England, this truly singular work is a venomous polemic against F.'s literary detractors in Milan, chiefly Urbano Lampredi, but it has significant comments on the Italian predicament during and after Napoleon's rule, and revelatory autobiographical touches regarding F.'s demise as a soldier and man of action and his survival as "Didymus." The atrabiliousness of the book is worthy of Swift. See *Opere di F.*, pp. 735-823 (with Italian translation *en face*), and *Edizione Nazionale*, VIII (*Prose politiche e letterarie dal 1811 al 1816*, ed. Luigi Fassò, 1933).

[5] See fn. 13, Ch. IV.

[6] See fn. 8, Ch. IV.

published there posthumously, in 1832); on the other hand, he refused to lock himself up in a ghetto of the mind, for he cultivated some of the best literate society in London. English literature, in fact, had always been dear to him from the Venice apprenticeship days when Cesarotti exposed him to "Ossian" and sepulchral poetry; he knew his Shakespeare, and devoted much zest and time to the translation of Sterne, a favorite author who was to suggest the Didymus persona, a providential device for final period of exile. The *Sepolcri*, as Giovanni Getto has recently shown,[7] owes a great deal to Young's and Gray's cues, and the favorable treatment of English mores and English representative men like Nelson and Newton in a poem written by an officer of the Napoleonic army preparing to invade England likewise catches the eye. The Jacobin ideas of Rousseau and Voltaire had also found a corrective, with Foscolo, in the empiricism of Locke and Hobbes—which strengthened his propensity for Vico.

It seems indeed that something in Ugo Foscolo had always "looked forward" to England, whose culture meant so much to him since the early stage of his career. Emigrating there from the Swiss way station of Hottingen in September 1816 was then more than a matter of circumstance, it came to fulfill a lifelong drive, as if the hospitable and free British island were a last reappearance—on the largest scale—of the native Greek island forever lost. And—to complete on the existential level the shape of the mythical destiny he was impelled to enact in word and deed alike—in England he was to find again, after a long separation, "miss Floriana," the illegitimate daughter he had had from an Englishwoman while stationed on the Channel shore with the Italian contingent of Napoleon's army in 1804.

London would also secretly conjure, in the Canaletto-like part of its waterfront, the image of Ugo's intermediate insular homeland, Venice—seafaring, busy, lately free Venice. Thus the traumatic, if exciting, experience of finding himself

[7] Giovanni Getto, *La composizione dei "Sepolcri" di Ugo Foscolo.* Florence: Olschki, 1977.

abroad would be compounded with the strange vibration of a
half-realized recognition, the familiar being mirrored in the
alien and new. The tension inherent in this ambivalent relation to his host culture posed a challenge to the expatriate
writer, who soon found himself stimulated to bridge the gap
newly opened between himself and his native audience by
winning an English audience for his eloquent surveys of Italian literary history from the lectern and from the printed
page, while also projecting a comparative description of English and Italian mores for the readers back home. The latter
project remained unfinished, like so much else, and never
saw the light until the twentieth century; but what did get
written or even just sketched has elicited Mario Fubini's
claim that the *Lettere scritte dall'Inghilterra* (Letters written
from England, including a "Gazzettino del bel mondo" or
Gazette of the Beau Monde) amounts to a novel in progress.[8]
Despite the prevalently essayistic, at times deceptively frivolous, tone, the partly inchoate work does have the ring of autobiographical fiction, since it revolves around the Didymean
persona of the exile who, poised between the world he has
just left behind and the world he is still endeavoring to appropriate, makes himself the inevitable touchstone of both.
The tragic shade of Ortis is exorcised though not forgotten;
the direct link is rather to that other unfinished novel, *Tomo
sesto dell'Io*, and of course to the translation of Sterne's *Sentimental Journey*.

Yet if Ortis is deliberately left behind—to the point that in
one of the fictional letters (the "Address to the reader")[9] the
writer castigates his own first novel as a dangerously romantic
outburst—the quality of his passion is not. It surfaces sporad-
ically from the humorous or erudite chitchat to remind us of
its underlying presence, and that is enough to dissuade us
from taking the stern self-criticism too literally. After all, in
1816 and 1817 Foscolo had reissued *Jacopo Ortis* in Zurich
and then London, with a preface that confirmed the novel's

[8] See Fubini's Introduction to *Edizione Nazionale*, v.
[9] See fn. 50, Ch. iv.

importance to him; and the prologue to *Lettere scritte dall'Inghilterra* is dated December 25, 1817. The Ortis persona acts as a foil to Didymus, and in the polytonal economy of this new style, the Didymus voice, modulating through its own gamut, from urbanity to mischievousness and downright satire, from amusement to candor and actual ferociousness, sets the key but uses the Ortis voice for recurrent counterpoint, with incidental chords that bring the tension to brilliant, momentary resolution. One could even say that Didymus is the daylight aspect of Foscolo's mature world, with Jacopo Ortis the nocturnal element, held at bay but unsubdued—were it not that Didymus himself has his dark moments, for he is acquainted with the night, with nothingness actually, *il Nulla*, as Foscolo has it in the *Notizia*. The *Hypercalypsis*, that savage satire of Napoleonic Milan society, is the work of Didymus, but of an atrabilious Didymus, one who, instead of smiling the benevolent smile of humor at the awkward, hopeless human world, destroys it in a peal of nihilist laughter. That side of the Didymean persona does not come from Sterne; it comes from Swift, and Swift is expressly quoted in one variant draft of the "Lettera sulla moda" (Letter on Fashion).

If Ortis was the side of Ugo that could live only for an absolute, and die for it, while Didymus was the side that had learned to live with the inescapably relative, the latter's wisdom could never feel quite at home in the unreliable world that had pushed Jacopo to suicide. In fact, Jacopo's self-destructive gesture, a matter of uncompromising passion, is paradoxically far more affirmative than the smile, or grin, of Didymus. Youth's turbulence says Yes even in death; not so the world-wise calm of the survivor. Eugenio Montale's poem on Foscolo comes here to mind:[10]

. . . Ottimista fu già chi si estasiava

[10] Eugenio Montale, from "Il mio ottimismo," in *Diario del '71 e del '72* (Milan: Mondadori, 1973), p. 108, and now in *Tutte le poesie* (Milan: Mondadori, 1977), p. 567. Montale's high opinion of F.'s poetry has been confirmed in a recent (1977) letter to me.

> tra i sepolcri inebriandosi del rauco gargarismo
> delle strigi;
> pessimista colui che con felpati versi
> lasciava appena un'orma di pantofola
> sul morbido velluto dei giardini inglesi . . .

> . . . An optimist once was he who rejoiced
> among sepulchers, relishing the hoarse gutturals
> of owls;
> a pessimist instead, he who with plush-padded lines
> left hardly the trace of a slipper
> on the soft velvet of English gardens . . .

No wonder that Montale should esteem Foscolo's work, whose Didymean phase seems poignantly mirrored in his own late development as a disenchanted, humorous, satirical poet since *La Bufera e altro.* No wonder either that Foscolo's Didymean prose should appeal to many of the Italian modernist writers in the early decades of the twentieth century, especially the members of the *La Voce* group,[11] with their commitment to existential autobiography, narrative-essayistic "fragmentarism," and earnestness capable of playful disguise—Soffici above all. Renzo Fasano has brought this fact to our attention,[12] and it is a further proof of Foscolo's renewed, or unceasing, viability.

---

[11] *La Voce* (The Voice) was an innovative cultural periodical founded by Giuseppe Prezzolini and Giovanni Papini in Florence, and edited by Prezzolini from 1908 to 1914. It dealt with social, political, educational, and literary issues, and it attracted as contributors or contributing editors some of the finest new writers of the time. The movement originated by *La Voce* made a difference in Italian poetry too, and it is hardly possible to exaggerate the importance of this lively journal in Italian twentieth-century culture at large. In 1974 Prezzolini himself, still living and active, has published a richly annotated anthology of *La Voce*: G.P., *La Voce 1908-1913—Cronaca, antologia e fortuna di una rivista,* con la collaborazione di Emilio Gentile e di Vanni Scheiwiller. Milan: Rusconi, 1974.

[12] Renzo Fasano, *Stratigrafie foscoliane.* Rome: Bulzoni, 1974, pp. 182-83.

There is little playfulness, to be sure, in the straightforward self-portrait the writer sketches in the introductory address to the reader, "Al lettore," one of the most revealing pages in Foscolo's work; there is, if anything, the detachment that comes from suffering weathered:

> Reader,
>
> These are the letters of an exile who, in using his free time to write his friends about the nation where he found shelter, was still thinking so much of his native country that comparisons suggested themselves between England and Italy.
>
> And do you also cast a glance at them in your spare time; nor read any of them in earnest except the only one I dictated for prospective publication—which is this one: and it is no preface either, for I do not presume to give you an authoritative book. Accordingly, I will converse with you just as I do in my other letters with my personal friends; and with the same sincerity. And even if you were not to receive it with equal trust, you will realize, I hope, that it is the letter of a man to another man.[13]

Rather than an author donning a mask, this is the writer laying himself bare; and he will proceed to outline a confession of his intellectual career, moral beliefs, and existential predicament involving the world at large and more particularly that part of it which is the motherland he has been forced to abandon in distress. There is talk of wounds, and the conclusion has the ring of muffled despair at the present condition and prospects of his fellow countrymen. Perhaps the sharpest wound is his knowledge that the letters he has been sending abroad may have been opened by police censorship (and the persecution in absentia that the reinstated Hapsburg government kept up against Foscolo is no invention: the documents

---

[13] *Lettere scritte dall'Inghilterra*, "Al lettore," p. 541 *Opere di F*.; p. 239 *Edizione Nazionale*, v. Translation mine.

at the Milan State Archive are there to prove it).[14] His most pressing need in the new circumstances is to communicate, to *write*, even if that means reopening the wounds that might be healing otherwise; "between grief and nothing," as a Faulkner character would eventually put it, "he chose grief." If the

[14] A report on F. by the Austrian police, dated September 7, 1814, months after the fall of the Napoleonic Italian Kingdom, says: "A certain Ugo Foscolo, soldier, poet, professor, constant hot head, atheist, with no manners or morality, manifold Proteus, infamous tongue at every time, another ringleader of the faction that in the last days of April agitated this region for independence, ousted by the [Austrian] Regency, was then recalled and is now in Milan going from one café to the next, living on a pension which both as a professor and as a soldier he has stolen, for he has always done nothing. He is from the Ionian islands." (Translation mine.) F. in that interim period appealed to the Count De Bellegarde, Commander of the Austrian Army, to grant him a professorship at Padua University (October 18, 1814; see *Epistolario*, v, p. 277; the original is in the Milan Archive), and some of the reports on him, including Baron von Hager's, were not unfavorable, Bellegarde himself taking a positive attitude. But F.'s application was eventually turned down, and one of the reasons must have been the Austrian authorities' suspicion that he had had a hand in inditing or inspiring an "Appeal to the Czar Alexander" published by the journal "Italico" in London during the Vienna Congress. This "Appeal" advocates an Italy politically united under an Italian prince, the Savoia king of Piedmont, and warns against the dire consequences of dismemberment and foreign domination. The anti-Austrian bent of the cleverly conceived appeal is evident, and Baron von Hager had reason to ascribe the document (now conserved in Folder No. 174 of Milan's State Archive) to a group of "reformist" officers of the Napoleonic Italian Army, of whom Foscolo was one.

In 1817 the Austrian police learns of Foscolo's plans to come to Lombardy (they now and then come up in his letters to Quirina Magiotti) and recommends vigilance in its secret reports to Count De Bellegarde (who was by now the Viceroy of Lombardy and Venetia in the name of the Austrian Emperor). It's October 18, 1817; Foscolo had aired to friends and correspondents the idea of going to his native Greek island, which involved Italy as a way station. As far as we know from his correspondence, he had no intention of plotting against the Hapsburg occupants of Northern Italy. In October 1819 the Austrian Viceroy's Chancery in Venice recommends "excluding from printing . . . Ugo Foscolo's tragedy entitled *Ricciarda* . . . because it might possibly arouse the factional spirit." Still in 1819 the Viceroy's Chancery recommends "exclusion from printing" for Foscolo's

pen draws your blood, then to write is to exist, and the conjuring of demons will be its own ever-renewed exorcism. What reopens the wound will heal it.

In a sense, what we have here is the expression of a man who already died once, and so can die no more; Jacopo Ortis has seen to that; and Ugo has adopted a posthumous voice, that voice materializing as Didymus, the necessary mask, or incarnation, which arises from the painfully achieved bareness in life itself and on the written page. Foscolo has imbibed the bitter doctrine of Machiavelli and Hobbes, to prevent his yielding to the utopian optimism of Rousseau. But having died to naive hope does not mean staying dead; it actually quickens the disabused consciousness into its most alert state, discounting all preconceptions for the sake of new experience, and thereby investing the act of writing with utter immediacy, a free convergence of observation, thought, and expression:

> . . . Too much pondering besets judgment with doubts and discourages imagination, which inspires us to express candidly the feelings and thoughts aroused in us by the presence of new things . . .

> . . . On England I was writing, so to speak, as a storyteller might; and meanwhile wounds bled in my memory. . . . I see that to fill gaps, and to avoid repetitiousness—to muster the dispersed facts—to spare you the

tragedy *Aiace*, against the favorable opinion of Austrian censorship. The same folder of Milan's Archive contains a letter by F., marked as "apocryphal," and dated November 21, 1820 from Oxford. It is addressed to the personnel of the Neapolitan periodical called *Giornale Italiano* and deals with a publication called "L'animo della Costituzione" (The spirit of the Constitution). In 1823 a high official of the Hapsburg Imperial police, Mr. D'Adda, asks the President of Pavia University for archive documents concerning Ugo Foscolo's appointment and service as incumbent of the quickly abolished Chair of Italian and Latin Eloquence between 1808 and 1809, and orders the President to omit U.F.'s name from the roster of Emeritus Professors.

desultory gait of my reflections—and to check the impatience and smooth out the stylistic unevenness of these letters, I should need more time than to start again from scratch for your sake—and they would come out the worse anyway: for I should then endeavor to compile a set of academic dissertations for you. Now I cannot belong to any academy—and were I even to encompass a vast horizon with philosophical eye, so as to paint whole nations for you by large brushstrokes, I would falter in defeat. I only look at the closest objects, and it is my lot to scrutinize them one by one and ever more deeply so as to be able to tell myself and my friends whatever I descry therein, until the very depth makes them seem invisible to me.[15]

The disclaimer of his ability to outline with vivid concision vast historical scenes has to be taken with a grain of salt, for that is exactly what he had done years before in the academic addresses of Pavia—on the origins and functions of literature, and on the problem of justice. He had done it even earlier, in the *Ortis* chapter on the hopelessness of history which has been discussed in another chapter, and which in turn had provided a cue for the essay on justice. Ugo did have the rare gift of narrative and expository foreshortening, to an extent that may evoke Tintoretto's and Tiepolo's dramatic handling of pictorial space. (They were also Venetian.) And this gift, which enabled him to respond creatively to the vision of a Hobbes, and of a Vico, is of a piece with the Pindaric sweep of *The Sepulchers*. It makes for a style of unique speed, forever risking discontinuity, or taking it in its stride; a style attuned to the dizzy rhythm of a restless thought, as the writer himself implies in the next paragraph when describing the native Italian language in its historical heyday:

The language I write, reader, besides the powers per-

[15] From *Lettere scritte dall'Inghilterra*, "Al lettore," p. 544 *Opere di F*.; pp. 239-43 *Edizione Nazionale*, v. Translation mine.

fected or fostered by age, . . . possesses a native one which three hundred years of inertia, foreign habits, and servitude would have utterly removed, were it not congenital; and it is a glowing, straightforward, manifest speed. Its first writers drew their ideas from their heart's feelings and from their experience of life; they ascertained those ideas through sincere meditation; therefore they could signify them without recourse to abstract words: and to make others feel and see them as well, these early writers lit their clauses with metaphors involving objects accessible to the senses; and thereby compressing their sentence into a conflation of emotions and images, they would fling it like an arrow which, noiseless and flameless, still left a whole visible track of heat and light and unfailingly hit the mark.

In translating this further exemplary passage from Foscolo's polished Italian (for the prefatory address to the reader is the only part of the projected work that reached final completion) I have tried to keep as close as possible to the original syntactical shape, a paramount factor of its effectiveness. The compression of emotion-charged imagery into cumulative clauses which succeed one another as a progression of impulses to achieve final release in the last phrase, metaphor, and word, perfectly illustrates the ideal style attributed by Foscolo to the early Italian writers. The glowing straightforwardness and rapidity he ascribes to them (and chiefly to Dante, witness the parallel between Dante and Petrarch in the *Essays on Petrarch* and the *Epochs of the Italian Language*, already mentioned in the preface under discussion as a projected "Letter from England") is first and foremost his own signature as a writer, and he avowedly feels called upon to recapture for his native language the buried energy of the forefathers. Thus a lost golden age myth serves the modern writer to sanction his innovations in the name of a cultural paradise to be regained, and certainly worth striving for. Over a century after Foscolo, Ezra Pound will make his case for revolutionary traditional-

ism in much the same terms and with the same emphasis on
Dante's example; and, again, the qualities discerned by Foscolo in the exemplary writing of the medieval and Renaissance authors remarkably fit the requirements set by his
twentieth-century American successor for the Imagist poetics. It is a pity, and an oddity, that the author of *Spirit of
Romance* should never have taken the trouble to read the
work of a man who had anticipated so much of his program to
"make it new."

For assuredly Foscolo's harking back to his Trecento and
Cinquecento models has nothing to do with imitative depend-
ence. The very innervations of his syntax and semantics,
which the above sampling has spotlighted only in minimal
part, bear his unique mark, and detailed analysis could yield
far richer results to confirm it. I will only add a few cursory
considerations. For instance, the passage under scrutiny
gains by its articulation in two sentences, the first of which
makes an axiomatic point while the second proves it by vivid
illustration. Both sentences embody their logical tenor in
their syntactical organization, since the first one begins with
"the language I write" to conclude with its attribute, "manifest speed," and the second rehearses this semantic trajectory by beginning with a homologous subject, "Its first writers," to achieve its dynamic design in an equally homologous
way with the imagery that shows the concrete medium and effect of "speed": "track of heat and light and unfailingly hit
the mark." In the same way, the subject of the second sentence's governing clause ("first writers") particularizes the
subject of the governing clause in the first sentence ("The
language I write"). Such symmetry, however, would make for
stasis, not heightening progression, if it were just a matter of
perfect balance between two equal members. Instead, the
symmetrical structure is corrected by a built-in imbalance
which tilts it forward—in keeping with the overall proleptic
bent of Foscolo's writing. For the second sentence semantically particularizes, and syntactically amplifies the first—it
occupies a far vaster syntactic space, and it populates it with

far more specific ideas. Both in the total semantic structure, and within each of its two syntactical members—the two sentences—the movement is from general to particular, from the abstract to the tangible. Taken together, sequentially, the two sentences speed toward their common resolution—the conclusive image of the target hit by the arrow which aptly renders the idea of propulsive thought. It is the whole verbal Gestalt that darts to the mark.

The rhetorical feat carries the day for the cause of intellectual mobility, and makes style an instrument of discovery, not camouflage. One can see a further dimension of this dialectic by correlating the passage under perusal to the preceding one, which touched on the rejection of academic systems for the sake of such an intense scrutiny of "the nearest objects" singly taken that they end up becoming "invisible." The relevant paragraph, it should be added, concludes on the statement that the writer's peculiar use of his language denies him the possibility of that style which painters call *"piazzoso,"* spacious, relaxed, and abundant. This triggers the initial consideration in the following paragraph which we have discussed; and the celebration of the native dynamism of the Italian language then makes room, in the rest of the long paragraph, for a concentrated survey of Italian social decadence from the Renaissance to the present post-Napoleonic era. But that flies in the face of the preceding disavowal of any ability to "paint a large historical canvas in big brushstrokes"; tenor and shape of paragraph No. 2 contradict the tenor of paragraph No. 1. The relation between the two moments of thought-expression is dialectical, however, rather than paralyzingly contradictory. In paragraph No. 1 the writer has repudiated the systematic and extensive treatment of history in favor of an open empiricism focused on accessible objects; of a method, that is, of intensive discovery. He has chosen the microscope over the telescope. Then he reverses his approach to range over wide historical vistas, as if to go himself one better. What we are witnessing is a central pulsation in thought and style, from microscopy to macroscopy, and it well suits the non-rationalist, nongeometric nature of Foscolo's thought, forever intent on seizing reality in motion.

And whether he chooses to focus on close objects and (as Stevens would have put it) "see [them] with the hottest fire of sight," actually "burn everything not part of [them] to ash,"[16] or to range over vast stretches of cultural time, intensity is still the point. His way of encompassing history is by fore-shortening, and not accidentally he himself has brought the painterly metaphor into the context in question. Both as writer and thinker, there could be no other way for him to cope with the complementary requirements of experiential contact with the object and of liberal perspective; the empiricism he found so congenial in such disparate sources as Bacon, Machiavelli, Hobbes, and Locke went hand in hahd with the amplitude of Vico's vision, a favorite source he somehow fails to mention in the revelatory letter "to the reader" even though at one point he paraphrases him. It all goes to confirm the sensorialist bent of his poetics, of which he gives here an incisive formulation. Sensorialist rather than sensualist, I would say, because its mainspring is kinetic, dramatic, ultimately cognitive, not hedonistic. And the dramatic impulse in writing cannot be sustained except by fulfilling it in comparatively short structural units: the letter (and the "letter"), the essay, the epigram, the scene, the ode, the sonnet, the hymn, and, within the hymn, the poignantly achieved and abruptly succeeded epiphany. Hence the compositional method we have seen at work in all of his writing from *Ortis* to *Letters from England*. That it could make for troubling discontinuity he knew, for in one of the *Letters from England*, the *Lettera sulla Moda* (Letter on Fashion), he says he can only "write letters in mosaic form"; and even though he refers to his habit of punctuating his epistolary prose with abundant verse quotations, the expression also evokes prehensile, complex, non-linear patterns in the act of his writing—

[16] Wallace Stevens, "Credences of Summer," in *Transport to Summer* (1947) and now *The Collected Poems of W.S.* New York: Knopf, 1957, p. 373.

patterns which only much later would be developed into elliptical juxtaposition, in true "mosaic form," by such poets as Eliot and Pound.

Yet the mosaic metaphor fails to do complete justice to Foscolo's compositional method, which is self-propelling rather than tessellating. With him, an image/idea evokes more, in a kind of chain-reaction. As a consequence, the open form of the "letter" proves most congenial to him, and in the literary enterprise we have been discussing, letter will follow letter as wave follows wave, except that each wave cancels the previous one, and these chapters of a work in progress are not supposed to supersede one another. In *Letters from England* we eavesdrop on the rhythms of nascent thought, we witness the genesis of writing. Literature is indeed *letter*, free message, informally taking shape and just as informally amalgamating—or transcending—the various fixed genres: confession, fiction, satire, essay, and poetry (at least as functional insert). The intellectual component— witness the "letter" on modern novels,[17] castigating Mme. de Staël as well as the notorious Marquis who invented sadism; or the tirade against German metaphysics—eventually emerges from salon causerie in rococo vignettes, and thus makes itself light, in Didymean fashion, though there is no mistaking the dead earnest under the mundane smile.

Opera-box glitter, boudoir frivolities, high-life civilities counterpoint the recurrent, if soft-pedaled, flashbacks to the Napoleonic past, to hopeless Italy, to the moment of hope that had gleamed when Continental patricians could no longer impunely make torch-bearing lackeys of the people's sons and then carelessly run them over; the tone is Mozartian. And through it all, the Foscolian persona intermittently comes to the limelight, irrepressible, as a man "with something barbarous in his heart," almost an Alceste compelled to survive in a world of alien fatuousness—though fatuousness is only

[17] *Lettere scritte dall'Inghilterra,* "Appendice al Gazzettino N.1, II (Frammento sui Romanzi)," pp. 598-603 *Opere di F.;* pp. 368-74 *Edizione Nazionale,* v.

incidental to the English *beau monde* he is describing and comparing to its Italian counterpart. He is neither naive nor jaundiced, in fact he is very appreciative and tactful, if shrewd in his observation of manners:

> Considering the effects of different education and character in England and Italy respectively, it seems to me they can be equitably distinguished and judged in this way: the Englishman will help you spontaneously, steadily, and very liberally, but if you are haughty he discourages your requests, and if you are importunate he rejects and despises you—the Italian will trade more abundantly in small favors, continuously, so as to bind human minds with the thinnest threads, and to please the more as less gratitude is implied. Therefore the English seem harder and at the same time more modest; the Italians, more helpful and importunate—I do not know which to prefer; I do know that I have something barbarous in my heart—and neither throw favors to people's faces nor ask for any. . . .[18]

And then, continuing:

> The other fashion of wandering out of sheer boredom is utterly dominant in England, much more so than in any other corner of earth, and the more they love their homeland, and they do have reasons to love it, the more they flee from it, to compare it with the other countries and enjoy like Addison Italy's sky and the memories it fosters, and then return to kiss their native land—they say this is curiosity—but curiosity itself comes from boredom.
>
> Hence it cannot be said that here the traveler is fashionable; but just that he who has not traveled can never

[18] *Ibid.*, p. 576 *Opere di F.*; p. 328 *Edizione Nazionale*, v ("Serie de Gazzetti scritti non volendo").

be fashionable, with a few exceptions. But in Italy he
who has traveled is fashionable. . . .

We can see here the verification of what had been promised
in the Address to the Reader:

Sixteen years ago I published another booklet [*Ortis*],
and not being able to express the opinions which seemed
true to me then—and to a great extent still do now—, I
inflamed them with the mournful passions that smoul-
dered in me. And I am afraid they may be a very dismal
light to darken prematurely the prospects of life's journey for youths and discourage them from undertaking it
with carefree mirth. The many readers I did not hope for
do not make up for the repentance I still did not fear;
and today I have some, and shall still have when that
booklet and the present one too have been forgotten by
you. Meanwhile you might get some profit from the latter
(the *Letters from England*) by considering in two so
diverse ages and through the vicissitudes and opinions
of our century the same human individual. . . .

This is the voice of Didymus, who has learned to bear his
burden, including the gravest, exile—witness the unfinished
letter that follows the address to the Reader and is written to a
Swiss scholar and friend, Mr. Heinrich Meister in Zurich:

. . . I would almost feel tempted to agree with Samuel
Johnson who said that Fielding wrote in taverns . . . and
that whoever has been through school can use epi-
graphs. The English are crazy about them, and of quotations as well, but to this my vice of quoting verse
throughout my letters, you and your friends are resigned
by now—I recite verse out of laziness, and also out of
affection, to spare the waste of time and the chatter involved in saying in bad prose the thought a poet
suggests;—and really I seem to hear him talk in my

ear—but it's that often I cannot recognize him; and
perhaps a word or two is missing; but laziness still pre-
vents me from checking it in the books. And what
books? They are a most burdensome impediment and
delay to the fleeing exile . . .

Yet even this is not totally so; nor do I hope any
longer that my age will . . . in Italy. And I'm afraid that I
shall never experience again the pleasure I had when,
returning after two years, I saw my books with joyfully
tear-filled eyes, with more joy than I felt at seeing my
friends. . . . The true pleasure is in exercising one's
faculties . . .[19]

The same wisdom can suggest, in Part III of an alternative
draft of the "Lettera sulla moda," the hilarious, and poker-
faced description of a visit to an English dandy in his parrot-
damasked dressing gown. It is parrots all over, and the gen-
tleman's grave disclaimer of fatuousness, and his resentment
of possible competitors in securing this brand-new novelty
from a tailor, compounds the subtlety and the amusement.
The scene has the ring of truth, and it counts among the finest
descriptions of that unsurpassed British social institution—
the fashionable eccentric.

Then there are the matchless antics of the ladies going to
the theater; and, in short, the comedy of manners Foscolo has
been able to sketch is a delightful ingredient in the rich fare
he is offering with these *Letters*. We can only regret that other
pressing engagements, and the difficulty of finding a publisher in the Continent or a readership in England, should
have induced him to abandon this work which promised to
become an accomplished piece of autobiographical fiction.
Even so, enough is there to recommend the incomplete book
to our attention, and its outspoken informality should not mis-
lead us into believing it hasty patchwork. The variant drafts
of the "Letter on Fashion" and of some "Gazettes" prove the

[19] *Ibid.*, p. 548 *Opere di F.*; p. 263 *Edizione Nazionale*, v, *cit.* ("Fram-
menti delle lettere; Esilio—Al Signor Enrico Meister a Zurigo").

contrary. Lucia Conti-Bertini has now edited the preliminary notes,[20] which testify to the scrupulous care the writer put in gathering information for this project, even if in the pretty advanced stage at which he left it, it sounds so self-deflating. It is all part of Didymus' humorous wisdom, fully ripened in the English climate.

Painstaking research eventuates in mercurial prose. But the distillation, needless to say, does not result from books alone. It exploits personal experience, present and past; and perhaps the best samples are to be found in Variant No. I of the "Lettera sulla moda," section entitled "Delle nove diverse fisionomie d'una donna" (Of the nine different physiognomies of a woman)[21] and, respectively, the "Frammento di una nuova redazione del Gazzettino N. 1" (Fragment of a new draft of Gazette No. 1),[22] third part of the Appendix to the "Gazzettino." The first passage, unfinished and desultory though it is, brings in a note of its own—a wistful reminiscence of the remote days spent on the Channel shore with the Napoleonic invasion army, when England loomed on the other side as a problematic target, and Didymus—the alter ego materializing on the beach ahead of galloping Ugo and a friend—in the moonlit night "turned his eyes toward England, and raised his head, and lifted his face in utter gladness, and suddenly exclaimed. . . . "I will," he said, "o land, I will also come to you in my wanderings"; and perhaps that was the first time he made up his mind to travel to England. . . ." Retrospective prophecy amounts to a recognition of the fact that emigration to England had been a way to make the best of exile, especially since that free country had stimulated the growth of Didymus in the troubled spirit of our wandering poet.

And Didymus again speaks in the "Fragment of the

[20] U.F., *Gli appunti per le "Lettere scritte dall'Inghilterra."* Edizione critica a cura di Lucia Conti Bertini. Florence: La Nuova Italia, 1975.

[21] Variant draft of the *Lettera sulla Moda* (Letter on Fashion); pp. 564-66 *Opere di F.*; pp. 304-07 *Edizione Nazionale*, v.

[22] Pp. 604-06 *Opere di F.*; pp. 375-79, *Edizione Nazionale*, v.

Gazette" to spice with self-deprecating humor the portrait of
Ugo Foscolo, whose name is said to derive from the Greek
words for "light" (*phos*) and "gall" (*cholos*)—a witty way to
pinpoint his psychological polarity and its variable literary
manifestations. It leads to a memorable description of his
unfettered kind of writing:

> . . . If anybody then wanted me to explain how so many
> wise, crazy, and indifferent thoughts—but many in any
> case—have entered my skull, all ready to spill over on
> the page, I really could not find an answer. It may well
> be a *combination of bilious matter and fiery motion*; but I
> have already confessed to you that I am innocent of
> physiology—and of chemistry; and here it would be
> necessary for conversation with young ladies.—I do
> know from experience that my ideas all come out of the
> inkwell—and writing I seem to discover things of which
> I knew myself to be quite ignorant—and then I go on
> with my pen because I like to learn from myself—and on
> the following day I would like to unlearn because my
> new knowledge. . . .

At one stroke Foscolo has caught his mind in motion, the
creative process as such. It is an experience recorded, not an
attempt at explanation. Powered by its emotional drives,
nourished by its disparate sensory accruals from the outside
world and from the store of memory, the imagination is released and flows—with the inkwell supplying its humorously
appropriate symbolic counterpart, for it is a kind of source.
And everything in and around finds its outlet in the act of
writing, which in turn originates knowledge, renews the consciousness of reality, because it essentially transcends its materials and motivation. That which came last in the physiolog-
ical and psychological chain of causes becomes first;
choleric, fiery Ugo is now reborn from his pen, and there is no
end to the flow of words, of ideas, of images. Even the unplanned interruption in mid-flow helps to dramatize the

open-ended nature of the process. The important thing is not to conclude, but to keep up, or renew, the act of discovery. That is the primal thing now.

Seldom has the primacy of imagination been so casually propounded. And this, by vatic Foscolo, the author of *Ortis*, of the melancholy sonnets, of the solemn *Sepulchers*. Ripeness is all. Didymus can laugh at himself, at his broken leg, at the unresponsiveness of many readers—and in the process make effortless contact with his creative source, the self beyond the ego. The beautiful thing about it all is that, true to his avowed allergy to metaphysics, he avoids making the quick self-analysis a matter of transcendental postulates. He simply captures the rhythm of inner experience, the "voice dictating within," and it certainly does not occur to him to reify it in any way. Gide and his "availability," Pirandello's fidelity to the inconclusiveness of experience, Joyce's reaching for the pre-logical stream of consciousness, Pavese's unpremeditated transformation of a soul-searching diary into a lived novel, a *roman-vérité*—these all loom ahead, and they make Foscolo a pathfinder, just when he least thinks of his literary role as epoch-making. For he has learned to play, long after proving his ability to celebrate, to denounce, and to prophesy. He, the lover of hyperbole, has learned to understate.

Something of that newly found freedom had of course been inherent in Foscolo's practical poetics for a long time; Didymus was not born like Minerva. There had been, for instance, the preliminary jottings for *Le Grazie*, notably the few prose pages that are an isolated diary entry, in the Florence MSS., on the just unveiled Venus of Canova.[23] And several

[23] Biblioteca Nazionale, Florence: Fas. IV ("Registro Mors"), pp. 5-6. See fn. 20, Ch. IV, and my translation of the diary pages dated Aug. 31 and Sept. 1, in the same chapter. It may be useful to know that the same "Registro Mors" contains, besides the Canova Venus diary entries, a "Notice" or foreword to the translation of Sterne's *Sentimental Journey* (pp. 7-10), with variants, not checking in every part with the printed version, then (pp. 14-21) fragments of *Le Grazie*; then (pp. 98-143) passages of *Ricciarda*, blank pages, and a copy of *Aiace*.

years earlier, when serving in Napoleon's army in France, he
filled notebook pages with disparate sketches, notations,
seminal impressions; Volume III of the Florence MSS., at the
Florence library, page 41, has a vivid entry on the vintage
activities in the French countryside, and immediately after,
on the same sheet, the prose sketch of a prayer to Father
Ocean which, hard to read as it is, and even undecipherable
in spots, conveys the exile's lament on the bleak Channel
shore, and the memory of brighter seas. Other contiguous
pages of these MSS. have grammatical notations on the English language. What connects such notebook entries to the
development of creative freedom as we have seen it emerge in
the *Letters from England* is their impromptu liveliness in the
very transitions of topic and tone.

And then of course there are the letters, in which Foscolo
lavishes so much of his gift. For, like the casual diary entry,
the letter affords a maximum of liberty to the professional
writer. He can let his pen do the work, unhampered by concerns of a formalist nature; he has a silent interlocutor to release in turn his expression of joy, sadness, anger, or humor,
and confession will shade into prayer, or subside into description, unselfconsciously, until the everyday becomes
pure invention. No wonder that, generations before Foscolo,
novelists should resort to the epistolary form. It was certainly
much more versatile, and potentially inclusive of the main
literary genres, than, say, the medical diagnosis or scientific
"impersonal" account or logbook that the Naturalist generation was to take as its functional model. No wonder either that
Foscolo's unfinished epistolary book penned in the first years
of his English stay should include as part of its fictional structure a letter addressed to a real person, Mr. Meister, to stress
the interchange of fiction and reality. In an analogous way,
there had been an exchange between the novel in progress,
Ortis, and the actual correspondence between its author and
the woman who inspired him in the decisive phase of its completion. And just as the letters to Antonietta Arese became an
unplanned novel, parallel and antiphonal to *Ortis*, the letters

written later from England to a number of friends in Italy—
the Countess of Albany, Silvio Pellico, Sigismondo Trechi,
and above all "la donna gentile," Quirina Magiotti—make up
another autobiographical novel to put alongside the fictional
Letters from England. The immediacy granted by the epistolary convention as such goes hand in hand with the ease of
the experienced writer, just as the trained purebred horse
cannot help ambling with style. Foscolo's tonal range, his
forcefulness and his humor, the modulated eloquence, are all
there.

A particularly spirited letter to his old friend and confidante, the Countess of Albany, who had been very close to
Vittorio Alfieri until his death in Florence, may well
exemplify Foscolo's unique literary temper and self-
understanding. The letter dates from October 15, 1814,[24]
and already reflects the transitional period that will lead to
the choice of exile in March of the following year; as a confession it ranks among the most valuable:

Madam the Countess—The little Englishman [a Mr.
Crackenthorpe] is touring the [Lombard] Lakes; and if ,
he tarries, I shall not have the pleasure of seeing him
again because I may well return to the countryside before long, though I have finally found an excellent lodg-
ing in Milan, where I shall hear no noise nor feel any
cold, but in the countryside I shall have more quiet for
the time being—The other Englishman, Mr. Rose,[25]
wrote me that to date I haven't done anything that corre-
sponds, as he puts it, to my talent; the rebuke perhaps is

[24] *Epistolario* v, pp. 267-71, letter numbered 1590. Translation mine.

[25] See fn. 4 to this chapter. William Stewart Rose translated Ariosto's
Orlando Furioso and Berni's *Orlando Innamorato*, among other Italian
poems, into polished English verse, and his version of *Orlando Furioso* has
been favored by some modern anthologists (like Prof. H. H. Blanchard,
author of *Prose and Poetry of the Continental Renaissance in Translation*,
New York: McKay, 1949, 1955) over the Elizabethan one by Sir John
Harington.

326 THE ACT OF WRITING

not fair; but the remark is very true, and its truth applies perhaps not just to the past as to my studies, and even more to the present and the future: and since I *believe, and believe myself to be believing the truth*,[26] that the rebuke derives from some affectionate complaint uttered by or with you, so I thank you, Madam the Countess; nor can you give me a better proof of your benevolence than by encouraging me anew to Glory. . . . but first of all . . . I happen to be very indifferent to this blessed Glory . . . and in the second place, though I am of utterly steadfast mind and heart in pursuing my goal, my strength and nature do not allow me to persist very long in the same work;—often, it's true, I do persist; but I sense the artifice, and the awkward effort, and the cold, and the smell of lamp oil, and finally my own soul's distaste in those things I write more out of wilful design than from natural impulse. When *the spirit is ready, and the flesh is weary*,[27] one fills many sheets of paper with lots of common sense and philosophical regularity of art, but the toil rises a hundredfold, and one gets neither a spontaneous smile nor a sigh from the readers. I, Madam the Countess, firmly believe that what little happiness one can obtain down here consists wholly of *pleasing oneself*; and, either I am the dumbest of mortals, or all the ancient philosophers who devised and upheld so many systems to find a shelter for human happiness, have lost their way in metaphysical worlds, by hunting for virtues that are humanly impossible, and have missed (and I don't know that anybody else ever said it) the only [authentic] maxim: *Please yourself, and you will be less unhappy on this earth*. But to please oneself, one must accommodate one's nature, and give to body and heart and talent the nourishment that is most

[26] "Credo, e creder credo il vero"; a Petrarchan quotation.

[27] "Lo spirto è pronto, e la carne stanca"; a slightly modified quotation from Petrarch's Sonnet 208, last line ("Lo spirto è pronto, ma la carne è stanca"), which is in turn a quotation from the Gospel of St. Mark (XIV: 38).

the honor and interest which depend on the whims of the rich and powerful few; not the glory of a name, which comes late; confused; after death; given or denied, like all other things, by luck; and dependent on the world's judgment; but the true fruit of our studies derives from the free, tranquil exercise of our faculties, from contempt for any base thing, which like a steel armor comes to arm our heart, and makes us disdain the opinion of the populace; and finally from the pleasant deceit practiced on time, which is utterly boring to the idle. With such occupations I have finished in these two months an excerpt of a new translation of two books from Homer, which I do not want to publish, also, part of an epistolary book made up of letters addressed to several men I esteem in Italy; and its theme is *the universal principles of Literature*; new ideas, and bizarre perhaps; and they will be published, if the Supervisor changes his opinion about who knows which paragraphs he thinks dangerous to the tranquility of minds. . . . Also, I am about to finish the *Grazie*; and when the little demon of versification, which has abruptly left my home for the time, returns to visit me, and to ring out the painterly harmony of verse, I shall give the last touch to the poem. Meanwhile who heard some of its parts says wonders of it, which I do not believe; . . . but of these *Grazie*, and of a certain intention of mine, I will write you another time, provided you assure me, or rather, frankly declare whether the lengthiness of my letters does not become to you, as I reasonably fear, a bother; the more so as I have gotten into the habit of writing as I talk, by parentheses, and clauses upon clauses, in long and loose sentences, and rehashing the same idea in different words, as I did today with *Pleasing oneself*. This way of writing prose almost ungrammatically comes, I think, from my having accustomed myself for so many weeks to thinking, idolizing my thoughts, and singing them in my mind on the meter of verse, and with phrases totally different

from prose; and the Greeks and Latins were shrewder,
who gave themselves entirely either to verse, or to prose;
and did not cherish like us the ambition of all trades.
But here I am, adrift in chatter; may God forgive me,
and preserve your eyesight. . . .

Although written two years before Foscolo's coming to England, this letter foreshadows the style and statements of *Letters from England*, particularly as regards the elvishness into
which self-criticism shades, to counterpoint the high serious-
ness of values entertained. As in the "letter" where he mock-
ingly describes himself as part light (*phos*) and part bile
(*cholos*), a graceful hilarity suffuses, or actually propels the
writing, until it becomes self-descriptive, its own best
illustration—one and the same thing with the free flowing of
associative thought it elicits and reflects in turn. Out of the
personal Slough of Despond, which prevails when the creative impulse flags, the dance of the Graces; and their visita-
tions are sustained if intermittent, and unpredictable. Definitions like self-indulgence or strenuous discipline become
irrelevant where the point is how to tap the deep source, how
to keep it flowing, whatever the name it is given ("nature,"
"inspiration," "Muse"). There has obviously been, and there
will be, a preparatory exercise; but the liberated dancer
forgets the training, and then, "how can we know the dancer
from the dance?"

The process takes over, and it matters more—at least
subjectively—than its successive results, the completed or
unfinished works. It makes the difference between living and
vegetating. It enlists in its service the various "demons," for
the Graces need—or are—demons. It supersedes emptiness,
irrelevance, tedium. It precedes and transcends "grammar"
and genre: poetry or prose? for it is an inner rhythm behind
and beyond all rules. A secret alchemy has made "phos" out
of "cholos." Nothing less would have done for the man who,
finally deprived of any possibility to act politically or militar-
ily for his cause, from now on was to depend on his pen for

moral (as well as physical) sustenance. From this he would get the strength to bridge the two worlds between which he had to exist, the one he had lost and the one he did not belong to.

Petrarch is quoted in the 1814 letter to the Countess, and Petrarch will elicit from Ugo Foscolo's exiled pen the finest completed work of his English period, the four connected essays that treat every conceivable aspect of the fourteenth-century poet's life, love, and art, finally to conclude with a keen comparison of Petrarch and Dante, those two founding fathers of Italian poetry in whom Ugo recognized many an essential trait of his own artistic vocation and earthly destiny. The book on Petrarch is essay and autobiography at the same time, with more than a touch of the novelist's flair for incident. How much bile, how much light, in Dante! What gift of the Graces, in Petrarch; and when Ugo ends the third chapter on the scene of the seventy-year-old Francesco found dead in his library, his head bent on a book, he is depicting the kind of death that he, Ugo, is secretly yearning for. A temporary Laura has even been granted him in the person of lovely Caroline Russell, the direct inspirer of the book. She can only be to him what Minna or Ulrike are to old Goethe—creatures of *Entsagung*, of renunciation, "Graces." The important thing is—to write.

And throughout these English years, another cynosure keeps beckoning him to cross an unbridgeable distance, and thus spurring him on to write: Homer. The 1807 translation of *Iliad* I contained several passages of such radiant firmness as to warrant their juxtaposition to the best of Foscolo's own verse in *Sepolcri*. He has been reworking it all, and indefatigably testing every line in the first seven books, and many in the following three. For most passages the deletions and reworkings are too many to be counted; this infinite approximation to the Platonic idea that Homer is to Ugo fills page upon page, day after day, year after year. It becomes the ascetic quintessence of the literary act, a sustaining *Entsagung*. Gennaro Barbarisi, the editor of these ceaseless "experiments" which in the 1812-1814 period intertwined with the analogous work on the *Grazie*, has thrown definitive light on the merit, background, and circumstances of this further unfinished (and life-long) enterprise.[29] It would seem that here the priestly side of Didymus came to the fore, to worship a transcendence in the world of signs with the supreme dedication that is the other side of the elvish freedom, and of the assumed worldliness, so vividly present in *Letters from England*. If in the last years poverty forced Foscolo to move for a while into the London slums, where he took sick and daily heard the angry shouts of the disinherited from the street, he still found the strength to keep translating the *Iliad*.[30] The letter reporting this situation must rank among the most telling human documents of the age. Observant, compassionate, and secure in his conversation with the father of all poets, the ailing, destitute poet is now sustained by what has claimed so much of his energy for such a long time. Homer is his Atlantis, both unreachable and intimate, and as long as Homer beams his silent call, the source of writing will not dry up. The thing to do is to tap the inner reservoir of freedom, and to translate the inimitable, both experiments converging into the one act that makes sense of a disjointed life: the act of writing, which comes last and first, for as long as Ugo's weary flesh permits, down to the final days in Turnham Green. In his end is his beginning.

[29] *Edizione Nazionale*, III (in three parts): *Esperimenti di traduzione dell'Iliade*, edizione critica a cura di G. Barbarisi. Florence: 1961 (Part I), 1965 (Part II), 1967 (Part III). Barbarisi's Introduction is masterly, and so is his essay "Introduzione alle versioni omeriche del F.," in *Giornale storico della letteratura italiana*, LXXII (1955), fas. 4, pp. 568-609.

[30] See Vincent, *U.F.*, p. 195 (in the chapter entitled "The Slums"), and his reference to F.'s letter in notes to p. 195.

Sample Translations

THE SEPULCHERS

In the shadow of cypresses and within
the urns solaced by tears is the sleep of death
any softer? Once the sun for me no more
fosters on earth this lovely family
of vegetal, of animal existences; and when
no more the dance of future hours will
dawn on my mind, and when from you, dear friend,
I shall no longer hear that subtle harmony
of melancholy verse, and when no more
the virgin soul of poetry and of love
will speak to me, my only inspiration
and sustenance along a roaming life,
what restoration can be to my lost days
a headstone placed to tell my bones apart
from the myriads death sows through land and sea?
It is true, Pindemonte! Hope itself,
last of godheads, deserts the tombs; oblivion
envelops everything in its night;
and a restless force drives all the elements
from motion on to motion; and man and his tombs
and the last images and relics of earth
and sky become only playthings of time.
    But then why should man, the deathbound, renounce
the illusion which, once he is bereft of life,

still retains him this side of the last threshold?
Does he not live on even under thick earth
when daylight's harmony is silent to him,
if he can rouse it with delicate thoughts
in the mind of his loved ones? It's heavenly,
this correspondence of unbroken love,
a heavenly gift in human beings; and often
through it we live with our departed friend,
and he with us, if only that piece of land
which welcomed him at birth and nursed him on
afford him the last shelter in its motherly
womb, thereby protecting his remains
from the assaults of the weather and the trampling
populace; if but a stone do keep his name
and a friendly tree redolent with flowers
do but console his ashes with soft shadow.
Only the man who leaves behind no inheritance
of love takes little joy in a burial urn:
and if he looks ahead, he sees his soul
wander among the mournful mansions of Hades
or take shelter under God's forgiving wings;
but his dust he will leave to a patch of nettles,
forlorn, with no woman to bring her prayer,
and no passerby to hear the gentle sigh
that Nature sends us from the burial place.
    And yet a new law nowadays bans all
burials from reach of compassionate eyes,
and strips the dead of their very names. Tombless
lies your priest, O Thalia, who singing for you
in his poor home raised a laurel with long
love; and he used to hang wreaths in your honor;
and you quickened with your exhilaration
the songs that stung Lombard Sardanapalus
who has ears only for one kind of music:
for the mooing of his cattle from the Adda
and the Ticino, promising fat idleness.
O lovely Muse, where are you? I don't feel

the breath of your divine presence among
these trees where I am sitting to sigh forth
my unabating homesickness. You came
and smiled to him under that linden tree
which now shakes through and through in its lush foliage
missing forever the old man on whom
it once bestowed the gift of peace and shade.
Are you perhaps looking around in the maze of
nondescript tombs for your Parini's sacred
resting place? No memorial grove for him
did the corrupt city set within its walls
so hospitable to emasculated singers,
no stone, no words; maybe his bones are tainted
by the foul gore of a beheaded robber
who ended a crime career on the scaffold.
There among the rubble and the briars one hears
the stray bitch, hunger driven, scratch the graves
and howl, and from a skull at moonset flutter
the hoopoe circling from cross to cross all over
the death-ridden countryside, with foul sobs
to insult the gentle starlight which the night sky
grants to all those forgotten graves. In vain,
o goddess, you beseech the bleak night to
effuse dew on your poet. Alas, no flower
grows on the dead unless it be well nursed
by human recognition, by fond tears.

    Ever since wedding rituals, law courts, and altars
taught us, the human beasts, to be compassionate
of one another and of ourselves, the living
have rescued from malevolence of weather
and of wild animals the poor remains
which Nature reappropriates for its ceaseless
chain of change. The graves witnessed to past glory
and were altars to each rising generation;
from there issued the answers of the household
gods, and awe surrounded the oath sworn
by the ancestors' dust: a common cult

through the manifold rites perpetuated
patriotic virtue and religious piety.
Sepulchral slabstones did not always pave
temple floors; nor corpse stench mixed to incense
contaminate the worshipers; nor cities gloom
with sculpted skeletons: the startled mother
jumps in terror from sleep and stretches bare
arms over her beloved baby's head
to ward off the long wailing of a dead man
who came to claim the bought prayers of his heirs
from a church. Cypresses, instead, and cedars
saturating the air with purest scent
would cover the urns with their perennial green
for memory perennial, and precious
vases would treasure votive tears. The friends
would wrest a spark from the sun to illuminate
the subterranean night, because the eyes
of a dying man seek the sun, and man's last breath
flies in pursuit of the fast ebbing light.
The fountains, steadily pouring lustral waters,
brought forth amaranths and violets from the
funereal clods; and whoever sat there
to offer milk and tell his troubles to his
beloved dead, could smell an all pervasive
fragrance as if of an Elysian breeze.
Compassionate delusion—it endears
verdant suburban graveyards to the British
maidens attracted there by love of lost
mother, where they implored a safe return
for the dauntless sailor who cut off the mainmast
from a conquered ship, therein to carve his coffin.
But where the zest for acts of valor sleeps
and civilized society submits
to opulence and fear, conspicuous luxury
and unhallowed effigies of Hades
sprout into a wilderness of marble monuments.
The oh so learned, rich and patrician crowd,

the decorum and mind of our Italian kingdom,
even alive has burial in its fawned-upon
palaces, with coats of arms for eulogy.
For us may death prepare a resting place
where destiny will desist from revenge
and may then our friends gather an inheritance
not of wealth, but of feeling and free song.

   The gravestones of the strong kindle the strong
mind to lofty deeds, my Pindemonte, and they
make beautiful and holy to the traveler
their host land. When I saw the monument
that shelters the remains of the great writer
who tempers the scepter of rulers and
strips it of laurel leaves to show the blood
and tears it soaks, for all people to see;
and when I saw the shrine of the man who raised
a new Olympus in Rome; and of him who descried
many worlds wheel around under the sky's
canopy, and the sun motionless light them,
to clear the vaults of heaven for the Englishman
who then ranged them on such bold wings—O blissful
city, I cried out, for your life-giving breezes
and for the waters Apennine pours out
to you! The moon rejoicing in your air
clothes with crystalline light your happy hills
astir with vintage, and the farm-studded valleys
thick with their olive groves exhale incense
from myriad blossoms: and you, Florence, were the first
to hear the song that alone gladdened the fugitive
Ghibelline's anger, and you gave both parents
and language to the sweet lyrist of love
who threw the whitest veil over the nakedness
of Eros to return him to celestial
Venus on high. Yet happier still for keeping
the Italian glories in one temple. None
other are left perhaps since the ill-defended Alps
and the fateful vicissitudes of human

power robbed you of weapons, of possessions,
of altars and of country and of all things
save memory alone. And to this marble
shrine Vittorio used to come for inspiration.
Angered at his country's fate, he would wander
silently in Arno's loneliest reaches, gazing
at fields and sky full of desire; and since
no living thing would soothe his worry, he
came here to seek stern quiet; and his face showed
death's pallor with a glimmer of new hope.
Now he dwells here forever with these great
ancestors, his bones still shuddering with love
for the ravaged homeland. Yes, from this awe-filled
peace a godhead speaks: the same that once in Marathon,
made holy by all those Athenian graves,
aroused Greek fury against Persian invaders.
Whoever sailed that sea off the Euboea
would see through the vast darkness sparks flash out
from clashing helmets and swords, pyres smoke ruddily,
and phantom warriors glittering with armor
rush into combat; and the awestruck night
would be flooded by a turmoil of phalanxes
and blaring bugles, and horses clattering upon
the helmets of the dying, and moans, and hymns,
and the weird threesome singing of the Fates.
    O happy Ippolito, who in the years of your youth
freely ranged through the huge kingdom of wind
and water! and if your pilot steered the course
beyond the Aegean islands, you then heard
Hellespont's surf roar with ancient memories
and the high tide bellow to bring Achilles'
arms to the beach where rest the bones of Ajax:
death is just: not astuteness, not the favor
of kings secured the long-coveted trophy
for Ulysses: his roaming ship soon lost it
to the waves that the nether gods let loose.
    And me, whom the complexion of the times

and steadfastness in honor drive to flee
through alien nations, me may the Muses summon
to evoke all heroes, for the Muses only
forever breathe life into human thought.
They sit to watch the sepulchers, and when
Time with its cold wings there sweeps away
even the last ruins, the Pierian sisters gladden
the desert wastes with their singing, and harmony
overwhelms the silence of a thousand ages.
And today still in the barren Trojan region
a spot shines forth to travelers forever,
forever hallowed by the Nymph whom Zeus
loved, and she gave him Dardanus, the son
from whom Troy sprang forth and Assaracus, and
the fifty marriage beds, and the Julian kingdom.
Because when Electra heard Atropos call her
away from daylight's breezes to the Elysian
choirs, she uttered her last and supreme wish
to Zeus, and said, If you did cherish my face
and hair and our sweet trysts, and fate denies me
any better reward, do then from heaven
look down upon your dead friend, to perpetuate
the name of your beloved, of Electra.
Thus praying she died. And the Olympian wept;
and with a nod of his immortal head
he rained ambrosia from his locks on the nymph
and made holy her body and her grave.
There rested Erychthonius, there sleep the just
ashes of Ilus; there the women of Ilion
loosened their hair, beseeching fate in vain
to spare their husbands; there Cassandra, stirred
in her heart by the Numen to proclaim
Troy's doomsday, came, and sang a song of love
to the sad shades, and led her nephews, and
taught those youths love's forlorn lamentation.
And she said sighing: O, if heaven ever
grant you return from Argos, where you will

pasture horses for Diomed and for the son
of Laertes, you will not find your home again!
The walls built by Phoebus will be a smoking rubble.
But Troy's Penates will forever dwell
in these tombs; for the gods bestow the gift
of retaining a proud name in adversity.
And you, palmtrees and cypresses that Priamus'
daughters-in-law are planting—and you will grow
quickly indeed, watered by widows' tears!—
do protect my ancestors: and whoever
piously keeps his axe away from you
will be spared much bereavement in his home
and will enjoy a blessed wedding rite.
Protect my ancestors. One day you will see
a blind beggar roam among your ancient shades,
and grope his way into the burial chambers,
and embrace the urns, and interrogate them.
At this, a moan will issue from the secret
vaults, and the whole tomb will tell the story
of Ilion twice razed and twice rebuilt
in tragic splendor on the silent streets
only to enhance the glory of Peleus'
children in their last trophy. The sacred bard,
soothing the hurt of those souls with his song,
will make Greek princes immortal through all
the lands that father Ocean embraces.
And you, Hector, will be honored by tears
wherever blood shed for one's homeland is
holy and revered, and as long as the sun
keeps shining on the disasters of mankind.

THE ERINYS' PASSAGE
(*Le Grazie*, worksheets Hymn I)

. . . invisible and silent through the forests
they wander. As when an Erinys comes out
to gloat over the lands all burnt by winter,
malevolently, and washes her limbs in
the abhorrent Icelandic springs, where desolate
waters exhale sulphur; or at Greenland's lakes
she lights her torch longing for the clear sky;
first perfidiously counterfeits pink splendor,
and peoples, thus deluded, call her
with the fair name of Aurora Borealis;
then runs along, changing the clouds into horrid
chimaeras and impending weapons; and then
you hear the eagles upset by the silent storm
swoop down through the air at the eerie sight
of snakes and lions sitting in their realm
and shadowy wolves ahowl. Blood-flooded roam
the planets in full view of cities, faintly
beaming their light through the airborne chaos;
the whole vault of heaven blazes into flame
and under that lurid light the hyperborean
lands redden into one glaring immensity.
From up there the evil-eyed goddess takes in
the unseeded countryside and the northern ocean
ice-blocked to sailors; and today perhaps
all over battle-ridden Russia weapons
and flags and the unmourned Italian corpses.

THEOPHANY AND ASCENSION OF VENUS
(*Hymn* I, Chiarini's reconstruction)

         . . . And when the goddesses
arrived at the foothills, disdainful Diana's
chariot drawn by the tame does Iris took
away to Crete, a handsome gift forever.
Cynthia was always a friend to the Graces,
and with their help she always gave protection
to the heart of innocent girls and of children.
And light, all alone, they skirted the slopes
of spring-rilled Ida; and as they got closer
to the sky, where a pink light bathes the summits
of the holy mountain, and the stars seem
all gold, the Goddess sent these inward words
to her trusted virgins who were following:
"Blissful indeed, o maidens, is the kingdom
of the Celestial Powers where I return;
you stay back to console the unhappy Earth
and its children; only through you the gods
will pour their gifts down there. And if they
should be vindictive rather than compassionate,
then through my Father's thunderclouds and lightnings
I will lead you to calm them. At my leaving
you will hear such a harmony from on high
as, spread further by you, will turn to joy
those mortal lives foredoomed to darkest frenzy,
and awaken them to the arts and stop the quivering
lust for the cry that bodes death. Friendly shelter
may the Elysian fields give you sometimes; do smile
there to the poets, if they gathered their laurels
in purity, and to indulgent princes,
and to the pious young mothers who kept
their children in their care, and to the girls
whom hidden love brought guiltless to the stake,

and to the youths who died for their own country.
Be immortal, be eternally beautiful!"
She no longer was speaking, but her eyes
effused on her daughters the eternal light
of cool sunrise; and she was leaving: and
they followed her with tear-filled eyes, they saw
her turn around from that height, and they heard
this voice: "The Fates will give you renewed grief
and perennial joy." And she vanished; and flying
through two first heavens, she enveloped herself
in the pure light of her own star. Harmony
heard her, and stirred the sky with jubilation.

TO EVENING

Perhaps because you are the very image
of the ultimate quiet, you are so welcome
to me, O evening, and whether the summer clouds
blithely court you along with the mild breezes
or through the snow-ridden air you bring
disquieting, long darkness to the world,
you always alight as a presence invoked,
and softly win secret access to my heart.
You make me roam with my thoughts along the way
that leads to eternal nothingness; meanwhile
this wretched age flees, and with it go the herds
of worries that devour me in its wake;
and while I contemplate your peace, there slumbers
in me the warlike spirit, its roars hushed.

WORKS CONSULTED

Primary Sources

Edizione Nazionale delle Opere di Ugo Foscolo. Florence: Le Monnier, 1933, vol. VII (*Lezioni, articoli di critica e di polemica—1809-1811*, a cura di E. Santini); 1933, vol. VIII (*Prose politiche e letterarie dal 1811 al 1816*, a cura di L. Fassò); 1949, vol. XIV (*Epistolario* I, a cura di P. Carli); 1951, vol. V (*Prose varie d'arte*, a cura di M. Fubini); 1952, vol. XV (*Epistolario* II, a cura di P. Carli); 1953, vol. X (*Saggi e discorsi critici*, a cura di C. Foligno); 1953, vol. XVI (Epistolario III, a cura di P. Carli); 1954, vol. XVII (*Epistolario* IV, a cura di P. Carli); 1955, vol. IV (*Ultime lettere di Jacopo Ortis*, a cura di G. Gambarin); 1956, vol. XVIII (*Epistolario* V, a cura di P. Carli); 1958, vol. XI (*Saggi di letteratura italiana*, Parte I e II, a cura di C. Foligno); 1961, vol. II (*Tragedie e poesie minori*, a cura di G. Bézzola); 1961, vol. III (*Esperimenti di traduzione dell'Iliade*, a cura di G. Barbarisi, Parte I); 1964, vol. XIII (*Prose politiche e apologetiche*, Parte I e II, a cura di G. Gambarin); 1965, vol. III (*Esperimenti di traduzione dell'Iliade*, a cura di G. Barbarisi, Parte II); 1966, vol. XIX (*Epistolario* VI, a cura di G. Gambarin e F. Tropeano); 1967, vol. III (*Esperimenti di traduzione dell'Iliade*, a cura di G. Barbarisi, Parte III); 1970, vol. XX (*Epistolario* VII, a cura di M. Scotti); 1972, vol. VI (*Scritti letterari e politici dal 1796 al 1808*, a cura di G. Gambarin).

Vol. I of this edition, the most authoritative to date, which was being edited by the late F. Pagliai to include the major poetical works, is yet to appear. Other volumes were scheduled to appear at a later date when the present book reached completion.

Opere di Foscolo, a cura di Mario Puppo (with critical introduction, bibliography, and notes). Milan: Mursia, 1966.

Ugo Foscolo: Opere, Tomo I, a cura di Franco Gavazzeni (with critical introduction, biographical chronology, extensive bibliography, and notes). Milan and Naples: Riccardo Ricciardi, 1974.

Ugo Foscolo: Dall'Ortis alle Grazie, antologia a cura di Saverio Orlando. Turin: Loescher, 1974.

Ugo Foscolo: Le Grazie, carme ad Antonio Canova. Edizione critica a cura di Saverio Orlando. Brescia: Paideia editrice, 1974.

Lettere amorose di Ugo Foscolo ad Antonietta Fagnani, a cura di Giovanni Mestica, con un discorso. Florence: Barbera, 1884.

Ugo Foscolo: Ultime lettere di Jacopo Ortis, edizione critica con riscontro su tutte le stampe originali . . . , a cura di G. A. Martinetti e C. A. Traversi. Saluzzo: Tipografia F. lli Lobetti-Bodoni, presso Enrico Molino, Roma, 1887 (With an important introduction containing a textual collation of related passages from the letters to Antonietta F. and from *Ortis*).

Ugo Foscolo: Lettere d'amore, a cura di Giuseppe Argentieri. Verona: Edizioni speciali del Club degli Editori, 1970.

Manuscript collections and related documents at the Biblioteca Nazionale of Florence, at the Biblioteca Labronica "Guerrazzi" of Leghorn, and at the Archivio di Stato of Milan.

Ministero della Pubblica Istruzione, *Indici e cataloghi*, II. Catalogo dei MSS foscoliani già proprietà Martelli della R. Biblioteca Nazionale di Firenze, a cura di Giuseppe Chiarini. Rome: 1885.

Viglione, Francesco. *Catalogo illustrato dei MSS| foscoliani della Biblioteca Labronica*. In: *Bollettino della Società pavese di storia patria*, anno IX, fas. III-IV, 1909. Pp. 383-556.

Ugo Foscolo: Gli appunti per le "Lettere scritte dall'Inghilterra," edizione critica a cura di Lucia Conti Bertini. Florence: La Nuova Italia, 1975.

Goethe, Johann Wolfgang. *Die Leiden des jungen Werthers*, in *Goethes Werke*, Hamburger Ausgabe, Band 6 (*Romane und Novellen*), herausgegeben von Erich Trunz. Hamburg: Christian Wegner Verlag, 1963.

Secondary Sources

Barbarisi, Gennaro. "Introduzione alle versioni omeriche del Foscolo," *Giornale storico della Letteratura Italiana* LXXII, 4 (1955), 568-609.

Barbi, Michele. *La nuova filologia e l'edizione dei nostri classici da Dante al Manzoni*. Florence: Sansoni, 1938.

Bézzola, Guido. "Pagine di Lucini sul Foscolo," *Il Verri* 33-34 (October 1970), 311-15.

Bigongiari, Piero. *Il senso della lirica italiana*. Florence: Sansoni, 1952.

Binni, Walter. *Carducci e altri saggi*. Turin: Einaudi, 1960: *Foscolo e la critica: storia e antologia della critica*. Florence: La Nuova Italia, 1957.

Borgese, G. A. *Storia della critica romantica in Italia*. Naples: Edizioni della Critica, 1905.

Caretti, Lanfranco. *Studi e ricerche di letteratura italiana*. Florence: La Nuova Italia, 1951.

Caretti, L., e Luti, G., eds. *La letteratura italiana per saggi storicamente disposti: l'Ottocento*. Milan: Mursia, 1973.

Circeo, Ermanno. *Le Grazie del Foscolo*. Naples: Loffredo, 1974.

Croce, Benedetto. *Poesia e non poesia, note sulla letteratura europea del secolo decimonono*. Bari: Laterza, 1922; tr. Ainslie, D., *European literature in the nineteenth century*, London, 1924—*Poesia antica e moderna*. Bari: Laterza, 1942.

De Robertis, Giuseppe. *Saggi*. Florence: Le Monnier, 1953.

De Sanctis, Francesco. *Saggi critici*, a cura di L. Russo. Bari: Laterza, 1952.

Donadoni, Eugenio. *Ugo Foscolo pensatore, critico, poeta*. Palermo: Sandron, 1910; Florence: Sandron, 1964.

Fasano, Pino. *Stratigrafie foscoliane*. Roma: Bulzoni, 1974.

Ferrucci, Franco. *Addio al Parnaso*. Milan: Bompiani, 1971.

Flora, Francesco. "Le Grazie capolavoro del Foscolo e dell'Ottocento lirico," in *Storia della letteratura italiana*, vol. III. Milan: Mondadori, 1940.

Fubini, Mario. *Ugo Foscolo*. Florence: La Nuova Italia, 1962.

Getto, Giovanni. *La composizione dei Sepolcri di Ugo Foscolo*. Florence: Olschki, 1977.

Goffis, G. F. *Studi foscoliani*. Florence: La Nuova Italia, 1942.

Highet, Gilbert. *The Classical Tradition: Greek and Roman Influences on Western Literature*. Oxford and New York: Oxford University Press, 1949.

Jacomuzzi, Angelo. *Il monologo tragico di Jacopo Ortis*. Turin: Fògola, 1974.

Kroeber, Karl. *The Artifice of Reality: Poetic Style in Wordsworth, Foscolo, Keats, and Leopardi*. Madison and Milwaukee: The University of Wisconsin Press, 1964.

Limentani, Uberto. "Testimonianze inglesi sul Foscolo," *Giornale storico della Letteratura Italiana* LXXIII (1956), 390-409.

Luti, Giorgio. *Foscolo*. Milan: C.E.I., 1967.

Luzi, Mario. *L'Inferno e il Limbo*. Florence: Il Marzocco, 1949.

Macrì, Oreste. "Mitopoiesi delle 'Grazie' e confronto coi 'Sepolcri,' " *L'Albero*, 57 (1977), 29-51. Part of a book in progress, to be called *Semantica e metrica dei Sepolcri di Foscolo*.

Manacorda, Giorgio. *Naturalismo e masochismo: il Werther, Foscolo e Leopardi*. Florence: La Nuova Italia, 1973.

Mandruzzato, Enzo. *Foscolo*. Milan: Rizzoli, 1978.

Marcazzan, Mario. *Didimo Chierico e altri saggi*. Milan: Libreria editrice degli Omenoni, 1930.

Martelli, Mario. *Linee generali per uno studio su Le Grazie di Ugo Foscolo*. Siena: Ticci, 1947—*Ugo Foscolo*. Florence: Le Monnier, 1969—"La parte del Sassoli," *Studi di filologia italiana*, XXVIII (1970), 177-251.

Masiello, Vitilio. "Il mito e la storia. Analisi delle strutture dialettiche delle 'Grazie' foscoliane," *Angelus Novus* 12-13 (1968), 130-70.

Muscetta, Carlo. Introduction to *Le ultime lettere di Jacopo Ortis*. Turin: Einaudi, 1973.

Natali, Giulio. *Ugo Foscolo*. Florence: La Nuova Italia, 1953.

Nicoletti, Giuseppe. *Il "metodo" dell' 'Ortis' e altri studi foscoliani*. Florence: La Nuova Italia, 1978.

Noferi, Adelia. "Appunti sulla critica foscoliana (dai saggi sul Petrarca al discorso sul Decamerone)," *Paragone*, 50 (February 1954), 3-16.

Orlando, Saverio. "La seconda redazione dell'*Inno alle Grazie* di Ugo Foscolo," *Paideia*, XXVIII (1973), 15-39.—"Il mito di Atlantide nelle *Grazie* del Foscolo,". *Italianistica*, III, 1 (January-April 1974), 33-53.

Pagliai, Francesco. "I versi dei Silvani nelle *Grazie* del Foscolo," *Studi di filologia italiana*, X (1952), 145-412.—"Prima redazione (fiorentina) dell'*Inno alle Grazie* di Ugo Foscolo," *Studi di filologia italiana*, XIX (1961), 45-442.—"Versi a Dante nelle *Grazie* del Foscolo," *Studi Danteschi*, XLI (1966), 135-92.

Praz, Mario. "Foscolo e Byron," *Rivista di Letterature Moderne eComparate*, June 1962, 177-84.

Presta, Vincenzo. "Sulle *Grazie*," *Cultura e Scuola*. 29 (January-March 1969), 17 ff.

Radcliffe-Umstead, Douglas. *Ugo Foscolo*. New York: Twayne Publishers, 1970.

Ramat, Raffaello. *Itinerario ritmico foscoliano*. Bari-Città di Castello: Macrì, 1946.

Romagnoli, Sergio. *Ottocento tra letteratura e storia*. Padua: Liviana editrice, 1961.

Rosada, Bruno. "Rassegna foscoliana (1965-1976)," *Lettere Italiane*, XXVIII (1976), 234-46.

Russo, Luigi. *Ritratti e disegni storici*. Bari: Laterza, 1946.

Schenk, H. G. *The Mind of the European Romantics: an essay in cultural history*. New York: Ungar, 1966.

Sterpa, Mario. *Le Grazie di Ugo Foscolo*. Catania: Tipografia Coniglione e Giuffrida, 1930.

Scotti, Mario. *Foscolo fra erudizione e poesia*. Roma: Borracci, 1973.

Tripet, Arnaud. *L'Inquiétude et la Forme: essai sur Ugo Foscolo*. Lausanne: L'Aire, Coopérative Rencontre, 1973.

Vallone, Aldo. *Linea della poesia foscoliana*. Florence: La Nuova Italia, 1957.—*Interpretazione delle Grazie di Foscolo*. Lecce: Milella, 1970-71.

Vincent, E. R. *Ugo Foscolo, an Italian in Regency England*. Cambridge: At the University Press, 1953.

Wellek, René. *A History of Modern Criticism, 1750-1950*, vol. 2 (*The Romantic Age*). New Haven: Yale University Press, 1955.

INDEX

Library of Congress Cataloging in Publication Data

Cambon, Glauco.
  Ugo Foscolo, poet of exile.

  Bibliography: p.
  Includes index.
    1.   Foscolo, Ugo, 1778-1827—Criticism and
interpretation.   I.   Title.
PQ4691.C27   858′.6′09   79-3193
ISBN 0-691-06424-5